# The Science of Fairy Tales
## An Inquiry into Fairy Mythology

Edwin Sidney Hartland

**The Science of Fairy Tales: An Inquiry into Fairy Mythology**

Copyright © 2011 by Indo-European Publishing

All rights reserved.

For information and contact visit our website at:
IndoEuropeanPublishing.com

The present edition is a revised version of 1891 of this work published by Scribner & Welford, produced in the current edition with completely new, easy to read format, and is set and proofread by Alfred Aghajanian for Indo-European Publishing.

Cover Design by Indo-European Design Team

ISBN: 978-1-60444-348-6

# PREFACE

The chief object of this volume is to exhibit, in a manner acceptable to readers who are not specialists, the application of the principles and methods which guide investigations into popular traditions to a few of the most remarkable stories embodying the Fairy superstitions of the Celtic and Teutonic peoples. Some of the subjects discussed have already been dealt with by more competent inquirers. But even in these cases I have sometimes been able to supply additional illustrations of the conclusions previously arrived at, and occasionally, I hope, to carry the argument a step or two further than had been done before. I have thus tried to render the following pages not wholly valueless to students.

A portion of the book incorporates the substance of some articles which I contributed to "The Archæological Review" and "Folk-Lore." But these have been to a considerable extent re-written; and it is hoped that in the process wider and more accurate generalizations have been attained.

My hearty thanks are due to the various friends whose generous assistance has been recorded in the footnotes, and especially to Professor Dr. George Stephens, the veteran antiquary of the North, and Mr. W. G. Fretton, who have not measured their pains on behalf of one whose only claim on them was a common desire to pry into the recesses of the past. I am under still deeper obligations to Mr. G. L. Gomme, F.S.A., who has so readily acceded to my request that he would read the proof-sheets, and whose suggestions have repeatedly been of the greatest value; and to Mr. Havelock Ellis for the counsel and suggestions which his experience has more than once enabled him to give as the book was passing through the press.

I have been anxious to enable the reader who cares to do so to verify every statement made; but some of them no doubt have escaped reference. Many books are cited again and again, and in similar cases the reader's time is frequently wasted in searching for the first mention of a book, so as to ascertain its title and other particulars. To avoid the trouble I have so many times experienced in this way, I have put together in an Appendix a list of the principal authorities made use of, indicating them by the short title by which they are cited in the footnotes, and giving sufficient bibliographical details to enable them to be identified. Classics and works which are in every one's hands I have not thought it necessary to include in the list.

E. S. H.

Barnwood Court, Gloucester,
24th October, 1890.

# CONTENTS

| | | |
|---|---|---|
| **PREFACE** | ................................................................. | iii |
| **CHAPTER I** | THE ART OF STORY-TELLING ............................ | 1 |
| **CHAPTER II** | SAVAGE IDEAS ................................................... | 14 |
| **CHAPTER III** | FAIRY BIRTHS AND HUMAN MIDWIVES ......... | 23 |
| **CHAPTER IV** | FAIRY BIRTHS AND HUMAN MIDWIVES (continued) ............................................................ | 37 |
| **CHAPTER V** | CHANGELINGS ................................................... | 58 |
| **CHAPTER VI** | ROBBERIES FROM FAIRYLAND ....................... | 84 |
| **CHAPTER VII** | THE SUPERNATURAL LAPSE OF TIME IN FAIRYLAND ........................................................ | 100 |
| **CHAPTER VIII** | THE SUPERNATURAL LAPSE OF TIME IN FAIRYLAND (continued) .................................... | 121 |
| **CHAPTER IX** | THE SUPERNATURAL LAPSE OF TIME IN FAIRYLAND (continued) .................................... | 137 |
| **CHAPTER X** | SWAN-MAIDENS ................................................ | 157 |
| **CHAPTER XI** | SWAN-MAIDENS (continued) ............................ | 174 |
| **CHAPTER XII** | CONCLUSION ..................................................... | 204 |
| **BIBLIOGRAPHY** | ................................................................. | 216 |

# CHAPTER I

# THE ART OF STORY-TELLING

The art of story-telling — Unity of human imagination — Definition of Fairy Tales — Variable value of Tradition — Story-telling and the story-teller among various peoples — The connection of folk-tales with folk-songs — Continuity of Tradition — Need of accuracy and good faith in reporting stories.

The art of story-telling has been cultivated in all ages and among all nations of which we have any record; it is the outcome of an instinct implanted universally in the human mind. By means of a story the savage philosopher accounts for his own existence and that of all the phenomena which surround him. With a story the mothers of the wildest tribes awe their little ones into silence, or rouse them into delight. And the weary hunters beguile the long silence of a desert night with the mirth and wonders of a tale. The imagination is not less fruitful in the higher races; and, passing through forms sometimes more, sometimes less, serious, the art of story-telling unites with the kindred arts of dance and song to form the epic or the drama, or develops under the complex influences of modern life into the prose romance and the novel. These in their various ways are its ultimate expression; and the loftiest genius has found no fitter vehicle to convey its lessons of truth and beauty.

But even in the most refined products of the imagination the same substances are found which compose the rudest. Something has, of course, been dropped in the process; and where we can examine the process stage by stage, we can discern the point whereat each successive portion has been purged away. But much has also been gained. To change the figure, it is like the continuous development of living things, amorphous at first, by and by shooting out into monstrous growths, unwieldy and half-organized, anon settling into compact and beautiful shapes of subtlest power and most divine suggestion. But the last state contains nothing more than was either obvious or latent in the first. Man's imagination, like every other known power, works by fixed laws, the existence and operation of which it is possible to trace; and it works upon the same material,—the external universe, the mental and moral constitution of man and his social relations. Hence, diverse as may seem at first sight the results among the cultured Europeans and the debased Hottentots, the philosophical Hindoos and the Red Indians of the Far West, they present, on a close examination, features absolutely identical. The outlines of a story-plot among savage races are wilder and more unconfined; they are often a vast unhidebound corpse, but one that bears no distant resemblance to forms we think more reasonable only because we find it difficult to let ourselves down to the level of savage ignorance, and to lay aside the data of thought which have been won for us by the painful efforts of civilization. The incidents, making all due allowance for these differences and those of climate and physical surroundings, are not merely alike; they are often indistinguishable. It cannot, of course, be expected that the characters of the actors in these stories will be drawn with skill, or indeed that any attention will be paid to them. Character-study is a late development. True: we ought not to overlook the fact that we have to do with barbarous ideals. In a rudimentary state of civilization the passions, like the arts, are distinguished not by subtlety and complexity, but by simplicity and violence of contrast. This may account to some extent for what seems to us repulsive, inconsistent or impossible. But we must above all things beware of crediting the story-teller with that degree of conscious art which is only possible in an advanced culture and under literary influences. Indeed, the researches which are constantly extending the history of human civilization into a remoter and remoter past, go everywhere to show that story-telling is an inevitable and wholly unconscious growth, probably arising, as we shall see in the next chapter, out of narratives believed to record actual events.

I need not stop now to illustrate this position, which is no new one, and the main lines of which I hope will be rendered apparent in the course of this volume. But it is necessary, perhaps, to point out that, although these are the premises from which I start, the limitations imposed by a work of the size and pretensions of this one will not allow me to traverse more than a very small corner of the field here opened to view. It is, therefore, not my intention to attempt any formal proof of the foregoing generalizations. Rather I hope that if any reader deem it proper to require the complete evidence on which they rest, he will be led to further investigations on his own behalf. His feet, I can promise him, will wander along flowery paths, where every winding will bring him fresh surprises, and every step discover new sources of enjoyment.

The stories with which we shall deal in the following pages are vaguely called Fairy Tales. These we may define to be: Traditionary narratives not in their present form relating to beings held to be divine, nor to cosmological or national events, but in which the supernatural plays an essential part. It will be seen that literary tales, such as those of Hans Andersen and Lord Brabourne, based though they often are upon tradition, are excluded from Fairy Tales as thus defined. Much no doubt might be said both interesting and instructive concerning these brilliant works. But it would be literary criticism, a thing widely different from the scientific treatment of Fairy Tales. The Science of Fairy Tales is concerned with tradition, and not with literature. It finds its subjects in the stories which have descended from mouth to mouth from an unknown past; and if reference be occasionally made to works of conscious literary art, the value of such works is not in the art they display, but the evidence they yield of the existence of given tales in certain forms at periods and places approximately capable of determination: evidence, in a word, which appropriates and fixes a pre-existing tradition. But even in this they are inferior in importance to historical or topographical works, where we frequently meet with records of the utmost importance in considering the origin and meaning of Folk-tales.

Literature, in short, of whatever kind, is of no value to the student of Fairy Tales, as that phrase is here used, save as a witness to Tradition. Tradition itself, however, is variable in value, if regard be had alone to purity and originality. For a tribe may conceivably be so isolated that it is improbable that any outside influence can have affected its traditions for a long series of generations; or on the other hand it may be in the highway of nations. It may be physically of a type unique and unalloyed by foreign blood; or it may be the progeny of a mingling of all the races on the earth. Now it is obvious that if we desire to reason concerning the wide distribution, or the innate and necessary character of any idea, or of any story, the testimony of a given tribe or class of men will vary in proportion to its segregation from other tribes and classes: where we can with most probability exclude outside influence as a factor in its mental evolution, there we shall gather evidence of the greatest value for the purpose of our argument.

Again: some nations have developed the art of story-telling more highly than others, since some stages of civilization are more favourable to this development than others, and all nations are not in the same stage. The further question may, therefore, be put whether these various stages of development may not produce differences of manner in story-telling—differences which may indicate, if they do not cause, deep-seated differences in the value of the traditions themselves. To make my meaning clear: a people which requires its story-tellers to relate their stories in the very words in which they have been conveyed from time immemorial, and allows no deviation, will preserve its traditions with the least possible blemish and the least possible change. In proportion as latitude in repetition is permitted and invention is allowed to atone for want of memory, tradition will change and become uncertain. Such latitude may be differently encouraged by different social states. A social state is part of, and inseparable from, the sum total of arts, knowledge, organization and customs which we call the *civilization*, or the *stage of civilization*, of a people. It may be worth while to spend a short time in examining the mode of story-telling and the requirements of a story-teller among nations in different stages of civilization. We shall thus endeavour to appreciate the differences in the manner of telling, and to ascertain in general terms how far these differences affect the value of the traditions.

If we turn first to some of the Celtic nations, we find a social state in which the art of story-telling has received a high degree of attention. The late Mr. J. F. Campbell, to whom the science of Folklore owes an incalculable debt, describes a condition of things in the Western Highlands extremely favourable to the cultivation of folk-tales. Quoting from one of his most assiduous collectors, he says that most of the inhabitants of Barra and South Uist are Roman Catholics, unable to speak English or to read or write. Hence it is improbable that they can have borrowed much from the literature of other nations. Among these people in the long winter nights the recitation of tales is very common. They gather in crowds at the houses of those who are reputed to be good tale-tellers. Their stories frequently relate to the exploits of the

Ossianic heroes, of whose existence they are as much convinced as ordinary English folk are of the existence and deeds of the British army in its most recent wars. During the tales "the emotions of the reciters are occasionally very strongly excited, and so also are those of the listeners, almost shedding tears at one time, and giving way to loud laughter at another. A good many of them firmly believe in all the extravagance of these stories." Another of his collectors, a self-educated workman in the employ of the Duke of Argyll, writing more than thirty years ago to him, speaks of what used to take place about Loch Lomond upwards of fifty years before—that is to say, about the beginning of the present century. The old people then would pass the winter evenings telling each other traditional stories. These chiefly concerned freebooters, and tribal raids and quarrels, and included descriptions of the manners, dress and weapons of their ancestors and the hardships they had to endure. The youngsters also would gather, and amuse themselves with games or the telling of tales of a more romantic cast. But the chief story-tellers appear to have been the tailors and shoemakers, who were literally journeymen, going from house to house in search of work. As they travelled about, they picked up great numbers of tales, which they repeated; "and as the country people made the telling of these tales, and listening to hear them, their winter night's amusement, scarcely any part of them would be lost." In these tales Gaelic words were often used which had dropped out of ordinary parlance, giving proof of careful adherence to the ancient forms; and the writer records that the previous year he had heard a story told identical with one he had heard forty years before from a different man thirty miles away; and this story contained old Gaelic words the meaning of which the teller did not know. A gamekeeper from Ross-shire also testified to similar customs at his native place: the assemblies of the young to hear their elders repeat, on winter nights, the tales they had learned from their fathers before them, and the renown of the travelling tailor and shoemaker. When a stranger came to the village it was the signal for a general gathering at the house where he stayed, to listen to his tales. The goodman of the house usually began with some favourite tale, and the stranger was expected to do the rest. It was a common saying: "The first tale by the goodman, and tales to daylight by the guest." The minister, however, came to the village in 1830, and the schoolmaster soon followed, with the inevitable result of putting an end to these delightful times.[1]

Not very different is the account given by M. Luzel of the *Veillées* in which he has often taken part in Brittany. In the lonely farmhouse after the evening meal prayers are said, and the life in Breton of the saint of the day read, all the family assemble with the servants and labourers around the old-fashioned hearth, where the fire of oaken logs spirts and blazes, defying the wind and the rain or snow without. The talk is of the oxen and the horses and the work of the season. The women are at their wheels; and while they spin they sing love ditties, or ballads of more tragic or martial tone. The children running about grow tired of their games, and of the tedious conversation of their elders, and demand a tale, it matters not what, of giants, or goblins, or witches—nay, even of ghosts. They are soon gratified; and if an old man, as frequently happens, be the narrator, he is fortified and rewarded for the toil by a mug of cider constantly replenished. One such depositary of tradition is described as a blind beggar, a veritable Homer in wooden shoon, with an inexhaustible memory of songs and tales of every kind. He was welcome everywhere, in the well-to-do farmhouse as in the humble cottage. He stayed as long as he pleased, sometimes for whole weeks; and it was with reluctance that he was allowed to leave in order to become for a time the charm of another fireside, where he was always awaited with impatience.[2]

M. Braga, the Portuguese scholar, quotes an old French writer, Jean le Chapelain, as recording a custom in Normandy similar to that of Ross-shire, that the guest was always expected to repay hospitality by telling tales or singing songs to his host. And he states that the emigrants from Portugal to Brazil took this custom with them. In Gascony M. Arnaudin formed his collection of tales a few years ago by assisting at gatherings like those just described in Brittany, as well as at marriages and at various agricultural festivals.[3]

Similar customs existed in Wales within living memory, and in remote districts they probably exist to-day. If they do not now continue in England, it is at least certain that our forefathers did not differ in this respect from their neighbours. A writer of the seventeenth century, in enumerating the causes of upholding "the damnable doctrine of witchcraft," mentions: "Old wives' fables, who sit talking and chatting of many false old stories of Witches and Fairies and Robin Goodfellow, and walking spirits and the dead walking again; all of which lying fancies people are more naturally inclined to listen after than to the Scriptures." And if we go further back we find in chapter clv. of the printed editions of the "Gesta Romanorum" an interesting picture of domestic life. The whole family is portrayed gathering round the fire in the winter evenings and beguiling the time by telling stories. Such we are informed was the custom among the higher classes. It was, indeed, the custom among all classes, not only in England but on the Continent, throughout the Middle Ages. The eminent French antiquary, Paul Lacroix, speaks of wakes, or evening parties, where fairy tales and other superstitions were propagated, as having a very ancient origin. He states that they are still (as we have already seen in Brittany and Gascony) the custom in most of the French provinces, and that they formed important events in the private lives of the peasants.[4]

It is difficult to sever the occasion and mode of the tale-telling from the character of the teller; nor would it be wise to do so. And in this connection it is interesting to pause for a moment on Dr. Pitré's description of Agatuzza Messia, the old woman from whom he derived so large a number of the stories in his magnificent collection, and whom he regarded as a model story-teller. I am tempted to quote his account at length. "Anything but beautiful," he says, "she has facile speech, efficacious phrases, an attractive manner of telling, whence you divine her extraordinary memory and the sallies of her natural wit. Messia already reckons her seventy years, and is a mother, grandmother, and great grandmother. As a child, she was told by her grandmother an infinity of tales which she had learned from her mother, and *she* in turn from her grandfather; she had a good memory and never forgot them. There are women who have heard hundreds of tales and remember none; and there are others who, though they remember them, have not the grace of narration. Among her companions of the Borgo, a quarter of Palermo, Messia enjoyed the reputation of a fine story-teller; and the more one heard her, the more one desired to hear. Almost half a century ago she was obliged to go with her husband to Messina, and lived there some time: a circumstance, this, worthy of note, since our countrywomen never go away from their own district save from the gravest necessity. Returning to her native home, she spoke of things of which the gossips of the neighbourhood could not speak: she spoke of the Citadel, a fortress which no one could take, not even the Turks themselves; she spoke of the Pharos of Messina, which was beautiful, but dangerous for sailors; she spoke of Reggio in Calabria, which, facing the walls of Messina, seemed to wish to touch hands with them; and she remembered and mimicked the pronunciation of the Milazzesi, who spoke, Messia said, so curiously as to make one laugh. All these reminiscences have remained most vivid in her memory. She cannot read, but she knows so many things that no one else knows, and repeats them with a propriety of tongue that is a pleasure to hear. This is a characteristic to which I call my readers' attention. If the tale turns upon a vessel which has to make a voyage, she utters, without remarking it, or without seeming to do so, sailors' phrases, and words which only seamen and those who have to do with seamen are acquainted with. If the heroine arrives, poor and desolate, at a baker's and takes a place there, Messia's language is so completely that of the trade that you would believe that the baking of bread had been her business, whereas at Palermo this occupation, an ordinary one in the families of the large and small communes of the island, is that of professional bakers alone.... As a young woman Messia was a tailoress; when through toil her sight became weakened, she turned to sewing winter quilts. But in the midst of this work, whereby she earns her living, she finds time for the fulfilment of her religious duties; every day, winter and summer, in rain or snow, in the gloaming she goes to her prayers. Whatever feast is celebrated in the church, she is solicitous to attend: Monday, she is at the Ponte dell' Ammiraglio praying for the Souls of the Beheaded; Wednesday, you find her at San Giuseppe keeping the festival of the Madonna della Providenza; every Friday she goes to San Francesco di Paola, reciting by the way her accustomed beads; and if one Saturday pass when she ought to go to the Madonna dei Cappuccini, another does not; and there she prays with a devotion which none can understand who has not experienced it. Messia witnessed my birth and held me in her arms: hence I have been able to collect from her mouth the many and beautiful traditions to which her name is appended. She has repeated to the grown man the tales she had told to the child thirty years before; nor has her narration lost a shade of the old sincerity, vivacity, and grace. The reader will only find the cold and naked words; but Messia's narration consists, more than in words, in the restless movement of the eyes, in the waving of the arms, in the gestures of the whole person, which rises, walks around the room, bends, and is again uplifted, making her voice now soft, now excited, now fearful, now sweet, now hoarse, as it portrays the voices of the various personages, and the action which these are performing."[5]

Such a woman as is here described is a born story-teller; and her art, as exhibited in the tales attributed to her in Dr. Pitré's collection, reaches perhaps the highest point possible in tradition. Women are usually the best narrators of nursery tales. Most of the modern collections, from that of the brothers Grimm downwards, owe their choicest treasures to women. In the Panjab, however, Captain Temple ascribes to children marvellous power of telling tales, which he states they are not slow to exercise after sunset, when the scanty evening meal is done and they huddle together in their little beds beneath the twinkling stars, while the hot air cools, the mosquito sings, and the village dogs bark at imaginary foes. The Rev. Hinton Knowles' collection was gathered in Cashmere apparently from men and boys only; but all classes contributed, from the governor and the pandit down to the barber and the day-labourer, the only qualification being that they should be entirely free from European influence.[6]

But nursery tales told simply for amusement are far from being the only kind of traditional narrative. Savage and barbarous races, to whom the art of writing is unknown, are dependent upon memory for such records as they have of their past; and sometimes a professional class arises to preserve and repeat the stories believed to embody these records. Among the Maories and their Polynesian kinsmen the priests are the great depositaries of tradition. It is principally from them that Mr. White and the Rev. W. W. Gill have obtained their collections. But the orators and chiefs are also fully conversant with the narratives; and their speeches are filled with allusions to them, and with quotations from ancient poems relating the deeds of their forefathers. The difficulty of following such allusions, and consequently of understanding the meaning of the chiefs when addressing him on behalf of their fellow-countrymen, first induced, or compelled, Sir George Grey, when Governor of New Zealand, to make the inquiries whose results are embodied in his work on Polynesian Mythology. The Eskimo of Greenland, at the other end of the world, divide their tales into two classes: the ancient and the modern. The former may be considered, Dr. Rink says, as more or less the property of the whole nation, while the latter are limited to certain parts of the country, or even to certain people who claim to be akin to one another. The art of telling these tales is "practised by certain persons specially gifted in this respect; and among a hundred people there may generally be found one or two particularly favoured with the art of the *raconteur*, besides several tolerable narrators." It is the narrators of the ancient tales "who compose the more recent stories by picking up the occurrences and adventures of their latest ancestors, handed down occasionally by some old members of the family, and connecting and embellishing them by a large addition of the supernatural, for which purpose resort is always had to the same traditional and mystic elements of the ancient folklore."[7]

But the art of story-telling has not everywhere given rise to a professional class. When the Malagasy receive friends at their houses, they themselves recount the deeds of their ancestors, which are handed down from father to son, and form the principal topic of conversation. So, too, the savage Ahts of Vancouver Island sit round their fires singing and chatting; "and the older men, we are told, lying and bragging after the manner of story-tellers, recount their feats in war, or the chase, to a listening group." Mr. Im Thurn has drawn an interesting picture of the habits at night of the Indian tribes of Guiana. The men, if at home, spend the greater part of the day in their hammocks, smoking, "and leisurely fashioning arrowheads, or some such articles of use or of ornament.... When the day has at last come to an end, and the women have gathered together enough wood for the fires during the night, they, too, throw themselves into their hammocks; and all talk together. Till far into the night the men tell endless stories, sometimes droning them out in a sort of monotonous chant, sometimes delivering them with a startling amount of emphasis and gesticulation. The boys and younger men add to the noise by marching round the houses, blowing horns and playing on flutes. There is but little rest to be obtained in an Indian settlement by night. These people sleep, as dogs do, without difficulty, for brief periods, but frequently and indifferently by day or night as may be convenient. The men, having slept at intervals during the day, do not need night-rest; the women are not considered in the matter. At last, in the very middle of their stories, the party drops off to sleep; and all is quiet for a short while. Presently some woman gets up to renew the fires, or to see to some other domestic work. Roused by the noise which she makes, all the dogs of the settlement break into a chorus of barks and yelps. This wakes the children, who begin to scream. The men turn in their hammocks, and immediately resume their stories, apparently from the point at which they left off, and as if they had never ceased. This time it is but a short interruption to the silence of the night; and before long everything again becomes quiet, till some new outbreak is caused, much as was the last. In the very middle of the night there are perhaps some hours of quiet. But about an hour before dawn, some of the men having to go out to hunt, effectually wake everybody about them by playing flutes, or beating drums, as they go to bathe before leaving the settlement."[8]

But the folk-tale cannot be separated in this inquiry from the folk-song with which, in its origin and development, it is so closely connected. In India there are, or were until recent years, everywhere professional bards; and the stories told in Indian villages are frequently the substance of the chants of these bards. More than this, the line between singing and narration is so faintly drawn, that the bards themselves often interpose great patches of prose between the metrical portions of their recitations. Fairs, festivals, and marriages all over India are attended by the bards, who are always ready to perform for pay and drink. Mr. Leland believes the stories he obtained from the Christian Algonkins of New England, concerning the ancient heroes of the race and other mythical personages, to have once been delivered as poems from generation to generation and always chanted. The deeds of Maori warriors are handed down in song; just as we find in Beowulf, the story of Hrothgar's ancestors was sung before his own companions-in-arms by his gleemen to the accompaniment of some instrument after the mead cup had gone round. The Roman historian attests the prevalence among the German tribes of ancient songs, which he expressly mentions as their only kind of memory or record,—thus showing that all their tales, whether mythologic or heroic, were for better preservation cast into metrical form. Some of these, enshrining the deeds of their heroes, were chanted on going into battle, in order to arouse the warriors' courage. And as far back as the light of history, or of literature, penetrates, not only the Teutonic, but also the Celtic nations loved to have their actions celebrated thus. To a Welsh king his household bard was as necessary as his domestic chaplain, or his court physician, and in the ancient laws his duties, his precedence, his perquisites, and even the songs he was expected to sing, are minutely prescribed. The bards were organized into a regular order, or college, with an official chief. They were not merely singers or poets, but also tale-tellers; and from the Mabinogion we gather that listening to songs and tales was one of the habitual, if not daily pastimes, of a court.[9]

It is needless to follow through the Middle Ages the history of the troubadour, the minstrel and the jongleur, who played so large part in the social life of those times. Many of them were retainers of noblemen and kings; but others roamed about from place to place, singing their lays and reciting their stories (for they dealt in prose as well as verse), very much in the manner of the Indian bards just mentioned. Their stock-in-trade must have been partly traditional and partly of their own composition. In this respect they were probably less hide-bound than their Indian brethren are. For the latter, whether retainers of the native grandees, as many of them are, or members of the humbler class of wandering minstrels, are expected to repeat their lays as they have received them. But, although in the main these professional gentlemen adhere to the traditional words which they know by heart, the temptation must be very strong to foist at suitable pauses into their tales impromptu passages—best described in stage language as "gag"—which they think will be acceptable to their audience. And whether or not this be actually the case with the Indian bards, we are expressly told that it is so with the Arab story-teller, and that it accounts for much of the ribaldry and filth which have become embedded in the immortal "Nights." A viol having only one string accompanies the passages in verse with which the stories are interlarded; and a similar instrument seems to be used for the like purpose among the orthodox Guslars of Bosnia and Herzegovina.[10] A description given by Sir Richard Burton of a story-teller at the bazaar at Tangier may stand, except as to the external details, for that of an Arab reciter throughout Northern Africa and the Moslem East. "The market people," he says, "form a ring about the reciter, a stalwart man, affecting little raiment besides a broad waist-belt into which his lower chiffons are tucked, and noticeable only for his shock hair, wild eyes, broad grin, and generally disreputable aspect. He usually handles a short stick; and, when drummer and piper are absent, he carries a tiny tomtom shaped like an hour-glass, upon which he taps the periods. This Scealuidhe, as the Irish call him, opens the drama with an extempore prayer, proving that he and the audience are good Moslems; he speaks slowly and with emphasis, varying the diction with breaks of animation, abundant action and the most comical grimace: he advances, retires, and wheels about, illustrating every point with pantomime; and his features, voice and gestures are so expressive that even Europeans who cannot understand a word of Arabic, divine the meaning of his tale. The audience stands breathless and motionless, surprising strangers by the ingenuousness and freshness of feeling hidden under their hard and savage exterior. The performance usually ends with the embryo actor going round for alms, and flourishing in the air every silver bit, the usual honorarium being a few *flús*, that marvellous money of Barbary, big coppers worth one-twelfth of a penny." Another writer, who has published modern Arab folk-tales, obtained eleven out of twelve from his cook, a man who could neither read nor write, but possessed an excellent memory. His stories were derived from his mother and aunts, and from old women who frequented his early home. The remaining tale was dictated by a sheikh with some, though small, pretensions to education, and this tale, though at bottom a genuine folk-tale, presented traces of literary manipulation.[11]

The literary touches here spoken of were probably not impromptu. But it must be admitted that the tendency to insert local colouring and "gag" is almost irresistible amongst the Arabs. Dr. Steere notices it as a characteristic of the story-tellers of the Swahili, a people of mixed Arab and Negro descent at Zanzibar;[12] and it is perhaps inevitable in a professional reciter whose audience, like himself, is restless and vivacious in so high a degree. The only case in which any restraint would be certain to be felt is where a narrative believed to be of religious import is given. Under the influence of religious feeling the most mobile of races become conservative; and traditions of a sacred character are the most likely of all to be handed down unchanged from father to son. Directly we get outside the charmed circle of religious custom, precept, and story, the awe which has the most powerful effect in preserving tradition intact ceases to work; and we are left to a somewhat less conservative force of habit to retain the old form of words and the time-honoured ceremonies. Still this force is powerful; the dislike of voluntary change forbids amendment even of formularies which have long ceased to be understood, and have often become ridiculous because their meaning has been lost. It is by no means an uncommon thing for the rustic story-teller to be unable to explain expressions, and indeed whole episodes, in any other way than Uncle Remus, when called upon to say who Miss Meadows was: "She wuz in de tale, Miss Meadows en de gals wuz, en de tale I give you like hi't wer' gun ter me." Dr. Steere, speaking of a collection of Swahili tales by M. Jablonsky which I think has never been published, tells us that almost all of the tales had "sung parts," and of some of these even they who sang them could scarcely explain the meaning. Here we may observe the connection with the folk-song; and it is a strong evidence of adherence to ancient tradition. Frequently in Dr. Steere's own experience the skeleton of the story seemed to be contained in these snatches of song, which were connected together by an account, apparently extemporized, of the intervening history. In these latter portions, if the hypothesis of extemporization were correct, the words of course would be different, but the substance might remain untouched. I suspect, however, that the extemporization was nothing like so complete as the learned writer imagined, but rather that the tale, as told with song and narrative mingled, was in a state of gradual decay or transition from verse to prose, and that the prose portions were, to almost as great an extent as the verse, traditional.

Be this as it may, the tenacity with which the illiterate story-teller generally adheres to the substance and to the very words of his narrative is remarkable—and this in spite of the freedom sometimes taken of dramatic illustration, and the license to introduce occasional local and personal allusions and "gag." These are easily separable from the genuine tale. What Dr. Rink says of the Eskimo story-telling holds good, more or less, all over the world. "The art," he states, "requires the ancient tales to be related as nearly as possible in the very words of the original version, with only a few arbitrary reiterations, and otherwise only varied according to the individual talents of the narrator, as to the mode of recitation, gesture, &c. The only real discretionary power allowed by the audience to the narrator is the insertion of a few peculiar passages from other traditions; but even in that case no alteration of these original or elementary materials used in the composition of tales is admissible. Generally, even the smallest deviation from the original version will be taken notice of and corrected, if any intelligent person happens to be present. This circumstance," he adds, "accounts for their existence in an unaltered shape through ages; for had there been the slightest tendency to variation on the part of the narrator, or relish for it on that of the audience, every similarity of these tales, told in such widely-separated countries, would certainly have been lost in the course of centuries." Here the audience, wedded to the accustomed formularies, is represented as controlling any inclination to variation on the reciter's part. How far such an attitude of mind may have been produced by previous repetitions in the same words we need not inquire. Certain it is that accuracy would be likely to generate the love of accuracy, and *that* again to react so as to compel adherence to the form of words which the ear had been led to expect. Readers of Grimm will remember the anxiety betrayed by a peasant woman of Niederzwehr, near Cassel, that her very words and expressions should be taken down. They who have studied the records collectors have made of the methods they have adopted, and the assistance they have received from narrators who have understood and sympathized with their purpose, will not find anything exceptional in this woman's conduct.[13]

Nor must we overlook the effect of dramatic and pantomimic action. At first sight action, like that of Messia or the Arab reciter, might seem to make for freedom in narration. But it may well be questioned if this be so to any great extent. For in a short time certain attitudes, looks, and gestures become inseparably wedded, not only in the actor's mind, but also in the minds of the audience who have grown accustomed to them, with the passages and the very words to which they are appropriate. The eye as well as the ear learns what to expect, with results proportioned to the comparative values of those two senses as avenues of knowledge. The history of the stage, the observation of our own nurseries, will show with how much suspicion any innovation on the mode of interpreting an old favourite is viewed.

To sum up: it would appear that national differences in the manner of story-telling are for the most part superficial. Whether told by men to men in the bazaar or the coffee-house of the East, or by old men or women to children in the sacred recesses of the European home, or by men to a mixed assembly during the endless nights of the Arctic Circle, or in the huts of the tropical forest, and notwithstanding the license often taken by a professional reciter, the endeavour to render to the audience just that which the speaker has himself received from his predecessors is paramount. The faithful delivery of the tradition is the principle underlying all variation of manner; and it is not confined to any one race or people. It is not denied that changes do take place as the story passes from one to another. This indeed is the inevitable result of the play of the two counteracting forces just described—the conservative tendency and the tendency to variation. It is the condition of development; it is what makes a science of Folk-tales both necessary and possible. Nor can it be denied that some changes are voluntary. But the voluntary changes are rare; and the involuntary changes are only such as are natural and unavoidable if the story is to continue its existence in the midst of the ever-shifting social organism of humanity. The student must, therefore, know something of the habits, the natural and social surroundings, and the modes of the thought of the people whose stories he examines. But this known, it is not difficult to decipher the documents.

There is, however, one caution—namely, to be assured that the documents are gathered direct from the lips of the illiterate story-teller, and set down with accuracy and good faith. Every turn of phrase, awkward or coarse though it may seem to cultured ears, must be unrelentingly reported; and every grotesquery, each strange word, or incomprehensible or silly incident, must be given without flinching. Any attempt to soften down inconsistencies, vulgarities or stupidities, detracts from the value of the text, and may hide or destroy something from which the student may be able to make a discovery of importance to science. Happily the collectors of the present day are fully alive to this need. The pains they take to ensure correctness are great, and their experiences in so doing are often very interesting. Happily, too, the student soon learns to distinguish the collections whose sincerity is certain from those furbished up by literary art. The latter may have purposes of amusement to serve, but beyond that they are of comparatively little use.

**FOOTNOTES:**

[1] Campbell, vol. i. pp. xii. xiv. lvii.

[2] Luzel, "Veillées," *passim.*

[3] Introduction to Romero, p. x.; Arnaudin, p. 5.

[4] Thomas Ady, "A Candle in the Dark" (1656) (*Cf.* Aubrey, "Remaines," p. 67); "Gesta Romanorum," Introd., p. xxv. (E.E.T.S.); Lacroix, p. 100.

[5] Pitré, vol. iv. p. xvii.

[6] "Wide-awake Stories," p. 1; Knowles, p. ix.

[7] White, vol. i. p. vi.; Sir G. Grey, p. vii.; Gill, p. xx.; Rink, pp. 83, 85.

[8] Ellis, "History of Madagascar," vol. i. p. 264; Sproat, "Scenes and Studies of Savage Life," p. 51; Im Thurn, pp. 215, 216.

[9] Temple, "Legends of the Panjab," vol. i. p. v.; Thorburn, p. 172; Leland, p. 12; Taylor, p. 306; "Beowulf," lay 16; Tacitus, "Germania," cc., 2, 3; "Ancient Laws and Institutions of Wales" (Public Record Commission, 1841), pp. 15, 35, &c.

[10] Burton, "Nights," vol. x. p. 163; "Revue des Trad. Pop." vol. iv. p. 6. In Greece and Albania, however, the viol would seem not to be used. Women are the chief reciters. Von Hahn, vol. i. p. ix.

[11] Spitta Bey, p. viii.

[12] Steere, pp. v., vii.

[13] Rink, p. 85; Grimm, "Märchen," p. vii.

# CHAPTER II
# SAVAGE IDEAS

Sagas and *Märchen* — Fairy Tales based upon ideas familiar to savages — The Doctrine of Spirits — The Doctrine of Transformation — Totemism — Death — Witchcraft — The predominance of imagination over reason in savages — Method of the inquiry.

Fairy Tales, as defined in the previous chapter, fall under two heads. Under the first we may place all those stories which relate to definite supernatural beings, or definite orders of supernatural beings, held really to exist, and the scenes of which are usually laid in some specified locality. Stories belonging to this class do not necessarily, however, deal with the supernatural. Often they are told of historical heroes, or persons believed to have once lived. For instance, the legends of Lady Godiva and Whittington and his Cat, which, however improbable, contain nothing of the supernatural, must be reckoned under this head equally with the story of the Luck of Edenhall, or the Maori tale of the Rending asunder of Heaven and Earth. In other words, this class is by no means confined to Fairy Tales, but includes all stories which are, or at all events have been up to recent years, and in the form in which they come to us, looked upon as narratives of actual occurrences. They are called *Sagas*. The other class of tales consists of such as are told simply for amusement, like Jack and the Beanstalk, Cinderella, Beauty and the Beast, and Puss in Boots. They may embody incidents believed in other countries, or in other stages of civilization, to be true in fact; but in the form in which we have them this belief has long since been dropped. In general, the reins are thrown upon the neck of the imagination; and, marvellous though the story be, it cannot fail to find acceptance, because nobody asserts that its events ever took place, and nobody desires to bring down its flights to the level either of logic or experience. Unlike the saga, it binds the conscience neither of teller nor of listener; its hero or heroine has no historical name or fame, either national or local; and being untrammelled either by history or probability, the one condition the tale is expected to fulfil is to end happily. Stories of this class are technically called *Märchen*: we have no better English name for them than *Nursery Tales*.

If we inquire which of these two species of tales is the earlier in the history of culture, it seems that the priority must be given to sagas. The matter, indeed, is not quite free from doubt, because low down in the scale of civilization, as among the Ainos of Japan, stories are told which appear to be no more than *märchen*; and because, on the other hand, it is at all times easier, even for experienced collectors, to obtain sagas than *märchen*. But among the lower races, a vastly preponderating number of tales recorded by Europeans who have lived with them on the terms of the greatest intimacy is told to account for the phenomena of nature, or their own history and organization. From many savage peoples we have no other stories at all; and it is not uncommon to find narratives at bottom identical with some of these told as *märchen* among nations that have reached a higher plane. In these cases, at all events, it looks as if the tales, or tales from which they had been derived, had been originally believed as true, and, having ceased to be thus received, had continued to be repeated, in a shape more or less altered, for mere amusement. If we may venture to affirm this and to generalize from such cases, this is the way in which *märchen* have arisen.

But sagas are not only perhaps the most ancient of tales, they are certainly the most persistent. By their attachment to places and to persons, a religious sanction is frequently given to them, a local and national pride is commonly felt in preserving them. Thus they are remembered when nursery tales are forgotten; they are more easily communicated to strangers; they find their way into literature and so are rendered imperishable.

Fairy Tales of both these classes are compounded of incidents which are the common property of many nations, and not a few whereof are known all over the habitable globe. In some instances the whole plot, a more or less intricate one, is found among races the most diverse in civilization and character. Where the plot is intricate, or contains elements of a kind unlikely to have originated independently, we may be justified in suspecting diffusion from one centre. Then it is that the history and circumstances of a nation become important factors in the inquiry; and upon the purity of blood and the isolation from neighbouring races may depend our decision as to the original or derivative character of such a tradition. Sometimes the passage of a story from one country to another can be proved by literary evidence. This is markedly the case with Apologues and Facetious Tales, two classes of traditions which do not come within the purview of the present work. But the story has then passed beyond the traditional stage, or else such proof could not be given. In tracing the history of a folk-tale which has entered into literature, the problem is to ascertain how far the literary variations we meet with may have been influenced by pre-existing traditional tales formed upon similar lines. In general, however, it may be safely said of Fairy Tales (with which we are more immediately concerned) that the argument in favour of their propagation from a single centre lacks support. The incidents of which they are composed are based upon ideas not peculiar to any one people, ideas familiar to savages everywhere, and only slowly modified and transformed as savagery gives way to barbarism, and barbarism to modern civilization and scientific knowledge of the material phenomena of the universe. The ideas referred to are expressed by races in the lower culture both in belief and in custom. And many of the tales which now amuse our children appear to have grown out of myths believed in the most matter-of-fact way by our remote forefathers; while others enshrine relics of long-forgotten customs and modes of tribal organization.

There is one habit of thought familiar to savage tribes that to us, trained through long centuries of progressive knowledge, seems in the highest degree absurd and even incomprehensible. As a matter of every-day practice we cannot, if we would, go back to that infantine state of mind which regards not only our fellow men and women, but all objects animate and inanimate around us, as instinct with a consciousness, a personality akin to our own. This, however, is the savage philosophy of things. To a large proportion of human beings at the present day beasts and birds, trees and plants, the sea, the mountains, the wind, the sun, the moon, the clouds and the stars, day and night, the heaven and the earth, are alive and possessed of the passions and the cunning and the will they feel within themselves. The only difference is that these things are vastly cleverer and more powerful than men. Hence they are to be dreaded, to be appeased—if possible, to be outwitted—even, sometimes, to be punished. We may observe this childish habit of thought in our nurseries to-day when one of our little ones accidentally runs against the table, and forthwith turns round to beat the senseless wood as if it had voluntarily and maliciously caused his pain; or when another, looking wistfully out of window, adjures the rain in the old rhyme:

"Rain, rain, go away!
Come again another day!"

Poets, too, and orators in their loftiest moods revert to language and modes of expression which have no meaning apart from this belief in the conscious animation of every object in the world. They may move us for the moment by their utterances; but we never take their raptures literally. To the savage, however, it is no figure of speech to call upon the sun to behold some great deed, or to declare that the moon hides her face; to assert that the ocean smiles, or that the river swells with rage, and overwhelms a wayfarer who is crossing it, or an unsuspecting village on its banks. These phrases for him fit the facts of nature as closely as those which record that the man eats or the boy runs. Nay, what would seem incredible to him would be to deny that the sun can see or the moon hide her face, the ocean smile or the river become enraged. Conscious personality and human emotions are visible to him everywhere and in all things.

It matters not to the savage that human form and speech are absent. These are not necessary, or, if they are, they can be assumed either at will or under certain conditions. For one of the consequences, or at least one of the accompaniments, of this stage of thought is the belief in change of form without loss of individual identity. The bear whom the savage meets in the woods is too cunning to appear and do battle with him as a man; but he could if he chose. The stars were once men and women. Sun and moon, the wind and the waters, perform all the functions of living beings: they speak, they eat, they marry and have children. Rocks and trees are not always as immovable as they appear: sometimes they are to be seen as beasts or men, whose shapes they still, it may be, dimly retain.

It follows that peoples in this stage of thought cannot have, in theory at all events, the repugnance to a sexual union between man and the lower animals with which religious training and the growth of civilization have impressed all the higher races. Such peoples admit the possibility of a marriage wherein one party may be human and the other an animal of a different species, or even a tree or plant. If they do not regard it as an event which can take place in their own time and neighbourhood, it does not seem entirely incredible as an event of the past; and sometimes customs are preserved on into a higher degree of culture—such as that of wedding, for special purposes, a man to a tree—unmistakably bespeaking former, if not present, beliefs. Moreover, tribes in the stage of thought here described, hold themselves to be actually descended from material objects often the most diverse from human form. These are not only animals (beasts, birds, fishes, reptiles, and even insects) or vegetables, but occasionally the sun, the sea, the earth, and other things unendowed with life. Such mythic ancestors are worshipped as divine. This superstition is called *Totemism*, and the mythic ancestor is known as the *Totem*. As a people passes gradually into a higher stage of culture, greater stress is constantly laid on the human qualities of the Totem, until it becomes at length an anthropomorphic god. To such deity the object previously reverenced as a Totem is attached, and a new and modified legend grows up to account for the connection.

The belief in metamorphosis involves opinions on the subject of death which are worth a moment's pause. Death is a problem to all men, to the savage as to the most civilized. Least of any can the savage look upon it as extinction. He emphatically believes that he has something within him that survives the dissolution of his outward frame. This is his spirit, the seat of his consciousness, his real self. As he himself has a spirit, so every object in the world has a spirit. He peoples the universe, as he knows it, with spirits akin to his own. It is to their spirits that all the varied objects around him, all the phenomena observable by day or by night, owe the consciousness, the personality, I have already tried to describe. These spirits are separable from the material form with which they are clad. When the savage sleeps, his spirit goes forth upon various adventures. These adventures he remembers as dreams; but they are as veritable as his waking deeds; and he awakes when his spirit returns to him. In his dreams he sees his friends, his foes; he kills imaginary bears and venison. He knows therefore that other men's spirits travel while their bodies sleep and undergo adventures like his own, and in company often with his spirit. He knows that the spirits of wild animals range abroad and encounter his spirit. What is death but the spirit going forth to return no more? Rocks and rivers perhaps cannot die, or at least their life immeasurably exceeds that of men. But the trees of the forest may, for he can cut them down and burn them. Yet, inasmuch as it is the nature of a body to have an indwelling spirit, death—the permanent severing of body and spirit—cannot occur naturally: it must be due to the machination of some enemy, by violence, by poison, or by sorcery.

The spirit that has gone forth for ever is not, by quitting its bodily tenement, deprived of power offensive and defensive. It is frequently impelled by hostile motives to injure those yet in the flesh; and it must, therefore, be appeased, or deceived, or driven away. This is the end and aim of funeral rites: this is the meaning of many periodical ceremonies in which the whole tribe takes part. For the same reason, when the hunter slays a powerful animal, he apologizes and lays the blame on his arrows or his spear, or on some one else. For the same reason the woodman, when he cuts down a tree, asks permission to do so and offers sacrifices, and he provides a green sprig to stick into the stump as soon as the tree falls, that it may be a new home for the spirit thus dislodged. For since the spirit is neither slain, nor deprived of power, by destruction of the body, or by severance from the body, it may find another to dwell in. Spirits of dead men, like other spirits, may assume fresh bodies, new forms, and forms not necessarily human. A favourite form is that of a snake: it was as a snake that the spirit of Anchises appeared and accepted the offerings made by his pious son. In their new forms the spirits of the dead are sometimes, as in this case, kindly, at other times malicious, but always to be treated with respect, always to be conciliated; for their power is great. They can in their turn cause disease, misfortune, death.

Another characteristic of the mental condition I am describing must not be omitted. Connection of thought, even though purely fortuitous, is taken to indicate actual connection of the things represented in thought. This connection is, of course, often founded on association of time or place, and once formed it is not easily broken. For example, any object once belonging to a man recalls the thought of him. The connection between him and that object is therefore looked upon as still existing, and he may be affected by the conduct shown towards it. This applies with special force to such objects as articles of clothing, and still more to footprints and to spittle, hair, nail-parings and excrement. Injury to these with malicious intent will hurt him from whom they are derived. In the same way a personal name is looked upon as inseparable from its owner; and savages are frequently careful to guard the knowledge of their true names from others, being content to be addressed and spoken of by a nickname, or a substituted epithet. The reason of this is that the knowledge of another's name confers power over that other: it is as though he, or at least an essential part of him, were in the possession of the person who had obtained the knowledge of his name. It is perhaps not an unfair deduction from the same premises that endows an image with the properties of its prototype—nay, identifies it with its prototype. This leads on the one hand to idol-worship, and on the other hand to the rites of witchcraft wherein the wizard is said to make a figure of a man, call it by his name, and then transfix it with nails or thorns, or burn it, with the object of causing pain and ultimately death to the person represented. Nor is a very different process of thought discernible in the belief that by eating human or other flesh the spirit (or at any rate some of the spiritual qualities) formerly animating it can be transferred to the eater. So a brave enemy is devoured in the hope of acquiring his bravery; and a pregnant woman is denied the flesh of hares and other animals whose qualities it is undesirable her children should have.

To minds guiltless of inductive reasoning an accidental coincidence is a sure proof of cause and effect. Travellers' tales are full of examples of misfortunes quite beyond foresight or control, but attributed by the savages among whom the narrators have sojourned to some perfectly innocent act on their part, or merely to their presence, or to some strange article of their equipment. Occasionally the anger of the gods is aroused by these things; and missionaries, in particular, have suffered much on this account. But sometimes a more direct causation is imagined, though it is probably not always easy to distinguish the two cases. Omens also are founded upon accidental coincidences. The most lively imagination may fail to trace cause and effect between the meeting of a magpie at setting out and a fruitless errand following, or between a certain condition of the entrails of an animal sacrificed and a victory or defeat thereafter. But the imagination is not to be beaten thus. If the magpie did not cause failure, at all events it foretold it; and the look of the entrails was an omen of the gain or loss of the battle.

Again, a merely fanciful resemblance is a sufficient association to establish actual connection. Why do the Bushmen kindle great fires in time of drought, if not because of the similarity in appearance between smoke and rain-clouds? Such resemblances, to give a familiar instance, have fastened on certain rocks and stones many legends of transformation in conformity with the belief already discussed; and they account for a vast variety of symbolism in the rites and ceremonies of nations all over the world.

The topic is well nigh endless; but enough has been said to enable the reader to see how widely pervasive in human affairs is the belief in real connection founded on nothing more substantial than association of thought, however occasioned. Nothing, indeed, is too absurd for this belief. It is one of the most fruitful causes of superstition; and it only disappears very gradually from the higher civilization as the reasoning powers become more and more highly trained. In magic, or witchcraft, we find it developed into a system, with professional ministers and well-established rules. By these rules its ministers declare themselves able to perform all the wonders of transformation referred to above, to command spirits, to bring distant persons and things into their immediate presence, to inflict injury and death upon whom they please, to bestow wealth and happiness, and to foretell the future. The terror they have thus inspired, and the horrors wrought under the influence of that terror, form one of the saddest chapters of history.[14]

I do not of course pretend that the foregoing is a complete account of the mental processes of savage peoples. Still less have I attempted to trace the history of the various characteristics mentioned, or to show the order of their evolution. To attempt either of these things would be beyond the scope of the present work. I have simply enumerated a few of the elements in the psychology of men in a low state of culture which it is needful to bear in mind in order to understand the stories we are about to examine. In those stories we shall find many impossibilities, many absurdities and many traces of customs repulsive to our modes of thought and foreign to our manners. The explanation is to be obtained, not by speculations based on far-fetched metaphors supposed to have existed in the speech of early races, nor in philological puzzles, but by soberly inquiring into the facts of barbarian and savage life and into the psychological phenomena of which the facts are the outcome. The evidence of these facts and phenomena is to be found scattered up and down the pages of writers of every age, creed and country. On hardly any subject have men of such different degrees of learning, such various and opposite prejudices, left us their testimony—testimony from the nature of the subject more than ordinarily liable to be affected by prejudice, and by the limitations of each witness's powers of observation and opportunities of ascertaining the truth. But after all deductions for prejudice, mistake, inaccuracy and every other shortcoming, there is left a strong, an invincible consensus of testimony, honest, independent and full of undesigned corroborations, to the development of the mind of all races in the lower culture along the lines here indicated. Nay, more; the numerous remains of archaic institutions, as well as of beliefs among the most advanced nations, prove that they too have passed through the very same stages in which we find the most backward still lingering—stages which the less enlightened classes even of our own countrymen at the present day are loth to quit. And the further we penetrate in these investigations, the more frequent and striking are the coincidences between the mental phenomena already described which are still manifested by savage peoples, and those of which the evidence has not yet disappeared from our own midst.

Nor need we be surprised at this, for the root whence all these phenomena spring is the predominance of imagination over reason in the uncivilized. Man, while his experience is limited to a small tract of earth, and his life is divided between a struggle with nature and his fellow-man for the permission and the means to live, on the one hand, and seasons of idleness, empty perforce of every opportunity and every desire for improving his condition, on the other, cannot acquire the materials of a real knowledge of his physical environment. His only data for interpreting the world and the objects it contains, so far as he is acquainted with them, are his own consciousness and his own emotions. Upon these his drafts are unbounded; and if he have any curiosity about the origin and government of things, his hypotheses take the shape of tales in which the actors, whatever form they bear, are essentially himself in motive and deed, but magnified and distorted to meet his wishes or his fears, or the conditions of the problem as presented to his limited vision. The thought which is the measure of his universe is as yet hardly disciplined by anything beyond his passions.

Nor does the predominance of the imagination issue only in these tales and in songs—the two modes of expression we most readily attribute to the imagination. In practical life it issues in superstitious observances, and in social and political institutions. Social institutions are sometimes of great complexity, even in the depth of savagery. Together with political institutions they supply the model on which are framed man's ideas of the relationship to one another and to himself of the supernatural beings whom he creates; and in turn they reflect and perpetuate those ideas in ceremonial and other observances. The student of Fairy Tales, therefore, cannot afford to neglect the study of institutions; for it often throws a light altogether unexpected on the origin and meaning of a story. Tradition must, indeed, be studied as a whole. As with other sciences, its division into parts is natural and necessary; but it should never be forgotten that none of its parts can be rightly understood without reference to the others. By Tradition I mean the entire circle of thought and practice, custom as well as belief, ceremonies, tales, music, songs, dances and other amusements, the philosophy and the superstitions and the institutions, delivered by word of mouth and by example from generation to generation through unremembered ages: in a word, the sum total of the psychological phenomena of uncivilized man. Every people has its own body of Tradition, its own Folklore, which comprises a slowly diminishing part, or the whole, of its mental furniture, according as the art of writing is, or is not, known. The invention of writing, by enabling records to be made and thoughts and facts to be communicated with certainty from one to another, first renders possible the accumulation of true knowledge and ensures a constantly accelerating advance in civilization. But in every civilized nation there are backward classes to whom reading and writing are either quite unknown, or at least unfamiliar; and there are certain matters in the lives even of the lettered classes which remain more or less under the dominion of Tradition. Culture, in the sense of a mode of life guided by reason and utilizing the discoveries and inventions that are the gift of science, finds its way but slowly among a people, and filters only sluggishly through its habits, its institutions and its creeds. Surely, however, though gradually it advances, like a rising tide which creeps along the beach, here undermining a heap of sand, there surrounding, isolating, and at last submerging a rock, here swallowing up a pool brilliant with living creatures and many-coloured weed, there mingling with and overwhelming a rivulet that leaps down to its embrace, until all the shore is covered with its waters. Meanwhile, he who would understand its course must know the conformation of the coast,—the windings, the crags (their composition as well as their shape), the hollows, the sands, the streams; for without these its currents and its force are alike inexplicable. The analogy must not be pressed too far; but it will help us to understand why we find a fragment of a custom in one place, a portion of a tale jumbled up with portions of dissimilar tales in another place, a segment of a superstition, and again a worn and broken relic of a once vigorous institution. They are the rocks and the sands which the flood of civilization is first isolating, then undermining, and at last overwhelming, and hiding from our view. They are (to change the figure) survivals of an earlier state of existence, unintelligible if regarded singly, made to render up their secret only by comparison with other survivals, and with examples of a like state of existence elsewhere. Taken collectively, they enable us to trace the evolution of civilization from a period before history begins, and through more recent times by channels whereof history gives no account.

These are the premises whence we set out, and the principles which will guide us, in the study on which we are about to enter. The name of Fairy Tales is legion; but they are made up of incidents whose number is comparatively limited. And though it would be impossible to deal adequately with more than a small fraction of them in a work like the present, still a selection may be so treated as to convey a reasonably just notion of the application of the principles laid down and of the results to be obtained. In making such a selection several interesting groups of stories, unconnected as between themselves, might be chosen for consideration. The disadvantage of this course would be the fragmentary nature of the discussions, and consequently of the conclusions arrived at. It is not wholly possible to avoid this disadvantage in any mode of treatment; but it is possible to lessen it. I propose, therefore, to deal with a few of the most interesting sagas relative to the Fairy Mythology strictly so called. We shall thus confine our view to a well-defined area, in the hope that we may obtain such an idea of it as in its main lines at all events may be taken to be fairly true to the facts, and that we may learn who really were these mysterious beings who played so large a part in our fathers' superstitions. As yet, however, we must not be disappointed if we find that the state of scientific inquiry will not admit of many conclusions, and such as we may reach can at present be stated only tentatively and with caution. Science, like Mr. Fox in the nursery tale, writes up over all the doors of her palace:

"Be bold, be bold, but not too bold."

Many a victim has found to his cost what it meant to disregard this warning.

**FOOTNOTES:**

[14] I have not thought it necessary to illustrate at length the characteristics of savage thought enumerated above. They are exhaustively discussed by Dr. Tylor in "Primitive Culture," Sir John Lubbock in "The Origin of Civilization," Mr. Andrew Lang in "Myth Ritual and Religion," and some of them by Mr. J. G. Frazer in "Totemism," and more recently in "The Golden Bough," published since these pages were written.

# CHAPTER III

# FAIRY BIRTHS AND HUMAN MIDWIVES

Stories of midwives who have been summoned to the birth of fairies — Human visitors to Fairyland must not eat there — The reason — Fairies' gratitude — The conditions of fairy gifts.

A tale, the scene of which is laid near Beddgelert, runs, as translated by Professor Rhys, in this way:—"Once on a time, when a midwife from Nanhwynan had newly got to the Hafodydd Brithion to pursue her calling, a gentleman came to the door on a fine grey steed and bade her come with him at once. Such was the authority with which he spoke, that the poor midwife durst not refuse to go, however much it was her duty to stay where she was. So she mounted behind him, and off they went, like the flight of a swallow, through Cwmllan, over the Bwlch, down Nant yr Aran, and over the Gadair to Cwm Hafod Ruffydd before the poor woman had time even to say Oh! When they got there, she saw before her a magnificent mansion, splendidly lit up with such lamps as she had never before seen. They entered the court, and a crowd of servants in expensive liveries came to meet them, and she was at once led through the great hall into a bed-chamber, the like of which she had never seen. There the mistress of the house, to whom she had been fetched, was awaiting her. She got through her duties successfully, and stayed there until the lady had completely recovered, nor had she spent any part of her life so merrily; there was naught but festivity day and night: dancing, singing, and endless rejoicing reigned there. But merry as it was, she found she must go, and the nobleman gave her a large purse, with the order not to open it until she had got into her own house; then he bade one of his servants escort her the same way she had come. When she reached home she opened the purse, and, to her great joy, it was full of money; and she lived happily on those earnings to the end of her life."[15]

It is a long leap from Carnarvonshire to Lapland, where this story is told with no great variation. A clergyman's wife in Swedish Lappmark, the cleverest midwife in all Sweden, was summoned one fine summer's evening to attend a mysterious being of Troll race and great might, called Vitra. At this unusual call she took counsel with her husband, who, however, deemed it best for her to go. Her guide led her into a splendid building, the rooms whereof were as clean and elegant as those of very illustrious folk; and in a beautiful bed lay a still more beautiful woman, for whom her services were required, and who was no other than Vitra herself. Under the midwife's care Vitra speedily gave birth to a fair girl, and in a few minutes had entirely recovered, and fetched all sorts of refreshments, which she laid before her benefactress. The latter refused to eat, in spite of Vitra's reassuring persuasion, and further refused the money which the Troll-wife pressed upon her. Vitra then sent her home, bidding her look on the table when next she entered her cowherd's hut and see what she would find there. She thought no more of the matter until the following spring, when on entering the hut she found on the table half a dozen large spoons of pure silver with her name engraved thereon in neat letters. These spoons long remained an heirloom in the clergyman's family to testify the truth of the story. A Swedish book, published in 1775, contains a tale, narrated in the form of a legal declaration solemnly subscribed on the 12th April 1671 by the fortunate midwife's husband, whose name was Peter Rahm, and who also seems to have been a clergyman. On the authority of this declaration we are called on to believe that the event recorded actually happened in the year 1660. Peter Rahm alleges that he and his wife were at their farm one evening late when there came a little man, swart of face and clad in grey, who begged the declarant's wife to come and help his wife then in labour. The declarant, seeing that they had to do with a Troll, prayed over his wife, blessed her, and bade her in God's name go with the stranger. She seemed to be borne along by the wind. After her task was accomplished she, like the clergyman's wife just mentioned, refused the food offered her, and was borne home in the same manner as she had come. The next day she found on a shelf in the sitting-room a heap of old silver pieces and clippings, which it is to be supposed the Troll had brought her.[16]

Apart from the need of human aid, common to all the legends with which we are dealing, the two points emphasized by these Swedish tales are the midwife's refusal of food and the gratitude of the Troll. In a Swabian story the Earthman, as he is called, apologizes for omitting to offer food. In this case the midwife was afraid to go alone with her summoner, and begged that her husband might accompany her. This was permitted; and the Earthman showed them the way through the forest with his lantern, for it was of course night. They came first to a moss door, then to a wooden door, and lastly to a door of shining metal, whence a staircase went down into the earth, and led them into a large and splendid chamber where the Earthwife lay. When the object of their visit was accomplished the Earthman thanked the woman much, and said: "You do not relish our meat and drink, wherefore I will bestow something else upon thee." With these words he gave her a whole apronful of black coals, and taking his lantern again he lighted the midwife and her husband home. On the way home she slily threw away one coal after another. The Earthman said nothing until he was about to take his leave, when he observed merely: "The less you scattered the more you might have." After he had gone the woman's husband remonstrated with her, bidding her keep the coals, for the Earthman appeared in earnest with his gift. When they reached home, however, she shook out her apron on the hearth, and behold! instead of coals, glittering true gold pieces. The woman now sought eagerly enough after the coals she had thrown away, but she found them not.[17]

Confining our attention for the moment to the refusal of food, it would seem that the Earthman's apology in the foregoing narrative is, as too many human apologies are, a mere excuse. The real reason for the midwife's abstention was not that fairy food was distasteful, but that she durst not touch it, under penalty of never again returning to the light of day. A Danish tradition tells of a woman who was taken by an elf on Christmas Eve down into the earth to attend his wife. As soon as the elfwife was delivered her husband took the child away; for if he could find two newly married persons in the bridal bed, before they had repeated their Paternoster, he could, by laying the child between them, procure for it all the good fortune intended for the newly wedded pair. During his absence the elfwife took the opportunity of instructing her helper as to her conduct when he returned; and the first and chief point of her advice was to eat nothing that was offered her. The elfwife was herself a Christian woman who had been inveigled down into the dwellings of the elves; she had eaten, and therefore had never escaped again. On the elf's return, accordingly, the midwife refused food, and he said: "They did not strike thee on the mouth who taught thee that." Late rabbinical writings contain a similar legend of a Mohel, a man whose office it was to circumcise, who was summoned one winter's night by a stranger to perform the ceremony upon a child who would be eight days old the following day. The stranger led him to a lofty mountain, into the bowels of which they passed, and after descending many flights of steps found themselves in a great city. Here the Mohel was taken to a palace, in one of whose apartments was the child's mother lying. When she saw the Mohel she began to weep, and told him that he was in the land of the Mazikin, but that she was a human being, a Jewess, who had been carried away when little from home and brought thither. And she counselled him to take good heed to refuse everything whether of meat or drink that might be offered him: "For if thou taste anything of theirs thou wilt become like one of them, and wilt remain here for ever."[18]

We touch here upon a very ancient and widespread superstition, which we may pause to illustrate from different parts of the world. A Manx tale, which can be traced back to Waldron, narrates the night adventure of a farmer who lost his way in returning home from Peel, and was led by the sound of music into a large hall where were a great number of little people feasting. Among them were some faces he seemed to know; but he took no notice of them until the little folk offered him drink, when one of them, whose features seemed not unknown to him, plucked him by the coat and forbade him, whatever he did, to taste anything he saw before him; "for if you do", he added, "you will be as I am, and return no more to your family."[19]

It is necessary for the hero of a Picard story to go and seek the devil in his own abode. The devil of popular imagination, though a terrific ogre, is not the entirely Evil One of theologians; and one of his good points in the story referred to is that he has three fair daughters, the fairest of whom is compelled by the hero to help him in overcoming her father. She accordingly instructs him to eat no meat and to drink no wine at the devil's house, otherwise he will be poisoned. This may remind us of Kan Püdäi, who in the Altaic ballad descends with his steed to the middle of the earth and encounters various monsters. There the grass and the water of the mountain forest through which he rode were poison. In both cases, what is probably meant is, that to eat or drink is to return no more from these mysterious abodes; and it may be to the intent to obviate any such consequence that Saint Peter, in sending a certain king's son down through a black and stinking hole a hundred toises deep underground, in a Gascon tale, to fetch Saint Peter's own sword, provides him with just enough bread in his wallet every morning to prevent his bursting with hunger. An extension of this thought sometimes even prohibits the hero from accepting a seat or a bed offered by way of hospitality on the part of the devil, or the sorceress, to whose dwelling his business may take him, or even to look at the fair temptress who may seek to entice him to eat.[20]

The meaning of the superstition is not easy to trace, but it should be remembered that in the lower stages of human civilization no distinction is drawn between supernatural or spiritual beings who have never been enclosed in human bodies, and the spirits of the dead. Savage philosophy mingles them together in one phantasmagoria of grotesquery and horror. The line which separates fairies and ogres from the souls of men has gradually grown up through ages of Christian teaching; and, broad as it may seem to us, it is occasionally hardly visible in these stories. Every now and then it is ignored, as in the case of the old friends found among the "little people" by the Manx farmer. Less startling than these, but quite as much in point, are the women, like some already mentioned, who are carried off into Fairyland, where they become wives and mothers. They can never come back to their old life, though they retain enough of the "mortal mixture" to require the adventurous human midwife to relieve their pains. Accordingly, we need not be surprised if the same incidents of story or fibres of superstition attach at one time to ghosts and at another to the non-human creatures of imagination, or if Hades and Fairyland are often confounded. Both are equally the realm of the supernatural. We may therefore inquire whether eating is forbidden to the chance sojourner in the place of the dead equally as to the sojourner in Fairyland, if he wish to return to the upper air. And we shall find that it is.

Proserpine ate seven grains of a pomegranate which grew in the Elysian Fields, and so was compelled to remain in the Shades, the wife of "the grisly king." Thus, too, when Morgan the Fay takes measures to get Ogier the Dane into her power she causes him to be shipwrecked on a loadstone rock near to Avalon. Escaping from the sea, he comes to an orchard, and there eats an apple which, it is not too much to say, seals his fate. Again, when Thomas of Erceldoune is being led down by the Fairy Queen into her realm, he desires to eat of the fruit of certain trees.

"He presed to pul the frute with his honde,
As man for fode was nyhonde feynte;
She seid, Thomas, lat them stande,
Or ellis the fiend will the ateynte.
If thou pulle the sothe to sey,
Thi soule goeth to the fyre of hell

Hit cummes never out til doomsday,
But ther ever in payne to dwelle."

An old story preserved for us by Saxo Grammaticus describes the visit of some Danish heroes to Guthmund, a giant who rules a delightful land beyond a certain river crossed by a golden bridge. Thorkill, their conductor, a Scandinavian Ulysses for cunning, warns his companions of the various temptations that will be set before them. They must forbear the food of the country, and be satisfied with that which they had brought with them; moreover, they must keep apart from the natives, taking care not so much as to touch them. In spite, however, of Thorkill's warnings to them, and his excuses in their behalf to the king, some of the heroes fell and were left behind when their friends were at last allowed to depart.[21] So far we see that the prohibition and the danger we found extant in the Fairyland of modern folk-tales apply also to the classic Hades; and we have traced them back a long way into the Middle Ages in French, British, and Danish traditions relating to fairies and other supernatural existences, with a special threat of Hell in the case of Thomas of Erceldoune.

On the other side of the globe the Banks' islanders believe, like the Greeks, in an underground kingdom of the dead, which they call Panoi. Only a few years ago a woman was living who professed to have been down there. Her object had been to visit her brother, who had recently died. To do this she perfumed herself with water in which a dead rat had been steeped, so as to give herself a death-like smell. She then pulled up a bird's nest and descended through the hole thus made. Her brother, whom of course she found, cautioned her to eat nothing, and by taking his advice she was able to return. A similar tale is told of a New Zealand woman of rank, who was lucky enough to come back from the abode of departed spirits by the assistance of her father and his repeated commands to avoid tasting the disgusting food of the dead. Wäinämöinen, the epic hero of the Finns, determined to penetrate to Manala, the region of the dead. We need not follow in detail his voyage; it will suffice to say that on his arrival, after a long parley with the maiden daughter of Tuoni, the king of the island, beer was brought to him in a two-eared tankard.

"Wäinämöinen, old and trusty,
Gaz'd awhile upon the tankard;
Lo! within it frogs were spawning,
Worms about its sides were laying.
Words in this wise then he utter'd:
'Not to drink have I come hither
From the tankard of Manala,
Not to empty Tuoni's beaker;
They who drink of beer are drowned,
Those who drain the can are ruin'd.'"[22]

The hero's concluding words might form a motto for our teetotallers; and in any case his abstinence enabled him to succeed in his errand and return. A point is made in the poem of the loathsome character of the beverage offered him, which thus agrees with the poison referred to in some of the narratives I have previously cited. The natives of the Southern Seas universally represent the sustenance of spirits as filthy and abominable. A most remarkable coincidence with the description of Tuoni's beer occurs in a curious story told on one of the Hervey Islands, concerning a Mangaian Dante. Being apparently near death, this man directed that, as soon as the breath was out of his body, a cocoa-nut should be cracked, and its kernel disengaged from the shell and placed upon his stomach under the grave-clothes. Having descended to the Shades, he beheld Miru, the horrible hag who rules them, and whose deformities need not now be detailed. She commanded him to draw near. "The trembling human spirit obeyed, and sat down before Miru. According to her unvarying practice she set for her intended victim a bowl of food, and bade him eat it quite up. Miru, with evident anxiety, waited to see him swallow it. As Tekanae took up the bowl, to his horror he found it to consist of living centipedes. The quick-witted mortal now recollected the cocoa-nut kernel at the pit of his stomach, and hidden from Miru's view by his clothes. With one hand he held the bowl to his lips, as if about to swallow its contents; with the other he secretly held the cocoa-nut kernel, and ate it—the bowl concealing the nut from Miru. It was evident to the goddess that Tekanae was actually swallowing *something*: what else could it be but the contents of the fatal bowl? Tekanae craftily contrived whilst eating the nourishing cocoa-nut to allow the live centipedes to fall on the ground one or two at a time. As the intended victim was all the time sitting on the ground it was no difficult achievement in this way to empty the bowl completely by the time he had finished the cocoa-nut. Miru waited in vain to see her intended victim writhing in agony and raging with thirst. Her practice on such occasions was to direct the tortured victim-spirit to dive in a lake close by, to seek relief. None that dived into that water ever came up alive; excessive anguish and quenchless thirst so distracting their thoughts that they were invariably drowned. Miru would afterwards cook and eat her victims at leisure. Here was a new event in her history: the bowl of living centipedes had been disposed of, and yet Tekanae manifested no sign of pain, no intention to leap into the cooling, but fatal, waters. Long did Miru wait; but in vain. At last she said to her visitor, 'Return to the upper world' (*i.e.*, to life). 'Only remember this—do not speak against me to mortals. Reveal not my ugly form and my mode of treating my visitors. Should you be so foolish as to do so, you will certainly at some future time come back to my domains, and I will see to it that you do not escape my vengeance a second time!' Tekanae accordingly left the Shades, and came back to life"; but he, it is needless to say, carefully disregarded the hag's injunction, or we should not have had the foregoing veracious account of what happens below.[23]

The tortures reserved for Miru's victims cast a weird light on the warning in the Picard story against eating and drinking what the devil may offer. But whether poisoning in the latter case would have been the preliminary to a hearty meal to be made off the unlucky youth by his treacherous host, or no, it is impossible to determine. What the tales do suggest, however, is that the food buried with the dead by uncivilized tribes may be meant to provide them against the contingency of having to partake of the hospitality of the Shades, and so afford them a chance of escaping back to the upper air. But, putting this conjecture aside, we have found the supposition that to eat of fairy food is to return no more, equally applicable to the world of the dead as to Fairyland. In seeking its meaning, therefore, we must not be satisfied without an explanation that will fit both. Almost all over the earth the rite of hospitality has been held to confer obligations on its recipient, and to unite him by special ties to the giver. And even where the notion of hospitality does not enter, to join in a common meal has often been held to symbolize, if not to constitute, union of a very sacred kind. The formation of blood relationship, or brotherhood, and formal adoption into a tribe or family (ceremonies well known in the lower culture), are usually, if not always, cemented in this way. The modern wedding breakfast, with its bridecake, is a survival from a very ancient mode of solemnizing the closest tie of all; and when Proserpine tasted a pomegranate she partook of a fruit of a specially symbolic character to signify acceptance of her new destiny as her captor's wife. Hence to partake of food in the land of spirits, whether they are human dead, or fairies, is to proclaim one's union with them and to renounce the fellowship of mortals.

The other point emphasized in the Swedish tales quoted just now is the Troll's gratitude, as evidenced by his gifts to the successful midwife. Before considering this, however, let us note that these supernatural beings do not like to be imposed upon. A German midwife who was summoned by a Waterman, or Nix, to aid a woman in labour, was told by the latter: "I am a Christian woman as well as you; and I was carried off by a Waterman, who changed me. When my husband comes in now and offers you money, take no more from him than you usually get, or else he will twist your neck. Take good care!" And in another tale, told at Kemnitz of the Nicker, as he is there called, when he asks the midwife how much he owes her, she answers that she will take no more from him than from other people. "That's lucky for thee," he replies; "hadst thou demanded more, it would have gone ill with thee!" But for all that he gave her an apron full of gold and brought her safely home.[24]

A Pomeranian story marks the transition to a type of tale wherein one special characteristic of elfin gifts is presented. For in this case, when the mannikin asked the midwife what her charge was, she modestly replied: "Oh, nothing; the little trouble I have had does not call for any payment." "Now then, lift up thy apron!" answered he; and it was quickly filled with the rubbish that lay in the corner of the room. Taking his lantern, the elf then politely guided her home. When she shook out the contents of her apron, lo! it was no rubbish which fell on the ground, but pure, shining minted gold. Hitherto she and her father had been very poor; thenceforth they had no more want their whole lives long. This gift of an object apparently worthless, which turns out, on the conditions being observed, of the utmost value, is a commonplace of fairy transactions. It is one of the most obvious manifestations of superhuman power; and as such it has always been a favourite incident in the stories of all nations. We have only to do here with the gift as it appears in the group under analysis; and in these cases it presents little variety. In a tale told on the lake of Zug the dwarf fills the woman's apron with something at which he bids her on no account look before she is in her own house. Her curiosity, however, is uncontrollable; and the moment the dwarf vanishes she peeps into her apron, to find simply black coals. She, in a rage, flings them away, keeping only two as evidence of the shabby treatment she had met with; but when she got home these two were nothing less than precious stones. She at once ran back to where she had shaken out the supposed coals; but they were all gone. So a recompense of straws, dust, birch leaves, or shavings becomes, as elsewhere told, pure gold, pure silver, or thalers. Nor is the story confined to Europe. In Dardistan it is related that a boy, taken down by a Yatsh, or demon, into an underground palace, is allowed to be present at a Yatsh wedding. He finds the Yatshes assembled in great force and in possession of a number of valuables belonging to the dwellers in his own village. On his return his guide presents him with a sack full of coals, which he empties as soon as he is out of sight. One little piece, however, remains, and is transformed into a gold coin when he reaches home.[25]

Conversely, when the midwife is rewarded with that which seems valuable it turns out worthless. An Irishwoman, in relating a professional experience among the Good People, wound up her story as follows: "The king slipped five guineas into my hand as soon as I was on the ground, and thanked me, and bade me good-night. I hope I'll never see his face again. I got into bed, and couldn't sleep for a long time; and when I examined my five guineas this morning, that I left in the table-drawer the last thing, I found five withered leaves of oak—bad scran to the giver!" This incident recalls the Barber's tale of his fourth brother in the "Arabian Nights." This unlucky man went on selling meat to a sorcerer for five months, and putting the bright new money in which the latter paid him into a box by itself; but when he came to open the box he found in it nothing but a parcel of leaves, or, as Sir Richard Burton has it, bits of white paper cut round to look like coin. Chinese folklore is full of similar occurrences, which we cannot now stay to discuss. But, returning to western traditions, there is a way of counteracting the elves' transforming magic. The wife of a farmer named Niels Hansen, of Uglerup, in Denmark, was summoned to attend a troll-wife, who told her that the troll, her husband, would offer her a quantity of gold; "but," she said, "unless you cast this knife behind you when you go out, it will be nothing but coal when you reach home". The woman followed her patient's advice, and so continued to carry safely home a costly present of gold.[26]

The objection of supernatural beings to iron, and its power of undoing their charms, will be considered in a future chapter. The good luck of Niels Hansen's wife offers meantime another subject of interest; for it was due to her own kindness of heart. A short time before she had been raking hay in a field, when she caught a large and fat toad between the teeth of her rake. She gently released it, saying: "Poor thing! I see that thou needest help; I will help thee." That toad was the troll-wife, and as she afterwards attended her she was horrified to see a hideous serpent hanging down just above her head. Her fright led to explanations and an expression of gratitude on the part of the troll-wife. This incident is by no means uncommon; but a very few examples must suffice here. Generally the woman's terror is attributed to a millstone hanging over her head. At Grammendorf, in Pomerania, a maid saw, every time she went to milk the cows, a hateful toad hopping about in the stable. She determined to kill it, and would have seized it one day had it not, in the very nick of time, succeeded in creeping into a hole, where she could not get at it. A few days after, when she was again busy in the stable, a little Ulk, as the elves there are called, came and invited her to descend with him into Fairyland. On reaching the bottom of a staircase with her conductor, she found her services were required for an Ulkwife, whose time was at hand. Entering the dwelling she was frightened to observe a huge millstone above her, suspended by a silken thread; and the Ulk, seeing her terror, told her she had caused him exactly the same, when she chased the poor toad and attempted to kill it. The girl was compelled to share in the feast which followed. When it was over she was given a piece of gold, that she was carefully to preserve; for so long as she did so she would never be in want of money. But her guide warned her at parting never to relate her experience, otherwise the elves would fetch her again, and set her under the millstone, which would then fall and crush her. Whether this was indeed the consequence of her narrating this very true story we do not know. After some of the beliefs we have been considering in the foregoing pages it is, however, interesting to note that no ill attended her eating and drinking in Fairyland, and that the gold she received did not turn to dross, though it possessed other miraculous qualities which might very well have led her to the bad end threatened by the Ulk. Perhaps a portion of the story has been lost.[27]

Sometimes a different turn is given to the tale. A Swabian peasant-woman was once in the fields with her servant-maid, when they saw a big toad. The woman told her maid to kill it. The latter replied: "No; I won't do that, and I will stand sponsor for it yet once more." Not long afterwards she was sent for to become sponsor, and was conducted into the lake, where she found the toad now in guise of a woman. After the ceremony was over, the lake-woman rewarded her with a bushel of straw, and sent by her hand a girdle for her mistress. On the way home the girl tried the girdle on a tree to see how it would look, and in a moment the tree was torn into a thousand pieces. This was the punishment devised by the lake-woman for her mistress, because she had wished to put her to death while in the form of a toad. The straw was, of course, pure gold; but the girl foolishly cast it all away except a few stalks which clung to her dress. So a countryman who accidentally spilt some hot broth on a witch, disguised as a toad, is presented by her another day with a girdle for his little son. Suspecting something wrong, he tries it on his dog, which at once swells up and bursts. This is a Saxon saga from Transylvania; an Irish saga brings us to the same catastrophe. There a girl meets a frog which is painfully bloated, and kicks it unfeelingly aside, with the words: "May you never be delivered till I am midwife to you!" Now the frog was a water-fairy dwelling in a lake, into which the girl soon after was conveyed and compelled to become the fairy's midwife. By way of reward she is presented with a red cloak, which, on her way home, she hangs up in admiration on a tree. Well was it for her that she did so, for it set the tree on fire; and had she worn it, as she meant to do, on the following Sunday at Mass, the chapel itself would have been in a blaze.[28]

The fairies' revenge here missed its mark, though calculated on no trifling scale. Indeed, the rewards they bestowed were never nicely balanced with the good or ill they intended to requite, but were showered in open-handed fashion as by those who could afford to be lavish. Of this we have already had several instances; a few more may be given. At Palermo a tale is told of a midwife who was one day cooking in her own kitchen when a hand appeared and a voice cried: "Give to me!" She took a plate and filled it from the food she was preparing. Presently the hand returned the plate full of golden money. This was repeated daily; and the woman, seeing the generous payment, became more and more free with her portions of food. At the end of nine months a knocking was heard at the door; and, descending, she found two giants, who caught her up on their shoulders, and unceremoniously ran off with her. They carried her to a lady who needed her offices, and she assisted to bring into the world two fine boys. The lady evidently was fully alive to her own dignity, for she kept the woman a proper human month, to the distress of her husband, who, not knowing what had become of her, searched the city night and day, and at last gave her up for dead. Then the lady (a fairy princess she was) asked her if she wished to go, and whether she would be paid by blows or pinches. The poor midwife deemed her last hour was come, and said to herself that if she must die it would be better to die quickly; so she chose blows. Accordingly the princess called the two giants, and sent her home with a large sack of money, which enabled her to relinquish business, set up her carriage, and become one of the first ladies in Palermo. Ten years passed; and one day a grand carriage stopped at her door. A lady alighted and entered her palace. When she had her face to face, the lady said: "Gossip, do you know me?" "No, madam." "What! do you not remember that I am the lady to whom you came ten years ago, when these children were born? I, too, am she who held out her hand and asked for food. I was the fairies' captive; and if you had not been generous enough to give me to eat, I should have died in the night. And because you were generous you have become rich. Now I am freed, and here I am with my sons." The quondam midwife, with tears in her eyes, looked at her, and blessed the moment she had done a generous act. So they became lifelong friends.[29]

I have given the foregoing tale almost at full length because it has not, so far as I know, appeared before in any other than its native Sicilian dress, and because analogous stories are not common in collections from Mediterranean countries. This rarity is not, I need hardly say, from any absence of the mythological material, and perhaps it may be due to accident in the formation of the collections. If the story were really wanting elsewhere in Southern Europe, we might be permitted the conjecture that its presence in Sicily was to be accounted for by the Norman settlements there. One such story, however, is recorded from the Island of Kimolos, one of the Cyclades, but without the human captivity in Elfland, without the acts of charity, and without the gratitude. The Nereids of the Kimoliote caves are of a grimmer humour than the kindly-natured underground folk of Celtic and Teutonic lands, or than the heroine of Palermo. The payment to their human help is no subject of jest to them. A woman whom they once called in was roundly told: "If it be a boy you shall be happy; but if it be a girl we will tear you in four parts, and hang you in this cave." The unhappy midwife of course determined that it should be a boy; and when a girl arrived she made believe it was a boy, swaddled it up tightly, and went home. When, eight days afterwards, the child was unpacked, the Nereids' rage and disappointment were great; and they sent one of their number to knock at her door in the hope that she would answer the first summons. Now to answer the first summons of a Nereid meant madness. Of this the woman was fully aware; and her cunning cheated them even of their revenge.[30]

Sometimes these supernatural beings bestow gifts of a more distinctly divine character than any of the foregoing. A midwife in Strathspey, on one such occasion, was desired to ask what she would, and it should be granted if in the power of the fairies. She asked that success might attend herself and her posterity in all similar operations. The gift was conferred; and her great-grandson still continued to exercise it when Mr. Stewart was collecting the materials for his work on the superstitions of the Highlanders, published in 1823. In like manner the Mohel, to whose adventure I have already referred, and who was originally an avaricious man, received the grace of benevolence to the poor, which caused him to live a long and happy life with his family, a pattern unto the whole world. The gift was symbolized by the restoration to him of his own bunch of keys, which he found with many others in the possession of his uncanny conductor. This personage had held the keys by virtue of his being lord over the hearts of those who never at any time do good: in other words, he was the demon of covetousness. Here we have an instance, more or less conscious, of the tendency, so marked in Jewish literature, to parable. But the form of the parable bears striking testimony to its origin in a myth common to many races. The keys in particular probably indicate that the recompense at one time took the shape of a palladium. This is not at all uncommon in the tales. The Countess Von Ranzau was once summoned from her castle of Breitenburg in Schleswig to the help of a dwarf-woman, and in return received, according to one account, a large piece of gold to be made into fifty counters, a herring and two spindles, upon the preservation of which the fortunes of the family were to depend. The gifts are variously stated in different versions of the tale, but all the versions agree in attaching to them blessings on the noble house of Ranzau so long as they were kept in the family. The Frau Von Hahnen, in a Bohemian legend, receives for her services to a water-nix three pieces of gold, with the injunction to take care of them, and never to let them go out of the hands of her own lineage, else the whole family would fall into poverty. She bequeathed the treasures to her three sons; but the youngest son took a wife, who with a light heart gave the fairy gold away. Misery, of course, resulted from her folly; and the race of Hahnen speedily came to an end.[31]

It is quite possible that the spoons bestowed by Vitra upon the clergyman's wife in Lappmark were once reputed to be the subject of a similar proviso. So common, forsooth, was the stipulation, that in one way or other it was annexed to well-nigh all fairy gifts: they brought luck to their possessor for the time being. Examples of this are endless: one only will content us in this connection; and, like Vitra's gift, we shall find it in Swedish Lappmark. A peasant who had one day been unlucky at the chase, was returning disgusted, when he met a fine gentleman who begged him to come and cure his wife. The peasant protested in vain that he was not a doctor. The other would take no denial, insisting that it was no matter, for if he would only put his hands upon the lady she would be healed. Accordingly the stranger led him to the very top of a mountain, where was perched a castle he had never seen before. On entering it he found the walls were mirrors, the roof overhead of silver, the carpets of gold-embroidered silk, and the furniture of the purest gold and jewels. The stranger took him into a room where lay the loveliest of princesses on a golden bed, screaming with pain. As soon as she saw the peasant she begged him to come and put his hands upon her. Almost stupefied with astonishment he hesitated to lay his coarse hands upon so fair a dame. But at length he yielded; and in a moment her pain ceased, and she was made whole. She stood up and thanked him, begging him to tarry awhile and eat with them. This, however, he declined to do, for he feared that if he tasted the food which was offered him he must remain there. The stranger whom he had followed then took a leathern purse, filled it with small round pieces of wood, and gave it to the peasant with these words: "So long as thou art in possession of this purse money will never fail thee. But if thou shouldst ever see me again, beware of speaking to me; for if thou speak thy luck will depart." When the man got home he found the purse filled with dollars; and by virtue of its magical property he became the richest man in the parish. As soon as he found the purse always full, whatever he took out of it, he began to live in a spendthrift manner and frequented the alehouse. One evening as he sat there he beheld the stranger with a bottle in his hand going round and gathering the drops which the guests shook from time to time out of their glasses. The rich peasant was surprised that one who had given him so much did not seem able to buy himself a single dram, but was reduced to this means of getting a drink. Thereupon he went up to him and said: "Thou hast shown me more kindness than any other man ever did, and I will willingly treat thee to a little." The words were scarce out of his mouth when he received such a blow on his head that he fell stunned to the ground; and when again he came to himself the stranger and his purse were both gone. From that day forward he became poorer and poorer, until he was reduced to absolute beggary.[32]

This story exemplifies every point that had had interested us in this discussion: the need of the Trolls for human help, the refusal of food, fairy gratitude, and the conditions involved in the acceptance of supernatural gifts. It mentions one further characteristic of fairy nature—the objection to be recognized and addressed by men who are privileged to see them. But the consideration of this requires another chapter.

**FOOTNOTES:**

[15] "Y Cymmrodor," vol. v. p. 70, translated from "Y Brython," vol. iv. p. 251.

[16] Poestion, p. 111; Grimm, "Teut. Myth." p. 457, note, quoting at length the declaration from Hülpher, "Samlingen om Jämtland." A translation will be found in Keightley, p. 122.

[17] Meier, p. 59.

[18] Thorpe, vol. ii. p. 128, from Thiele, "Danmark's Folkesagn"; Keightley, p. 506.

[19] Waldron, p. 28.

[20] "Mélusine," vol. i. p. 446; Radloff, vol. i. p. 78; Bladé, vol. i. p. 161; Cosquin, vol. ii. p. 10; Cavallius, p. 281; "Revue des Trad. Pop." vol. iv. p. 222.

[21] Child, vol. i. p. 319; "Thomas of Erceldoune," p. 11 (Cambridge Text); Saxo, "Gesta Dan." l. viii.

[22] *Journal of Anthrop. Inst.* vol. x. p. 282; Shortland, p. 150; "Kalewala," rune xvi. l. 293.

[23] Gill, p. 172.

[24] Keightley, p. 261; Kuhn und Schwartz, p. 93.

[25] Jahn, p. 72; Keightley, p. 275, quoting Müller, "Bilder und Sagen aus der Schweiz," p. 119; Birlinger, "Volksthümliches," vol. i. p. 42; Kuhn, p. 82; Thorpe, vol. ii. p. 128; vol. iii. p. 54, quoting Müllenhoff, "Sagen, &c., der Herzogthümer Schleswig, Holstein und Lauenburg"; Kuhn und Schwartz, p. 173; Wratislaw, p. 40; Wenzig, p. 198; Liebrecht, p. 100, citing "Results of a Tour in Dardistan", part iii. p. 3.

[26] Kennedy, p. 106; Thorpe, vol. ii. p. 130, quoting Thiele, "Danmark's Folkesagn."

[27] Jahn, p. 64; *cf.* p. 74, where there are two maidens, one of whom had saved the toad when the other desired to kill it. They stand sponsors for the fairy child, and are rewarded with sweepings which turn to gold; also Bartsch, vol. i. p. 50, where a sword is suspended.

[28] Meier, p. 69; Müller, p. 140; "N. and Q.," 7th ser. vol. v. p. 501.

[29] Pitré, vol. v. p. 23. The story in its present form does not say that the human food enabled the lady to return from Fairyland, but only that it saved her life. Probably, however, an earlier version may have shown the incident in a more primitive form.

[30] Bent, p. 46.

[31] Keightley, p. 388, citing Stewart; Thorpe, vol. iii. p. 50 *et seq.*, quoting Müllenhoff and Thiele; Grohmann, p. 145; see also Thorpe, vol. iii. p. 51.

[32] Poestion, p. 119.

# CHAPTER IV

# FAIRY BIRTHS AND HUMAN MIDWIVES

## (*continued*)

The magical ointment — Human prying punished by fairies, and by other supernatural beings — Dame Berchta — Hertha — Lady Godiva — Analogous stories in Europe — In the East — Religious ceremonies performed by women only — Lady Godiva a pagan goddess.

Before we quit the subject of fairy births, we have a few more stories to discuss. They resemble in their general tenor those already noticed; but instead of one or other of the incidents considered in the previous chapter we are led to a different catastrophe by the introduction of a new incident—that of the Magical Ointment. The plot no longer hinges upon fairy gratitude, but upon human curiosity and disobedience.

The typical tale is told, and exceedingly well told—though, alas! not exactly in the language of the natives—by Mrs. Bray in her Letters to Southey, of a certain midwife of Tavistock. One midnight, as she was getting into bed, this good woman was summoned by a strange, squint-eyed, little, ugly old fellow to follow him straightway, and attend upon his wife. In spite of her instinctive repulsion she could not resist the command; and in a moment the little man whisked her, with himself, upon a large coal-black horse with eyes of fire, which stood waiting at the door. Ere long she found herself at the door of a neat cottage; the patient was a decent-looking woman who already had two children, and all things were prepared for her visit. When the child—a fine, bouncing babe—was born, its mother gave the midwife some ointment, with directions to "strike the child's eyes with it." Now the word *strike* in the Devonshire dialect means not to give a blow, but to rub, or touch, gently; and as the woman obeyed she thought the task an odd one, and in her curiosity tried the effect of the ointment upon one of her own eyes. At once a change was wrought in the appearance of everything around her. The new mother appeared no longer as a homely cottager, but a beautiful lady attired in white; the babe, fairer than before, but still witnessing with the elvish cast of its eye to its paternity, was wrapped in swaddling clothes of silvery gauze; while the elder children, who sat on either side of the bed, were transformed into flat-nosed imps, who with mops and mows were busied to no end in scratching their own polls, or in pulling the fairy lady's ears with their long and hairy paws. The nurse, discreetly silent about what she had done and the wonderful metamorphoses she beheld around her, got away from the house of enchantment as quickly as she could; and the sour-looking old fellow who had brought her carried her back on his steed much faster than they had come. But the next market-day, when she sallied forth to sell her eggs, whom should she see but the same ill-looking scoundrel busied in pilfering sundry articles from stall to stall. So she went up to him, and with a nonchalant air addressed him, inquiring after his wife and child, who, she hoped, were both as well as could be expected. "What!" exclaimed the old pixy thief, "do you *see* me to-day?" "See you! to be sure I do, as plain as I see the sun in the skies; and I see you are busy into the bargain," she replied. "Do you so?" cried he; "pray, with which eye do you see all this?" "With the right eye, to be sure." "The ointment! the ointment!" exclaimed the old fellow; "take that for meddling with what did not belong to you: you shall see me no more." He struck her eye as he spoke, and from that hour till the day of her death she was blind on the right side, thus dearly paying for having gratified an idle curiosity in the house of a pixy.[33]

In this tale the midwife acquired her supernatural vision through gratifying her curiosity; but perhaps in the larger number of instances it is acquired by accident. Her eye smarts or itches; and without thinking, she rubs it with a finger covered with the Magical Ointment. In a Breton variant, however, a certain stone, perfectly polished, and in the form of an egg, is given to the woman to rub the fairy child's eyes. In order to test its virtue she applies it to her own right eye, thus obtaining the faculty of seeing the elves when they rendered themselves invisible to ordinary sight. Sometimes, moreover, the eye-salve is expressly given for the purpose of being used by the nurse upon her own eyes. This was the case with a doctor who, in a north country tale, was presented with one kind of ointment before he entered the fairy realm and another when he left it. The former gave him to behold a splendid portico in the side of a steep hill, through which he passed into the fairies' hall within; but on anointing one eye with the latter ointment, to that eye the hill seemed restored to its natural shape. Similarly in Nithsdale a fairy rewards the kindness of a young mother, to whom she had committed her babe to suckle, by taking her on a visit to Fairyland. A door opened in a green hillside, disclosing a porch which the nurse and her conductor entered. There the lady dropped three drops of a precious dew on the nurse's left eyelid, and they were admitted to a beautiful land watered with meandering rivulets and yellow with corn, where the trees were laden with fruits which dropped honey. The nurse was here presented with magical gifts, and when a green dew had baptized her right eye she was enabled to behold further wonders. On returning, the fairy passed her hand over the woman's eye and restored its normal powers; but the woman had sufficient address to secure the wonder-working balm. By its means she retained for many years the gift of discerning the earth-visiting spirits; but on one occasion, happening to meet the fairy lady who had given her the child, she attempted to shake hands with her. "What ee d' ye see me wi'?" whispered she. "Wi' them baith," answered the matron. The fairy accordingly breathed on her eyes; and even the power of the box failed afterwards to restore their enchanted vision. A Carnarvonshire story, probably incomplete, makes no mention of the ointment conferring supernatural sight; but when the midwife is to be dismissed she is told to rub her eyes with a certain salve, whereupon she at once finds herself sitting on a tuft of rushes, and not in a palace: baby and all had disappeared. The sequel, however, shows that by some means she had retained the power of seeing fairies, at least with one eye; for when she next went to the town, lo and behold! busily buying was the elf whose wife she had attended. He betrayed the usual annoyance at being noticed by the woman; and on learning with which eye she saw him he vanished, never more to be looked upon by her. A tale from Guernsey attributes the magical faculty to some of the child's saliva which fell into the nurse's eye. And a still more extraordinary cause is assigned to it in a tradition from Lower Brittany, where it is said to be due to the sacred bond formed between the woman and a masculine elf when she became godmother and he godfather to the babe.[34]

The effect of the wonder-working salve or water is differently described in different tales. The fairy maiden Rockflower speaks of it to her lover, in a Breton tale from Saint Cast, as "clearing his eyes like her own." And this is evidently to be understood in all cases. Accordingly, we find the invariable result is that the favoured mortal beholds swarms of fairies who were invisible before. But their dwellings, their clothing, and their surroundings in general suffer a transformation by no means always the same. A hovel or a cavern becomes a palace, whose inhabitants, however ugly they may be, are attired like princesses and courtiers, and are served with vessels of silver and gold. On the other hand a castle is changed by the magical balm into "a big rough cave, with water oozing over the edges of the stones, and through the clay; and the lady, and the lord, and the child, weazened, poverty-bitten crathurs—nothing but skin and bone, and the rich dresses were old rags." This is an Irish picture; but in the north of England it is much the same. Instead of a neat cottage the midwife perceives the large overhanging branches of an ancient oak, whose hollow and moss-grown trunk she had before mistaken for the fireplace, where glow-worms supplied the place of lamps. And in North Wales, when Mrs. Gamp incautiously rubbed an itching eye with the finger she had used to rub the baby's eyes, "then she saw with that eye that the wife lay on a bundle of rushes and withered ferns, in a large cave of big stones all round her, with a little fire in one corner of it; and she also saw that the lady was only Eilian, her former servant-girl, whilst with the other eye she beheld the finest place she had ever seen." More terrible still, in another story, evidently influenced by the Welsh Methodist revival, the unhappy woman beheld "herself surrounded by fearful flames; the ladies and gentlemen looked like devils, and the children appeared like the most hideous imps of hell, though with the other parts of her eyes all looked grand and beautiful as before."[35]

However disturbing these visions may have been, the nurse was generally discreet enough to maintain perfect silence upon them until she got back to the safety of her own home. But it is not very surprising if her tongue sometimes got the better of her, as in a story obtained by Professor Rhys at Ystrad Meurig. There the heroine said to the elf-lady in the evening, as she was dressing the infant: "You have had a great many visitors to-day." To this the lady sharply replied: "How do you know that? Have you been putting the ointment to your eyes?" Thereupon she jumped out of bed, and blew into her eyes, saying: "Now you will see no more." The woman could never afterwards see the fairies, nor was the ointment entrusted to her again. So in the Cornish tale of Cherry of Zennor, that young damsel, being hired by a fairy widower to keep house for him, has the assurance to fall in love with him. She touches her own eyes with the unguent kept for anointing the eyes of her master's little boy, and in consequence catches her master kissing a lovely lady. When he next attempts to kiss Cherry herself she slaps his face, and, mad with jealousy, lets slip the secret. No fairy widower with any self-respect could put up with such conduct as this; and Cherry has to quit Fairyland. Her parents had supposed her dead; and when she returned they believed at first it was her ghost. Indeed, it is said she was never afterwards right in her head; and on moonlight nights, until she died, she would wander on to the Lady Downs to look for her master.[36]

The earliest writer who mentions a story of this type is Gervase of Tilbury, marshal of the kingdom of Arles, who wrote about the beginning of the thirteenth century. He professes to have himself met with a woman of Arles who was one day washing clothes on the banks of the Rhone, when a wooden bowl floated by her. In trying to catch it, she got out of her depth and was seized by a Drac. The Dracs were beings who haunted the waters of rivers and dwelt in the deep pools, appearing often on the banks and in the towns in human form. The woman in question was carried down beneath the stream, and, like Cherry of Zennor, made nurse to her captor's son. One day the Drac gave her an eel pasty to eat. Her fingers became greasy with the fat; and she happened to put them to one of her eyes. Forthwith she acquired a clear and distinct vision under the water. After some years she was allowed to return to her husband and family; and going early one morning to the market-place of Beaucaire, she met the Drac. Recognizing him at once, she saluted him and asked after the health of his wife and child. "With which eye do you see me?" inquired the Drac. The woman pointed to the eye she had touched with the eel-fat; and thrusting his finger into it, the Drac vanished from sight.[37]

The only punishment suffered in these cases is the deprivation of the power of seeing fairies, or banishment from their society. This seems mild enough: much more was generally inflicted. The story first quoted relates what seems to be the ordinary form of vengeance for disregard of the prohibition to use the fairy eye-salve, namely, loss of sight in the offending eye. Spitting or striking is usually the means adopted by the elves to effect this end. Sometimes, however, the eye is torn from its socket. Whether there is much to choose between these different ways of undergoing the punishment is doubtful; but it should be noted that the last-mentioned mode is a favourite one in Brittany, and follows not so much on recognition as on denunciation by the virtuous mortal of the elf's thieving propensities. "See what thieves these fairies are!" cried a woman who watched one of them putting her hand into the pocket of a country woman's apron. The fairy instantly turned round and tore out her eye. "Thieves!" bawled another on a similar occasion, with the same result. In a Cornish tale a woman is entrusted in her own house with the care of an elf-child. The child brought remarkable prosperity to the house, and his foster-mother grew very fond of him. Finding that a certain water in which she was required to wash his face made it very bright, she determined to try it on her own, and splashed some of it into her eye. This conferred the gift of seeing the little people, who played with her boy, but had hitherto been invisible to her; and one day she was surprised to meet her nursling's father in the market—stealing. Recognition followed, and the stranger exclaimed:

"Water for elf, not water for self,
You've lost your eye, your child, and yourself."

From that hour she was blind in the right eye. When she got home the boy was gone; and she and her husband, who had once been so happy, became poor and wretched.[38]

Here poverty and wretchedness, as well as the loss of an eye, were inflicted. In a Northumbrian case the foster-parent lost his charge and both eyes. So in a story from Guernsey, the midwife, on the Saturday following her attendance on the lady, meets the husband and father in a shop filling his basket to right and left. She at once comprehends the plenty that reigned in his mysterious dwelling. "Ah, you wicked thief, I see you!" she cried. "You see me; how?" he inquired. "With my eyes," she replied. "In that case I will soon put you out of power to play the spy," he answered. So saying, he spat in her face, and she became blind on the spot. A Danish story also relates that a midwife, who had inadvertently anointed her eyes with the salve handed to her by the elf-folk for the usual purpose, was going home afterwards and passed by a rye-field. The field was swarming with elves, who were busy clipping off the ears of rye. Indignantly she cried out: "What are you doing there?" The little people thronged round her, and angrily answered: "If thou canst see us, thus shalt thou be served;" and suiting the action to the word, they put out her eyes.[39]

Human beings, however, betray their meddling with fairy ointment in other ways than by speech. The following curious story was related as current at his native place, by Dr. Carré of St. Jacut-de-la-Mer, to M. Sébillot. A fisherman from St. Jacut was the last to return one evening at dusk from the scene of his labours; and as he walked along the wet sand of the seashore, he suddenly came upon a number of sea-fairies in a cavern, talking and gesticulating with vivacity, though he could not hear what they said. He beheld them rub their eyes and bodies with a sort of pomade, when, lo! their appearance changed, and they were enabled to walk away in the guise of ordinary women. Hiding carefully behind a large rock, he watched them out of sight; and then, impelled by curiosity, he made straight for the cave. There he found what was left of the pomade, and taking a little on his finger, he smeared it around his left eye. By this means he found himself able to penetrate the various disguises assumed by the fairies for the purpose of robbing or annoying mankind. He recognized as one of that mischievous race a beggar-woman whom he saw a few days afterwards going from door to door demanding charity. He saw her casting spells on certain houses, and peering eagerly into all, as if she were seeking for something to steal. He distinguished, too, when out in his boat, fish which were real fish from fish which were in reality "ladies of the sea," employed in entangling the nets and playing other tricks upon the seamen. Attending the fair of Ploubalay, he saw several elves who had assumed the shapes of fortune-tellers, showmen, or gamblers, to deceive the country folk; and this permitted him to keep clear of their temptations. But as he smiled to himself at what was going on around him, some of the elves, who were exhibiting themselves on a platform in front of one of the booths, caught sight of him; and he saw by the anger in their looks that they had divined his secret. Before he had time to fly, one of them, with the rapidity of an arrow, struck his clairvoyant eye with a stick and burst it. That is what happened to him who would learn the secrets of the sea-fairies.[40]

Such was the punishment of curiosity; nor is it by fairies alone that curiosity is punished. Cranmere Pool on Dartmoor is, we are told, a great penal settlement for refractory spirits. Many of the former inhabitants of the parish are supposed to be still there expiating their ghostly pranks. Of the spirit of one old farmer it is related that it took seven clergymen to secure him. They, however, succeeded at last in transforming him into a colt, which was given in charge to a servant-boy with directions to take him to Cranmere Pool, and there on the brink of the pool to slip off the halter and return instantly without looking round. He did look round, in spite of the warning, and beheld the colt in the form of a ball of fire plunge into the water. But as the mysterious beast plunged he gave the lad a parting kick, which knocked out one of his eyes, just as the Calender was deprived of his eye in the "Arabian Nights." Still worse was the fate that overtook a woman, who, at midnight on New Year's Eve, when all water is turned into wine, was foolhardy enough to go to a well. As she bent over it to draw, one came and plucked out her eye, saying:

"All water is wine,
And thy two eyes are mine."

A variant of the story relates that the woman herself disappeared, and gives the rhyme as

"All water is wine,
And what is thereby is mine."[41]

At the end of the last chapter we noted as a characteristic of fairy nature the objection to be recognized and addressed by men who are privileged to see them. We are now able to carry the generalization a step further. For, from the instances adduced in the foregoing pages, it is obviously a common belief that supernatural personages, without distinction, dislike not merely being recognized and addressed, but even being seen, or at all events being watched, and are only willing to be manifested to humanity at their own pleasure and for their own purposes. In the stories of the Magical Ointment it is not so much the theft as the contravention of the implicit prohibition against prying into fairy business that rouses elfin anger. This will appear more clearly from the fuller consideration of cases like those mentioned in the last paragraph, in which punishment follows directly upon the act of spying. In

Northamptonshire, we learn that a man whose house was frequented by fairies, and who had received many favours from them, became smitten with a violent desire to behold his invisible benefactors. Accordingly, he one night stationed himself behind a knot in the door which divided the living-room of his cottage from the sleeping-apartment. True to their custom, the elves came to disport themselves on his carefully-swept hearth, and to render to the household their usual good offices. But no sooner had the man glanced upon them than he became blind; and so provoked were the fairies at this breach of hospitality that they deserted his dwelling, and never more returned to it. In Southern Germany and Switzerland, a mysterious lady known as Dame Berchta is reputed to be abroad on Twelfth Night. She is admittedly the relic of a heathen goddess, one of whose attributes was to be a leader of the souls of the dead; and as such she is followed by a band of children. For her the peasants on Twelfth Night set a repast, of which, if she be pleased, she and her troop partake. A servant boy at a peasant's farm in the Tirol on one such occasion perceived Lady Berchta's approach, and hid himself behind the kneading-trough to watch what she would do. She immediately became aware of his presence as he peeped through a chink, and called to one of her children to go and stop that chink. The child went and blew into it, and the boy became stark-blind. Thus he continued for a year, nor could any doctor help him, until an old experienced man advised him to go to the same place on the following Twelfth-tide, and falling down on his knees behind the kneading-trough, to bewail his curiosity. He accordingly did so. Dame Berchta came again, and taking pity on him, commanded one of her children to restore his sight. The child went and blew once more through the chink, and the boy saw. Berchta, however, and her weird troop he saw not; but the food set out for them had disappeared.[42]

The tradition of the goddess Hertha lingered until recently, and perchance lingers still, in the island of Rügen. She had her dwelling, it is believed, in the Herthaburg; and often yet, in the clear moonlight, out of the forest which enfolds that hill, a fair lady comes surrounded by her maids to bathe in the lake at its foot. After awhile they emerge from the waters, and, wrapt again in their long white veils, they vanish flickering among the trees. But to the belated wanderer, if any such there be, who looks upon this scene, it is a vision of dread; for he is drawn by irresistible might to the lake wherein the white lady is bathing, to be swallowed up in its depths. And it is said that every year the lady must lure one unhappy mortal into the flood. So in the classic mythology, if Ovid report aright, Actæon met the fearful fate of transformation into a stag by "gazing on divinity disrobed," and was torn in pieces by his own hounds. Hertha was, indeed, according to Tacitus, more terrible than Diana, since death was the penalty even when duty called her slaves to the awful sight.[43]

These traditions have led us away from the Magical Ointment, which thus appears to be only one aspect of the larger theme of the objection on the part of supernatural beings to human prying. Nor need we regret having strayed; for we are brought naturally to one of the most interesting of our national legends, namely, that of Lady Godiva; and it will well repay a little consideration. As generally told to-day it bears an unmistakable resemblance to the foregoing stories; but there seems some difficulty in classing it with them, because Peeping Tom is wanting in the most ancient version known to us.

Godiva, properly Godgifu, was an undoubted historical personage, the wife of Leofric, Earl of the Mercians, and mother of the Earls Morcar and Edwin, and of Edith, wife first of Gruffydd, Prince of North Wales, and afterwards of King Harold the Second. The earliest mention of her famous ride through Coventry is by Roger of Wendover, who wrote in the beginning of the thirteenth century, or a hundred and fifty years or thereabout after her death. His account of the matter is as follows: "The countess Godiva, who was a great lover of God's mother, longing to free the town of Coventry from the oppression of a heavy toll, often with urgent prayers besought her husband, that from regard to Jesus Christ and His mother, he would free the town from that service, and from all other heavy burdens; and when the earl sharply rebuked her for foolishly asking what was so much to his damage, and always forbade her evermore to speak to him on the subject; and while she, on the other hand, with a woman's pertinacity, never ceased to exasperate her husband on that matter, he at last made her this answer: 'Mount your horse, and ride naked before all the people, through the market of the town from one end to the other, and on your return you shall have your request.' On which Godiva replied: 'But will you give me permission if I am willing to do it?' 'I will,' said he. Whereupon the countess, beloved of God, loosed her hair and let down her tresses, which covered the whole of her body like a veil, and then mounting her horse and attended by two knights, she rode through the market place without being seen, except her fair legs; and having completed the journey, she returned with gladness to her astonished husband, and obtained of him what she had asked, for Earl Leofric freed the town of Coventry and its inhabitants from the aforesaid service, and confirmed what he had done by a charter."[44] According to the more modern version, the inhabitants were enjoined to remain within doors, and, in the Laureate's words:

"one low churl, compact of thankless earth,
The fatal byword of all years to come,
Boring a little auger-hole in fear,
Peep'd—but his eyes, before they had their will,
Were shrivell'd into darkness in his head,
And dropt before him. So the powers who wait
On noble deeds, cancell'd a sense misus'd."

It is not my business now to prove that the legend is untrue in fact, or I should insist, first, that its omission by previous writers, who refer both to Leofric and Godgifu and their various good deeds, is strong negative testimony against it; and I should show, from a calculation made by the late Mr. M. H. Bloxam, and founded on the record of Domesday Book, that the population of Coventry in Leofric's time could scarcely have exceeded three hundred and fifty souls, all in a greater or less degree of servitude, and dwelling probably in wooden hovels each of a single story, with a door, but no window.[45] There was, therefore, no market on the scale contemplated by Roger of Wendover,— hardly, indeed, a town through which Godgifu could have ridden; and a mere toll would have been a matter of small moment when the people were all serfs. The tale, in short, in the form given by the chronicler, could not have been told until after Coventry had risen to wealth and importance by means of its monastery, whereof Godgifu and her husband were the founders. Nobody, however, now asserts that Roger of Wendover's narrative is to be taken seriously. What therefore I want to point out in it is that Godgifu's bargain was that she should ride naked *before all the people*. And this is what the historian understands her to have done; for he states that she rode through the market-place without being seen, *except her fair legs*, all the rest of her body being covered by her hair like a veil. He tells us nothing about a proclamation to the inhabitants to keep within doors; and of course Peeping Tom is an impossibility in this version of the tale.

Coventry has for generations honoured its benefactress by a periodical procession, wherein she is represented by a girl dressed as nearly like the countess on her ride as the manners of the day have permitted. When this procession was first instituted, is unknown. The earliest mention of it seems to be in the year 1678. Its object then was to proclaim the Great Fair, and Lady Godiva was merely an incident in it. The Lansdowne MSS. in the British Museum contain an account of a visit to Coventry by the "captain, lieutenant, and ancient" of the military company of Norwich, who travelled in the Midland Counties in August 1634. These tourists describe St. Mary's Hall as adorned at the upper end "with rich hangings, and all about with fayre pictures, one more especially of a noble lady (the Lady Godiva) whose memory they have cause not to forget, for that shee purchas'd and redeem'd their lost infringed liberties and ffreedomes, and obtained remission of heavy tributes impos'd upon them, by undertaking a hard and unseemly task, w'ch was to ride naked openly at high noone day through the city on a milk-white steed, w'ch she willingly performed, according to her lord's strict injunction. It may be very well discussed heere whether his hatred or her love exceeded. Her fayre long hayre did much offend the wanton's glancing eye." In this record we have no additional fact except the mention of "high noone day" as the time of the journey; for the allusion to "the wanton's glancing eye" is too vague to be interpreted of Peeping Tom, and the writer does not refer to any commemorative procession. It has been supposed, therefore, that the carnival times of Charles the Second both begot the procession and tacked Peeping Tom to the legend. But it is more likely that the procession is as old as the fair, which was held under a charter of Henry the Third, granted in 1217. Such pageants were not uncommon in municipal life, and were everywhere to the taste of the people. Whether Lady Godiva was a primitive part of it is another question. The mention of the procession in 1678 occurs in a manuscript volume of annals of the city, in a handwriting of the period. The entry in question is as follows: "31 May 1678 being the great Fair at Coventry there was an extraordinary" [Here the bottom of the page is reached; and in turning over the chronicler has omitted a word, for on the top of the next page we read:] "Divers of the Companies" [*i.e.*, the City Guilds] "set out each a follower, The Mayor Two, and the Sheriffs each one and 2 at the publick charge, there were divers Streamers with the Companies arms and Ja. Swinnertons Son represented Lady Godiva."

This brief entry is by no means free from ambiguity. Perhaps all that we are warranted in inferring from it is that the annual procession was, that year, of unusual splendour. Whether, as has been conjectured, it was the first time Lady Godiva had ever made her appearance, there seems more doubt. Apart from any evidence, there is no improbability in supposing that she may have formed part of earlier processions; though it may be that during the period of Puritan ascendency the show had been neglected and the lady in particular had been discountenanced. If this be so, however, it is difficult to account for the manner in which her figure is referred to by the writer, unless there were some personal reason connected with James Swinnerton, or his son, undiscoverable by us at this distance of time.

But whatever doubt may exist as to Godiva's share in the early processions, there appears no less as to the episode of Peeping Tom. Looking out of an upper story of the King's Head, at the corner of Smithford Street, is an oaken figure called by the name of the notorious tailor. It is in reality a statue of a man in armour, dating no further back than the reign of Henry the Seventh; and, as a local antiquary notes, "to favour the posture of his leaning out of window, the arms have been cut off at the elbows."[47] This statue, now generally believed to have been intended for St. George, could not have been thus appropriated and adapted to its present purpose until its original design had been forgotten and the incongruity of its costume passed unrecognized. This is said to have been in 1678, when a figure, identified with the one in question, was put up in Grey Friars Lane by Alderman Owen.

It must not be overlooked that there may have been from the first more than one version of the legend, and that a version rejected by, or perhaps unknown to, Roger of Wendover and the writers who followed him may have always included the order to the inhabitants to keep within doors, of which Peeping Tom would seem to be the necessary accompaniment. Unfortunately, we have no evidence on this point. The earliest record of such a version appears in one of the manuscript volumes already alluded to. It has not been hitherto printed; and it is so much at variance, alike with the legend preserved in the thirteenth century, and the poem of the nineteenth century, that I quote it entire:—"The Franchisment and Freedome of Coventry was purchased in manner Following. Godiva the wife of Leofric Earle of Chester and Duke of March requesting of her Lord freedome for this That Towne, obtained the same upon condition that she should ride naked through the same; who for the Love she bare to the Inhabitants thereof, and the perpetuall remembrance of her Great Affection thereunto, performed the same as Followeth. In the forenoone all householders were Commanded to keep in their Families shutting their doores and windows close whilst the Dutchess performed this good deed, which done she rode naked through the midst of the Towne, without any other Coverture save only her hair. But about the midst of the Citty her horse neighed, whereat one desirous to see the strange Case lett downe a Window, and looked out, for which fact or for that the Horse did neigh, as the cause thereof, Though all the Towne were Franchised, yet horses were not toll-free to this day."[48]

The manuscript in which this passage occurs is copied from an older manuscript which appears to have been compiled in the sixteenth century. Unfortunately, however, the latter is imperfect, a leaf having been torn out at this very point. We cannot, therefore, say with certainty that the account of the famous ride was ever comprised in it. But the expressions made use of imply that the windows were closed with shutters rather than glass, and that they were opened by letting down the shutters, which were either loose or affixed by a hinge to the bottom sills. It is a question exactly at what period glass came into general use for windows in the burgesses' houses at Coventry. Down almost to the middle of the fifteenth century all glass was imported; and consequently it was not so common in the midlands as near the coast, especially the south-eastern coast. We shall probably be on the safe side if we assume that in the early years of the sixteenth century, at all events, the ordinary dwelling-house at Coventry was no longer destitute of this luxury. It would seem, therefore, that the story, in the form here given, cannot be later, and may be much earlier, than the latter years of the fifteenth century.

Failing definite evidence to carry us back further, it becomes of importance to inquire whether there are any traditions in other places from which we may reason. In the "History of Gloucestershire," printed by Samuel Rudder of Cirencester in 1779, we read that the parishioners of St. Briavels, hard by the Forest of Dean, "have a custom of distributing yearly upon Whitsunday, after divine service, pieces of bread and cheese to the congregation at church, to defray the expenses of which every householder in the parish pays a penny to the churchwardens; and this is said to be for the privilege of cutting and taking the wood in Hudnolls. The tradition is that the privilege was obtained of some Earl of Hereford, then lord of the Forest of Dean, at the instance of his lady, upon the same hard terms that Lady Godiva obtained the privileges for the citizens of Coventry." It appears that Rudder, while in the main accurately relating both custom and tradition, has made the mistake of supposing that the payment was made to the churchwardens, whereas it was in all probability made to the constable of the castle of St. Briavels as warden of the Forest of Dean. The custom is now in a late stage of decadence, and local inquiries have failed to elicit any further details throwing light on the point under consideration.[49]

I am not aware of any other European tradition that will bear comparison with that of Godiva, but Liebrecht relates that he remembers in his youth, about the year 1820, in a German newspaper, a story according to which a countess frees her husband's subjects from a heavy punishment imposed by him. She undertakes to walk a certain course clad only in her shift, and she performs it, but clad in a shift of iron.[50] The condition is here eluded rather than fulfilled; and the point of the story is consequently varied. It would be interesting to have the tale unearthed from the old newspaper, and to know where its scene was laid, and whether it was a genuine piece of folklore.

Eastern tales, however, furnish us repeatedly with incidents in which a lady parades the streets of a city, and during her progress all folk are bidden to close their shops and withdraw into their houses on pain of death. The example of the Princess Badroulbadour will occur to every reader of the "Arabian Nights." This, however, is by no means a solitary example. In the story of Kamar Al-Zaman and the Jeweller's Wife, one of the stories of the "Nights" rejected on moral grounds by Lane, but translated by Burton, a dervish relates that he chanced one Friday to enter the city of Bassorah, and found the streets deserted. The shops were open; but neither man nor woman, girl nor boy, dog nor cat was to be seen. By and by he heard a sound of drums, and hiding himself in a coffee-house, he looked out through a crevice and saw forty pairs of slave girls, with uncovered heads and faces displayed, come walking through the market, and in their midst a lady riding unveiled and adorned with gold and gems. In front of her was a damsel bearing in baldric a great sword with haft of emerald and tassels of jewel-encrusted gold. Pausing close to the dervish, the lady said to her maidens: "I hear a noise of somewhat within yonder shop; so do ye search it, lest haply there be one hidden there, with intent to enjoy a look at us while we have our faces unveiled." Accordingly they searched the shop opposite the coffee-house, and brought forth a man. At the lady's command the damsel with the sword smote off his head, and leaving the corpse lying on the ground, the procession swept on. It turned out that the lady was the wife of a jeweller to whom the King of Bassorah was desirous of granting a boon, and at her request the boon obtained was a proclamation commanding that all the townsfolk should every Friday enter the mosques two hours before the hour of prayer, so that none might abide in the town, great or small, unless they were in the mosques or in the houses with the doors locked upon them; but all the shops were to be left open. Then the lady had permission to ride with her slave-women through the heart of the town, and none were to look on her from window or lattice; and every one whom she found abroad she was at liberty to kill. A similar incident is related in the life of Kurroglú, the robber-poet of Persia, where a beautiful princess passes in state through the bazaars every Friday on her way to the mosque, while all the men are banished.[51] Here, again, some one was of course found playing the spy.

A version of the incident, which can be traced further back in literary form than either of the foregoing, occurs in the "Ardshi-Bordshi." This book is a Mongolian recension of a Sanskrit collection of stories concerning Vikramâditya, a monarch who, if he ever lived, seems to have flourished about the beginning of the Christian era. He was celebrated, like Solomon, for his wisdom and his might; and his name became the centre of a vast accretion of legends. Some of these legends were translated into Mongolian late in the Middle Ages, and formed a small collection called after Ardshi-Bordshi, the nominal hero. In the story to which I wish to direct attention, a certain king has a daughter bearing the name of Sunshine, of whom he was so jealous that if any one looked upon her his eyes were put out, and the man who entered her apartments had his legs broken. Naturally, the young lady got tired of being thus immured, and complained to her father that, as she had no opportunity of seeing man or beast, the time hung heavily on her hands; and she begged him to let her go out on the fifteenth of the month and look about her. The king agreed to this; but, the sly old rascal! nothing was further from his intention than to gratify his daughter's longing for masculine converse. Wherefore he issued a decree that all objects for sale were to be exposed openly to the view, all cattle to be left indoors, the men and women were to withdraw into their houses and close their doors and windows, and if any one came forth he should be severely punished. On the appointed day, Sunshine, surrounded by her ladies, and seated in a brand-new chariot, drove through the town, and viewed the merchandise and goods exposed for sale. The king had a minister, named Moon, who could not restrain his curiosity; and he peeped at her from a balcony. The princess, as he did so, caught sight of him and made signs to him, which were interpreted by the penetration of his wife to be an invitation to meet her clandestinely. The wife hardly displayed what most ladies would deem "a proper spirit" in advising compliance; and the consequence of taking that advice would have been serious trouble both to himself and to the princess, had it not been for the ready wit of the two women, who got over the difficulty by contriving an ingenious equivocation not unknown in other stories, by which the princess cleared herself and her lover on oath.[52]

It is true that in these tales the lady who rides forth is not naked; but to ride openly and unveiled would be thought almost as immodest in countries where strict seclusion is imposed upon women. All these tales include the Peeping Tom incident; and it appears, indeed, so obvious a corollary to the central thought of Lady Godiva's adventure that it is hardly likely to have required centuries for its evolution. From some traditions, however, it is absent. A story belonging to the Cinderella cycle, found at Smyrna, relates that when a certain king desired to marry his own daughter, the maiden, by the advice of her Fate, demanded as the price of compliance three magnificent dresses. Having obtained these, she asked permission to go unseen (like Badroulbadour) to the bath. The king, to gratify her, forbade his subjects on pain of death to open their shops or to show themselves in the streets while she passed by. She thus got an opportunity of escaping from the city, of which she did not fail to make use,—greatly, no doubt, to her unnatural father's disgust. An Indian tradition also tells us that the inhabitants of Chamba were under the necessity of digging a canal for irrigation, but when it was dug, owing to the enchantments of an evil spirit, not a drop of water could be got to flow along its course. A magician at last found out that the spell could be dissolved if the beautiful and virtuous young princess of Chamba would consent to traverse a given distance of the plain entirely naked, in full view of the populace, and to lose her head when the journey was accomplished. After much hesitation, her compassion triumphed over her shame; and she undertook the task. But lo! as she advanced, a thick line of young trees arose to right and left, completely hiding her from cynical eyes. And the shady canal is shown to-day by the good people of Chamba as one of the most authentic monuments of their history.[53]

So far the stories. Concerning which it must be observed that they are evidence that the myth of Lady Godiva is widely diffused in the East, and that the spy is usually, though not always, part of the tale. The Smyrnœan version must probably be thrown out of the reckoning. It is, as I have already mentioned, a variant of the Cinderella cycle. The problem of the plot is how to get the heroine unseen out of her father's clutches. This is commonly effected by the simple mechanism of a disguise and a night escape. Other methods, I need not now detail, are, however, sometimes adopted; and the excuse of going to the bath, with the order to the people to close their shops and keep within doors, would seem to reveal nothing more than the unconscious influence of Aladdin or some other of the Eastern stories. Throwing this out, then, as accidental, an overwhelming proportion of the analogues cited contains the spy. It would be dangerous to reason on the supposition that the proportions of all the Asiatic variants extant correspond with those of the variants cited; but we are at liberty to assume that a large number, if not the majority, comprise the incident of Peeping Tom. None of them was known in Europe until Galland published his translation of the "Arabian Nights" in the year 1704—upwards of two centuries later than the latest period at which the story as given in the Coventry manuscript can have come into existence.

But the stories, though they may go a little way to help us in regard to the incident of Peeping Tom, throw no light on the origin of the legend, or of the procession. Let us therefore turn to one or two curious religious ceremonies, which may have some bearing upon it. A potent spell to bring rain was reported as actually practised during the Gorakhpur famine of 1873-4. It consisted of a gang of women stripping themselves perfectly naked, and going out by night to drag the plough across a field. The men were kept carefully out of the way, as it was believed that peeping by them would not only vitiate the spell, but bring trouble on the village. It would not be a long step from this belief to a story in which peeping was alleged to have taken place with disastrous effects, either to the village, or (by favour of the deities intended to be propitiated) to the culprit himself. At the festival of the local goddess in the village of Serúr, in the Southern Mahratta country, the third and fourth days are devoted to private offerings. Many women, we are told, on these days walk naked to the temple in fulfilment of vows, "but they were covered with leaves and boughs of trees, and surrounded by their female relations and friends."[54]

The performance of religious rites by women alone, when men are required under heavy penalties to absent themselves, is, indeed, not very uncommon in savage life. Nor is it confined to savage life. When Rome was at the height of her civilization and her triumphs, the festival of the Bona Dea was rendered notorious by the divorce of Cæsar's wife and by legal proceedings against an aristocratic scoundrel, who, for the purposes of an intrigue with her, had violated the sacred ceremonies. The Bona Dea, or Good Goddess, was a woodland deity, the daughter and wife of Faunus. Her worship had descended from a remote antiquity; and her annual festival was held in the month of December, and was attended only by women. The matrons of the noblest families of Rome met by night in the house of the highest official of the state to perform the traditional ceremonies of the goddess, and to pray for the well-being of the Roman people. Only women, and those of the most unsullied character, were permitted to attend; and the breach of this rule by Clodius, disguised in woman's garb, constituted a heinous offence against the state, from the penalties of which he only escaped, if we may believe Cicero, by bribing the judges.[55]

At the village of Southam, not far from Coventry, another procession in honour of Godiva formerly took place. Very little is known about it now, save one singular fact, namely, that there were two Godivas in the cavalcade, and one of them was black. Southam was part of the property possessed by Earl Leofric; and it has been suggested that this is enough to account for the commemoration of Godgifu. It would no doubt be an excellent reason for affixing her renowned name to a periodical ceremony already performed there. But it would hardly be a reason for commemorating her extortion of privileges in which the inhabitants of Southam did not share; and it would leave the black lady unexplained. She may, indeed, have been a mere travesty, though the hypothesis would be anything but free from difficulty. Here, again, if we have recourse to the comparison of ceremonies, we may obtain some light. Among the tribes of the Gold Coast of Africa the wives of men who have gone to war make a daily procession through the town. They are stark naked, painted all over with white, and decorated with beads and charms. Any man who is found in the town is attacked and driven away. And on the occasion of a battle the women imitate the actions the men are thought to be performing, with guns, sticks, and knives. The Gold Coast is a long way off; but not only do black women there paint themselves white in their sacred rites, white women in Britain have painted themselves, if not black, at least a dark blue. Pliny records that both matrons and unmarried girls among the Britons in the first century of the Christian era were in the habit of staining themselves all over with the juice of the woad; and he adds that, thus rivalling the swarthy hue of the Æthiopians, they go on these occasions in a state of nature. We are sometimes taught that when the English invaded Britain, the natives whom they found here were all driven out or massacred. There are, however, many reasons for doubting that this wholesale destruction was as complete as has been imagined. The name of Coventry betrays in its termination a Celtic element; and this could hardly have entered into it had there not been in the neighbourhood a considerable British-speaking population. What is more likely than that at Southam this population continued and preserved its customs, and that one of such customs was that very religious rite of which Pliny speaks? Unhappily he tells us nothing about the rite itself, nor the deity in whose honour it was performed. But it would not involve a great stretch of fancy to suppose that in the black lady of Southam we have a survival of the performance. It is not too much to say that this explanation would have the merit of being intelligible and adequate.[56]

In all countries ceremonies of a special character are usually dramatic. They represent, or are believed to represent, actions of the divinities in whose honour they are performed. The rites of the Bona Dea, we know, were of this kind; and they consequently degenerated into orgies of a shameful character. The Coventry procession is admittedly a representation of Godgifu's ride. It is not now, nor has it been so long as we have any records of it—that is to say for two hundred years—connected with any professed act of worship; but this is not incompatible with its being the long-descended relic of some such observance as those I have described. The introduction of Christianity did not annihilate the older cults. The new religion incorporated some of them; and although the rest were no longer regarded as sacred, the feeling of obligation remained attached to them for centuries. They were secularized, and ultimately degraded for the most part into burlesque. Such as were connected with municipal life, or, as we shall see in a future chapter, with family life, retained a measure of solemnity long after it had passed away from rites which had been abandoned to an unorganized mob. This is well illustrated by the contrast between the ceremonial at Coventry (whatever its origin) and that at St. Briavels. The stronger hand of a municipality would have a restraining power wanting to that of a village community, or a parish—especially if the latter had been governed by a lord, who in later times had been shorn of his authority, or had ceased to reside among, or take an interest in the affairs of, his tenantry. Something like this I take to have been the history of St. Briavels. There does not appear from Rudder's account to have been, in his time at least, any pageant commemorative of the achievement of the lady to whom the parishioners reckoned themselves to owe their privileges; nor have I been able to trace one by local inquiries. But the tradition is at St. Briavels unmistakably connected with a religious and social rite. The distribution of food on a day of high and holy festival in the church to the congregation, and paid for by a levy upon every householder in the parish, can point to nothing else than a feast of the whole community as a solemn act of worship. Its degeneracy in more recent times has been thus described to me by the Rev. W. Taprell Allen:— "For many years it was customary to bring to the church on Whitsunday afternoon baskets of the stalest bread and hardest cheese, cut up into small pieces the size of dice. Immediately after the service the bread and cheese were scrambled for in the church, and it was a custom to use them as pellets, the parson coming in for his share as he left the pulpit. About 1857, or perhaps a year or two later, the unseemly custom was transferred from the church to the churchyard, the bread and cheese being thrown down from the church tower. Later on it was transferred to the road outside the church gates. It now lasts but a few minutes. A few years ago all the roughs of the Forest used to come over, and there was much drinking and fighting; but now it is very different. The custom has in fact been dying out." From these later stages of decay the Godiva pageant was saved by becoming a municipal festival. And while at St. Briavels we can watch the progress of degeneration from a point at which the religious character of the ceremony had not quite vanished, down to the most unblushing burlesque, and to its ultimate expulsion from consecrated precincts,—at Coventry we see but one phase, one moment, at which the rite, if it ever had any title to that name, seems to have been photographed and rendered permanent.

It is obvious, however, that a feast is not a dramatic representation of a ride; and the point requiring elucidation is the intimate relation of the feast at St. Briavels with a story apparently so irrelevant as that of the countess' ride. To explain this, we must suppose that the feast was only part—doubtless the concluding part—of a ceremony, and that the former portion was a procession, of which the central figure was identical with that familiar to us at Coventry. But such a procession, terminating in a sacred feast, would have had no meaning if the naked lady represented a creature merely of flesh and blood. It is only explicable on the hypothesis that she was the goddess of a heathen cult, such as Hertha (or Nerthus), whose periodical progress among her subject tribes is described in a well-known passage by Tacitus,[57] and yet survives, as we have seen, in the folklore of Rügen. Now the historian tells us that Hertha was Mother Earth, the goddess of the soil, whose yearly celebration would appropriately take place in the spring or early summer. To her the produce of the land would be ascribed; and in her name and by her permission would all agricultural operations be performed. Such a goddess it must be who is honoured by the ceremonies already noticed in India. Such a goddess, at any rate, was the Bona Dea; and to such a goddess we may readily believe would be ascribed the privilege of cutting wood. It is quite consistent with this that the payment by every household at St. Briavels should be made to the warden of the forest, and that it should be spent by him on the goddess' festival. We are left to surmise what were the tolls and burdens at Coventry, so vaguely referred to by Roger of Wendover. Pigs and horses, we learn from two different sources, were not included in the exemptions obtained by the countess; and the reason for this in the latter case is accounted for by the incident of Peeping Tom.

One other point is worthy of mention: both at St. Briavels and at Coventry the commemoration takes place nearly at the same time of year. The Great Fair at Coventry opens on the day after Corpus Christi Day—that is to say, the Friday after Trinity Sunday. Corpus Christi Day itself was the day on which the celebrated Coventry Miracle Plays were performed; and the Fair opened the next morning. At the same time of year too—namely, on Ascension Day—a custom, for which there is no explanation in any record, was observed at St. Michael's Church, York, when ale and bread and cheese were yearly given away in the church to the poor of the parish.[58] Although Ascension Day is separated by three weeks from Corpus Christi, the movable character of the feasts would bridge this gulf without any difficulty; and heathen observances of the same nature, and referring to the same season, when they had to be reconciled to the Christian calendar, might easily find places in some instances on one day and in others on another day. Godgifu and her husband were honoured as founders of the Benedictine monastery at Coventry, which rose upon the ruins of an earlier house of Benedictine nuns founded by Osburg, a lady of the royal house, nearly two hundred years before. This nunnery had been destroyed in the Danish wars about the year 1016.

Consequently, if any legend, or ceremony, was known or practised at Coventry in connection with some traditional patroness, the name of Godgifu was ready to hand to be identified with it. Through the monastery Coventry first rose to wealth and repute; and the townsfolk on this score owed a debt of gratitude to the foundress, though there is no record whether any special day was set apart in her honour.

On the whole, then, there is ground for supposing that the legend and procession of Lady Godiva are survivals of a pagan belief and worship located at Coventry; that the legend was concerned with a being awful and mysterious as Dame Berchta, or Hertha herself; and that the incident of Peeping Tom was from the first, or at all events from an early date, part of the story. The evidence upon which these conclusions rest may be shortly recapitulated thus:—

1. The absence of historical foundation for the tradition.
2. The close resemblance between the tradition and other stories and superstitions which unquestionably deal with heathen goddesses, such as Berchta and Hertha.
3. The equally close analogy between the procession and that described in Eastern stories, which, so far as we know, could not have reached England at the latest period when the procession could possibly have been instituted; and between the procession and certain heathen rites practised not only in the East, but as near home as Rome and Germany,—nay, in Britain itself.
4. The occurrence of a similar procession at Southam, in the same county, having the special feature of a black lady, best explained as a survival of certain rites practised by the ancient Britons.
5. The connection between the analogous legend at St. Briavel's and the remains of a sacred communal feast that can hardly be anything else than the degraded remnant of a pagan observance.

The want of historical evidence cannot, of course, be overlooked; but we must remember that in investigating traditions and traditional observances we are dealing with a phase of civilization of which history only yields rare and indirect glimpses. It is the absence of direct evidence that, not only in the science of Folklore, but also in the physical sciences, causes resort to the evidence afforded by comparison of other structures and processes. On the validity of this evidence, and the reasoning based upon it, nearly all our scientific learning depends. In spite, therefore, of the defects in the historical evidence, and in the absence of evidence to the contrary, it can scarcely be denied that the analogies in both custom and legend here brought together amount to a fairly strong presumption in favour of the conclusions I have ventured to draw from them.

If I may formulate my conjecture as to the course of development actually pursued, it would be something like this. The ceremony at Coventry is a survival of an annual rite in honour of a heathen goddess, from which men were excluded. This rite, like all such, would have been a part of the tribal cult, and intimately associated with the tribal life and organization. Side by side with it a myth would have been evolved, accounting for the performance as a dramatic representation of an event in the goddess' career. This myth would have been similar in outline to those recited above, and would have comprised an explanation of the exclusion of men. When Christianity spread through the district the inhabitants would still cling to their old custom and their old myth, as we know was done elsewhere, because it was bound up with their social life. But, if not violently put down by the rulers of the land, both custom and myth would, little by little, lose their sacred character as the new religion increased in influence, and would become transformed into municipal ceremonies. This process would be slow, centuries being required for its completion; but it would be aided by the gradual development of the tribe first into a settled village community, and thence into a mediæval township. With the loss of sanctity the reason for prohibiting the attendance of men would vanish; but the tradition of it would be preserved in the incident of the story which narrated Peeping Tom's treachery.[59]

**FOOTNOTES:**

[33] Mrs. Bray, vol. i. p. 174.

[34] "Revue Celtique," vol. i. p. 231; Keightley, p. 312, citing "The Local Historian's Table-Book," by M. A. Richardson. Cromek, p. 242; "Y Cymmrodor," vol. iv. p. 209; "Revue des Trad. Pop." vol. iii. p. 426; "Revue Celtique," vol. i. p. 232.

[35] Sébillot, "Contes," vol. ii. p. 34; "Revue des Trad. Pop." vol. iii. p. 428; Sébillot, "Litt. Orale," p. 21; Kennedy, p. 106; Keightley, p. 311; "Y Cymmrodor," vol. vi. p. 166; Wirt Sikes, p. 87. This story purports to be quoted from Howells, p. 349—an impossible reference, seeing that the volume in question only contains 194 pages. The peculiarities of Mr. Sikes' authorities, however, need very little comment.

[36] "Y Cymmrodor," vol. vi. p. 194; Hunt, p. 120.

[37] Gerv. Tilb. *Dcc.* iii. c. 85.

[38] Sébillot, "Contes," vol. ii. p. 42; "Litt. Orale," p. 23; "Trad. et Super." p. 109. But in these cases the operation was performed painlessly enough, for the victims were unaware of their loss until they came to look in the glass. In one of Prof. Rhys' stories the eye is pricked with a green rush; "Y Cymmrodor," vol. vi. p. 178: Hunt, p. 83. See also Sébillot, "Contes," vol. i. p. 119.

[39] Keightley, p. 310; "Revue des Trad. Pop." vol. iii. p. 426; Thorpe, vol. ii. p. 129, quoting Thiele. In another Danish tale given on the same page, the

woman's blindness is attributed to her having divulged what she had seen in Fairyland.

[40] Sébillot, "Litt. Orale," p. 24.

[41] "Choice Notes," p. 170; Thorpe, vol. iii. p. 8. The latter form of the story seems more usual. See Gredt, pp. 28, 29, where we are plainly told that the hapless mortals are fetched away by the devil.

[42] Sternberg, p. 132 (see also Thorpe, vol. ii. p. 12); Von Alpenburg, p. 63. See a similar story in Grimm, "Teut. Myth." p. 276, from Börner, "Folk-tales of the Orlagau." In the latter case, however, the punishment seems to have been inflicted for jeering.

[43] Jahn, p. 177, quoting Temme, "Volkssagen"; Ovid, "Metam." l. iii. fab. 3; Tacitus, "Germ." c. 40.

[44] Roger of Wendover, "Flowers of History," sub anno 1057. I quote from Dr. Giles' translation.

[45] See his Presidential Address to the Warwickshire Naturalists' and Archæologists' Field Club, 1886.

[46] MS. marked D. This entry is an interpolation in a list of mayors and sheriffs in a different handwriting. There are several such interpolations in the volume. Coventry possesses a number of MS. volumes of annals, one of which (see below) seems to date from the latter part of the sixteenth century, and the rest from the latter part of the seventeenth. In the MS. marked F. (considered by Mr. W. G. Fretton, F.S.A., to be in the handwriting of John Tipper, of Bablake, Coventry, a schoolmaster and local antiquary at the end of the seventeenth and beginning of the eighteenth centuries), and also in the MS. in the British Museum (Additional MSS. 11,364), the entry runs simply:—"1678 Michaell Earle (Mercer) Mayor; Francis Clark, George Allatt, Sherriffs. This year ye severall Companies had new streamers, and attended ye Mayor to proclaim ye faire, and each company cloathed one boy or two to augment ye show." The latter MS. elsewhere speaks of the story of Godiva's ride as "comonly known, and yearly comemorated by the Mayor, Aldermen, and ye severall companies."

[47] This statue used to be decked out on the occasion of the procession in the long peruke and neckcloth of the reign of Charles II. See T. Ward, "Collections for the Continuation of Dugdale's Antiquities of Warwickshire" (2 vols., fol. MS., Brit. Mus., Additional MSS., Nos. 29,264, 29,265), vol. ii. fol. 143.

[48] MS. marked E, Coventry, seventeenth century. A careful examination of the language of Roger of Wendover, Matthew Paris, John of Brompton, and Matthew of Westminster, shows that Roger of Wendover's account is the source of the other three, Matthew Paris copying most closely, and John of Brompton most freely. John of Brompton and Matthew of Westminster omit the escort. Their statement as to Godiva's being unseen refers to the hair

which covered her; and the latter informs us, with a touch of rhetoric, that Leofric regarded it as a miracle.

[49] Rudder, p. 307. The Rev. W. Taprell Allen, M.A., Vicar of St. Briavels, has been kind enough to supply me with the correction from local inquiries and intimate acquaintance with the traditions and affairs of the parish extending over many years. See also "Gent. Mag. Lib." (Manners and Customs), p. 230.

[50] Liebrecht, p. 104.

[51] Burton, "Nights," vol. ix. p. 255; Burton, "Supp. Nights," vol. iii. p. 570 (Appendix by Mr. W. A. Clouston). Kurroglú flourished in the second half of the seventeenth century.

[52] This story is edited by Jülg in Mongolian and German (Innsbruck, 1867). Miss Busk gives a free adaptation rather than a translation of the German version, "Sagas," p. 315. Prof. De Gubernatis, "Zool. Myth." vol. i. p. 138, of course interprets it as a sun-myth—an interpretation to which the names Sunshine and Moon, and the date of the adventure (the fifteenth of the month), lend themselves.

[53] Von Hahn, vol. ii. p. 225; "Tour du Monde," vol. xxi. p. 342, quoted by Liebrecht, p. 105.

[54] "Panjab N. and Q." vol. iii. pp. 41, 115; "Journal Ethnol. Soc. London," N. S., vol. i. p. 98.

[55] The information relating to the Bona Dea has been collected by Preller, "Röm. Myth." vol. i. p. 398; and see the authorities he has cited.

[56] Ellis, p. 226; Pliny, "Nat. Hist." l. xxii. c. 1. For the information as to the procession at Southam I am indebted to Mr. W. G. Fretton, who formerly lived there.

[57] "Germania," c. 40; cf. c. 9.

[58] Nicholson, p. 32.

[59] I am indebted to Mr. Samuel Timmins, F.S.A., and to Mr. W. G. Fretton, F.S.A., for a great amount of local information and other assistance which they have spared no pains to render me, and to the Town Clerk of Coventry for permission to inspect the invaluable local manuscripts belonging to the Corporation.

# CHAPTER V

# CHANGELINGS

The belief in changelings — Precautions against changing — Motives assigned for changing — Attempts frustrated — How changelings may be known — Their physical characteristics — Devices to lead them to betray themselves — Their subsequent treatment — Journey to Fairyland to fetch back the true child — Adult changelings.

A new-born babe, of all human beings the most helpless, has always roused compassion and care. Nor is it a matter for wonder if its helplessness against physical dangers have led to the assumption that it is exposed to spiritual or supernatural evils more than its elders. At all events it seems a widespread superstition that a babe, when first it makes its appearance in this world, must be protected not merely against the natural perils of its condition, but also against enemies of an even more subtle and fearful description. The shape taken by this superstition in north-western Europe is the belief in Changelings—a belief which I propose to examine in the present chapter.[60]

By the belief in changelings I mean a belief that fairies and other imaginary beings are on the watch for young children, or (as we shall see hereafter) sometimes even for adults, that they may, if they can find them unguarded, seize and carry them off, leaving in their place one of themselves, or a block of wood animated by their enchantments and made to resemble the stolen person. Wise mothers take precautions against such thefts. These precautions are tolerably simple, and for the most part display the same general character. First and foremost among them is the rite of baptism, whereby the little one is admitted into the Christian Church. Faith in the efficacy of baptism as a protection from the powers hostile to man is not less strong among communities nominally Protestant than among Roman Catholics, and has doubtless operated to bring many children within the pale of the visible Church who might otherwise have been long in reaching that sacred enclosure. Examples of the belief in the power of baptism against the depredations of fairies could easily be cited from all Protestant countries. Without doing this, we may just pause to note that baptism was also reckoned a remedy for disease. This is doubtless a relic of the old creed which refers all human ailments to witchcraft and other spiritualistic origins. Mr. Henderson, speaking of the notion prevalent in the north of England that sickly infants never thrive until they are christened, relates a story communicated to him by a clergyman, within whose personal knowledge it had happened. He says: "The infant child of a chimney-sweeper at Thorne, in the West Riding of Yorkshire, was in a very weak state of health, and appeared to be pining away.

A neighbour looked in, and inquired if the child had been baptized. On an answer being given in the negative, she gravely said, 'I would try having it christened.' The counsel was taken, and I believe with success." The same belief is found both in North and South Wales. It is also testified to by a Scottish clergyman, who moreover adduces the following conversation as illustrative of it and of "an undefinable sort of awe about unbaptized infants, as well as an idea of uncanniness in having them without baptism in the house," which is entertained among the labouring classes in the north-east of Scotland. "Oh, sir," said the wife of a working man to the minister, on asking him to baptize her child along with others, whose mothers were present, "this registration's the warst thing the queentry ever saw; it sud be deen awa' wee athegeethir!" "Why?" asked the minister, in astonishment at the woman's words and earnestness of manner. "It'll pit oot kirsnin athegeethir. Ye see the craitirs gets their names, an we jist think that aneuch, an' we're in nae hurry sennin for you." How far, as this anecdote dimly suggests, it was the giving of a name which was supposed to protect a child, I cannot say: more probably it was the dedication to God involved in baptism. This is countenanced by the precaution said to have been observed in Nithsdale when a pretty child was born to consecrate it to God, and sue for its protection by "taking the Beuk" and other acts of prayer and devotion.[61]

Putting aside such ceremonies as these which may be supposed distinctly Christian, there were other charms looked upon as efficacious. Thus in Scotland it was deemed highly judicious to keep an open Bible always near a child, and even to place the holy volume beneath the head of a woman in labour. In some parts of Germany it is enough to lay a single leaf out of a Bible or prayer-book in the cradle, until by the baptism of the infant the danger of robbery passes away; and a prayer-book is also placed under the pillow of the newly-made mother, who is at that time specially liable to fall under the power of the underground folk. Indeed a prayer-book, or the mere repetition of a Paternoster, is equally valuable with a Bible for these purposes; and if, by the neglect of any of these precautions, an opportunity be given to the foe, the child may yet be saved by the utterance of the name of Jesus Christ at the moment when the change is being effected. Holy water and the sign of the cross, in Ireland, or a rosary blessed by a priest, in Picardy, enjoy a similar reputation.[62]

All these means of prevention are veneered with some sort of Christianity; but there are others which display Heathenism naked and unblushing. While a child in Mecklenburg remains unbaptized it is necessary to burn a light in the chamber. Nor is the superstition confined to one district: it is common all over Germany and Denmark; it was once common in England; it is found in Ireland; it is found among the Lithuanians on the shores of the Baltic; it was practised by the ancient Romans, and appears to be a relic of the sacred character anciently imputed to fire. In the island of Lewis fire used to be carried round women before they were churched and children before they were christened, both night and morning; and this was held effectual to preserve both mother and infant from evil spirits, and (in the case of the infant) from being changed. The Sad Dar, one of the sacred books of the Parsees, contains directions to keep a continual fire in the house during a woman's pregnancy, and after the child is born to burn a lamp for three nights and days—a fire, indeed, is declared to be better—"so that the demons and fiends may not be able to do any damage and harm." By way of enforcing this precept we are told that when Zoroaster was born, a demon came at the head of a hundred and fifty other demons, every night for three nights, to slay him, but they were put to flight by seeing the fire, and were consequently unable to hurt him.[63]

Iron or steel, in the shape of needles, a key, a knife, a pair of tongs, an open pair of scissors, or in any other shape, if placed in the cradle, secured the desired end. In Bulgaria a reaping-hook is placed in a corner of the room for the same purpose. I shall not stay now to discuss the reason why supernatural beings dread and dislike iron. The open pair of scissors, however, it should be observed, has double power; for it is not only of the abhorred metal,—it is also in form a cross. The use of the cross in baptism was probably one of the reasons for the efficacy of that rite against felonious fairies. At all events, over a very wide area the cross is thought a potent protection; nor is the belief by any means confined to Christian lands. Mr. Mitchell-Innes tells us that the fear of changelings exists in China. "To avert the calamity of nursing a demon, dried banana-skin is burnt to ashes, which are then mixed with water. Into this the mother dips her finger and paints a cross upon the sleeping babe's forehead. In a short time the demon soul returns—for the soul wanders from the body during sleep and is free—but, failing to recognize the body thus disguised, flies off. The true soul, which has been waiting for an opportunity, now approaches the dormant body, and, if the mark has been washed off in time, takes possession of it; but if not, it, like the demon, failing to recognize the body, departs, and the child dies in its sleep."[64] How to hit the exact moment between the flight of the demon and the advent of the true soul doubtless puzzles many a Chinese mother fully as much as the cross puzzles the two competing souls. But when she is successful she baffles the evil spirit by deceit, of which the cross is made the instrument; though we may well believe that the child is not disguised in this way without reference to the cross's inherent sanctity; for it is a religious symbol among nations who never heard the gospel of the Crucified.

Spirits whose baleful influences are feared by man are happily easily tricked. To this guilelessness on their part must be attributed another strange method of defeating their evil designs on children. It appears to be enough to lay over the infant, or on the bed beside the mother, a portion of the father's clothes. A shepherd's wife living near Selkirk was lying in bed one day with her new-born boy at her side, when she heard a sound of talking and laughter in the room. Suspecting what turned out to be the case, she seized in great alarm her husband's waistcoat, which was lying at the foot of the bed, and flung it over herself and the child. The fairies, for it was they who were the cause of the noise, set up a loud scream, crying out: "Auld Luckie has cheated us o' our bairnie!" Soon afterwards the woman heard something fall down the chimney, and looking out she saw a waxen effigy of her baby, stuck full of pins, lying on the hearth. The would-be thieves had meant to substitute this for the child. When her husband came home he made up a large fire and threw the doll upon it; but, instead of burning, the thing flew up the chimney amid shouts of laughter from the unseen visitors. The suggestion seems to be that the sight of the father's clothes leads "the good people" to think that he himself is present watching over his offspring. Some articles of clothing, however, seem to have special virtue, such as a right shirt-sleeve or a left stocking, though wherefore is not very clear; and in China, about Canton, a fisherman's net is employed with as little apparent reason. In Sweden the babe is wrapped in red cloth, which we may be allowed to conjecture is intended to cozen the fairies by simulating fire.[65]

Moreover, certain plants are credited with a similar gift. In Germany orant (whatever that may be), blue marjoram, and black cumin; and in Denmark garlic—nasty enough surely to keep any beings off—and bread are used. The Danes, too, place salt in the cradle or over the door. The Italians fear not only fairies who rob them of their children, but also witches who tear the faces of unbaptized infants. These are both old superstitions, dating in one form or other from classic times. To baulk the witches of their prey it is in some places customary to keep a light burning in the chamber at night, and to affix at the door of the house the image of a saint, hanging to it a rosary and an unravelled napkin; while behind the door are put a jar full of salt and a brush. A twofold defence is thus built up; for the witch, beholding the image of the saint and the rosary, will straightway retire; or if these fail to warn her off, she will on entering be compelled to count the grains of salt, the broken threads of the napkin, and the twigs of the brush—a task that will keep her occupied from midnight, when at the earliest she can dare appear, until dawn, when she must slink away without having been able to attain her object. Among the Greeks witches are believed to have great power. They seek new-born babes to suck their blood or to prick them to death with sharp instruments. Often they inflict such injuries that a child remains for ever a cripple or an invalid. The Nereids of the fountains and springs are also on the watch "to exchange one of their own fractious offspring for a mortal babe." Constant watchfulness, and baptism as soon as the Church permits it, are therefore necessary. In England it seems to have been held in former days that witches stole children from their cradles before baptism to make an oil or unguent by boiling them to a jelly. A part of this jelly they used to drink, and with the remainder they rubbed their bodies. This was the orthodox means of acquiring magical powers. It is a Sicilian belief that the hands of unbaptized children are used by witches in their sorceries.[66]

As we might expect, the reason why unbaptized babes are held to be so liable to these attacks is that until the initiatory rite has been performed they are looked upon as heathen, and therefore peculiarly under the dominion of evil spirits. In Sicily and in Spain an infant until baptism is called by the opprobrious epithets of *Pagan, Turk, Moor, Jew*. Even women will not kiss it, for to kiss a Moor, at all events in Spain, is sin; though, on the other hand, to kiss an unbaptized child, if no one else have kissed it, is sovereign against toothache. By the Greeks these little innocents are regarded not merely as not Christians, but as really less human than demoniac in their nature. This is said, indeed, to be the teaching of the Church. The lower classes, at least (and, presumably therefore, not long ago the upper classes) believe it firmly; so that an unbaptized babe is called *Drakos* (feminine, *Drakoula*), that is to say, serpent or dragon. This is the same opprobrious title that we found Gervase of Tilbury applying to the evil spirits infesting the waters of the Rhone; and we cannot doubt that it is intended to convey an imputation of Satanic nature.[67] The extent of this superstition would form an interesting subject of inquiry. If it could be established as existing now or formerly among other Christian nations (and the superstitions of Sicily and Spain just cited point to this) it would help to clear up much of the difficulty surrounding the subject of changelings, especially the motives actuating both fairies and witches in their depredations. And, as infant baptism is by no means exclusively a Christian rite, research among heathen nations would be equally pertinent.

Meanwhile the motive usually assigned to fairies in northern stories is that of preserving and improving their race, on the one hand by carrying off human children to be brought up among the elves and to become united with them, and on the other hand by obtaining the milk and fostering care of human mothers for their own offspring. Doubts have been expressed by the German poet and mythologist, Karl Simrock, whether this was the primitive motive. He suggests that originally these spirits were looked upon as wholly beneficent, and even the theft of children was dictated by their care for the best interests of mankind. Nor does he hesitate to lay it down that the selfish designs just mentioned were first attributed to them when with growing enlightenment the feeling manifested itself that the kindly beings were falling into decay.[68]

It might be sufficient to reply that no spiritual existences imagined by men in a state of civilization such as surrounded our Celtic and Teutonic forefathers were ever regarded as unswervingly benevolent: caprice and vindictiveness, if not cruelty, are always elements of their character. Beyond this general consideration, however, there is a further and conclusive answer in the fact that there is no warrant in tradition for the supposition that could we penetrate to the oldest strata of mythical belief we should not discover selfish designs imputed to "the good people." The distinguished commentator himself is bound to admit that the belief in their need of human help is entwined in the very roots of the Teutonic myths. It is, indeed, nothing but the mediæval and Teutonic form of tenets common to all the nations upon earth. The changeling superstition and the classic stories of children and adults beloved by gods of high and low degree are consistent with this belief, and inseparable from it. The motive is so far comprehensible: what is wanted is to know whether any special relations, such as are pointed at by the Greek epithet *Drakos*, were held to exist between the mysterious world and newly-born babes which would render the latter more obnoxious to attack than elder children or adults; or whether, as I have put it at the beginning of this chapter, their helplessness alone suggested their exceeding danger. To solve the riddle we must wait for a larger accumulation of documents.[69]

But in the best regulated families it is not always possible to prevent the abduction from being attempted, and sometimes accomplished, in spite of every precaution. One night a Welsh woman, waking in a fright in her husband's absence, missed her baby. She sought for it and caught it upon the boards above the bed: the fairies had not succeeded in bearing it any further away. Another felt her boy being taken from her arms; whereupon she screamed and held him tightly, and, according to her own expression, "God and me were too hard for them." The child grew up to become a famous preacher. A peasant woman in Mecklenburg who ventured to sleep without a light was attacked by an elf-woman. The stranger seized the child, but was baffled by the woman's determination; for she struggled and shrieked for her husband, and when he hurried in with a light the fairy vanished.[70]

Nor is it always the mother who arrests the theft. A trick frequently played by the dwarfs in Northern Germany on the birth of a child was to pinch a cow's ear; and when the animal bellowed and everybody ran out to know why, a dwarf would slip indoors and effect the change. On one such occasion the father saw his infant being dragged out of the room. In the nick of time he grasped it and drew it towards himself. The changeling left in its place was found in the bed; and this he kept too, defying the efforts of the underground folk to regain it. At a place in North Jutland it happened many years ago in a lying-in room that the mother could get no sleep while the lights were burning. So her husband resolved to take the child in his arm, in order to keep strict watch over it so long as it was dark. But, unfortunately, he fell asleep; and on being awakened by a shake of the arm, he saw a tall woman standing by the bed, and found that he had an infant in each arm. The woman instantly vanished; and as he had forgotten in which arm he had held his child, there he lay without knowing which of the two children was his own. A boy, who was watching his younger sister while his parents were both from home, saw a small man and woman come from behind the oven. They told him to give them the little one; and when he refused they stepped to the cradle and endeavoured to take the babe by force. The boy, however, was strong and bold, and laid about him with such determination that the robbers at length took to flight. On the Lithuanian coast of the Baltic substantially the same tale is told with more humour. There a farmer's boy sleeping in the living-room of the house is awakened by the proceedings of two *laumes*, or elves. They stealthily fetch out of the bedroom the new-born babe and swathe it in swaddling clothes of their own, while they wrap in its clothes the oven-broom. Then they began to quarrel which of them should carry the broom thus rolled up into the bedroom; and as they were unable to agree they resolved to carry it together. No sooner had they disappeared into the inner apartment than the boy leaped out of bed, picked up his mistress' child and took it into his own bed. When the *laumes* returned the infant was not to be found. They were both very angry and began to scold one another: "It's your fault." "No, it's your fault; didn't I say, You carry it, while I stay here and keep watch? I said it would be stolen!" While they wrangled thus, kakary ku! crew the cock, and, foiled and enraged, they had to make off. The boy had great difficulty in wakening his mistress, who was in a deep sleep, dreaming a horrible dream that a stock of wood had been placed on her breast so that she could hardly breathe. He told her what had happened, but she would not believe it until she saw that she had *two* children—one to which she had given birth, the other fashioned out of the oven-broom.[71]

Prayer and the utterance of a holy name are to the full as effectual as physical strength. A fisherwoman in the north-east of Scotland was once left alone in bed with her baby, when in came a little man dressed in green, and proceeded to lay hold of the child. The woman knew at once with whom she had to do, and ejaculated: "God be atween you an' me!" Out rushed the fairy in a moment, and mother and babe were left without further molestation. A curious tale is told of two Strathspey smugglers who were one night laying in a stock of whiskey at Glenlivat when they heard the child in the cradle give a piercing cry, just as if it had been shot. The mother, of course, blessed it; and the Strathspey lads took no further notice, and soon afterwards went their way with their goods. Before they had gone far they found a fine healthy child lying all alone on the roadside, and recognized it as their friend's. They saw at once how the affair stood. The fairies had taken away the real infant and left a stock; but owing to the pious ejaculation of the mother, they had been forced to drop it. As the urgency of their business did not admit of their return they took the child with them, and kept it until they went to Glenlivat again. On their arrival here they said nothing about the child, which they kept concealed. In the course of conversation the woman remarked that the disease which had attacked the little one the last time they were there had never left it, and she had now scarce any hope of its recovery. As if to confirm her statement, it continued uttering most piercing cries. The smugglers thereupon produced the real babe healthy and hearty, and told her how they had found it. The mother was, of course, pleased to recover it; and the next thing was to dispose of the changeling. For this purpose the Strathspey lads got an old creel to put him in and some straw to light under it. Seeing the serious turn matters were likely to take he resolved not to await the trial, but flew up the smoke-hole and cried out from the top that but for the guests events would have gone very differently.[72]

Two pixies of Dartmoor, in the shape of large bundles of rags, led away one of two children who were following their mother homeward. It was eventually found, on a search being made by the neighbours with lanterns, under a certain large oak tree known to be pixy-haunted. This is hardly a changeling story, as no attempt was made to foist a false child on the parent. A tale from the Isle of Man contains two similar incidents of attempted robbery without replacing the stolen child by one of superhuman birth. The fairies there adopted artifices like those of the North German dwarfs above mentioned. A few nights after a woman had been delivered of her first child a cry of fire was raised, and every one ran out of the house to see whence it proceeded, leaving the helpless mother alone with her babe. On returning they found the infant lying on the threshold of the house. The following year, when another little stranger had presented itself, a noise was heard in an out-house among the cattle. Again everybody that was stirring, including the nurse, hurried forth to learn what was the matter, believing that the cattle had got loose. But finding all safe, they came back, only to discover that the new-born babe had been taken out of bed, as the former had been, and on their coming dropped in the middle of the entry. It might have been supposed that these two warnings would have been enough; but a third time the trick was played, and then more successfully. Forgetting what had previously happened, all who were in the house ran out one night on hearing a noise in the cow-house—all, that is, except the mother, who could not move, and the nurse, who was sleeping off the effects of alcohol. The former was lying broad awake and saw her child lifted from the bed by invisible hands and carried clean away. She shrieked at once to the nurse, but failed to arouse her; and when her husband returned, an infant was indeed lying beside her, but a poor, lean, withered, deformed creature, very different from her own. It lay quite naked, though the clothes of the true child had been considerately left for it by the ravishers.[73]

One of the difficulties experienced by the fairies on two of the three occasions here narrated in making off with the little one occurred at the door of the house. That they should have tried, repeatedly at all events, to pass out that way is almost as remarkable as that they should have been permitted more than once to attempt the theft. For the threshold is a part of the dwelling which from of old has been held sacred, and is generally avoided by uncanny beings. Wiser, though still doomed to failure, were those Irish elves who lifted up a window and handed the infant out. For it happened that a neighbour who was coming to pay a visit that moment stopped before the house, and exclaimed: "God keep all here from harm!" No sooner had she uttered the words than she saw the child put forth, how, or by whom, she did not know; and without hesitation she went up and took it away home with her. The next morning when she called to see how her friend fared great was the moan made to her over the behaviour of the child—so different from what it had ever been before—crying all the night and keeping awake its mother, who could not quiet it by any means. "I'll tell you what you'll do with the brat," she replied; "whip it well first, and then bring it to the cross-roads, and leave the fairy in the ditch there for any one to take that pleases; for I have your child at home safe and sound as he was handed out of the window last night to me." When the mother heard this, she just stepped out to get a rod; but before she returned the changeling had vanished, and no one either saw or heard of it again.[74]

Fairies, however, when bent upon mischief, are not always baulked so easily. They effect the exchange, sometimes in the house, and sometimes when the parent is at work in the fields and incautiously puts her offspring down the while. In these circumstances, grievous as may be the suspicion arising from the changed conduct of the nursling, it is not always easy to be sure of what has taken place. Tests, therefore, have to be applied. Often the appearance is enough. A "mighty big head," or an abnormally thick head and neck, is in

Germany deemed sufficient credentials from Fairyland; while in a case from Lapland, where the hand and foot grew so rapidly as to become speedily nearly half an ell in length and the child was unable to learn to speak, whereas she readily understood what was said to her, these deviations from the course of nature were looked upon as conclusive evidence.[75] A reputed changeling shown to Waldron in the Isle of Man early in the last century is thus described: "Nothing under heaven could have a more beautiful face; but though between five and six years old, and seemingly healthy, he was so far from being able to walk, or stand, that he could not so much as move any one joint; his limbs were vastly long for his age, but smaller than an infant's of six months; his complexion was perfectly delicate, and he had the finest hair in the world; he never spoke, nor cried, eat scarce anything, and was very seldom seen to smile, but if any one called him a fairy-elf, he would frown and fix his eyes so earnestly on those who said it, as if he would look them through. His mother, or at least his supposed mother, being very poor, frequently went out a-charing, and left him a whole day together. The neighbours, out of curiosity, have often looked in at the window to see how he behaved when alone, which, whenever they did, they were sure to find him laughing and in the utmost delight. This made them judge that he was not without company more pleasing to him than any mortal's could be; and what made this conjecture seem the more reasonable was, that if he were left ever so dirty, the woman at her return saw him with a clean face, and his hair combed with the utmost exactness and nicety."[76] Luther tells us that he saw and touched at Dessau a changed child which was twelve years of age. The account he gives of the child is that "he had his eyes and all members like another child; he did nothing but feed, and would eat as much as two clowns or threshers were able to eat. When one touched it, then it cried out. When any evil happened in the house, then it laughed and was joyful; but when all went well, then it cried and was very sad." So much for the Reformer's testimony of what he saw and was told. His theories and generalizations are in their way not less interesting than his testimony: as might have been expected, they are an adaptation of the ordinary superstitions to his own grim scheme of things. "Such changelings and killcrops," he goes on to say, "*supponit Satan in locum verorum filiorum*; for the devil hath this power, that he changeth children, and instead thereof layeth devils in the cradles, which thrive not, only they feed and suck: but such changelings live not above eighteen or nineteen years. It sometimes falleth out that the children of women in child-bed are thus changed, and Devils laid in their stead, one of which more fouleth itself than ten other children do, so that the parents are much therewith disquieted; and the mothers in such sort are sucked out, that afterwards they are able to give suck no more."[77]

Making allowance for the influence of imagination, there can be no doubt, on comparison of these passages, that the children to whom the character of changelings was ascribed were invariably deformed or diseased. The delightful author of the "Popular Romances of the West of England" says that some thirty or forty years before the date of writing he had seen several reputed changelings. And his evidence is express that "in every case they have been sad examples of the influence of mesenteric disease." After describing their external symptoms, he adds: "The wasted frame, with sometimes strumous swellings, and the unnatural abdominal enlargement which accompanies disease of mesenteric glands, gives a very sad, and often a most unnatural, appearance to the sufferer." Professor Rhys' description of a reputed changeling, one Ellis Bach, of Nant Gwrtheyrn, in Carnarvonshire, is instructive as showing the kind of being accredited among the Welsh with fairy nature. The professor is repeating the account given to him of this poor creature, who died nearly half a century ago. He tells us: "His father was a farmer, whose children, both boys and girls, were like ordinary folks, excepting Ellis, who was deformed, his legs being so short that his body seemed only a few inches from the ground when he walked. His voice was also small and squeaky. However, he was very sharp, and could find his way among the rocks pretty well when he went in quest of his father's sheep and goats, of which there used to be plenty there formerly. Everybody believed Ellis to have been a changeling, and one saying of his is well known in that part of the country. When strangers visited Nant Gwrtheyrn, a thing which did not frequently happen, and when his parents asked them to their table, and pressed them to eat, he would squeak out drily: *'B'yta 'nynna b'yta'r cwbwl,'* that is to say—'Eating—that means eating all.'" A changeling in Monmouthshire, described by an eye-witness at the beginning of the present century, was simply an idiot of a forbidding aspect, a dark, tawny complexion, and much addicted to screaming.[78]

But a changeling was to be known in other ways than by his physical defects; under careful management he might be led to betray himself in speech or action. A Kirkcudbrightshire tale represents a child as once left in charge of a tailor, who "commenced a discourse" with him. "'Will, hae ye your pipes?' says the tailor. 'They're below my head,' says the tenant of the cradle. 'Play me a spring,' says the tailor. Like thought, the little man, jumping from the cradle, played round the room with great glee. A curious noise was heard meantime outside; and the tailor asked what it meant. The little elf called out: 'It's my folk wanting me,' and away he fled up the chimney, leaving the tailor more dead than alive." In the neighbouring county of Dumfries the story is told with more gusto. The gudewife goes to the hump-backed tailor, and says: "Wullie, I maun awa' to Dunse about my wab, and I dinna ken what to do wi' the bairn till I come back: ye ken it's but a whingin', screechin', skirlin' wallidreg—but we maun bear wi' dispensations. I wad wuss ye,' quoth she, 'to tak tent till't till I come hame—ye sall hae a roosin' ingle, and a blast o' the goodman's tobacco-pipe forbye.' Wullie was naething laith, and back they gaed the-gither. Wullie sits down at the fire, and awa' wi' her yarn gaes the wife; but scarce had she steekit the door, and wan half-way down the close, when the bairn cocks up on its doup in the cradle, and rounds in Wullie's lug: 'Wullie Tylor, an' ye winna tell my mither when she comes back, I'se play ye a bonny spring on the bagpipes.' I wat Wullie's heart was like to loup the hool—for tylors, ye ken, are aye timorsome—but he thinks to himsel': 'Fair fashions are still best,' an' 'It's better to fleetch fules than to flyte wi' them'; so he rounds again in the bairn's lug: 'Play up, my doo, an' I'se tell naebody.' Wi' that the fairy ripes amang the cradle strae, and pu's oot a pair o' pipes, sic as tylor Wullie ne'er had seen in a' his days—muntit wi' ivory, and gold, and silver, and dymonts, and what not. I dinna ken what spring the fairy played, but this I ken weel, that Wullie had nae great goo o' his performance; so he sits thinkin' to himsel': 'This maun be a deil's get, Auld Waughorn himsel' may come to rock his son's cradle, and play me some foul prank;' so he catches the bairn by the cuff o' the neck, and whupt him into the fire, bagpipes and a'!"[79]

In Nithsdale the elf-child displays a superhuman power of work. The mother left it on one occasion in the charge of a servant-girl, who sat bemoaning herself. "Wer't nae for thy girning face I would knock the big, winnow the corn, and grun the meal!" "Lowse the cradle band," cried the child, "and tent the neighbours, an' I'll work yere wark." With that he started up, the wind arose, the corn was winnowed, the outlyers were foddered, the hand-mill moved around as by instinct, and the knocking mell did its work with amazing rapidity. The lass and the elf meanwhile took their ease, until, on the mistress's return, he was restored to the cradle and began to yell anew.[80]

Most of the stories of changelings, in fact, assume that, though the outward characteristics might justify vehement suspicion, yet they were not absolutely decisive, and that to arrive at certainty the elf must be brought to betray himself. No great subtlety, however, was needful; for the stratagem employed varies but little, as the following examples will show. The child of a married couple in Mecklenburg at two years of age was no longer than a shoe, but had a mighty big head, and, withal, was unable to learn to speak. Its parents were led by an old man to suspect that it had been changed, and their adviser told them: "If you wish to become certain, take an empty egg-shell, and in the child's presence pour in new beer and cause it to ferment by means of yeast. If then the child speak, my conjecture is right." His counsel was followed, and scarcely had the beer fermented when the child cried out from the cradle:

"I am as old
As Bohemian gold,
Yet for the first time now I see
Beer in an egg-shell brew'd to be."

The parents determined to fling the babe into the river the following night; but when at midnight they rose for the purpose they found in the cradle a strong, blooming child. In a Welsh tale from Radnorshire the egg-shell is boiled full of pottage in the children's sight (there are twins in this case) and taken out as a dinner for the reapers who happened to be cutting the rye and oats. In Glamorganshire the woman declares she is mixing a pasty for the reapers. An Icelandic legend makes a woman set a pot containing food to cook on the fire and fasten twigs end to end in continuation of the handle of a spoon until the topmost one appears above the chimney, when she puts the bowl in the pot. Another woman in a Danish tale engaged to drive a changeling out of the house he troubled; and this is how she set about it. In his temporary absence she killed a pig and made a black pudding of it, hide, hair and all. On his return she set it before him, for he was a prodigious eater. He began gobbling it up as usual; but as he ate his efforts gradually slackened, and at last he sat quite still, eyeing it thoughtfully. Then he exclaimed: "A pudding with hide! and a pudding with hair! a pudding with eyes! and a pudding with bones in it! Thrice have I seen a young wood spring upon Tiis Lake, but never yet did I see such a pudding! The devil will stay here no longer!" And so saying he ran off and never returned.[81]

Of these devices, however, the normal one is that of the egg-shells. Sometimes one egg-shell only is employed, sometimes two—a dozen—or an indefinite number. At seaside places, like Normandy and the Channel Islands, egg-shells are sometimes replaced by shells of shell-fish.[82] In all the stories the end is the same, namely, to excite the curiosity and wonder of the imp to such a pitch that he gives expression to it in language akin to that of the North German or the Danish tale just quoted. The measure of age given in his exclamation is usually that of the trees in the forest, or indeed the forest itself. In the instance from Mecklenburg, Bohemian gold (*Böhmer Gold*) is made the measure, and this runs through quite a number of Low Dutch stories. There can be little doubt, however, that it is a corruption, and that the true form is, as given in a Schleswig-Holstein tale, Bohemian Forest (*Behmer Woelt*).[83] In Hesse Wester Forest (*Westerwald*) is found, and so on in other countries, the narrator in each case referring to some wood well known to his audience. The Lithuanian elf, or *laumes*, says: "I am so old, I was already in the world before the Kamschtschen Wood was planted, wherein great trees grew, and *that* is now laid waste again; but anything so wonderful I have never seen." In Normandy the changeling declares: "I have seen the Forest of Ardennes burnt seven times, but I never saw so many pots boil." The astonishment of a Scandinavian imp expressed itself even more graphically, for when he saw an egg-shell boiling on the fire having one end of a measuring rod set in it, he crept out of the cradle on his hands, leaving his feet still inside, and stretched himself out longer and longer until he reached right across the floor and up the chimney, when he exclaimed: "Well! seven times have I seen the wood fall in Lessö Forest, but never till now have I seen so big a ladle in so small a pot!" And the Danish story I have cited above represents the child as saying that he has seen a young wood thrice upon Tiis Lake.[84] The Welsh fairies are curiously youthful compared with these hoary infants, which is all the more remarkable when the daring exaggerations of Cambrian story-tellers are considered. It is a modest claim only to have seen the acorn before the oak and the egg before the hen, yet that is all that is put forward. In one of the Lays of Marie de France the wood of Brézal is indicated as the spot where the oak was seen.[85] The formula thus variously used would appear to be a common one to describe great antiquity, and in all probability itself dates back to a very remote period.

But changelings frequently conform to the more civilized usage of measuring their age by years. And various are the estimates given us, from fifteen hundred years in the Emerald Isle down to the computation, erring perhaps on the other side, of the young gentleman in the English tale, who remarks: "Seven years old was I before I came to the nurse, and four years have I lived since, and never saw so many milk-pans before." A yet more mysterious hint as to her earlier life is dropped by an imp in Brittany. She has been treated to the sight of milk boiling in egg-shells, and cries: "I shall soon be a hundred years old, but I never saw so many shells boiling! I was born in Pif and in Paf, in the country where cats are made; but I never saw anything like it!"[86] To all right-minded persons this disclosure contained sufficient warrant for her reputed mother to repudiate her as a witch, though cats are no less intimate with fairies than with conjurers.

Simrock, in his work on German mythology already cited, inclines to the opinion that the object of the ceremony which the suspected child is made to witness is to produce laughter. He says: "The dwarf is no over-ripe beauty who must keep her age secret. Rather something ridiculous must be done to cause him to laugh, because laughter brings deliverance."[87] The problem set before the heroes of many folk-tales is to compel laughter, but that does not seem to be intended in these changeling stories. At least I have only met with it in one, and it certainly is not common. The confession of age which the ceremony draws forth is really much more. It is a confession that the apparently human babe is an imposture, that it belongs in fact to a different race, and has no claim on the mother's care and tenderness. Therefore it is not always enough for the fraud to be discovered: active means must sometimes be taken to rid the family of their supernatural burden and regain their own little one. In Grimm's story, in which the child laughs, a host of elves comes suddenly bringing back the true and carrying away the false one; and in many of the German and Northern tales the changeling disappears in one way or other immediately after its exclamation. We are sometimes even told in so many words that the changeling had betrayed himself, and the underground folk were obliged to give back the stolen child. And in the Lithuanian story we have cited the *laumes* straightway falls sick and dies.[88] Such conduct accords entirely with the resentment at being recognized which we have in a previous chapter found to be a characteristic of spiritual existences. It is much more like the dislike of being found out attributed to beings who are in the habit of walking invisible, than any mystical effect of laughter.

If this be so, still less do the stories where it is required actually to drive the imp away support the learned German's contention. The means taken in these stories are very various. Sometimes it is enough to let the child severely alone, as once in the Isle of Man where a woman laid her child down in the field while she was cutting corn, and a fairy changed it there and then. The changeling began to scream, but the mother was prevented by a man who had been a witness to the transaction from picking it up; and when the fairy found that no notice was taken the true child was brought back. In the island of Lewis the custom was to dig a grave in the fields on Quarter Day and lay the goblin in it until the next morning, by which time it was believed the human babe would be returned. In the north of Germany one is advised not to touch the changeling with the hands, but to overturn the cradle so that the child falls on the floor. The elf must then be swept out of the door with an old broom, when the dwarfs will come and bring back the stolen child. Putting it on the dunghill and leaving it there to cry has been practised successfully in England; but in Ireland this is only one part of a long and serious ceremony directed by a wizard or "fairy-man." In dealing with these stories we must always remember that not merely are we concerned with sagas of something long past, but with a yet living superstition, and that the practices I am about to mention—even the most cruel and the most ridiculous of them—so far respond to the actual beliefs of the people that instances of their occurrence are quite recent and well authenticated, as we shall presently see. An anonymous but well-informed writer describes, as if it were by no means an unusual ceremony, that just referred to; and Kennedy gives the same in the shape of a legend. It seems to consist in taking a clean shovel and seating the changeling on its broad iron blade, and thus conveying the creature to the manure heap. The assistants would then join hands and circle about the heap thrice while the fairy-man chanted an incantation in the Irish language. At its conclusion all present would withdraw into the house, leaving the child where it had been placed, to howl and cry as it pleased. Says Mr. Kennedy: "They soon felt the air around them sweep this way and that, as if it was stirred by the motion of wings, but they remained quiet and silent for about ten minutes. Opening the door, they then looked out, and saw the bundle of straw on the heap, but neither child nor fairy. 'Go into your bedroom, Katty,' said the fairy-man, 'and see if there's anything left on the bed!' She did so, and they soon heard a cry of joy, and Katty was among them in a moment, kissing and hugging her own healthy-looking child, who was waking and rubbing his eyes, and wondering at the lights and all the eager faces."[89]

Whether it was the noise made by the child or the incantation that drew the "good people's" attention, we are left in doubt by this story. A Norman woman was, however, advised to make her child cry lustily "in order to bring its *real* mother to it." And this is probably the meaning of the many tales in which the elf is beaten, or starved and subjected to other ill-usage, or is threatened with death.[90] In the Pflöckenstein Lake in Bohemia wild women are believed to dwell, who, among other attributes common to elves or fairies, are believed to change infants. In order to compel a re-exchange, directions are given to bind with a weed growing at the bottom of the lake and to beat with a rod of the same, calling out therewithal: "Take thine own and bring me mine." A mother in a Little Russian tale had a baby of extraordinary habits. When alone, he jumped out of the cradle, no longer a baby but a bearded old man, gobbled up the food out of the stove, and then lay down again a screeching babe. A wise woman who was consulted placed him on a block of wood and began to chop the block under his feet. He screeched and she chopped; he screeched and she chopped; until he became an old man again and made the enigmatical confession: "I have transformed myself not once nor twice only. I was first a fish, then I became a bird, an ant, and a quadruped, and now I have once more made trial of being a human being. It isn't better thus than being among the ants; but among human beings—it isn't worse!" Here the chopping was evidently a threat to kill. Nor, if we may trust the stories, was this threat always an empty one. The changeling fashioned out of a broom in the Lithuanian story already cited, was disposed of, by the parish priest's advice, by hewing its head off. The reason given by the holy man was that it was not yet four and twenty hours old, and it would not be really alive until the expiration of that time. Accordingly when the neck was severed nothing but a wisp of straw was found inside, though blood flowed as if there were veins.[91]

But even more truculent methods are represented by the story-tellers as resorted to free the afflicted household. Nothing short of fire is often deemed sufficient for the purpose. There were various methods of applying it. Sometimes we are told of a shovel being made red-hot and held before the child's face; sometimes he is seated on it and flung out into the dung-pit, or into the oven; or again, the poker would be heated to mark the sign of the cross on his forehead, or the tongs to take him by the nose. Or he is thrown bodily on the fire, or suspended over it in a creel or a pot; and in the north of Scotland the latter must be hung from a piece of the branch of a hazel tree. In this case we are told that if the child screamed it was a changeling, and it was held fast to prevent its escape. Generally, however, it is related that the elf flies up the chimney, and when safely at the top he stops to make uncomplimentary remarks upon his persecutors. In the Nithsdale story which I have already cited, the servant girl at midnight covers up the chimney and every other inlet, makes the embers glowing hot, and undressing the changeling tosses it on them. In answer to its yells the fairies are heard moaning and rattling at the window boards, the chimney-head, and the door. "In the name o' God, bring back the bairn," she exclaims. In a moment up flew the window, the human child was laid unharmed on the mother's lap, while its guilty substitute flew up the chimney with a loud laugh.[92]

Frightful as this cruelty would seem to every one if perpetrated on the mother's own offspring, it was regarded with equanimity as applied to a goblin; and it is not more frightful than what has been actually perpetrated on young children, and that within a very few years, under the belief that they were beings of a different race. Instances need not be multiplied; it will be enough to show that one of the horrible methods of disposing of changelings referred to in the last paragraph came under judicial notice no longer ago than the month of May 1884. Two women were reported in the "Daily Telegraph" as having been arrested at Clonmel on the 17th of that month, charged with cruelly ill-treating a child three years old. The evidence given was to the effect that the neighbours fancied that the child, who had not the use of his limbs, was a changeling. During the mother's absence the prisoners accordingly entered her house and placed the child naked on a hot shovel, "under the impression that this would break the charm." As might have been expected the poor little thing was severely burnt, and, when the women were apprehended, it was in a precarious condition. The prisoners, on being remanded, were hooted by an indignant crowd. It might be thought that this was an indication of the decay of superstition, even in Ireland, however much to be condemned as an outburst of feeling against unconvicted and even untried persons. But we must regard it rather as a protest against the prisoners' inhumanity than against their superstition: in either case, of course, the product of advancing civilization. For if we may trust the witness of other sagas we find the trial by fire commuted to a symbolic act, as though men had begun to be revolted by the cruelty, even when committed only on a fairy who had been found out, but were unwilling to abandon their belief in the power of the exorcism. In the north-east of Scotland, for example, where a beggar, who had diagnosed a changeling, was allowed to try his hand at disposing of it, he made a large fire on the hearth and held a black hen over it till she struggled, and finally escaped from his grasp, flying out by the "lum." More minute directions are given by the cunning man in a Glamorganshire tale. After poring over his big book, he told his distracted client to find a black hen without a single feather of any other colour. This she was to bake (not living, but dead, as appears by the sequel) before a fire of wood (not, as usual, of peat), with feathers and all intact. Every window and opening was to be closed, except one—presumably the chimney; and she was not to watch the *crimbil*, or changeling, until the hen had been done enough, which she would know by the falling off of all her feathers. The more knowing woman, in an Irish story, attributes the fact of the infant's being changed to the Evil Eye; and her directions for treatment require the mother to watch for the woman who has given it the Evil Eye, inveigle her into the house and cut a piece secretly out of her cloak. This piece of the cloak was then to be burnt close to the child until the smoke made him sneeze, when the spell would be broken and her own child restored. The writer who records this tale mentions the following mode of proceeding as a common one, namely: to place the babe in the middle of the cabin and light a fire round it, fully expecting it to be changed into a sod of turf, but manifestly not intending to do bodily harm to it independently of any such change. In Carnarvonshire a clergyman is credited with telling a mother to cover a shovel with salt, mark a cross in the salt, and burn it in the chamber where the child was, judiciously opening the window first.[93] It is satisfactory to know that, so far as the recorded cases go, the ceremony lost nothing of its power by being thus toned down.

Fire, however, was not the only element efficacious for turning to flight these troublesome aliens. Water's antagonism to witches is notorious; and ample use was made of it in the old witch trials. It is equally obnoxious to fairies and their congeners. In a Welsh story from Radnorshire, when the mother has been by the egg-shell device convinced of the exchange of her own twin children, she takes the goblin twins and flings them into Llyn Ebyr; but their true kinsmen clad in blue trousers (their usual garb) save them, and the mother receives her own again. In other tales she drops the twins into the river; but in one case the witch who has been credited with the change bathes the child at a mountain spout, or *pistyll*, and exacts a promise from the mother to duck him in cold water every morning for three months. It is not very surprising to learn that "at the end of that time there was no finer infant in the Cwm."[94]

There is an oft-quoted passage in Luther's "Table Talk," in which he relates that he told the Prince of Anhalt that if he were prince he would venture *homicidium* upon a certain changeling with which he had been brought into contact, and throw it into the river Moldaw. The great Reformer was only on a level with his countrymen in their superstitions in reference to changelings, or Killcrops, as they were then called. I have already quoted his opinion of them as devils; and the test of their true nature, which he seems to have thought infallible, was their inordinate appetite; nor did he attach any value to baptism as a means of exorcism. One excellent tale he tells on the subject concerns a peasant who lived near Halberstadt, in Saxony. This good man, in accordance with advice, was taking the child to Halberstadt to be rocked at the shrine of the Virgin Mary, when in crossing a river another devil that was below in the river called out "Killcrop! Killcrop!" Then, says Luther, the child in the basket, that had never before spoken one word, answered "Ho, ho!" The devil in the water asked, "Whither art thou going?" and the child replied, "I am going to Halberstadt to our Loving Mother, to be rocked." In his fright the man threw the basket containing the child over the bridge into the water, whereupon the two devils flew away together and cried "Ho, ho, ha!" tumbling themselves one over another, and so vanished.[95] This may be taken as a type of many a story current in North Germany and the neighbouring Slavonic lands. It is not, however, unknown in this country. Mr. Hunt has versified a Cornish tale in which the mother took her brat to the chapel well to plunge it at dawn and pass it round slowly three times *against* the sun, as she had been advised to do on the first three Wednesdays in the month of May. Reaching the top of the hill on one of these occasions, she heard a shrill voice in her ear: "Tredrill, Tredrill! thy wife and children greet thee well." The little one of course replied, much to her astonishment, repudiating all concern for his wife and children, and intimating his enjoyment of the life he was leading, and the spell that was being wrought in his behalf. In the end she got rid of him by the homely process of beating and leaving him on the ground near the old church stile. A Sutherlandshire tradition tells of a child less than a year old who suddenly addressed his mother in verse as he was being carried through a wild glen. Translated, the youth's impromptu lines run thus:—

"Many is the dun hummel cow
(Each having a calf)
In the opposite dun glen,
Without the aid of dog,
Or man, or woman, or gillie,
One man excepted,
And he grey——"

At that moment his remarks were interrupted by the terrified woman throwing him down in the plaid which wrapt him, and scampering home, where to her joy she found her true babe smiling in the cradle.[96]

These verses carry us back to the egg-shell episode, from which the consideration of the means adopted to drive away the intrusive goblin has diverted us. They contain a vague assertion of age like those then before us, but not a hint of laughter. Nor have we found anything throughout the whole discussion to favour Simrock's suggestion, or to shake the opinion that the dissolution of the fairy spell was derived either from the vexation of the supernatural folk at their own self-betrayal, or from the disclosure to the human foster-parents of the true state of the facts, and their consequent determination to exorcise the demon.

It is true we have a few more stories to examine, but we shall find that they all confirm this conclusion. The cases we have yet to deal with, except the first, exhibit a different and much more humane treatment of the changeling than the foregoing. The case excepted is found in Carnarvonshire, where one infallible method of getting rid of the child was to place it on the floor and let all present in the house throw a piece of iron at it. The old woman who mentioned this to Professor Rhys conjectured that the object was to convince the *Tylwyth Teg*, or fairy people, of the intention to kill the babe, in order to induce them to bring the right child back.[97] This would be the same motive as that which threatened death by fire or other ill-usage, in some of the instances mentioned above. But we could not thus account for the requirement that iron, and only iron, was to be used; and here we have, in fact, a superstition carefully preserved, while its meaning has quite passed out of memory. In a future chapter we shall examine the attitude of mythical beings in folklore to metals, and especially to iron; in the meantime we may content ourselves with noting this addition to the examples we have already met with of the horror with which they regarded it.

So far from its being always deemed wise to neglect or injure the changeling, it was not infrequently supposed to be necessary to take the greatest care of it, thereby and by other means to propitiate its elvish tribe. This was the course pursued with the best results by a Devonshire mother; and a woman at Strassberg, in North Germany, was counselled by all her gossips to act lovingly, and above all not to beat the imp, lest her own little one be beaten in turn by the underground folk. So in a Hessian tale mentioned by Grimm, a *wichtel-wife* caught almost in the act of kidnapping refused to give up the babe until the woman had placed the changed one to her breast, and "nourished it for once with the generous milk of human kind." In Ireland, even when the child is placed on a dunghill, the charm recited under the direction of the "fairy-man" promises kindly entertainment in future for the "gambolling crew," if they will only undo what they have done. A method in favour in the north of Scotland is to take the suspected elf to some known haunt of its race, generally, we are told, some spot where peculiar soughing sounds are heard, or to some barrow, or stone circle, and lay it down, repeating certain incantations the while. What the words of these incantations are we are not informed, but we learn that an offering of bread, butter, milk, cheese, eggs, and flesh of fowl must accompany the child. The parents then retire for an hour or two, or until after midnight; and if on returning these things have disappeared, they conclude that the offering is accepted and their own child returned.[98]

Neither ill-usage nor kindness, neither neglect nor propitiation, was sometimes prescribed and acted upon, but—harder than either—a journey to Fairyland to fetch back the captive. A man on the island of Rügen, whose carelessness had occasioned the loss of his child, watched until the underground dwellers sallied forth on another raid, when he hastened to the mouth of the hole that led into their realm, and went boldly down. There in the Underworld he found the child, and thus the robbers were forced to take their own again instead. In a more detailed narrative from Islay, the father arms himself with a Bible, a dirk, and a crowing cock, and having found the hill where the "Good People" had their abode open, and filled with the lights and sounds of festival, he approached and stuck the dirk into the threshold. The object of this was to prevent the entrance from closing upon him. Then he steadily advanced, protected from harm by the Bible at his breast. Within, his boy (who was thirteen or fourteen years of age) was working at the forge; but when the man demanded him the elves burst into a loud laugh, which aroused the cock in his arms. The cock at once leaped upon his shoulders, flapped his wings, and crowed loud and long. The enraged elves thereupon cast the man and his son both out of the hill, and flung the dirk after them; and in an instant all was dark. It should be added that for a year and a day afterwards the boy did no work, and scarcely spoke; but he ultimately became a very famous smith, the inventor of a specially fine and well-tempered sword. The changeling himself in one of Lady Wilde's tales directs his foster-mother to Fairyland. The way thither was down a well; and she was led by the portress, an old woman, into the royal palace. There the queen admits that she stole the child, "for he was so beautiful," and put her own instead. The re-exchange is effected, and the good woman is feasted with food which the fairies cannot touch, because it has been sprinkled with salt. When she found herself again at home, she fancied she had only been away an hour: it was three years.[99]

But it was not always necessary to incur the risk of going as far as the other world. The Glamorganshire woman, whose successful cooking of a black hen has been already referred to, had first to go at full moon to a place where four roads met, and hide herself to watch the fairy procession which passed at midnight. There in the midst of the music and the *Bendith eu mammau* she beheld her own dear little child. One of the most interesting changeling stories was gravely related in the "Irish Fireside" for the 7th of January 1884, concerning a land-leaguer who had been imprisoned as a suspect under the then latest Coercion Act. When this patriot was a boy he had been stolen by the fairies, one of themselves having been left in his place. The parish priest, however, interfered; and by a miracle he caused the elf for a moment to disappear, and the boy to return to tell him the conditions on which his captivity might be ended. The information given, the goblin again replaced the true son; but the good priest was now able to deal effectually with the matter. The imp was accordingly dipped thrice in Lough Lane (a small lake in the eastern part of Westmeath), when "a curl came on the water, and up from the deep came the naked form of the boy, who walked on the water to meet his father on shore. The father wrapped his overcoat about his son, and commenced his homeward march, accompanied by a line of soldiers, who also came out of the lake. The boy's mother was enjoined not to speak until the rescuing party would reach home. She accidentally spoke; and immediately the son dropped a tear, and forced himself out of his father's arms, piteously exclaiming: 'Father, father, my mother spoke! You cannot keep me. I must go.'

He disappeared, and, reaching home, the father found the sprite again on the hearth." The ghostly father's services were called into requisition a second time; and better luck awaited an effort under his direction after the performance of a second miracle like the first. For this time the mother succeeded in holding her tongue, notwithstanding that at every stream on the way home from the lake the car on which the boy was carried was upset, and he himself fainted.[100] This is declared to have happened no longer ago than the year 1869. The writer, apparently a pious Roman Catholic, who vouches for the fact, probably never heard the touching tale of Orpheus and Eurydice.

The foregoing story, as well as some of those previously mentioned, shows that fairy depredations were by no means confined to babes and young children. Indeed adults were often carried off; and, although this chapter is already far too long, I cannot close it without briefly examining a few such cases. Putting aside those, then, in which boys or young men have been taken, as already sufficiently discussed, all the other cases of robbery, as distinguished from seduction or illusion, are concerned with matrons. The elfin race were supposed to be on the watch for unchurched or unsained mothers to have the benefit of their milk. In one instance the captive was reputed to have freed herself by promising in exchange her husband's best mare under milk, which was retained by the captors until it was exhausted and almost dead. More usually the story relates that a piece of wood is carved in the likeness of the lady and laid in her place, the husband and friends being deceived into believing it to be herself. A man returning home at night overhears the supernatural beings at work. He listens and catches the words: "Mak' it red cheekit an' red lippit like the smith o' Bonnykelly's wife." Mastering the situation he runs off to the smith's house, and sains the new mother and her babe. And he is only just in time, for hardly has he finished than a great thud is heard outside. On going out a piece of bog-fir is found,— the image the fairies intended to substitute for the smith's wife. In North German and Danish tales it is the husband who overhears the conspirators at work, and he often has coolness enough to watch their proceedings on his return home and, bouncing out upon them, to catch them just as they are about to complete their crime. Thus, one clever fellow succeeded in retaining both his wife and the image already put into her bed, which he thrust into the oven to blaze and crackle in the sight and hearing of his wife's assembled friends, who supposed he was burning her until he produced her to their astonished gaze. A tale from Badenoch represents the man as discovering the fraud from finding his wife, a woman of unruffled temper, suddenly turned a shrew. So he piles up a great fire and threatens to throw the occupant of the bed upon it unless she tells him what has become of his own wife. She then confesses that the latter has been carried off, and she has been appointed successor; but by his determination he happily succeeds in recapturing his own at a certain fairy knoll near Inverness.[101]

It happens occasionally that these victims of elfin gallantry are rescued by other men than their husbands. A smith at work one day hears a great moaning and sobbing out of doors. Looking out he sees a troll driving a pregnant woman before him, and crying to her continually: "A little further yet! a little further yet!" He instantly springs forward with a red-hot iron in his hand, which he holds between the troll and his thrall, so that the former has to abandon her and take to flight. The smith then took the woman under his protection, and the same night she was delivered of twins. Going to the husband to console him for his loss, he is surprised to find a woman exactly resembling his friend's wife in her bed. He saw how the matter stood, and seizing an axe he killed the witch on the spot, and restored to the husband his real wife and new-born children. This is a Danish legend; but there is a Highland one very similar to it. A man meets one night a troop of fairies with a prize of some sort. Recollecting that fairies are obliged to exchange whatever they may have with any one who offers them anything, no matter what its value, for it, he flings his bonnet to them, calling out: "Mine is yours, and yours is mine!" The prize which they dropped turned out to be an English lady whom they had carried off, leaving in her place a stock, which, of course, died and was buried. The Sassenach woman lived for some years in the Highlander's house, until the captain in command of an English regiment came to lodge in his house with his son, while the soldiers were making new roads through the country. There the son recognized his mother, and the father his wife long mourned as dead.[102]

The death and burial of changelings, though, as here, occurring in the tales, are not often alluded to; and there are grounds for thinking them a special deduction of the Scottish mind. Sometimes the incident is ghastly enough to satisfy the devoted lover of horrors. The west of Scotland furnishes an instance in which the exchange was not discovered until after the child's apparent death. It was buried in due course; but suspicion having been aroused, the grave and coffin were opened, and not a corpse but only a wooden figure was found within. A farmer at Kintraw, in Argyllshire, lost his wife. On the Sunday after the funeral, when he and his servants returned from church, the children, who had been left at home, reported that their mother had been to see them, and had combed and dressed them. The following Sunday they made the same statement, in spite of the punishment their father had thought proper to inflict for telling a lie on the first occasion. The next time she came the eldest child asked her why she came, when she said that she had been carried off by "the good people," and could only get away for an hour or two on Sundays, and should her coffin be opened it would be found to contain nothing but a withered leaf. The minister, however, who ridiculed the story, refused to allow the coffin to be opened; and when, some little time after, he was found dead near the Fairies' Hill, above Kintraw, he was held by many to be a victim to the indignation of the fairy world he had laughed at. Sir Walter Scott mentions the tale of a farmer's wife in Lothian, who, after being carried off by the fairies, reappeared repeatedly on Sunday to her children, and combed their hair. On one of these occasions the husband met her, and was told that there was one way to recover her, namely, by lying in wait on Hallowe'en for the procession of fairies, and stepping boldly out, and seizing her as she passed among them. At the moment of execution, however, his heart failed, and he lost his wife for ever. In connection with this, Scott refers to a real event which happened at the town of North Berwick. A widower, who was paying addresses with a view to second marriage, was troubled by dreams of his former wife, to whom he had been tenderly attached. One morning he declared to the minister that she had appeared to him the previous night, stating that she was a captive in Fairyland, and begged him to attempt her deliverance. The mode she prescribed was to bring the minister and certain others to her grave at midnight to dig up her body, and recite certain prayers, after which the corpse would become animated and flee from him. It was to be pursued by the swiftest runner in the parish, and if he could catch it before it had encircled the church thrice, the rest were to come to his help and hold it notwithstanding its struggles, and the shapes into which it might be transformed. In this way she would be redeemed. The minister, however, declined to take part in so absurd and indecent a proceeding.[103]

Absurd and indecent it would undoubtedly have been to unearth a dead body in the expectation of any such result; but it would have been entirely in harmony with current superstition. The stories and beliefs examined in the present chapter prove that there has been no superstition too gross, or too cruel, to survive into the midst of the civilization of the nineteenth century; and the exhumation of a corpse, of the two, is less barbarous than the torture by fire of an innocent child. The flight, struggles, and transformation of a bespelled lady are found both in *märchen* and saga: some examples of the latter will come under our notice in a future chapter.

**FOOTNOTES:**

[60] The belief in changelings is not confined to Europe, though the accounts we have of it elsewhere are meagre. It is found, as we shall see further on, in China. It is found also among the natives of the Pacific slopes of North America, where it is death to the mother to suckle the changeling. Dorman, p. 24, citing Bancroft.

[61] See a curious Scottish ballad given at length, "F. L. Record," vol. i. p. 235; Henderson, p. 15; "Cymru Fu N. and Q." vol. ii. p. 144; Gregor, p. 11 (*cf.* Harland and Wilkinson, p. 221); Cromek, p. 247. See Webster, p. 73, where a witch carries away a child who is not blessed when it sneezes.

[62] Napier, p. 40; "F. L. Journal," vol. i. p. 56; Kuhn, pp. 365, 196; Knoop, p. 155; "Zeits. f. Volksk." vol. ii. p. 33; Kennedy, p. 95; Carnoy, p. 4; "F. L. Journal," vol. ii. p. 257.

[63] Bartsch, vol. i. pp. 64, 89; vol. ii. p. 43; Kuhn, p. 195; Knoop, *loc. cit.*; Jahn, pp. 52, 71; Thorpe, vol. ii. p. 174; "Zeits. f. Volksk." vol. ii. *loc. cit.* W. Map, Dist. ii. c. 14; Brand, vol. ii. p. 8, note; Lady Wilde, vol. i. pp. 71, 73; Schleicher, p. 93; Tertullian, "Adv. Nationes," l. ii. c. 11; Brand, vol. ii. p. 334 note, quoting Martin, "History of the Western Islands"; Train, vol. ii. p. 132; "Sacred Books of the East," vol. xxiv. p. 277. As to the use of fire in China, see

"F. L. Journal," vol. v. p. 225; and generally as to the efficacy of fire in driving off evil spirits see Tylor, vol. ii. p. 177.

[64] Grimm, "Teut. Myth." p. 468; Thorpe, vol. ii. p. 2, vol. iii. p. 45; Train, vol. ii. p. 133; Garnett, pp. 231, 315; "F. L. Journal," vol. v. p. 225. In Eastern Prussia a steel used for striking a light, a hammer, or anything else that will strike fire, is used. This seems to combine the dread of steel with that of fire (Lemke, p. 41).

[65] Grimm, "Teut. Myth." *loc. cit.*; Train, vol. ii. *loc. cit.*; Henderson, p. 14; "F. L. Journal," vol. v. p. 224; "Zeits. f. Volksk." vol. ii, p. 33; "N. and Q." 7th ser. vol. x. p. 185.

[66] Henderson, *loc. cit.*; Bartsch, vol. ii. p. 192; Pitré, vol. xv. pp. 154 note, 155; vol. xvii. p. 102, quoting Castelli, "Credenze ed usi"; Horace, "Ep. ad Pison," v. 340; Dorsa, p. 146; Wright, "Middle Ages," vol. i. p. 290; Garnett, p. 70; "Mélusine," vol. v. p. 90, quoting English authorities. Map, Dist. ii. c. 14, gives a story of babies killed by a witch. St. Augustine records that the god Silvanus was feared as likely to injure women in child-bed, and that for their protection three men were employed to go round the house during the night and to strike the threshold with a hatchet and a pestle and sweep it with a brush; and he makes merry over the superstition ("De Civ. Dei," l. vi. c. 9).

[67] Pitré, vol. xii. p. 304, note; vol. xv. p. 154; "F. L. Españ." vol. ii. p. 51; De Gubernatis, "Usi Natal." p. 219, quoting Bézoles, "Le Baptême."

[68] Bartsch, vol. i. p. 46; Jahn, p. 89; Grimm, "Teut. Myth." p. 468; Simrock, p. 418.

[69] There is another motive for the robbery of a human creature, mentioned only, I think, in the Romance of Thomas the Rhymer, namely, that at certain seasons the foul fiend fetches his fee, or tribute of a living soul, from among the underground folk. Several difficulties arise upon this; but it is needless to discuss them until the motive in question be found imputed elsewhere than in a literary work of the fifteenth century, and ballads derived therefrom.

Since the foregoing note was written my attention has been drawn to the following statement in Lady Wilde, vol. i. p. 70: "Sometimes it is said the fairies carry off the mortal child for a sacrifice, as they have to offer one every seven years to the devil in return for the power he gives them. And beautiful young girls are carried off, also, either for sacrifice or to be wedded to the fairy king." It is easier to generalize in this manner than to produce documents in proof. And I think I am expressing the opinion of all folklore students when I say that, with all respect for Lady Wilde, I would rather not lay any stress upon her general statements. Indeed, those of anybody, however great an authority, need to be checked by the evidence of particular instances. I await such evidence.

[70] Sikes, p. 62; *cf.* Brand, vol. ii. p. 334 note; Bartsch, vol. i. p. 46.

[71] Thorpe, vol. ii. p. 175; vol. iii. p. 43; Kuhn, p. 195; Schleicher, p. 92.

[72] Gregor, p. 61; Keightley, p. 393; Campbell, vol. ii. p. 64.

[73] Hunt, p. 96; Waldron, p. 30. This account was given to the author by the mother herself.

[74] Croker, p. 81. See a similar tale in Campbell, vol. ii. p. 58. Gregor, p. 61, mentions the dog-hole as the way by which children are sometimes carried off.

[75] Bartsch, vol. i. p. 46; Kuhn, p. 196; Grimm, "Teut. Myth." p. 468; Poestion, p. 114; Grohmann, p. 113.

[76] Waldron, p. 29. The same writer gives a similar account of the changeling mentioned above, p. 107.

[77] "Colloquia Mensalia," quoted by Southey, "The Doctor" (London, 1848), p. 621. As to the attribute of greed, *cf.* Keightley, p. 125.

[78] Hunt, p. 85; "Y Cymmrodor," vol. vi. p. 175; Rev. Edmund Jones, "A Relation of Apparitions," quoted by Wirt Sikes, p. 56. Thiele relates a story in which a wild stallion colt is brought in to smell two babes, one of which is a changeling. Every time he smells one he is quiet and licks it; but on smelling the other he is invariably restive and strives to kick it. The latter, therefore, is the changeling. (Thorpe, vol. ii. p. 177.) Sir John Maundeville also states that in Sicily is a kind of serpent whereby men assay the legitimacy of their children. If the children be illegitimate the serpents bite and kill them; if otherwise they do them no harm—an easy and off-hand way of getting rid of them! ("Early Trav." p. 155).

[79] Campbell, vol. ii. p. 58; Chambers, p. 70.

[80] Cromek, p. 246.

[81] Bartsch, vol. i. p. 42; Sikes, p. 59, quoting from the "Cambrian Quarterly," vol. ii. p. 86; "Y Cymmrodor," vol. vi. p. 209; Arnason's "Icelandic Legends," cited in Kennedy, p. 89; Thorpe, vol. ii. p. 174, quoting Thiele, "Danmark's Folkesagn samlede." See also Keightley, p. 125.

[82] Fleury, p. 60; "Revue des Trad. Pop." vol. iii. p. 162.

[83] Cf. *Böhmen-Gold*, Bartsch, vol. i. p. 22; *Böhmegold*, ibid. p. 47; *Böhmer Gold*, ibid. pp. 65, 79, and presumably p. 89; *Böhma gold*, Kuhn und Schwartz, p. 30; *Boehman gold*, ibid. p. 31; *böm un gold* (timber and gold), ibid. p. 105; *Boem un holt* (timber and wood), Jahn, p. 90; *Bernholt in den Wolt* (firewood in the forest), and *Bremer Wold*, Müllenhoff, cited Grimm, "Tales," vol. i. p. 388. These variations while preserving a similar sound are suspicious.

[84] Grimm, "Tales," vol. i. pp. 163, 388; Schleicher, p. 91; Fleury, p. 60; Thorpe, vol. ii. p. 176; quoting Asbjörnsen, "Huldreeventyr," vol. ii. p. 165. *Cf.* Sébillot, "Contes Pop." vol. ii. p. 78.

[85] Sikes, pp. 58, 59; Howells, p. 138; "Y Cymmrodor," vol. iv. p. 208, vol. vi. pp. 172, 204; Keightley, p. 436.

[86] Croker, p. 65; "A Pleasant Treatise of Witches," p. 62, quoted in Hazlitt, "Fairy Tales," p. 372; Sébillot, "Contes," vol. ii. p. 76; Carnoy, p. 4; Thorpe, vol. iii. p. 157; Campbell, vol. ii. p. 47; "Revue des Trad. Pop." vol. iii. p. 162. *Cf.* a Basque tale given by Webster, where the Devil is tricked into telling his age (Webster, p. 58).

[87] Simrock, p. 419.

[88] Jahn, p. 89; Schleicher, p. 91.

[89] "Choice Notes," p. 27; (this seems to have been a common prescription in Wales: see "Y Cymmrodor," vol. vi, pp. 175, 178; and in the Western Highlands: see Campbell, vol. ii. p. 64.) Brand, vol. ii. p. 335, note; (this seems also to be the case in some parts of Ireland, Lady Wilde, vol. i. p. 70.) Thorpe, vol. iii. p. 157; Kennedy, p. 94; "Irish Folk Lore," p. 45.

[90] *Beaten*—Lay of Marie de France, quoted Keightley, p. 436; Costello, "Pilgrimage to Auvergne," vol. ii. p. 294, quoted Keightley, p. 471; Fleury, p. 62, citing Bosquet, "Normandie Romanesque"; Howells, p. 139; Aubrey, "Remains," p. 30; Jahn, pp. 98, 101; Kuhn und Schwartz, p. 29; Croker, p. 81. *Starved, beaten, &c.*—Croker, p. 77. *Threatened to be killed*—Sébillot, "Trad. et Super." vol. i. p. 118; "Contes," vol. i. p. 28, vol. ii. p. 76; Carnoy, p. 4.

[91] Grohmann, p. 135; Wratislaw, p. 161; Schleicher, p. 92.

[92] "Y Brython," vol. ii. p. 20; Kennedy, p. 90; Thorpe, vol. ii. p. 174; Napier, p. 40; Lady Wilde, vol. i. pp. 72, 171; Keightley, p. 393; "Revue des Trad. Pop." vol. iii. p. 162; Campbell, vol. ii. pp. 47, 61; Croker, p. 65; Chambers, p. 70; "F. L. Journal," vol. i. p. 56; Gregor, pp. 8, 9; Cromek, p. 246.

[93] "Daily Telegraph," 19 May 1884; Gregor, p. 61; Lady Wilde, vol. i. pp. 38, 173; "Y Cymmrodor," vol. vi. p. 209, vol. v. p. 72.

[94] "Cambrian Quarterly," vol. ii. p. 86, quoted, Sikes, p. 59; "Y Cymmrodor," vol. iv. p. 208, vol. vi. pp. 172, 203. Mr. Sikes refers to a case in which the child was bathed in a solution of foxglove as having actually occurred in Carnarvonshire in 1857, but he gives no authority.

[95] Quoted in Southey, *loc. cit.* Müllenhoff relates a similar tale, see Thorpe, vol. iii. p. 46; also Grohmann, p. 126; Kuhn und Schwartz, p. 30. Bowker, p. 73, relates a story embodying a similar episode, but apparently connected with Wild Hunt legends. See his note, ibid. p. 251.

[96] Hunt, p. 91; "F. L. Journal," vol. vi. p. 182.

[97] "Y Cymmrodor," vol. vi. p. 181.

[98] Mrs. Bray, vol. i. p. 167; Kuhn, p. 196; Grimm, "Teut. Myth." p. 468, note; "Irish F. L." p. 45; Napier, p. 42.

[99] Jahn, p. 52; Campbell, vol. ii. p. 47; Lady Wilde, vol. i. p. 119.

[100] "F. L. Journal," vol. ii. p. 91, quoting the "Irish Fireside."

[101] Gregor, p. 62; Thorpe, vol. ii. p. 139, quoting Thiele; vol. iii. p. 41, quoting Müllenhoff; Campbell, vol. ii. p. 67; Cromek, p. 244.

[102] Thorpe, vol. ii. p. 133, quoting Thiele; Keightley, p. 391, quoting Stewart, "The Popular Superstitions of the Highlanders."

[103] Napier, p. 41; Lord A. Campbell, "Waifs and Strays," p. 71; "Border Minstrelsy," vol. ii. p. 173.

# CHAPTER VI

# ROBBERIES FROM FAIRYLAND

The tale of Elidorus — Celtic and Teutonic stories of theft from supernatural beings — The thief unsuccessful — Cases of successful robbery — Robbery from the king of the serpents — Robbery of a drinking-cup, or horn — The horn of Oldenburg and similar vessels — The Luck of Edenhall — The cup of Ballafletcher — These vessels sacrificial and pagan.

The earliest writers who allude to the Welsh fairy traditions are Giraldus Cambrensis and Walter Map, two members of that constellation of literary men which rendered brilliant the early years of the Plantagenet dynasty. Giraldus, with whom alone we have to do in this chapter, lays the scene of what is perhaps his most famous story near Swansea, and states that the adventures narrated occurred a short time before his own days. The story concerns one Elidorus, a priest, upon whose persistent declarations it is founded. This good man in his youth ran away from the discipline and frequent stripes of his preceptor, and hid himself under the hollow bank of a river. There he remained fasting for two days; and then two men of pigmy stature appeared, and invited him to come with them, and they would lead him into a country full of delights and sports. A more powerful temptation could not have been offered to a runaway schoolboy of twelve years old; and the invitation was speedily accepted. He accompanied his guides into a subterranean land, where he found a people of small stature but pure morals. He was brought into the presence of the king, and by him handed over to his son, who was then a boy. In that land he dwelt for some time; but he often used to return by various paths to the upper day, and on one of these occasions he made himself known to his mother, declaring to her the nature, manners, and state of the pigmy folk. She desired him to bring her a present of gold, which was plentiful in that region; and he accordingly stole a golden ball while at play with the king's son, and ran off with it to his mother, hotly pursued. Reaching home, his foot stumbled on the threshold, and, dropping the ball, he fell into the room where his mother was sitting. The two pigmies who had followed him at once seized the ball and made off with it, not without expressing their contempt for the thief who had returned their kindness with such ingratitude; and Elidorus, though he sought it carefully with penitence and shame, could never again find the way into the underground realm.[104]

Narratives of the theft of valuables from supernatural beings are found all the world over. In this way, for example, in the mythology of more than one nation mankind obtained the blessing of fire. Such tales, however, throw but little light on this one of Elidorus; and it will therefore be more profitable in considering it to confine our attention to those generally resembling it current among Celts and Teutons. They are very common; and the lesson they usually teach is that honesty is the best policy—at all events, in regard to beings whose power is not bounded by the ordinary human limitations. Beginning with South Wales, we find one of these tales told by the Rev. Edward Davies, a clergyman in Gloucestershire at the beginning of this century, who was the author of two curious works on Welsh antiquities, stuffed with useless, because misdirected, learning. The tale in question relates to a small lake "in the mountains of Brecknock," concerning which we are informed that every Mayday a certain door in a rock near the lake was found open. He who was bold enough to enter was led by a secret passage to a small island, otherwise invisible, in the middle of the lake. This was a fairy island, a garden of enchanting beauty, inhabited by the *Tylwyth Teg* (or Fair Family), and stored with fruits and flowers. The inhabitants treated their visitors with lavish hospitality, but permitted nothing to be carried away. One day this prohibition was violated by a visitor, who put into his pocket a flower with which he had been presented. The Fair Family showed no outward resentment. Their guests were dismissed with the accustomed courtesy; but the moment he who had broken their behest "touched unhallowed ground" the flower disappeared, and he lost his senses. Nor has the mysterious door ever been found again.[105]

In both these cases the thief is unsuccessful, and the punishment of his crime is the loss of fairy intercourse; perhaps the mildest form which punishment could take. But sometimes the *chevalier d'industrie* is lucky enough to secure his spoils. It is related that certain white ghosts were in the habit of playing by night at skittles on a level grass-plot on the Lüningsberg, near Aerzen, in North Germany. A journeyman weaver, who was in love with a miller's daughter, but lacked the means to marry her, thought there could be no harm in robbing the ghosts of one of the golden balls with which they used to play. He accordingly concealed himself one evening; and when the harmless spectres came out he seized one of their balls, and scampered away with it, followed by the angry owners. A stream crossed his path, and, missing the plank bridge which spanned it, he sprang into the water. This saved him, for the spirits had no power there; and a merry wedding was the speedy sequel of his adventure. In like manner a fairy, who, in a Breton saga, was incautious enough to winnow gold in broad daylight in a field where a man was pruning beeches, excited the latter's attention by this singular proceeding; and the man possessed himself of the treasure by simply flinging into it a hallowed rosary. In Germany the water-nix has the reputation of being a good shoemaker. It is related that a man, who once saw a nix on the shore of the March busy at his work, threw a rosary upon it. The nix disappeared, leaving the shoe; and a variant states that the shoe was so well made that the owner wore out successively twelve other shoes which he had caused to be made to match it, without its being any the worse.[106]

We have already seen in the last chapter that the performance of Christian rites and the exhibition of Christian symbols and sacred books have a powerful effect against fairies. But further, the invocation, or indeed the simple utterance, of a sacred name has always been held to counteract enchantments and the wiles of all supernatural beings who are not themselves part and parcel of what I may, without offence and for want of a better term, call the Christian mythology, and who may therefore at times, if not constantly, be supposed to be hostile to the Christian powers and to persons under their protection. These beliefs are, of course, in one form or another part of the machinery of every religion. The tales just quoted are examples of the potency of a symbol. A North German story is equally emphatic as to the value of a holy name. We are told that late one evening a boy saw a great number of hares dancing and leaping. Now hares are specially witch-possessed animals. As he stood and watched them one of them sprang towards him and tried to bite his leg. But he said: "Go away! thou art not of God, but of the devil." Instantly the whole company vanished; but he heard a doleful voice exclaiming: "My silver beaker, my silver beaker!" On reaching home he told his adventure; and his father at once started back with him to the place, where they found a silver beaker inscribed with a name neither they nor the goldsmith, to whom they sold the goblet for a large sum of money, could read. The district whence this story comes furnishes us also with an account of a man who, being out late one night, came upon a fire surrounded by a large circle of women sitting at a table. He ventured to seat himself among them. Each one had brought something for the meal; and a man-cook went round them asking each what she had got. When he came to the hero of the story the latter struck him with his stick, saying: "I have a blow which our Lord God gave the devil." Thereupon the whole assembly disappeared, leaving nothing behind but the kettle which hung over the fire, and which the man took and long preserved to testify the truth of his story. A Cornish fisherman was scarcely less lucky without the protection of a pious exclamation. For one night going home he found a crowd of "little people" on the beach. They were sitting in a semicircle holding their hats towards one of their number, who was pitching gold pieces from a heap into them. The fisherman contrived to introduce his hat among them without being noticed, and having got a share of the money, made off with it. He was followed by the piskies, but had a good start, and managed to reach home and shut the door upon them. Yet so narrow was his escape that he left the tails of his sea-coat in their hands.[107]

Vengeance, however, is sometimes swift and sure upon these robberies. It is believed in Germany that the king of the snakes is wont to come out to sun himself at noon; and that he then lays aside his crown, a prize for any one who can seize it. A horseman, coming at the opportune moment, did so once; but the serpent-king called forth his subjects and pursued him. By the help of his good steed the man succeeded in arriving at home; and, thankful to have escaped the danger, he patted the beast's neck as he jumped down, saying: "Faithfully hast thou helped me!" At that instant a snake, which had hidden herself unnoticed in the horse's tail, bit the man; and little joy had he of his crime. In another story the girl who steals the crown is deafened by the cries of her victim; and elsewhere, when the serpent-king is unable to reach the robber, he batters his own head to pieces in ineffectual rage. Perhaps he deserved his fate in some of these cases, for it seems he had a foolish liking to lay down his crown on a white cloth, or a white, or blue, silk handkerchief,—a predilection which the robber did not fail to provide him with the opportunity of gratifying, and of repenting.[108]

Other tales represent the thief as compelled to restore the stolen goods. Thus a man who found the trolls on the Danish isle of Fuur carrying their treasures out into the air, shot thrice over them, and thereby forced the owners to quit them. He caught up the gold and silver and rode off with it, followed by the chief troll. But after he got into the house and shut the doors there was such a storming and hissing outside, that the whole house seemed ablaze. Terrified, he flung the bag wherein he had secured the treasures out into the night. The storm ceased, and he heard a voice crying: "Thou hast still enough." In the morning he found a heavy silver cup, which had fallen behind a chest of drawers. Again, a farm servant of South Kongerslev, in Denmark, who went at his master's instance, on Christmas Eve, to see what the trolls in a neighbouring hill were doing, was offered drink from a golden cup. He took the cup, and casting out its contents, spurred his horse from the spot, hotly pursued. On the way back he passed the dwelling of a band of trolls at enmity with those from whom he had stolen the cup. Counselled by them, he took to the ploughed field, where his pursuers were unable to follow him, and so escaped. The farmer kept the goblet until the following Christmas Eve, when his wife imprudently helped a tattered beggar to beer in it. It is not wonderful that both the cup and the beggar vanished; but we are to understand that the beggar was a troll. Perhaps he was. In Thyholm, a district of Denmark, there is a range of lofty mounds formerly inhabited by trolls. Some peasants who were once passing by these mounds prayed the trolls to give them some beer. In a moment a little creature came out and presented a large silver can to one of the men, who had no sooner grasped it than he set spurs to his horse, with the intention of keeping it. But the little man of the mound was too quick for him, for he speedily caught him and compelled him to return the can. In a Pomeranian story the underground folk forestalled the intention to rob them on the part of a farmer's boy whose thirst they had quenched with a can of delicious brown-beer. Having drunk, he hid the can itself, with the object of taking it home when his day's work was done, for it was of pure silver; but when he afterwards went to look for it, it had disappeared.[109]

Moreover, ungrateful mortals are sometimes punished, even when they are lucky enough to secure their prize. Thus it is told of a man of Zahren, in Mecklenburg, who was seized with thirst on his way home from Penzlin, that he heard music in a barrow known to be the haunt of the underground folk. People were then on familiar terms with the latter; and the man cried out and asked for a drink. Nor did he ask in vain; for his appeal was at once answered by the appearance of a little fellow with a flask of delicious drink. After slaking his thirst the man took the opportunity to make off with the flask; but he was pursued by the whole troop of elves, only one of whom, and he had only one leg, succeeded in keeping up with him. The thief, however, managed to get over a cross-road where One-leg could not follow him; and the latter then, making a virtue of necessity, cried out: "Thou mayst keep the flask; and henceforth always drink thereout, for it will never be empty; but beware of looking into it." For some years the elf's injunction was observed; but one day, in a fit of curiosity, the peasant looked into the bottom of the flask, and there sat a horrid toad! The toad disappeared, and so did the liquor; and the man in a short time fell miserably sick. In a Norse tale, a man whose bride is about to be carried off by Huldre-folk, rescues her by shooting over her head a pistol loaded with a silver bullet. This has the effect of dissolving the witchery; and he is forthwith enabled to seize her and gallop off, not unpursued. One of the trolls, to retard his flight, held out to him a well-filled golden horn. He took the horn, but cast the liquor away, and rode away with both horn and girl. The trolls, when they found themselves unable to catch him, cried after him in their exasperation: "The red cock shall crow over thy dwelling!" And behold! his house stood in a blaze. Similarly, a Swedish tradition relates that one of the serving-men of the lady of Liungby, in Scania, one night of Christmas in the year 1490, rode out to inquire the cause of the noise at the Magle stone. He found the trolls dancing and making merry. A fair troll-woman stepped forth and offered him a drinking-horn and a pipe, praying he would drink the troll-king's health and blow in the pipe. He snatched the horn and pipe from her, and spurring back to the mansion, delivered them into his lady's hands. The trolls followed and begged to have their treasures back, promising prosperity to the lady's race if she would restore them. She kept them, however; and they are said to be still preserved at Liungby as memorials of the adventure. But the serving-man who took them died three days after, and the horse on the second day; the mansion has been twice burnt, and the family never prospered after. On the eve of the first of May the witches of Germany hold high revel. Every year the fields and farmyards of a certain landowner were so injured by these nocturnal festivities that one of his servants determined to put a stop to the mischief. Going to the trysting-place, he found the witches eating and drinking around a large slab of marble which rested on four golden pillars; and on the slab lay a golden horn of wondrous form. The sorceresses invited him to join the feast; but a fellow-servant whom he met there warned him not to drink, for they only wished to poison him. Wherefore he flung the proffered beverage away, seized the horn, and galloped home as hard as he could. All doors and gates had been left open for him; and the witches consequently were unable to catch him. The next day a gentleman in fine clothes appeared and begged his master to restore the horn, promising in return to surround his property with a wall seven feet high, but threatening, in case of refusal, to burn his farms down thrice, and that just when he thought himself richest. Three days were allowed to the landowner for consideration, but he declined to restore the horn. The next harvest had hardly been housed when his barns were in flames. Three times did this happen, and the landowner was reduced to poverty. By the king's kindness he was enabled to rebuild; and he then made every effort to discover the owner of the horn, sending it about for that purpose even as far as Constantinople; but no one could be found to claim it.[110]

Somewhat more courteous was a Danish boy whom an Elf-maiden met and offered drink from a costly drinking-horn one evening as he rode homeward late from Ristrup to Siellevskov. He received the horn, but fearing to drink its contents, poured them out behind him, so that, as in several of these stories, they fell on the horse's back, and singed the hair off. The horn he held fast, and the horse probably needed no second hint to start at the top of its speed. The elf-damsel gave chase until horse and man reached a running water, across which she could not follow them. Seeing herself outwitted, she implored the youth to give her back the horn, promising him in reward the strength of twelve men. On this assurance he returned the horn to her, and got what she had promised him. But the exchange was not very profitable; for with the strength of twelve men he had unfortunately acquired the appetite of twelve. Here it may well be thought that the supernatural gift only took its appropriate abatement. In a story from the north of Scotland the cup was stolen for the purpose of undoing a certain spell, and was honourably returned when the purpose was accomplished. Uistean, we are told, was a great slayer of Fuathan, supernatural beings apparently akin to fairies. He shot one day into a wreath of mist, and a beautiful woman fell down at his side. He took her home; and she remained in his house for a year, speechless. On a day at the end of the year he was benighted in the mountains, and seeing a light in a hill, he drew nigh, and found the fairies feasting. He entered the hill, and heard the butler, as he was handing the drink round, say: "It is a year from this night's night that we lost the daughter of the Earl of Antrim. She has the power of the draught on her that she does not speak a word till she gets a drink from the cup that is in my hand." When the butler reached Uistean, he handed him the cup. The latter, on getting it in his hand, ran off, pursued by the fairies until the cock crew. When he got home, he gave the lady in his house to drink out of the cup; and immediately her speech returned. She then told him she was the Earl of Antrim's daughter, stolen by the fairies from child-bed. Uistean took back the cup to the hill whence he had brought it, and then restored the lady to her father safe and sound, the fairy woman who had been left in her place vanishing meantime in a flame of fire.[111]

There are also legends in which a hat conferring invisibility, or a glove, figures; but the stolen article is usually, as in most of the instances cited above, a cup or a drinking-horn. Many such articles are still preserved in various parts of Northern Europe. Of these the most celebrated are the Luck of Edenhall and the Oldenburg horn. But before discussing these I must refer to some other stories, the material evidence of which is no longer extant. Gervase of Tilbury relates that in a forest of Gloucestershire there is a glade in the midst whereof stands a hillock rising to the height of a man. Knights and hunters were wont, when fatigued with heat and thirst, to ascend the hillock in question to obtain relief. This had to be done singly and alone. The adventurous man then would say: "I thirst," when a cupbearer would appear and present him with a large drinking-horn adorned with gold and gems, as, says the writer, was the custom among the most ancient English, and containing liquor of some unknown but most delicious flavour. When he had drunk this, all heat and weariness fled from his body, and the cupbearer presented him with a towel to wipe his mouth withal; and then having performed his office he disappeared, waiting neither for recompense nor inquiry. One day an ill-conditioned knight of the city of Gloucester, having gotten the horn into his hands, contrary to custom and good manners kept it. But the Earl of Gloucester, having heard of it, condemned the robber to death, and gave the horn to King Henry I., lest he should be thought to have approved of such wickedness if he had added the rapine of another to the store of his own private property. Gervase of Tilbury wrote near the beginning of the thirteenth century. His contemporary, William of Newbury, relates a similar story, but lays its scene in Yorkshire. He says that a peasant coming home late at night, not very sober, and passing by a barrow, heard the noise of singing and feasting. Seeing a door open in the side of the barrow, he looked in, and beheld a great banquet. One of the attendants offered him a cup, which he took, but would not drink. Instead of doing so, he poured out the contents, and kept the vessel. The fleetness of his beast enabled him to distance all pursuit, and he escaped. We are told that the cup, described as of unknown material, of unusual colour and of extraordinary form, was presented to Henry I., who gave it to his brother-in-law, David, King of the Scots. After having been kept for several years in the Scottish treasury it was given by William the Lion to King Henry II., who wished to see it.[112]

By a fortune somewhat rare, this story, having been written down in the days of the early Plantagenet kings, has been lately found again among the folk in the East Riding. The how, or barrow, where it is now said to have occurred is Willey How, near Wold Newton, on the Bridlington road, a conspicuous mound about three hundred feet in circumference and sixty feet in height. The rustic to whom the adventure happened was an inhabitant of Wold Newton, who had been on a visit to the neighbouring village of North Burton, and was belated. Another tale resembling the Gloucestershire saga is found in Swabia, though the object of which the mysterious benefactor was deprived was not a cup, but a knife. Some farm servants, while at work in the fields, were approached by an unusually beautiful maiden clad in black. Every day about nine or ten o'clock in the morning, and again about four o'clock in the afternoon, she brought them a small pitcher of wine and a loaf of snow-white bread—greater luxuries, probably, to peasants then even than they would be now. She always brought a very pretty silver knife to cut the bread, and always begged them to be sure to give it back to her, else she were lost. Her visits continued until one of the servants took it into his head to keep the knife, which he was ungrateful enough to do in spite of her tears and prayers. Finding all entreaties vain, she uttered piercing cries of distress, tore her fair hair, rent her silken clothes, and vanished, never to be seen again. But often you may hear on the spot where she once appeared sobs and the sound of weeping.[113]

A Cornish tale relates that a farmer's boy of Portallow was one night sent to a neighbouring village for some household necessaries. On the way he fell in with some piskies, and by repeating the formula he heard them use, transported himself with them, first to Portallow Green, then to Seaton Beach, and finally to "the King of France's cellar," where he joined his mysterious companions in tasting that monarch's wines. They then passed through magnificent rooms, where the tables were laden for a feast. By way of taking some memorial of his travels he pocketed one of the rich silver goblets which stood on one of the tables. After a very short stay the word was passed to return, and presently he found himself again at home. The good wife complimented him on his despatch. "You'd say so, if you only know'd where I've been," he replied; "I've been wi' the piskies to Seaton Beach, and I've been to the King o' France's house, and all in five minutes." The farmer stared and said the boy was *mazed*. "I thought you'd say I was mazed, so I brort away this mug to show vor et," he answered, producing the goblet. With such undeniable evidence his story could not be any longer doubted. Stealing from a natural enemy like the King of France was probably rather meritorious than otherwise; and the goblet remained in the boy's family for generations, though unfortunately it is no longer forthcoming for the satisfaction of those who may still be sceptical.[114]

This story differs from the others I have detailed, in narrating a raid by supernatural beings on the dwelling of a human potentate—a raid in which a human creature joined and brought away a substantial trophy. In the seventeenth century there was in the possession of Lord Duffus an old silver cup, called the Fairy Cup, concerning which the following tradition was related to John Aubrey, the antiquary, by a correspondent writing from Scotland on the 25th of March 1695. An ancestor of the then Lord Duffus was walking in the fields near his house in Morayshire when he heard the noise of a whirlwind and of voices crying: "Horse and Hattock!" This was the exclamation fairies were said to use "when they remove from any place." Lord Duffus was bold enough to cry "Horse and Hattock" also, and was immediately caught up through the air with the fairies to the King of France's cellar at Paris, where, after he had heartily drunk, he fell asleep. There he was found lying the next morning with the silver cup in his hand, and was promptly brought before the King, to whom, on being questioned, he repeated this story; and the King, in dismissing him, presented him with the cup. Where it may be now I do not know, nor does Aubrey's correspondent furnish us with any description of it, save the negative but important remark that it had nothing engraven upon it beside the arms of the family.[115]

On this vessel, therefore, if it be yet in existence, there is nothing to warrant the name of Fairy Cup, or to connect it with the adventure just related. Nor does the Oldenburg Horn itself bear any greater marks of authenticity. That famous vessel is still exhibited at the palace of Rosenborg at Copenhagen. It is of silver gilt, and ornamented in paste with enamel. It bears coats of arms and inscriptions, showing that it was made for King Christian I. of Denmark in honour of the Three Kings of Cologne, and cannot therefore be older than the middle of the fifteenth century. The legend attached to it claims for it a much greater antiquity. The legend itself was narrated in Hamelmann's "Oldenburger Chronik" at the end of the sixteenth century, and is even yet current in the mouths of the Oldenburg folk. Hamelmann dates it in the year 990, when the then Count of Oldenburg was hunting in the forest of Bernefeuer. He had followed a roe from that forest to the Osenberg, and had distanced all his attendants. It was the twentieth of July, the weather was hot, and the count thirsty. He cried out for a draught of water, and had scarcely uttered the words, when the hill opened and a beautiful damsel appeared and offered him drink in this horn. Not liking the look of the beverage, he declined to drink. Whereupon she pressed him to do so, assuring him that it would go well with him and his thenceforth, and with the whole house of Oldenburg; but if the count would not believe her and drink there would be no unity from that time in the Oldenburg family. He had no faith in her words, and poured out the drink, which took the hair off his horse wherever it splashed him, and galloped away with the horn.[116]

Other drinking-horns, of which precisely analogous tales are told, are still to be seen in Norway. Of the one at Halsteengaard it is related that the posterity of the robber, down to the ninth generation, were afflicted, as a penalty, with some bodily blemish. This horn is described as holding nearly three quarts, and as being encircled by a strong gilt copper ring, about three inches broad, on which, in monkish characters, are to be read the names of the Three Kings of Cologne, Melchior, Baltazar, and Caspar. It is further ornamented with a small gilt copper plate, forming the setting of an oval crystal. Another horn, preserved in the museum at Arendal, was obtained in a similar manner. A father, pursuing his daughter and her lover, was stopped by a troll, and offered drink in it. Instead of drinking, he cast out the contents, with the usual result, and put spurs to his horse. He was counselled by another troll, who was not on good terms with the first, to ride through the rye and not through the wheat; but even when his pursuer was impeded by the tall rye-stalks, only the crowing of the cock before dawn rescued him. The vessel is encircled by three silver gilt rings, bearing an inscription, which seems not quite correctly reported, as follows: "Potum servorum benedic deus alme tuorum reliquam unus benede le un Caspar Melchior Baltazar."[117]

The legend of which I am treating attaches also to a number of sacred chalices. At Aagerup, in Zealand, is one of these. The thief, nearly overtaken by the trolls he had robbed, prayed to God in his distress, and vowed to bestow the cup upon the church if his prayer were heard. The church of Vigersted, also in Zealand, possesses another. In the latter case the man took refuge in the church, where he was besieged by the trolls until morning. In Bornholm a chalice and paten belonging to the church are said to have been made out of a cup stolen in the same way by a peasant whose mother was a mermaid, and who had inherited some portion of her supernatural power; hence, probably, his intercourse with the trolls, of which he took so mean an advantage. At Viöl, near Flensborg, in Schleswig, is a beaker belonging to the church, and, like the chalice at Aagerup, of gold, of which it is narrated that it was presented full of a liquor resembling buttermilk to a man who was riding by a barrow where the underground folk were holding high festival. He emptied and rode off with it in the usual manner. A cry arose behind him: "Three-legs, come out!" and, looking round, he saw a monster pursuing him. Finding this creature unable to come up with him, he heard many voices calling: "Two-legs, come out!" But his horse was swifter than Two-legs. Then One-leg was summoned, as in the story already cited from Mecklenburg, and came after him with gigantic springs, and would have caught him, but the door of his own house luckily stood open. He had scarcely entered, and slammed it to, when One-leg stood outside, banging against it, and foiled. The beaker was presented to the church in fulfilment of a vow made by the robber in his fright; and it is now used as the communion-cup. At Rambin, on the island of Rügen, is another cup, the story of which relates that the man to whom it was offered by the underground folk did not refuse to drink, but having drunk, he kept the vessel and took it home. A boy who was employed to watch horses by night on a turf moor near the village of Kritzemow, in Mecklenburg, annoyed the underground folk by the constant cracking of his whip. One night, as he was thus amusing himself, a mannikin came up to him and offered him drink in a silver-gilt beaker. The boy took the beaker, but being openly on bad terms with the elves, argued no good to himself from such an offering. So he instantly leaped on horseback and fled, with the vessel in his hand, along the road to Biestow and Rostock. The mannikin, of course, followed, but, coming to a crossway, was compelled to give up the chase. When the boy reached Biestow much of the liquid, as was to be expected, had been shaken out of the cup, and wherever on the horse it had fallen the hair had been burnt away. Glad of escaping this danger, the boy thanked God and handed the vessel over to the church at Biestow. In none of these instances, however, do I find any description of the goblet.[118]

Fortunately there is one, and that the most celebrated of all the cups to which a fairy origin has been ascribed, which has been often and accurately delineated both with pen and pencil. I refer to the Luck of Edenhall. It belongs to Sir George Musgrave of Edenhall in Cumberland, in the possession of whose family it has been for many generations. The tradition is that a butler, going to fetch water from a well in the garden, called St. Cuthbert's Well, came upon a company of fairies at their revels, and snatched it from them. As the little, ill-used folk disappeared, after an ineffectual attempt to recover it, they cried:

"If this glass do break or fall,
Farewell the luck of Edenhall!"

The most recent account of it was written in the year 1880, by the Rev. Dr. Fitch, for "The Scarborough Gazette," from which it has been reprinted for private circulation in the shape of a dainty pamphlet. He speaks of it, from a personal examination, as "a glass stoup, a drinking vessel, about six inches in height, having a circular base, perfectly flat, two inches in diameter, gradually expanding upwards till it ends in a mouth four inches across. The material is by no means fine in quality, presenting, as it does on close inspection, several small cavities or air-bubbles. The general hue is a warm green, resembling the tone known by artists as *brown pink*. Upon the transparent glass is traced a geometric pattern in white and blue enamel, somewhat raised, aided by gold and a little crimson. It will, of course, stand on its base, but it would be far from wise to entrust it, when filled, to this support." Dr. Fitch is in accord with the common opinion of antiquaries in pronouncing it to be of Venetian origin, though Mr. Franks thought it Saracenic. He describes the case in which it is kept as evidently made for it, being of the same shape. "The lid of this case," he says, "rather unevenly fits the body by overlapping it. There is no hinge; the fastenings are certain hooks or catches, not in good condition; the security and better apposition of the lid is maintained by a piece of leather, not unlike a modern boot-lace, or thin thong. The case dates, probably, from the fifteenth century, as articles made of similar material, viz., *cuir bouilli*, softened or boiled leather, were much in use in that age. This case bears an elegantly varied pattern that has been recognized in an inkstand of Henry the Seventh's, yet extant. Upon the lid of this case, in very chaste and well-formed characters, is the sacred monogram I.H.S." These three letters, which do not really form a monogram, have possibly given rise to the surmise, or tradition, that the Luck was once used as a sacred vessel. Dr. Fitch goes on to quote several authorities, showing that chalices of glass were sanctioned by the church, and were, in fact, made and used; and the Luck may have been such a vessel. But I can see no sufficient evidence of it. There is nothing to show that the leathern case is of the same date as the glass itself; and it may have been made long afterwards. The earliest mention of the relic seems to have been by Francis Douce, the antiquary, who was at Edenhall in 1785, and wrote some verses upon it; nor is there any authentic family history attaching to it. The shape of the goblet, its unsteadiness when full, and the difficulty of drinking from it without spilling some of its contents, of which Dr. Fitch had some experience, would point to its being intended rather for convivial than sacred uses.

The hypothesis of the Luck's having once been a chalice explains nothing; because, as we have seen, several of the cups alleged to have been stolen from supernatural beings are chalices to this day. Moreover, what are we to think of the drinking-horns of which the same tale is told? Some of these already mentioned bear, not indeed the sacred letters, but prayers and the names of the sainted Kings of Cologne, though, unlike the cups, they are not found in churches. One drinking-horn, however, was preserved in the cathedral at Wexiö, in Sweden, until carried away by the Danes in 1570. This horn, stated to be of three hundred colours, was received by a knight on Christmas morning from a troll-wife, whose head he there and then cut off with his sword. The king dubbed him Trolle in memory of the deed, and bestowed on him a coat-of-arms containing a headless troll.[119] How the horn came into the possession of the cathedral I do not know; but at all events it could never have been a chalice.

A silver cup, perhaps still used for sacramental purposes at the parish church of Malew, in the Isle of Man, is the subject of the following legend. A farmer returning homeward to the parish of Malew from Peel was benighted and lost his way among the mountains. In the course of his wanderings he was drawn by the sound of sweet music into a large hall where a number of little people were banqueting. Among them were some faces he thought he had formerly seen; but he forbore to take any notice of them. Nor did they take any notice of him until he was offered drink, when one of them, whose features seemed not unknown to him, plucked him by the coat and forbade him, whatever he did, to taste anything he saw before him; "for if you do," he added, "you will be as I am, and return no more to your family." Accordingly, when a large silver beaker was put into his hand, filled with liquor, he found an opportunity to throw its contents on the ground. The music forthwith ceased, and the company disappeared, leaving the cup in his hand. On finding his way home, he told the minister of the parish what had occurred; and the latter, with the instincts of his profession, advised him to devote the cup to the service of the Church. We are indebted to Waldron's well-known "Description of the Isle of Man," originally published in 1731, for this story. A later writer, annotating Waldron's work rather more than a quarter of a century ago, refers to the vessel in question as a paten; he states that it was still preserved in the church, and that it bore engraved the legend: "Sancte Lupe ora pro nobis."[120] There are no fewer than eleven saints named Lupus in the calendar. Whichever of them was invoked here, the inscription points to a continental origin for the vessel, whether cup or paten, and is not inconsistent with its being of some antiquity.

Mr. Train, who quotes the tradition in his account of the Isle of Man, states that several similar tales had been placed at his disposal by friends in the island; but it was naturally beneath the dignity of an historian to do more than give a single specimen of this "shade of superstition," as he calls it. He does, however, mention (though apparently without being conscious of any close relationship with the cup of Kirk Malew) an antique crystal goblet in the possession, when he wrote, of Colonel Wilks, the proprietor of the Estate of Ballafletcher, four or five miles from Douglas. It is described as larger than a common bell-shaped tumbler, uncommonly light and chaste in appearance, and ornamented with floral scrolls, having between the designs, on two sides, upright *columellæ* of five pillars. The history of this cup is interesting. It is said to have been taken by Magnus, the Norwegian King of Man, from St. Olave's shrine. On what ground this statement rests does not appear. What is really known about the goblet is that having belonged for at least a hundred years to the Fletcher family, the owners of Ballafletcher, it was sold with the effects of the last of the family in 1778, and was bought by Robert Cæsar, Esq., who gave it to his niece for safe keeping. This niece was, perhaps, the "old lady, a connection of the family of Fletcher," who is mentioned by Train as having presented the cup to Colonel Wilks. The tradition is that it had been given to the first of the Fletcher family more than two centuries ago, with the injunction "that as long as he preserved it peace and plenty would follow; but woe to him who broke it, as he would surely be haunted by the *lhiannan Shee*," or "peaceful spirit" of Ballafletcher. It was kept in a recess, whence it was never taken except on Christmas and Easter days, or, according to Train's account, at Christmas alone. Then, we are told, it was "filled with wine, and quaffed off at a breath by the head of the house only, as a libation to the spirit for her protection."[121]

Here is no mention of the theft of the goblet unless from St. Olave's sanctuary;

but yet I think we have a glimpse of the real character of the cups to which the legend I am discussing attaches. They were probably sacrificial vessels dedicated to the old pagan worship of the house-spirits, of which we find so many traces among the Indo-European peoples. These house-spirits had their chief seat on the family hearth; and their great festival was that of the New Year, celebrated at the winter solstice. The policy of the Church in early and mediæval times was to baptize to Christian uses as many of the heathen beliefs and ceremonies as possible. The New Year festival thus became united with the anniversary of the birth of Christ; and it is matter of history that as the Danes used, previously to their conversion, to drink to Odin and the Anses, so after that event they were in the habit of solemnly pledging Our Lord, His Apostles and the Saints. Such of the old beliefs and practices, however, as the Church could neither impress with a sacred character, nor destroy, lingered on. Among them were the superstitions of the fairies and the household spirits; and there is nothing unlikely in the supposition that special vessels were kept for the ceremonies in which these beings were propitiated. For this purpose a horn would serve as well as any goblet; if, indeed, it were not actually preferred, as being older, and therefore more sacred in shape and material. As these ceremonies gradually fell into desuetude, or were put down by clerical influence, it would be both natural and in accordance with policy that the cups devoted to the supposed rites should be transferred to the service of the Church.[122] They would all be old-fashioned, quaint, and, many of them, of foreign and unknown provenance. Already connected in the minds of the people with the spirit world, a supernatural origin would be ascribed to them; and gift or robbery would be the theory of acquisition most readily adopted. Now, theory in a certain stage of culture is indistinguishable from narrative.

In this chapter I have dealt entirely with stolen goods; but, as we have seen in previous chapters, tales of cups and other articles lent or given by elves in exchange for services rendered are by no means unknown. I cannot, however, recall any of such gifts which are now extant. It were much to be wished that all the drinking-vessels—nay, all the articles of every kind—to which legends of supernatural origin belong were actually figured and described. Much light would thereby be thrown upon their true history. I will only now point out, with regard to the Luck of Edenhall, and the three horns of Oldenburg, of Halsteengaard, and of Arendal, of which we have full descriptions, that what we know of them is all in confirmation of the theory suggested. In particular, the names of the Three Kings connect the horns with a Christmas, or Twelfth Night, festival, which is exactly what the theory of the sacrificial nature of these vessels would lead us to expect. If we turn from the actual beakers to the stories, it is surprising how many of these we find pointing to the same festival. The cup of South Kongerslev was won and lost on Christmas Eve. The horn and pipe of Liungby were stolen "one night of Christmas." It was at Christmas-time that the Danish boy acquired his supernatural strength by giving back to the elf-maiden the horn he had taken from her. The Halsteengaard horn and the golden beaker of Aagerup were both reft from the trolls on Christmas Eve, and the horn of Wexiö on Christmas morning. The night of St. John's Day is mentioned as the time when the horn now at Arendal was obtained. The saint here referred to is probably St. John the Evangelist, whose feast is on December the 27th. And in more than one case the incident is connected with a marriage, which would be an appropriate occasion for the propitiation of the household spirit. The only instance presenting any difficulty is that of the cup at Kirk Malew; and there the difficulty arises from the name of the saint to whom the cup was apparently dedicated. Nor is it lessened by the number of saints bearing the name of Lupus. The days on which these holy men are respectively commemorated range through the calendar from January to October; and until we know which of them was intended it is useless to attempt an explanation. The question, however, is of small account in the face of the probability called forth by the coincidences that remain.

There is one other matter to which I would call attention, namely, that while stories of the type discussed in the foregoing pages are common to both Celts and Teutons, the stolen cup is exclusively a Teutonic possession. More than that, no authentic record of the preservation of the relic itself is found save in the homes and conquests of the Scandinavian race. Is this to be accounted for by the late date of Christianity, and, therefore, the more recent survival of heathen rites among Teutonic, and especially Scandinavian, peoples?

## FOOTNOTES:

[104] Girald. Cambr., l. i. c. 8.

[105] Davies, "Mythology," p. 155. Mr. Wirt Sikes quotes this story without acknowledgment, stating that the legend, "varying but little in phraseology, is current in the neighbourhood of a dozen different mountain lakes." As if he had collected it himself! (Sikes, p. 45). Compare an Eskimo story of a girl who, having acquired *angakok* power, visited the *ingnersuit*, or underground folk, "and received presents from them; but while carrying them homewards the gifts were wafted out of her hands and flew back to their first owners" (Rink, p. 460).

[106] Thorpe, vol. iii. p. 120, apparently quoting Harry's "Sagen, Märchen und Legenden Niedersachsens"; Sébillot, "Trad. et Sup." vol. i. p. 115; "Zeits. f. Volksk." vol. ii. p. 415, quoting Vernaleken.

[107] Kuhn und Schwartz, pp. 305, 306; "Choice Notes," p. 76.

[108] Niederhöffer, vol. iv. p. 130; Bartsch, vol. i. p. 278; Thorpe, vol. iii. p. 56, quoting Müllenhoff; Birlinger, "Volksthümliches," vol. i. p. 103; Grimm, "Tales," vol. ii. p. 77. A Lusatian tradition quoted by Grimm in a note represents the waternake-king's crown as not only valuable in itself, but like other fairy property, the bringer of great riches to its possessor. Ibid. 406. *Cf.* a Hindoo story to the same effect, Day, p. 17; and many other tales.

[109] Thorpe, vol. ii. pp. 148, 146, 121, quoting Thiele, "Danmarks Folkesagn;" Jahn, p. 75.

[110] Bartsch, vol. i. p. 83 (see also p. 41); Thorpe, vol. ii. p. 6, quoting Faye, "Norske Folkesagn"; ibid. p. 89, quoting Afzelius, "Svenske Folkets Sago-Häfder"; Kuhn und Schwartz, p. 26.

[111] Thorpe, vol. ii. p. 142, quoting Thiele. See also Keightley, p. 88; Campbell, vol. ii. p. 97.

[112] Gerv. Tilb., Decis. iii. c. 60; Guil. Neub. "Chronica Rerum Anglic." lib. i. c. 28, quoted by Liebrecht in a note to Gerv. Tilb.

[113] Nicholson, p. 83. Mr. Nicholson in a letter to me says that he had the story as given by him from an old inhabitant of Bridlington, and that it is current in the neighbourhood. Birlinger, "Volkst." vol. i. pp. 3, 5.

[114] "Choice Notes," p. 73.

[115] Aubrey, "Miscellany," p. 149.

[116] Thorpe, vol. iii. p. 128; Kuhn und Schwartz, p. 280. The latter is the version still found as traditional. Its details are not so full, and are in some respects different.

[117] Thorpe, vol. ii. pp. 15, 14, apparently quoting Faye. Dr. Geo. Stephens of the University of Copenhagen very kindly made a great number of inquiries for me with a view to obtain information, and, if possible, drawings of the Scandinavian horns and cups, but unhappily with little success. The answer to his inquiries in reference to the horns of Halsteengaard and Arendal, sent by Prof. Olaf Rygh, the learned Keeper of the Norwegian Museum at Christiania, will be read with interest. He says: "Mr. Hartland's notice of 'Halsteengaard' in Norway doubtless refers to a local tale about a drinking-horn formerly in the hands of the owner of Holsteingaard, Aal parish, Hallingdal. It was first made public in the year 174-, in 'Ivar Wiels Beskriveke over Ringerige og Hallingdals Fogderi,' in 'Topografisk Journal for Norge,' Part XXXI., Christiania, 1804, pp. 179-183. I know nothing more as to the fate of this horn than what is said in Nicolaysen's 'Norske Fornlevninger,' p. 152, that it is said to have been sent to the Bergen Museum in 1845. Should this be so, it will be almost impossible to identify it among the many such horns in that collection. As described by Wiel, it was merely a very simple specimen of the kind with the common inscription JASPAR X MELCHIOR X BALTAZAR. This class of horn was largely imported to Norway from North Germany in the 15th and 16th centuries.

"Meanwhile I beg to point out that the oldest legend of this kind which has come down to us is found in 'Biskop Jens Nilssons Visitatsböger og Reiseoptegnelser, udgivne af Dr. Yngvar Nielsen,' p. 393. It was written by the bishop or his amanuensis during his visitation, 1595, in Flatdal parish, Telemarken. What has become of the horn spoken of by the bishop I cannot say.

"I have no idea of what is meant by Mr. Hartland's reference to Arendal. Possibly it may concern something in the museum there, but of which I never heard. The printed catalogue of the museum (Arendal, 1882) includes nothing from the middle age or later."

[118] Thorpe, vol. ii. p. 144, quoting Thiele. Keightley, pp. 109, 111, note; (The latter mentions another theft of a silver jug where the thief was saved by crossing running water.) Thorpe, vol. ii. p. 140; vol. iii. p. 70, quoting Müllenhoff; Jahn, p. 53; Bartsch, vol. i. p. 60.

[119] Thorpe, vol. ii. p. 91, quoting Afzelius.

[120] Waldron, pp. 28, 106.

[121] Train, vol. ii. p. 154; and see a note by Harrison to his edition of Waldron, p. 106. The cup is stated by Harrison to have been, when he wrote, in the possession of Major Bacon, of Seafield House. Mrs. Russell, of Oxford, kindly made inquiries for me in the Isle of Man as to its present whereabouts, and that of the cup of Kirk Malew, and inserted a query in *Yn Livar Manninagh*, the organ of the Isle of Man Natural History and Antiquarian Society, but without eliciting any information.

[122] It is not irrelevant to observe in this connection that several of the chalices in Sweden are said to have been presented to the churches by priests to whom a Berg-woman had offered drink in these very cups or bowls (Thorpe, vol. ii. p. 90, quoting Afzelius).

# CHAPTER VII

# THE SUPERNATURAL LAPSE OF TIME IN FAIRYLAND

The story of Rhys and Llewelyn — Dancing for a twelvemonth — British variants — Lapse of time among the Siberian Tartars — German and Slavonic stories — The penalty of curiosity and greed — A Lapp tale —The mother leaving her child in the mysterious cave — Rip van Winkle — Eastern variants — King Herla — The Adalantado of the Seven Cities — The Seven Sleepers — King Wenzel and the smith — Lost brides and bridegrooms — The Monk Felix — Visits to Paradise — A Japanese tale.

In previous chapters we have seen that human beings are sometimes taken by fairies into Fairyland, and that they are there kept for a longer or shorter period, or, it may be, are never permitted to return to earth at all. We have noted cases in which they are led down for temporary purposes and, if they are prudent, are enabled to return when those purposes are accomplished. We have noted other cases in which babes or grown women have been stolen and retained until their kindred have compelled restoration. The story cited in the last chapter from Giraldus describes a seduction of a different kind. There the visit to Fairyland was of a more voluntary character, and the hero was able to go to and fro as he pleased. We have also met with tales in which the temptation of food, or more usually of drink, has been held out to the wayfarer; and we have learned that the result of yielding would be to give himself wholly into the fairies' hands. I propose now to examine instances in which temptation of one kind or other has been successful, or in which a spell has been cast over man or woman, not merely preventing the bewitched person from regaining his home and human society, but also rendering him, while under the spell, impervious to the attacks of time and unconscious of its flight.

These stories are of many types. The first type comes, so far as I know, only from Celtic sources. It is very widely known in Wales, and we may call it, from its best-known example, the "Rhys and Llewelyn type." A story obtained between sixty and seventy years ago in the Vale of Neath relates that Rhys and Llewelyn were fellow-servants to a farmer; and they had been engaged one day in carrying lime for their master. As they were going home, driving their mountain ponies before them in the twilight, Rhys suddenly called to his companion to stop and listen to the music. It was a tune, he said, to which he had danced a hundred times, and he must go and have a dance now. So he told his companion to go on with the horses and he would soon overtake him. Llewelyn could hear nothing, and began to remonstrate; but away sprang

Rhys, and he called after him in vain. Accordingly he went home, put up the ponies, ate his supper and went to bed, thinking that Rhys had only made a pretext for going to the alehouse. But when morning came, and still no sign of Rhys, he told his master what had occurred. Search proving fruitless, suspicion fell on Llewelyn of having murdered his fellow-servant; and he was accordingly imprisoned. A farmer in the neighbourhood, skilled in fairy matters, guessing how things might have been, proposed that himself and some others, including the narrator of the story, should accompany Llewelyn to the place where he parted with Rhys. On coming to it, "Hush!" cried Llewelyn, "I hear music, I hear sweet harps." All listened, but could hear nothing. But Llewelyn's foot was on the outward edge of the fairy-ring. "Put your foot on mine, David," he said to the narrator. The latter did so, and so did each of the party, one after the other, and then heard the sound of many harps, and saw within a circle, about twenty feet across, great numbers of little people dancing round and round. Among them was Rhys, whom Llewelyn caught by the smock-frock, as he came by him, and pulled him out of the circle. "Where are the horses? where are the horses?" cried he. "Horses, indeed!" said Llewelyn. Rhys urged him to go home and let him finish his dance, in which he averred he had not been engaged more than five minutes. It was only by main force they got him away; and the sequel was that he could not be persuaded of the time that had passed in the dance: he became melancholy, took to his bed, and soon after died.[123]

Variants of this tale are found all over Wales. At Pwllheli, Professor Rhys was told of two youths who went out to fetch cattle and came at dusk upon a party of fairies dancing. One was drawn into the circle; and the other was suspected of murdering him, until, at a wizard's suggestion, he went again to the same spot at the end of a year and a day. There he found his friend dancing, and managed to get him out, reduced to a mere skeleton. The first question put by the rescued man was as to the cattle he was driving. Again, at Trefriw, Professor Rhys found a belief that when a young man got into a fairy-ring the fairy damsels took him away; but he could be got out unharmed at the end of a year and a day, when he would be found dancing with them in the same ring. The mode of recovery was to touch him with a piece of iron and to drag him out at once. We shall consider hereafter the reason for touching the captive with iron. In this way was recovered, after the expiration of a year and a day, a youth who had wandered into a fairy-ring. He had new shoes on at the time he was lost; and he could not be made to understand that he had been there more than five minutes until he was asked to look at his new shoes, which were by that time in pieces. Near Aberystwyth, Professor Rhys was told of a servant-maid who was lost while looking for some calves. Her fellow-servant, a man, was taken into custody on a charge of murdering her. A "wise man," however, found out that she was with the fairies; and by his directions the servant-man was successful at the end of the usual period of twelve months and a day in drawing her out of the fairy-ring at the place where she was lost. As soon as she was released and saw her fellow-servant (who was carefully dressed in the same clothes as he had on when she left him), she asked about the calves. On their way home she told her master, the servant-man, and the others, that she would stay with them until her master should strike her with iron. One day, therefore, when she was helping her master to harness a horse the bit touched her, and she disappeared instantly and was never seen from that time forth. In another case, said to have happened in Anglesea, a girl got into a fairy-circle while looking, with her father, for a lost cow. By a "wise man's" advice, however, he rescued her by pulling her out of the circle the very hour of the night of the anniversary of his loss. The first inquiry she then made was after the cow, for she had not the slightest recollection of the time she had spent with the fairies.[124]

A ghastly sequel, more frequently found in a type of the story considered later on, sometimes occurs. In Carmarthenshire it is said that a farmer going out one morning very early was lost; nor were any tidings heard of him for more than twelve months afterwards, until one day a man passing by a lonely spot saw him dancing, and spoke to him. This broke the spell; and the farmer, as if waking out of a dream, exclaimed: "Oh dear! where are my horses?" Stepping out of the magical circle, he fell down and mingled his dust with the earth. In North Wales a story was generally current a couple of generations since of two men travelling together who were benighted in a wood. One of them slept, but the other fell into the hands of the fairies. With the help of a wizard's advice, some of his relatives rescued him at the end of a year. They went to the place where his companion had missed him, there found him dancing with the fairies and dragged him out of the ring. The unfortunate man, imagining it was the same night and that he was with his companion, immediately asked if it were not better to go home. He was offered some food, which he began to eat; but he had no sooner done so than he mouldered away. A similar tradition attaches to a certain yew-tree near Mathafarn in the parish of Llanwrin. One of two farm-servants was lost at that spot, and found again, a year after, dancing in a fairy-circle. On being dragged out he was asked if he did not feel hungry. "No," he replied, "and if I did, have I not here in my wallet the remains of my dinner that I had before I fell asleep?" He did not know that a year had passed by. His look was like a skeleton; and as soon as he had tasted food he too mouldered away.[125]

In Scotland the story is told without this terrible end. For example, in Sutherlandshire we learn that a man who had been with a friend to the town of Lairg to enter his first child's birth in the session-books, and to buy a keg of whisky against the christening, sat down to rest at the foot of the hill of Durchâ, near a large hole from which they soon heard a sound of piping and dancing. Feeling curious, he entered the cavern, and disappeared. His friend was accused of murder, but being allowed a year and a day to vindicate himself, he used to repair at dusk to the fatal spot and call and pray. One day before the term ran out, he sat, as usual, in the gloaming by the cavern, when, what seemed his friend's shadow passed within it. It was his friend himself, tripping merrily with the fairies. The accused man succeeded in catching him by the sleeve and pulling him out. "Why could you not let me finish my reel, Sandy?" asked the bewitched man. "Bless me!" rejoined Sandy, "have you not had enough of reeling this last twelvemonth?" But the other would not believe in this lapse of time until he found his wife sitting by the door with a yearling child in her arms. In Kirkcudbrightshire, one night about Hallowe'en two young ploughmen, returning from an errand, passed by an old ruined mill and heard within music and dancing. One of them went in; and nothing was seen of him again until a year after, when his companion went to the same place, Bible in hand, and delivered him from the evil beings into whose power he had fallen.[126]

The captive, however, does not always require to be sought for: he is sometimes released voluntarily by his captors. A man who lived at Ystradgynlais, in Brecknockshire, going out one day to look after his cattle and sheep on the mountain, disappeared. In about three weeks, after search had been made in vain for him and his wife had given him up for dead, he came home. His wife asked him where he had been for the past three weeks. "Three weeks! Is it three weeks you call three hours?" said he. Pressed to say where he had been, he told her he had been playing on his flute (which he usually took with him on the mountain) at the Llorfa, a spot near the Van Pool, when he was surrounded at a distance by little beings like men, who closed nearer and nearer to him until they became a very small circle. They sang and danced, and so affected him that he quite lost himself. They offered him some small cakes to eat, of which he partook; and he had never enjoyed himself so well in his life. Near Bridgend is a place where a woman is said to have lived who was absent ten years with the fairies, and thought she was not out of the house more than ten minutes. With a woman's proverbial persistency, she would not believe her husband's assurances that it was ten years since she disappeared; and the serious disagreement between them which ensued was so notorious that it gave a name to the place where they lived. A happier result is believed to have attended an adventure that foreboded much worse to a man at Dornoch, in Sutherlandshire. He was present at a funeral in the churchyard on New Year's Day, and was so piqued at not being invited, as all the others were, to some of the New Year's festivities, that in his vexation, happening to see a skull lying at his feet, he struck it with his staff and said: "Thou seemest to be forsaken and uncared-for, like myself. I have been bidden by none; neither have I invited any: I now invite thee!" That night as he and his wife were sitting down alone to supper, a venerable old man entered the room in silence and took his share of the delicacies provided. In those days the New Year's feast was kept up for eleven days together; and the stranger's visit was repeated in the same absolute silence for six nights. At last the host, alarmed and uneasy, sought the priest's advice as to how he was to get rid of his unwelcome guest. The reverend father bade him, in laying the bannocks in the basket for the seventh day's supper, reverse the last-baked one. This, he declared, would induce the old man to speak. It did; and the speech was an invitation—nay, rather a command—to spend the remainder of the festival with him in the churchyard. The priest, again consulted, advised compliance; and the man went trembling to the tryst. He found in the churchyard a great house, brilliantly illuminated, where he enjoyed himself, eating, drinking, piping and dancing. After what seemed the lapse of a few hours, the grey master of the house came to him, and bade him hasten home, or his wife would be married to another; and in parting he advised him always to respect the remains of the dead. Scarcely had he done speaking when the grey old man himself, the guests, the house, and all that it contained, vanished, leaving the man to crawl home alone in the moonlight as best he might after so long a debauch. For he had been absent a year and a day; and when he got home he found his wife in a bride's dress, and the whole house gay with a bridal party. His entrance broke in upon the mirth: his wife swooned, and the new bridegroom scrambled up the chimney. But when she got over her fright, and her husband had recovered from the fatigue of his year-long dance, they made it up, and lived happily ever after.[127]

A story of this type has been elaborated by a Welsh writer who is known as "Glasynys" into a little romance, in which the hero is a shepherd lad, and the heroine a fairy maiden whom he weds and brings home with him. This need not detain us; but a more authentic story from the Vale of Neath may be mentioned. It concerns a boy called Gitto Bach, or Little Griffith, a farmer's son, who disappeared. During two whole years nothing was heard of him; but at length one morning when his mother, who had long and bitterly mourned for him as dead, opened the door, whom should she see sitting on the threshold but Gitto with a bundle under his arm. He was dressed and looked exactly as when she last saw him, for he had not grown a bit. "Where have you been all this time?" asked his mother. "Why, it was only yesterday I went away," he replied; and opening the bundle, he showed her a dress the "little children," as he called them, had given him for dancing with them. The dress was of white paper without seam. With maternal caution she put it into the fire.[128]

I am not aware of many foreign examples of this type; but among the Siberian Tartars their extravagant heroes sometimes feast overlong with friends as mythical as themselves. On one occasion

"They caroused, they feasted.
That a month had flown
They knew not;
That a year had gone by
They knew not.
As a year went by
It seemed like a day;
As two years went by
It seemed like two days;
As three years went by
It seemed like three days."

Again, when a hero was married the time very naturally passed rapidly. "One day he thought he had lived here—he had lived a month; two days he believed he had lived—he had lived two months; three days he believed he had lived—he had lived three months." And he was much surprised to learn from his bride how long it really was, though time seems always to have gone wrong with him. For after he was born it is recorded that in one day he became a year old, in two days two years, and in seven days seven years old; after which he performed some heroic feats, ate fourteen sheep and three cows, and then lying down slept for seven days and seven nights—in other words, until he was fourteen years old. In a Breton tale a girl who goes down underground, to become godmother to a fairy child, thinks, when she returns, that she has been away but two days, though in the meantime her god-child has grown big: she has been in fact ten years. In a Hessian legend the time of absence is seven years.[129]

Turning away from this type, in which pleasure, and especially the pleasure of music and dancing, is the motive, let us look at what seem to be some specially German and Slavonic types of the tale. In the latter it is rather an act of service (sometimes under compulsion), curiosity or greed, which leads the mortal into the mysterious regions where time has so little power. At Eldena, in Pomerania, are the ruins of a monastery and church, formerly very wealthy, under which are said to be some remarkable chambers. Two Capuchin monks came from Rome many years ago, and inquired of the head of the police after a hidden door which led under the ruins. He lent them his servant-boy, who, under their direction, removed the rubbish and found the door. It opened at the touch of the monks, and they entered with the servant. Passing through several rooms they reached one in which many persons were sitting and writing. Here they were courteously received; and after a good deal of secret conference between the monks and their hosts, they were dismissed. When the servant came back to the upper air, he found he had been absent three whole years. Blanik is the name of a mountain in Bohemia, beneath which are lofty halls whose walls are entirely fashioned of rock-crystal. In these halls the Bohemian hero, the holy King Wenzel, sleeps with a chosen band of his knights, until some day the utmost need of his country shall summon him and them to her aid. A smith, who dwelt near the mountain, was once mowing his meadow, when a stranger came and bade him follow him. The stranger led him into the mountain, where he beheld the sleeping knights, each one upon his horse, his head bent down upon the horse's neck. His guide then brought him tools that he might shoe the horses, but told him to beware in his work of knocking against any of the knights. The smith skilfully performed his work, but as he was shoeing the last horse he accidentally touched the rider, who started up, crying out: "Is it time?" "Not yet," replied he who had brought the smith thither, motioning the latter to keep quiet. When the task was done, the smith received the old shoes by way of reward. On returning home he was astonished to find two mowers at work in his meadow, whereas he had only left one there. From them he learned that he had been away a whole year; and when he opened his bag, behold the old horse-shoes were all of solid gold! On Easter Sunday, during mass, the grey horse belonging to another peasant living at the foot of the Blanik disappeared. While in quest of him the owner found the mountain open, and, entering, arrived in the hall where the knights sat round a large table of stone and slept. Each of them wore black armour, save their chief, who shone in gold and bore three herons' feathers in his helm. Ever and anon one or other of the knights would look up and ask: "Is it time?" But on their chief shaking his head he would sink again to rest. While the peasant was in the midst of his astonishment he heard a neighing behind him; and turning round he left the cavern. His horse was quietly grazing outside; but when he got home every one shrank in fright away from him. His wife sat at the table in deep mourning. On seeing him she shrieked and asked: "Where have you been for a whole year?" He thought he had only been absent a single hour. A servant-man driving two horses over the Blanik heard the trampling of steeds and a battle-march played. It was the knights returning from their mimic combat; and the horses he was driving were so excited that he was compelled to follow with them into the mountain, which then closed upon them. Nor did he reach home until ten years had passed away, though he thought it had only been as many days.[130]

We shall have occasion to return to Blanik and its knights. Parallel traditions attach, as is well known, to the Kyffhäuser, a mountain in Thuringia, where Frederick Barbarossa sleeps. A peasant going with corn to market at Nordhausen, drove by the Kyffhäuser, where he was met by a little grey man, who asked him whither he was going, and offered to reward him if he would accompany him instead. The little grey man led him through a great gateway into the mountain till they came at last to a castle. There he took from the peasant his waggon and horses, and led him into a hall gorgeously illuminated and filled with people, where he was well entertained. At last the little grey man told him it was now time he went home, and rewarding him bountifully he led him forth. His waggon and horses were given to him again, and he trudged homeward well pleased. Arrived there, however, his wife opened her eyes wide to see him, for he had been absent a year, and she had long accounted him dead. It fared not quite so well with a journeyman joiner from Nordhausen, by name Thiele, who found the mountain open, as it is every seven years, and went in. There he saw the Marquis John (whoever he may have been), with his beard spreading over the table and his nails grown through it. Around the walls lay great wine-vats, whose hoops and wood had alike rolled away; but the wine had formed its own shell and was blood-red. A little drop remained in the wine-glass which stood before the Marquis John. The joiner made bold to drain it off, and thereupon fell asleep. When he awoke again he had slept for seven years in the mountain.[131]

Curiosity and greed caused this man to lose seven years of his life. This is a motive often met with in these stories. A young girl during the midday rest left a hayfield in the Lavantthal, Carinthia, to climb the Schönofen, whence there is a fine view over the valley. As she reached the top she became aware of an open door in the rock. She entered, and found herself in a cellar-like room. Two fine black steeds stood at the fodder-trough and fed off the finest oats. Marvelling how they got there, she put a few handfuls of the oats into her pocket, and passed on into a second chamber. A chest stood there, and on the chest lay a black dog. Near him was a loaf of bread, in which a knife was stuck. With ready wit she divined, or recollected, the purpose of the bread; and cutting a good slice she threw it to the dog. While he was busy devouring it she filled her apron from the treasure contained in the chest. But meantime the door closed, and there was nothing for it but to lie down and sleep. She awoke to find the door wide open, and at once made the best of her way home. But she was not a little astounded to learn that she had been gone for a whole year.[132]

A Lapp tale presents this mysterious lapse of time as the sequel of an adventure similar to that of Ulysses with Polyphemus. An old Lapp, having lost his way while hunting, came to a cottage. The door was open; and he entered to remain there the night, and began to cook in a pot he carried with him the game he had caught that day. Suddenly a witch entered, and asked him: "What is your name?" "Myself," answered the Lapp; and taking a spoonful of the boiling liquid he flung it in her face. She cried out: "Myself has burnt me! Myself has burnt me!" "If you have burnt yourself you ought to suffer," answered her companion from the neighbouring mountain. The hunter was thus delivered for the moment from the witch, who, however, as she went away, exclaimed: "Self has burnt me; Self shall sleep till the new year!" When the Lapp had finished his repast he lay down to repose. On awaking he rummaged in his provision-sack: he found its contents mouldy and putrid. Nor could he understand this before he got home and learned that he had been missing for six months.[133]

This story is unlike the previous ones, inasmuch as it represents the six months' disappearance as in no way due to any enticements, either of supernatural beings or of the hero's own passions. Neither music, nor dancing, neither greed nor curiosity, led him astray. The aboriginal inhabitants of Japan in like manner tell of a certain man who went out in his boat to fish and was carried off by a storm to an unknown land. The chief, an old man of divine aspect, begged him to stay there for the night, promising to send him home to his own country on the morrow. The promise was fulfilled by his being sent with some of the old chief's subjects who were going thither; but the man was enjoined to lie down in the boat and cover up his head. When he reached his native place the sailors threw him into the water; and ere he came to himself sailors and boat had disappeared. He had been away for a whole year; and the chief appeared to him shortly afterwards in a dream, revealing himself as no human being, but the chief of the salmon, the divine fish; and he required the man thenceforth to worship him. Curiously similar to the Japanese tale is a tale told to M. Sébillot by a cabin-boy of Saint Cast in Brittany. A fisherman caught one day the king of the fishes, in the shape of a small gilded fish, but was persuaded to let him go under promise to send (such is the popular belief in the unselfishness of kings) at all times as many of his subjects as the fisherman wanted into his nets. The promise was royally fulfilled. More than this, when the fisherman's boat was once capsized by a storm the king of the fishes appeared, gave its drowning owner to drink from a bottle he had brought for the purpose, and conveyed him under the water to his capital,—a beautiful city whose streets, surpassing those of London in the traditions of English peasant children, were paved not only with gold but with diamonds and other gems. The fisherman promptly filled his pockets with these paving-stones; and then the king politely told him: "When you are tired of being with us, you have only to say so." There is a limit to hospitality; so the fisherman took the hint, and told the king how delighted he should be to remain there always, but that he had a wife and children at home who would think he was drowned. The king called a tunny and commanded him to take the fisherman on his back and deposit him on a rock near the shore, where the other fishers could see and rescue him. Then, with the parting gift of an inexhaustible purse, he dismissed his guest. When the fisherman got back to his village he found he had been away more than six months. In the chapter on Changelings I had occasion to refer to some instances of women being carried off at a critical time in their lives. One more such instance may be added here. Among the Bohemians a mythical female called Polednice is believed to be dangerous to women who have recently added to the population; and such women are accordingly warned to keep within doors, especially at noon and after the angelus in the evening. On one occasion a woman, who scorned the warnings she had received, was carried off by Polednice in the form of a whirlwind, as she sat in the harvest-field chatting with the reapers, to whom she had brought their dinner. Only after a year and a day was she permitted to return.[134]

In some of the German and Bohemian tales a curious incident occurs. Beneath the Rollberg, near Niemes, in Bohemia, is a treasure-vault, the door of which stands open for a short time every Palm Sunday. A woman once found it open thus and entered with her child. There she saw a number of Knights Templars sitting round a table, gambling. They did not notice her; so she helped herself from a pile of gold lying near them, having first set down her child. Beside the gold lay a black dog, which barked from time to time. The woman knew that the third time it barked the door would close; wherefore she hastened out. When she bethought herself of the child it was too late: she had left it behind in her haste, and the vault was closed. The following year she returned at the hour when the door was open, and found the little one safe and sound, in either hand a fair red apple. Frequently in these tales a beautiful lady comes and ministers to the child during its mother's absence; at other times, a man. The treasure of King Darius is believed to be buried beneath the Sattelburg in Transylvania. A Wallachian woman, with her yearling babe in her arms, once found the door open and went in. There sat an old, long-bearded man, and about him stood chests full of silver and gold. She asked him if she might take some of this treasure for herself. "Oh, yes," answered he, "as much as you like." She put down the child and filled her skirts with gold, put the gold outside and re-entered. Having obtained permission, she filled and emptied her skirts a second time. But when she turned to enter a third time the door banged-to, and she was left outside. She cried out for her child, and wept—in vain. Then she made her way to the priest and laid her case before him. He advised her to pray daily for a whole year, and she would then get her child again. She carried out his injunction; and the following year she went again to the Sattelburg. The door was open, and she found the babe still seated in the chest where she had put it down. It was playing with a golden apple, which it held up to her, crying: "Look, mother, look!" The mother was astonished to hear it speak, and asked: "Whence hast thou that beautiful apple?" "From the old man, who has given me to eat too." The man was, however, no longer to be seen; and as the mother took her child and left the place, the door closed behind her.[135]

But the most numerous, and assuredly the most weird and interesting, of these stories belong to a type which we may call, after the famous Posthumous Writing of Diedrich Knickerbocker, the "Rip van Winkle type." Here the hero remains under the spell of the supernatural until he passes the ordinary term of life; and he comes back to find all his friends dead and himself nothing but a dim memory. It will be needless here to recapitulate the tale of Rip van Winkle himself. Whether any such legend really lingers about the Kaatskill mountains I do not know; but I have a vehement suspicion that Washington Irving was indebted rather to Otmar's "Traditions of the Harz," a book published at Bremen in the year 1800. In this book the scene of the tale is laid on the Kyffhäuser, and with the exception of such embellishments as the keen tongue of Dame van Winkle and a few others, the incidents in the adventures of Peter Claus the Goatherd are absolutely the same as those of Rip van Winkle.[136]

Of all the variants of this type it is in China that we find the one most resembling it. Wang Chih, afterwards one of the holy men of the Taoists, wandering one day in the mountains of Kü Chow to gather firewood, entered a grotto in which some aged men were playing at chess. He laid down his axe and watched their game, in the course of which one of them handed him something in size and shape like a date-stone, telling him to put it into his mouth. No sooner had he done so than hunger and thirst passed away. After some time had elapsed one of the players said: "It is long since you came here; you should go home now." Wang Chih accordingly proceeded to pick up his axe, but found that its handle had mouldered into dust; and on reaching home he became aware that not hours, nor days, but centuries had passed since he left it, and that no vestige of his kinsfolk remained. Another legend tells of a horseman who, riding over the hills, sees several old men playing a game with rushes. He ties his horse to a tree while he looks on at them. In a few minutes, as it seems to him, he turns to depart; but his horse is already a skeleton, and of the saddle and bridle rotten pieces only are left. He seeks his home; but that too is gone; and he lies down and dies broken-hearted. A similar story is told in Japan of a man who goes into the mountains to cut wood, and watches two mysterious ladies playing at chess while seven generations of mortal men pass away. Both these legends omit the supernatural food which seems to support life, not only in the case of Wang Chih, but also in that of Peter Claus. In another Chinese tale two friends, wandering in the T'ien-t'ai mountains, are entertained by two beautiful girls, who feed them on a kind of haschisch, a drug made from hemp; and when they return they find that they have passed seven generations of ordinary men in the society of these ladies. Another Taoist devotee was admitted for a while into the next world, where he was fed on cakes, and, as if he were a dyspeptic, he received much comfort from having all his digestive organs removed. After awhile he was sent back to this world, to find himself much younger than his youngest grandson.[137]

Feasts in Fairyland occupy an unconscionable length of time. Walter Map, writing in the latter half of the twelfth century, relates a legend concerning a mythical British king, Herla, who was on terms of friendship with the king of the pigmies. The latter appeared to him one day riding on a goat, a man such as Pan might have been described to be, with a very large head, a fiery face, and a long red beard. A spotted fawn-skin adorned his breast, but the lower part of his body was exposed and shaggy, and his legs degenerated into goat's feet. This queer little fellow declared himself very near akin to Herla, foretold that the king of the Franks was about to send ambassadors offering his daughter as wife to the king of the Britons, and invited himself to the wedding. He proposed a pact between them, that when he had attended Herla's wedding, Herla should the following year attend his. Accordingly at Herla's wedding the pigmy king appears with a vast train of courtiers and servants, and numbers of precious gifts. The next year he sends to bid Herla to his own wedding. Herla goes. Penetrating a mountain cavern, he and his followers emerge into the light, not of sun or moon, but of innumerable torches, and reach the pigmies' dwellings, whose splendour Map compares with Ovid's description of the palace of the sun. Having given so charming, and doubtless so accurate, a portrait of the pigmy king, it is a pity the courtier-like ecclesiastic has forgotten to inform us what his bride was like. He leaves us to guess that her attractions must have corresponded with those of her stately lord, telling us simply that when the wedding was over, and the gifts which Herla brought had been presented, he obtained leave to depart, and set out for home, laden, he too, with gifts, among which are enumerated horses, dogs, hawks, and other requisites of a handsome outfit for hunting or fowling. Indeed, the bridegroom himself accompanied them as far as the darkness of the cavern through which they had to pass; and at parting he added to his presentations that of a bloodhound, so small as to be carried, forbidding any of the train to alight anywhere until the hound should leap from his bearer. When Herla found himself once more within his own realm he met with an old shepherd, and inquired for tidings of his queen by name. The shepherd looked at him astonished, scarcely understanding his speech; for he was a Saxon, whereas Herla was a Briton. Nor, as he told the king, had he heard of such a queen, unless it were a queen of the former Britons, whose husband, Herla, was said to have disappeared at yonder rock with a dwarf, and never to have been seen again. That, however, was long ago, for it was now more than two hundred years since the Britons had been driven out and the Saxons had taken possession of the land. The king was stupefied, for he deemed he had only been away three days, and could hardly keep his seat. Some of his followers, forgetful of the pigmy king's prohibition, alighted without waiting for the dog to lead the way, and were at once crumbled into dust. Herla and those who were wiser took warning by the fate of their companions. One story declared that they were wandering still; and many persons asserted that they had often beheld the host upon its mad, its endless journey. But Map concludes that the last time it appeared was in the year of King Henry the

Second's coronation, when it was seen by many Welshmen to plunge into the Wye in Herefordshire.[138]

Cases in which dancing endures for a whole twelvemonth have already been mentioned. This might be thought a moderate length of time for a ball, even for a fairy ball; but some have been known to last longer. Two celebrated fiddlers of Strathspey were inveigled by a venerable old man, who ought to have known better, into a little hill near Inverness, where they supplied the music for a brilliant assembly which lasted in fact for a hundred years, though to them it seemed but a few hours. They emerged into daylight again on a Sunday; and when they had learned the real state of affairs, and recovered from their astonishment at the miracle which had been wrought in them, they went, as was meet, to church. They sat listening for awhile to the ringing of the bells; but when the clergyman began to read the gospel, at the first word he uttered they both fell into dust. This is a favourite form of the legend in Wales as well as Scotland; but, pathetic and beautiful as the various versions are, they present no variations of importance.[139]

Often the stranger's festive visit to Fairyland is rounded with a sleep. We have seen this in the instance of Rip van Winkle. Another legend has been put into literary form by Washington Irving, this time from a Portuguese source. It relates the adventures of a noble youth who set out to find an island in which some of the former inhabitants of the Peninsula had taken refuge at the time of the Moorish conquest, and where their descendants still dwelt. The island was believed to contain seven cities; and the adventurer was appointed by the king of Portugal Adalantado, or governor, of the Seven Cities. He reached the island, and was received as Adalantado, was feasted, and then fell asleep. When he came to himself again he was on board a homeward-bound vessel, having been picked up senseless from a drifting wreck. He reached Lisbon, but no one knew him. His ancestral mansion was occupied by others; none of his name had dwelt in it for many a year. He hurried to his betrothed, only to fling himself, not, as he thought, at her feet, but at the feet of her great-granddaughter. In cases like this the supernatural lapse of time may be conceived as taking place during the enchanted sleep, rather than during the festivities. According to a Coptic Christian romance, Abimelek, the youthful favourite of King Zedekiah, preserved the prophet Jeremiah's life when he was thrown into prison, and afterwards persuaded his master to give him charge of the prophet, and to permit him to release him from the dungeon. In reward, Jeremiah promised him that he should never see the destruction of Jerusalem, nor experience the Babylonish captivity, and yet that he should not die. The sun should take care of him, the atmosphere nourish him; the earth on which he slept should give him repose, and he should taste of joy for seventy years until he should again see Jerusalem in its glory, flourishing as before. Accordingly, going out one day, as his custom was, into the royal garden to gather grapes and figs, God caused him to rest and fall asleep beneath the shadow of a rock. There he lay peacefully slumbering while the city was besieged by Nebuchadnezzar, and during the horrors of its capture and the whole of the seventy sad years that followed. When he awoke, it was to meet the prophet Jeremiah returning from the captivity, and he entered the restored city with him in triumph. But the seventy years had seemed to him but a few hours; nor had he known anything of what passed while he slumbered. Mohammed in the Koran mentions a story referred by the commentators to Ezra. He is represented as passing by a village (said to mean Jerusalem) when it was desolate, and saying: "How will God revive this after its death?" And God made him die for a hundred years. Then He raised him and asked: "How long hast thou tarried?" Said the man: "I have tarried a day, or some part of a day." But God said: "Nay, thou hast tarried a hundred years. Look at thy food and drink, they are not spoiled; and look at thine ass; for we will make thee a sign to men. And look at the bones, how we scatter them and then clothe them with flesh." And when it was made manifest to him, he said: "I know that God is mighty over all."[140]

Mohammed probably was unconscious that this is to all intents and purposes the same story as that of the Seven Sleepers, to which he refers in the chapter on the Cave. Some of the phrases he uses are, indeed, identical. As usually told, this legend speaks of seven youths of Ephesus who had fled from the persecutions of the heathen emperor Decius, and taken refuge in a cave, where they slept for upwards of three hundred years. In Mohammed's time, however, it should be noted, the number of the sleepers was undetermined; they were credited with a dog who slept with them, like Ezra's ass; and Mohammed's notion of the time they slept was only one hundred years. One of the wild tribes on the northern frontier of Afghanistan is said to tell the following story concerning a cavern in the Hirak Valley, known as the cave of the Seven Sleepers. A king bearing the suspicious name of Dakianus, deceived by the devil, set himself up as a god. Six of his servants, however, having reason to think that his claim was unfounded, fled from him and fell in with a shepherd, who agreed to throw in his lot with theirs and to guide them to a cavern where they might all hide. The shepherd's dog followed his master; but the six fugitives insisted on his being driven back lest he should betray their whereabouts. The shepherd begged that he might go with them, as he had been his faithful companion for years; but in vain. So he struck the dog with his stick, breaking one of his legs. The dog still followed; and the shepherd repeated the blow, breaking a second leg. Finding that the dog continued to crawl after them notwithstanding this, the men were struck with pity and took it in turns to carry the poor animal. Arrived at the cave, they all lay down and slept for three hundred and nine years. Assuming the genuineness of the tradition, which perhaps rests on no very good authority, its form is obviously due to Mohammedan influence. But the belief in this miraculous sleep is traceable beyond Christian and Mohammedan legends into the Paganism of classical antiquity. Pliny, writing in the first century of our era, alludes to a story told of the Cretan poet Epimenides, who, when a boy, fell asleep in a cave, and continued in that state for fifty-seven years. On waking he was greatly surprised at the change in the appearance of everything around him, as he thought he had only slept for a few hours; and though he did not, as in the Welsh and Scottish tales, fall into dust, still old age came upon him in as many days as the years he had passed in slumber.[141]

Nor is it only in dancing, feasting, or sleeping that the time passes quickly with supernatural folk. A shepherd at the foot of the Blanik, who missed one of his flock, followed it into a cavern, whence he could not return because the mountain closed upon him with a crash. A dwarf came and led him into a large hall. There he saw King Wenzel sleeping with his knights. The king awoke, and bade him stay and clean the armour. One day—perhaps the criticism would be too carping which inquired how he knew the day from the night—he received permission to go, and a bag which he was told contained his reward. When he reached the light of day, he opened the bag and found it filled with oats. In the village all was changed, for he had been a hundred years in the mountain, and nobody knew him. He succeeded in getting a lodging, and on again opening his bag, lo! all the grains of oats had turned to gold pieces and thalers, so that he was able to buy a fine house, and speedily became the richest man in the place. This was a pleasanter fate than that of the Tirolese peasant who followed his herd under a stone, where they had all disappeared. He presently came into a lovely garden; and there a lady came, and, inviting him to eat, offered to take him as gardener. He readily assented; but after some weeks he began to be homesick, and, taking leave of his mistress, went home. On arriving there he was astounded that he knew no one, and no one knew him, save an old crone, who at length came to him and said: "Where have you been? I have been looking for you for two hundred years." Thus saying, she took him by the hand and he fell dead; for the crone who had sought him so long was Death.[142]

Save in the legends that tell of a mother leaving her child in the mountain from her eagerness to gather treasure, we have encountered but few instances of women being beguiled. They are, indeed, not so numerous as those where the sterner sex is thus overcome; nor need we be detained by most of them. A Danish tradition, however, runs that a bride, during the dancing and festivities of her wedding-day, left the room and thoughtlessly walked towards a mound where the elves were also making merry. The hillock was standing, as is usual on such occasions, on red pillars; and as she drew near, one of the company offered her a cup of wine. She drank, and then suffered herself to join in a dance. When the dance was over she hastened home. But alas! house, farm, everything was changed. The noise and mirth of the wedding was stilled. No one knew her; but at length, on hearing her lamentation, an old woman exclaimed: "Was it you, then, who disappeared at my grandfather's brother's wedding, a hundred years ago?" At these words the aged bride fell down and expired. A prettier, if not a more pathetic, story is widely current on the banks of the Rhine. A maiden who bore an excellent character for piety and goodness was about to be married. She was fond of roses; and on the wedding morning she stepped into the garden to gather a small bunch. There she met a man whom she did not know. He admired two lovely blossoms which she had, but said he had many finer in his garden: would she not go with him? "I cannot," she said; "I must go to the church: it is high time." "It is not far," urged the stranger. The maiden allowed herself to be persuaded; and the man showed her beautiful, beautiful flowers—finer she had never seen—and gave her a wonderful rose of which she was very proud. Then she hastened back, lest she should be too late. When she mounted the steps of the house she could not understand what had happened to her. Children whom she knew not were playing there: people whom she did not recognize were within. And every one ran away from her, frightened to see a strange woman in an antiquated wedding-dress stand there bitterly weeping. She had but just left her bridegroom to go for a moment into the garden, and in so short a time guests and bridegroom had all vanished. She asked after her bridegroom, and nobody knew him. At last she told her story to the folk around her. A man said he had bought the house, and knew nothing at all of her bridegroom or her parents. They took her to the parish priest. He reached his church-books down, and there he found recorded that almost two hundred years before, a certain bride on the wedding-day had disappeared from her father's house. Burdened thus with two centuries of life, she lingered on a few lonely years, and then sank into the grave; and the good, simple villagers whisper that the strange gardener was no other than the Lord Jesus, who thus provided for His humble child an escape from a union which would have been the source of bitterest woe. After this it is almost an anti-climax to refer to a Scottish tale in which a bridegroom was similarly spirited away. As he was leaving the church after the ceremony, a tall dark man met him and asked him to come round to the back of the church, for he wanted to speak to him. When he complied, the dark man asked him to be good enough to stand there until a small piece of candle he held in his hand should burn out. He good-humouredly complied. The candle took, as he thought, less than two minutes to burn; and he then rushed off to overtake his friends. On his way he saw a man cutting turf, and asked if it were long since the wedding party had passed. The man replied that he did not know that any wedding party had passed that way to-day, or for a long time. "Oh, there was a marriage to-day," said the other, "and I am the bridegroom. I was asked by a man to go with him to the back of the church, and I went. I am now running to overtake the party." The turf-cutter, feeling that this could not be, asked him what date he supposed that day was. The bridegroom's answer was in fact two hundred years short of the real date: he had passed two centuries in those two minutes which the bit of candle took, as he thought, to burn. "I remember," said he who cut the turf, "that my grandfather used to tell something of such a disappearance of a bridegroom, a story which his grandfather told him as a fact which happened when he was young." "Ah, well then, I am the bridegroom," sighed the unfortunate man, and fell away as he stood, until nothing remained but a small heap of earth.[143]

Every reader of Longfellow loves the story of the Monk Felix, so exquisitely told in "The Golden Legend." Its immediate source I do not know; but it is certain that the tradition is a genuine one, and has obtained a local habitation in many parts of Europe. Southey relates it as attached to the Spanish convent of San Salvador de Villar, where the tomb of the Abbot to whom the adventure happened was shown. And he is very severe on "the dishonest monks who, for the honour of their convent and the lucre of gain, palmed this lay (for such in its origin it was) upon their neighbours as a true legend." In Wales, the ruined monastery at Clynnog-Fawr, on the coast of Carnarvonshire, founded by St.

Beuno, the uncle of the more famous St. Winifred, has been celebrated by a Welsh antiquary as the scene of the same event, in memory whereof a woodland patch near Clynnog is said to be called Llwyn-y-Nef, the Grove of Heaven. At Pantshonshenkin, in Carmarthenshire, a youth went out early one summer's morning and was lost. An old woman, Catti Madlen, prophesied of him that he was in the fairies' power and would not be released until the last sap of a certain sycamore tree had dried up. When that time came he returned. He had been listening all the while to the singing of a bird, and supposed only a few minutes had elapsed, though, seventy years had in fact gone over his head. In the Mabinogi of Branwen, daughter of Llyr, Pryderi and his companions, while bearing the head of Bran the Blessed, to bury it in the White Mount in London, were entertained seven years at Harlech, feasting and listening to the singing of the three birds of Rhiannon—a mythical figure in whom Professor Rhys can hardly be wrong in seeing an old Celtic goddess. In Germany and the Netherlands the story is widely spread. At the abbey of Afflighem, Fulgentius, who was abbot towards the close of the eleventh century, received the announcement one day that a stranger monk had knocked at the gate and claimed to be one of the brethren of that cloister. His story was that he had sung matins that morning with the rest of the brotherhood; and when they came to the verse of the 90th Psalm where it is said: "A thousand years in Thy sight are but as yesterday," he had fallen into deep meditation, and continued sitting in the choir when the others had departed, and that a little bird had then appeared to him and sung so sweetly that he had followed it into the forest, whence, after a short stay, he had now returned, but found the abbey so changed that he hardly knew it. On questioning him about his abbot and the name of the king whom he supposed to be still reigning, Fulgentius found that both had been dead for three hundred years. The same tale is told of other monasteries. In Transylvania it is told concerning a student of the school at Kronstadt that he was to preach on the fifteenth Sunday after Trinity in St. John's Church, now known as the Church of the Franciscans, and on the Saturday previous he walked out on the Kapellenberg to rehearse his sermon. After he had learned it he saw a beautiful bird, and tried to catch it. It led him on and on into a cavern, where he met a dwarf, who showed the astonished and curious student all the wealth of gold and jewels stored up in the vaults of the mountain. When he escaped again to the upper air the trees and the houses were altered; other and unknown faces greeted him at the school; his own room was changed—taken by another; a different rector ruled; and in short a hundred years had elapsed since he had gone forth to study his sermon for the next day. The old record-book, bound in pigskin, reposed on the rector's shelves. He took it down: it contained an entry of the student's having quitted the school and not returned, and of the difficulty caused thereby at St. John's Church, where he was to have preached the following day. By the time the entry was found and the mystery solved, it was noon. The student was hungry with his hundred-years' fast; and he sat down with the others at the common table to dine. But he had no sooner tasted the first spoonful of soup than his whole frame underwent a change. From a ruddy youth he became an old man in the last stage of decrepitude. His comrades scarce had time to hurry him upon a bed ere he breathed his last. Some pretty verses, attributed to Alaric A. Watts, commemorate a similar incident, said to have happened to two sisters who were nuns at Beverley Minister. They disappeared one evening after vespers. After some months they were found in a trance in the north tower. On being aroused they declared they had been admitted into Paradise, whither they would return before morning. They died in the night; and the beautiful monument called the Sisters' Shrine still witnesses to the truth of their story.[144]

From monastic meditations we may pass without any long interval to a type of the story that perhaps appears at its best in M. Luzel's charming collection of distinctively Christian traditions of Lower Brittany. In this type we are given the adventures of a youth who undertakes to carry a letter to *"Monsieur le Bon Dieu"* in Paradise. Proceeding by the directions of a hermit, he is guided by a ball to the hermit's brother, who points out the road and describes the various difficulties through which he will have to pass. Accordingly he climbs the mountain before him; and the path then leads him across an arid meadow filled with fat cattle, and next over a lush pasture tenanted only by lean and sickly kine. Having left this behind he enters an avenue where, under the trees, youths and damsels richly clad are feasting and making merry; and they tempt the traveller to join them. The path then becomes narrow and steep, and encumbered with brambles and nettles and stones. Here he meets a rolling fire, but standing firm in the middle of the path, the fire passes harmlessly over his head. Hardly has it gone by, however, when he hears a terrible roar behind him, as though the sea in all its fury were at his heels ready to engulf him. He resolutely refuses to look back; and the noise subsides. A thick hedge of thorns closes the way before him; but he pushes through it, only to fall into a ditch filled with nettles and brambles on the other side, where he faints with loss of blood. When he recovers and scrambles out of the ditch, he reaches a place filled with the sweet perfume of flowers, with butterflies, and with the melody of birds. A clear river waters this beautiful land; and there he sits upon a stone and bathes his cruelly torn feet. No wonder he falls asleep and dreams that he is already in Paradise. Awaking, he finds his strength restored, and his wounds healed. Before him is Mount Calvary, the Saviour still upon the cross, and the blood yet running from His body. A crowd of little children are trying to climb the mountain; but ere they reach the top they roll down again continually to the foot, only to recommence the toil. They crowd round the traveller, and beseech him to take them with him; and he takes three, one on each shoulder and one by the hand; but with them he cannot get to the top, for he is hurled back again and again. Leaving them therefore behind, he climbs with ease, and throws himself at the foot of the cross to pray and weep. On rising, he sees before him a palace that proves to be Paradise itself. St. Peter, the celestial porter, receives his letter and carries it to its destination. While the youth waits, he finds St. Peter's spectacles on the table and amuses himself by trying them on. Many and marvellous are the things they reveal to him; but the porter comes back, and he hastily takes off the glasses, fearing to be scolded. St. Peter, however, tells him: "Fear nothing, my child. You have already been looking through my glasses for five hundred years!" "But I have only just put them on my nose!" "Yes, my child," returned the door-keeper, "it is five hundred years, and I see you find the time short." After this it is a trifle that he spends another hundred years looking at the seat reserved for himself in Paradise and thinks them only a moment. The Eternal Father's reply to the letter is handed to him; and since his master and the king who sent him on the errand have both long been dead and in Paradise (though on lower seats than that which he is to occupy), he is bidden to take the reply to his parish prices. The priest will in return hand him a hundred crowns, which he is to give to the poor, and when the last penny has been distributed he will die and enter Paradise, to obtain the seat he has been allowed to see. As he makes his way back, one of the hermits explains to him the various sights he beheld and the difficulties he conquered during his outward journey. I shall not stop to unveil the allegories of this traditional Pilgrim's Progress, which is known from Brittany to Transylvania, from Iceland to Sicily. Other Breton tales exist, describing a similar journey, in all of which the miraculous lapse of time is an incident. In one the youth is sent to the sun to inquire why it is red in the morning when it rises. In another a maiden is married to a mysterious stranger, who turns out to be Death. Her brother goes to visit her, and is allowed to accompany her husband on his daily flight, in the course of which he sees a number of remarkable sights, each one of them a parable.[145]

A story is told at Glienke, near New Brandenburg, of two friends who made mutual promises to attend one another's weddings. One was married, and his friend kept his word; but before the latter's turn to marry came the married man had fallen into want, and under the pressure of need had committed robbery, a crime for which he had been hanged. Shortly afterwards his friend was about to be married; and his way a few days before, in the transaction of his business, led him past the gallows where the body still swung. As he drew near he murmured a Paternoster for the dead man, and said: "At your wedding I enjoyed myself; and you promised me to come to mine, and now you cannot come!" A voice from the gallows distinctly replied: "Yes, I will come." To the wedding feast accordingly the dead man came, with the rope round his neck, and was placed between the pastor and the sacristan. He ate and drank in silence, and departed. As he left, he beckoned the bridegroom to follow him; and when they got outside the village the hanged man said: "Thanks to your Paternoster, I am saved." They walked a little further, and the bridegroom noticed that the country was unknown to him. They were in a large and beautiful garden. "Will you not return?" asked the dead man; "they will miss you." "Oh! let me stay; it is so lovely here," replied his friend. "Know that we are in Paradise; you cannot go with me any further. Farewell!" So saying the dead man vanished. Then the bridegroom turned back; but he did not reach the village for three days. There all was changed. He asked after his bride: no one knew her. He sought the pastor and found a stranger. When he told his tale the pastor searched the church-books and discovered that a man of his name had been married one hundred and fifty years before. The bridegroom asked for food; but when he had eaten it he sank into a heap of ashes at the pastor's feet. The Transylvanian legend of "The Gravedigger in Heaven" also turns upon an invitation thoughtlessly given to a dead man and accepted. The entertainment is followed by a counter-invitation; and the gravedigger is forced to pay a return visit. He is taken to Heaven, where, among other things, he sees at intervals three leaves fall slowly one after another from off a large tree in the garden. The tree is the Tree of Life, from which a leaf falls at the end of every century. He was three hundred years in Heaven and thought it scarce an hour. The Icelandic version concerns a wicked priest. His unjust ways are reproved by a stranger who takes him to the place of joy and the place of torment, and shows him other wonderful things such as the youth in the Breton tale is permitted to behold. When he is brought back, and the stranger leaves him, he finds that he has been absent seven years, and his living is now held by another priest.[146]

Here, perhaps, is a fitting place to mention the Happy Islands of Everlasting Life as known to Japanese tradition, though the story can hardly be said to belong to the type we have just discussed,—perhaps not strictly to any of the foregoing types. A Japanese hero, the wise Vasobiove, it was who succeeded in reaching the Happy Islands, and in returning to bring sure tidings of them. For, like St. Brendan's Isle in western lore, these islands may be visible for a moment and afar off to the seafarer, but a mortal foot has hardly ever trodden them. Vasobiove, however, in his boat alone, set sail from Nagasaki, and, in spite of wind and waves, landed on the green shore of Horaisan. Two hundred years he sojourned there; yet wist he not how long the period was, there where everything remained the same, where there was neither birth nor death, where none heeded the flight of time. With dance and music, in intercourse with wise men and lovely women, his days passed away. But at length he grew weary of this sweet round of existence: he longed for death—an impossible wish in a land where death was unknown. No poison, no deadly weapons were to be found. To tumble down a chasm, or to fling oneself on sharp rocks was no more than a fall upon a soft cushion. If he would drown himself in the sea, the water refused its office, and bore him like a cork. Weary to death the poor Vasobiove could find no help. In this need a thought struck him: he caught and tamed a giant stork and taught him to carry him. On the back of this bird he returned over sea and land to his beloved Japan, bringing the news of the realm of Horaisan. His story took hold of the hearts of his fellow-countrymen; and that the story-tellers might never forget it, it has been emblazoned by the painters in a thousand ways. Nor can the stranger go anywhere in Japan without seeing the old, old man depicted on his stork and being reminded of his voyage to the Happy Islands.[147]

**FOOTNOTES:**

[123] Croker, vol. iii. p. 215. This tale is given by Sikes, p. 70, of course without any acknowledgment. It is also found in Keightley, p. 415.

[124] "Y Cymmrodor," vol. vi. pp. 174, 157, 196, 187.

[125] Howells, pp. 141, 145; Sikes, p. 73. I have not been able to trace Mr. Sikes' authority for the last story; but his experience and skill in borrowing from other books are so much greater than in oral collection that it is probably from some literary source, though no doubt many of the embellishments are his own. The foundation, however, appears to be traditional.

[126] Campbell, vol. ii. pp. 63, 55.

[127] "F. L. Journal," vol. vi. p. 191. (This story was told to the present writer and Mr. G. L. Gomme by Alderman Howel Walters, of Ystradgynlais, who had it from an old man who knew the hero well and gave implicit credit to the narrative.) "Trans. Aberd. Eistedd." p. 227; "F. L. Journal," vol. vi. p. 183. A similar tale is referred to in Jones' "Account of the Parish of Aberystruth," 1779, quoted in "Choice Notes," p. 157.

[128] "Cymru Fu," p. 177 (a translation is given by Professor Rhys in "Y Cymmrodor," vol. v. p. 81); Croker, vol. iii. p. 208.

[129] Radloff, vol. i. p. 95, vol. iv. p. 109; Sébillot, "Contes," vol. ii. p. 8; Grimm, "Tales," vol. i. p. 162.

[130] Jahn, p. 199; Grohmann, pp. 19, 20, 18.

[131] Kuhn und Schwartz, pp. 220, 222.

[132] Rappold, p. 34.

[133] "Archivio," vol. vi. p. 398.

[134] "F. L. Journal," vol. vi. p. 33; "Archivio," vol. ix. p. 233 Grohmann, p. 112.

[135] Grohmann, pp. 29, 289, 296, 298; Müller, p. 83.

[136] See Thorpe's translation of the story, "Yule Tide Stories," p. 475.

[137] Dennys, p. 98; Giles, vol. ii. pp. 89 note, 85; Brauns, p. 366.

[138] Map, Dist. i. c. 11. But see below, p. 234.

[139] Croker, vol. iii. p. 17; Howells, p. 123; "Y Cymmrodor," vol. iv. p. 196, vol. v. pp. 108, 113.

[140] "Wolfert's Roost, and other Sketches," by Washington Irving (London, 1855) p. 225; Amélineau, vol. ii. p. 111; Koran, c. 2 ("Sacred Books of the East," vol. vi. p. 41); "Masnavi i Ma'navi," p. 214.

[141] Koran, c. 18 ("Sacred Books of the East," vol. ix. p. 14); "Indian N. and Q." vol. iv. p. 8, quoting the "Pall Mall Gazette" (The story of the Seven Sleepers is also localized at N'gaous in Algeria; Certeux et Carnoy, vol. i. p. 63.) Pliny, "Nat. Hist." l. vii. c. 33.

[142] Grohmann, p. 16; Schneller, p. 217.

[143] Thorpe, vol. ii. p. 138; Birlinger, "Volkst." vol. i. p. 257 (*cf.* Bartsch, vol. i, p. 326, where there is no wedding, and curiosity is the lady's motive for venturing into the fairy cavern); "Celtic Mag." Oct. 1887, p. 566.

[144] Southey, "Doctor," p. 574; "Y Brython," vol. iii. p. 111, and Cymru Fu, p. 183; Howells, p. 127; "Y Llyvyr Coch," p. 40 (Lady Charlotte Guest's translation, p. 381); Thorpe, vol. iii. p. 297, quoting Wolf; Müller, p. 50 (*cf.* Jahn, p. 96). The reader will not fail to remark the record-book bound in pigskin as a resemblance in detail to Longfellow's version. Thorpe alludes in a note to a German poem by Wegener, which I have not seen. Nicholson, p. 58.

[145] Luzel, "Légendes Chrét." vol. i. pp. 225, 216, 247, 249; "Contes," vol. i. pp. 14, 40; *cf.* Pitré, vol. vi. p. 1; and Gonzenbach, vol. ii. p. 171, in neither of which the lapse of time is an incident. Dr. Pitré says that the tale has no analogues (*riscontri*) outside Sicily; by which I understand him to mean that it has not been hitherto found in any other Italian-speaking land.

[146] Bartsch, vol. i. p. 282; Müller, p. 46; Powell and Magnusson, vol. ii. p. 37.

[147] Brauns, p. 146.

# CHAPTER VIII

# THE SUPERNATURAL LAPSE OF TIME IN FAIRYLAND

## (continued)

Ossian in the Tir na n'Og — The Island of Happiness — The Mermaid — Thomas of Erceldoune — Olger the Dane — The Sleeping Hero — King Arthur — Don Sebastian — The expected deliverer — British variants — German variants — Frederick Barbarossa — Nameless heroes — Slavonic variants.

The stories we have hitherto considered, relating to the supernatural lapse of time in fairyland, have attributed the mortal's detention there to various motives. Compulsion on the part of the superhuman powers, and pleasure, curiosity, greed, sheer folly, as also the performance of just and willing service on the part of the mortal, have been among the causes of his entrance thither and his sojourn amid its enchantments. Human nature could hardly have been what it is if the supreme passion of love had been absent from the list. Nor is it wanting, though not found in the same plenteous measure that will meet us when we come to deal with the Swan-maiden myth—that is to say, with the group of stories concerning the capture by men of maidens of superhuman birth.

We may take as typical the story of Oisin, or Ossian, as told in Ireland. In County Clare it is said that once when he was in the full vigour of youth Oisin lay down under a tree to rest and fell asleep. Awaking with a start, he saw a lady richly clad, and of more than mortal beauty, gazing on him. She was the Queen of Tir nan'Og, the Country of Perpetual Youth. She had fallen in love with Oisin, as the strange Italian lady is said to have done with a poet of whose existence we are somewhat better assured than of Oisin's; and she invited him to accompany her to her own realm and share her throne. Oisin was not long in making up his mind, and all the delights of Tir na n'Og were laid at his feet. In one part of the palace garden, however, was a broad flat stone, on which he was forbidden to stand, under penalty of the heaviest misfortune. Probably, as is usual in these cases, if he had not been forbidden, he would never have thought of standing on it. But one day finding himself near it, the temptation to transgress was irresistible. He yielded, and stepping on the stone he found himself in full view of his native land, the very existence of which he had forgotten till that moment. Even in the short space of time since he left it much had changed: it was suffering from oppression and violence. Overcome with grief, he hastened to the queen and prayed for leave to go back, that he might help his people. The queen tried to dissuade him, but in vain. She asked him how long he supposed he had been absent. Oisin told her: "Thrice seven days." She replied that three times thrice seven years had passed since he arrived in Tir na n'Og; and though Time could not enter that land, it would immediately assert its dominion over him if he left it. At length she persuaded him to promise that he would return to his country for one day only, and then come back to dwell with her for ever. She accordingly gave him a beautiful jet-black horse, from whose back he was on no account to alight, or at all events not to allow the bridle to fall from his hand; and in parting she gifted him with wisdom and knowledge far surpassing that of men. Mounting the steed, he soon found himself near his former home; and as he journeyed he met a man driving a horse, across whose back was thrown a sack of corn. The sack had fallen a little aside; and the man asked Oisin to assist him in balancing it properly. Oisin, good-naturedly stooping, caught it and gave it such a heave that it fell over on the other side. Annoyed at his ill-success, he forgot his bride's commands, and sprang from the horse to lift the sack from the ground, letting go the bridle at the same time. Forthwith the steed vanished; and Oisin instantly became a blind, feeble, helpless old man—everything lost but the wisdom and knowledge bestowed upon him by his immortal bride.[148]

A variant adds some particulars, from which it appears that Oisin was not only husband of the queen, but also rightful monarch of Tir na n'Og. For in that land was a strange custom. The office of king was the prize of a race every seven years. Oisin's predecessor had consulted a Druid as to the length of his own tenure, and had been told that he might keep the crown for ever unless his son-in-law took it from him. Now the king's only daughter was the finest woman in Tir na n'Og, or indeed in the world; and the king naturally thought that if he could so deform his daughter that no one would wed her he would be safe. So he struck her with a rod of Druidic spells, which turned her head into a pig's head. This she was condemned to wear until she could marry one of Fin Mac Cumhail's sons in Erin. The young lady, therefore, went in search of Fin Mac Cumhail's sons; and having chosen Oisin she found an opportunity to tell him her tale, with the result that he wedded her without delay. The same moment her deformity was gone, and her beauty as perfect as before she was enchanted. Oisin returned to Tir na n'Og with her; and on the first race for the crown he won so easily that no man ever cared to dispute it with him afterwards. So he reigned for many a year, until one day the longing seized him to go to Erin and see his father and his men. His wife told him that if he set foot in Erin he would never come back to her, and he would become a blind old man; and she asked him how long he thought it was since he came to Tir na n'Og. "About three years," he replied. "It is three hundred years," she said. However, if he must go she would give him a white steed to bear him; but if he dismounted, or touched the soil of Erin with his foot, the steed would return that instant, and he would be left a poor old man. This inevitable catastrophe occurred in his eagerness to blow the great horn of the Fenians, in order to summon his friends around him. His subsequent adventures with Saint Patrick, interesting though they are, are unimportant for our present purpose.[149]

Perhaps the nearest analogue to this is the Italian Swan-maiden *märchen*, of the Island of Happiness. There a youth sets out to seek Fortune, and finds her in the shape of a maiden bathing, whose clothes he steals, obtaining possession thereby of her book of command, and so compelling her to wed him. But in his absence his mother gives her the book again, which enables her to return to her home in the Island of Happiness. Thither her husband goes to seek her, and after a variety of adventures he is reunited to her. All goes smoothly until he desires to visit his mother, supposing that he had only been in the island for two months, whereas in fact he has been there two hundred years. Fortune, finding he was bent on going, was more prudent than the queen of Tir na n'Og, for she went with him on the magic horse. In their way they met with a lean woman who had worn out a carriage-load of shoes in travelling. She feigned to fall to the ground to see if Fortune's husband would lift her up. But Fortune cried out to him: "Beware! that is Death!" A little further on they met a devil in the guise of a great lord riding a horse whose legs were worn out with much running. He also fell from his horse. This was another trap for Fortune's husband; but again she cried out to him: "Beware!" Then, having reached his own neighbourhood and satisfied himself that no one knew him, and that none even of the oldest remembered his mother, he allowed his wife to lead him back to the Island of Happiness, where he still dwells with her.[150]

In an Annamite saga a certain king wished to build a town on a site he had fixed upon. All at once a tree bearing an unknown foliage and strange flowers sprang up on the spot. It was determined to offer these flowers to the king; and sentinels were placed to see that no one plucked the blossoms. A rock still pointed out in the north of Annam was the home of a race of genii. A young and lovely maiden belonging to that race visited the tree, and was unlucky enough to touch one of the flowers and to cause it to drop. She was at once seized by the guards, but was released at the intercession of a certain mandarin. The mandarin's heart was susceptible: he fell in love with her, and, pursuing her, he was admitted into the abodes of the Immortals and received by the maiden of his dreams. His happiness continued until the day when it was his lady's turn to be in attendance on the queen of the Immortals. Ere she left him she warned him against opening the back door of the palace where they dwelt, otherwise he would be compelled to return home, and his present abode would be forbidden to him from that moment. He disobeyed her. On opening the door he beheld once more the outside world, and his family came to his remembrance. The Immortals who were within earshot drove him out, and forbade him to return. He thought he had only been there a few days, but he could no longer find his relatives. No one knew the name he asked for. At last an old man said: "There existed once, under the reign of I do not now remember what sovereign, an old mandarin of the name, but you would have some difficulty in finding him, for he has been dead three or four hundred years." An Esthonian tale represents a mermaid, the daughter of the Water-Mother, as falling in love with a loutish boy, the youngest son of a peasant, and taking him down to dwell with her as her husband in her palace beneath the waves. The form in which she appeared to him was a woman's; but she passed her Thursdays in seclusion, which she forbade him to break, enjoining him, moreover, never to call her Mermaid. After little more than a year, however, he grew curious and jealous, and yielded to the temptation of peeping through the curtain of her chamber, where he beheld her swimming about, half woman and half fish. He had broken the condition of his happiness, and might no longer stay with her. Wherefore he was cast up again on the shore where he had first met the mermaid. Rising and going into the village he inquired for his parents, but found that they had been dead for more than thirty years, and that his brothers were dead too. He himself was unconsciously changed into an old man. For a few days he wandered about the shore, and the charitable gave him bread. He ventured to tell his history to one kind friend; but the same night he disappeared, and in a few days the waves cast up his body on the beach.[151]

The foregoing tales all combine with the characteristics of the group under discussion, either those of the Swan-maiden group or those of the Forbidden Chamber group. In the myth of the Swan-maidens, as in some types of the myth of the Forbidden Chamber, the human hero weds a supernatural bride; and a story containing such an incident seems to have a tendency to unite itself to one or other of these two groups. This tendency is not, however, always developed. The two ladies in the Chinese legend, cited in the last chapter, were neither Swan-maidens nor female Bluebeards; and this is not the only tale from the Flowery Land in which these superhuman beauties appear without promoting the development in question. Nor do I find any hint of it in the tradition of Bran Mac Fearbhall, King of Ireland, who was one day lulled asleep by a strain of fairy music. On awaking he found the silver branch of a tree by his side; and a strange lady appeared at his court and invited him to a land of happiness. He handed her the silver branch; and the next morning with a company of thirty persons he sailed out on the ocean. In a few days they landed on an island inhabited only by women, of whom the strange lady appeared to be the chieftainess. Here Bran Mac Fearbhall remained several ages before returning to his own palace near Lough Foyle. An Arab tale in the Bibliothèque Nationale at Paris shows us a king's son who in his wanderings lands on a strange island, where he marries the king's daughter and becomes his father-in-law's vizier. The country was watered by a river which flowed at certain seasons from a great mountain. Every year it was the vizier's duty to enter the cavern, having first received instructions from the king and a mysterious gift. At the end of an hour he reappeared, followed by the stream, which continued to flow during the time needful for the fertilization of the country. When the prince as vizier entered the cavern he found a negro, who led him to his mistress, the queen of a people of Amazons. In her hands was the management of the river; and she had caused the periodical drought in order to exact a tribute of date-stones which she had to pass on to an Ifrit, to purchase his forbearance towards her own subjects. The prince ingratiates himself with her: she suppresses the periodical droughts and marries him. After two centuries of wedded life she dies, leaving him ten daughters, whom he takes back, together with considerable wealth, to the city formerly governed by his father-in-law, and now by his great-great-grandson. The latter was a hundred years old, and venerable by the side of his great-great-grandfather, over whose head the years had passed in that enchanted realm without effect. He made himself known to his descendant and stayed ten years with him; but whether he succeeded in marrying off any of his daughters, of ages so very uncertain, the abstract of the story I have before me does not say. At last he returned to his native land, and reigned there for a long time.[152]

In the hero of the Island of Happiness we found just now one who, having returned to earth for a season, had been taken back again by his supernatural spouse to a more lasting enjoyment. But he is not alone in his good fortune. Thomas of Erceldoune, a personage less shadowy than some of those commemorated in this chapter, is known to have lived in the thirteenth century. His reputation for prophetic powers has been wide and lasting. These powers were said to be, like Oisin's, a gift from the Fairy Queen. She met him under the Eildon Tree, which stood on the easternmost of the three Eildon Hills. Having got him into her power, she took him down with her into Fairyland, where he abode, as he deemed, for three days, but in reality for three years. At the end of that time the lady carries him back to Eildon Tree and bids him farewell. He asks her for some token whereby he may say that he had been with her; and she bestows on him a prophetic tongue that cannot lie, and leaves him with a promise to meet him again on Huntley Banks. Here both the old ballads and the older romance desert us; but if we may trust Sir Walter Scott's report of the tradition current in the neighbourhood, Thomas was under an obligation to return to Fairyland whenever he was summoned. "Accordingly, while Thomas was making merry with his friends in the tower of Ercildoune, a person came running in, and told, with marks of fear and astonishment, that a hart and hind had left the neighbouring forest, and were, composedly and slowly, parading the street of the village. The prophet instantly arose, left his habitation, and followed the wonderful animals to the forest, whence he was never seen to return. According to the popular belief, he still 'drees his weird' in Fairyland, and is one day expected to revisit earth. In the meanwhile his memory is held in the most profound respect."[153]

In the romance of Ogier, or Olger, the Dane, one of the Paladins of Charlemagne, it is related that six fairies presided at his birth and bestowed various gifts upon him. Morgan the Fay, the last of the six, promised that after a long and glorious career he should never die, but dwell with her in her castle of Avalon. Wherefore, after he had lived and fought and loved for more than a hundred years, Morgan caused him to be shipwrecked. All men thought he had perished. In reality Morgan had taken this means of bringing him to Avalon, where she met him and put a ring on his finger, which restored him to youth, and a golden crown of myrtle and laurel on his brow—the crown of forgetfulness. His toils, his battles, even his loves were forgotten; and his heart was filled with a new devotion, namely, for the fairy queen Morgan. With her he dwelt in pleasures ever new for two hundred years, until there came a day when France and Christendom fell into trouble and danger, and the peoples cried out for a deliverer. Morgan heard them, and resolved that Olger must go to fight for them. She lifted the crown from his brow, and his memory came back. She bade him guard well his ring, and gave him a torch: if that torch were lighted his life would burn out with the last spark. He returned to France, fought the Paynim and conquered, freeing France and Christendom. The widowed queen of France then intrigued to marry him; but as she was on the point of attaining her purpose Morgan appeared and caught him away. In Avalon he still dreams in her arms; and some day when France is in her direst need, Olger will come back on his famous charger to smite and to deliver her.

Here we come upon another type, the story and the superstition of the expected deliverer, which is widely scattered through Europe. In this country the most noted example is that of King Arthur, who may fitly give his name to the type. King Arthur, according to the romances, is, like Olger, in the Island of Avalon, where indeed the romance of Olger declares that the two heroes met. Sir Thomas Malory tells us: "Some men yet say in many parts of England that King Arthur is not dead, but had by the will of our Lord Jesus Christ into another place; and men say that hee will come againe, and he shall winne the holy crosse. I will not say that it shall bee so, but rather I will say that heere in this world hee changed his life. But many men say that there is written upon his tombe this verse: Hic jacet Arthurus, rex quondam, rexque futurus." This is a belief dear to the heart of many an oppressed people. It was told of Harold that he was not slain at Senlac, and that he would yet come back to lead his countrymen against the hated Normans. Even of Roderick, the Last of the Goths, deeply stained as he was with crime, men were loth to believe that he was dead. In the latter part of the sixteenth century, after Don Sebastian had fallen in the ill-fated expedition to Morocco, Philip the Second of Spain took advantage of the failure of the male line on the death of the cardinal-king, Henry, to add Portugal to his dominions, already too large. His tyranny roused a popular party whose faith was that Don Sebastian was not really dead: he was reigning in the Island of the Seven Cities, and he would return by and by to drive out the Spaniards and their justly execrated king. Even in the year 1761 a monk was condemned by the Inquisition as a Sebastianist, a believer and a disseminator of false prophecies,—so long did the tradition linger. In the Spanish peninsula, indeed, the superstition has been by no means confined to Christians. The Moors who were left in the mountains of Valentia looked for the return of their hero Alfatimi upon a green horse, from his place of concealment in the Sierra de Aguar, to defend them and to put their Catholic tyrants to the sword.[154]

Oppression nourishes beliefs of this kind. It was under the Roman dominion that the Jewish expectation of a Messiah grew to its utmost strength; and the manifestation of the Messiah was to be preceded by the reappearance of Elijah, a prophet who was not dead but translated to heaven. And strange sometimes are the gods from whom salvation is to come. Only a few years ago, if we may trust Bishop Melchisedech of Roumania, there was a Slavonic sect, the object of whose worship was Napoleon the First. He, said his worshippers, had not really died; he was only at Irkousk, in Siberia, where, at the head of a powerful, an invincible, army, he was ready once more to overrun the world.[155]

But, however the belief in a deity, or hero, who is to return some day, may be strengthened by political causes, it is not dependent upon them. Many races having traditions of a Culture God—that is, of a superior being who has taught them agriculture and the arts of life, and led them to victory over their enemies—add that he has gone away from them for awhile, and that he will some day come back again. Quetzalcoatl and Viracocha, the culture gods of Mexico and Peru, are familiar instances of this. In the later Brahminism of India, Vishnu, having already accomplished nine avatars, or incarnations, for special emergencies in the past, was yet to have one more avatar for the final destruction of the wicked and the restoration of goodness at the end of the present age; he would then be revealed in the sky seated on a white horse and wielding a blazing sword. I need not specify others: it will be manifest that the traditions of modern Europe we have been considering contain the same thought. Nor is it unlikely that they have been influenced by the Christian doctrine of the Second Advent. Many of them have received the polish of literature. The stories of Olger and Arthur, for example, have descended to us as romances written by cultivated men. Don Sebastian was the plaything of a political party, if not the symbol of religious heresy, for nearly two centuries. In all these stories we encounter the belief that the god or hero is in heaven, or in some remote land. Such a belief is the sign of a civilization comparatively advanced. The cruder and more archaic belief is that he sleeps within the hills.

This cruder belief is more familiar in the folklore of Europe than the other. King Arthur was believed to lie with his warriors beneath the Craig-y-Ddinas (Castle Rock) in the Vale of Neath. Iolo Morganwg, a well-known Welsh antiquary, used to relate a curious tradition concerning this rock. A Welshman, it was said, walking over London Bridge with a hazel staff in his hand, was met by an Englishman, who told him that the stick he carried grew on a spot under which were hidden vast treasures, and if the Welshman remembered the place and would show it to him he would put him in possession of those treasures. After some demur the Welshman consented, and took the Englishman (who was in fact a wizard) to the Craig-y-Ddinas and showed him the spot. They dug up the hazel tree on which the staff grew and found under it a broad flat stone. This covered the entrance to a cavern in which thousands of warriors lay in a circle sleeping on their arms. In the centre of the entrance hung a bell which the conjurer begged the Welshman to beware of touching. But if at any time he did touch it and any of the warriors should ask if it were day, he was to answer without hesitation: "No; sleep thou on." The warriors' arms were so brightly polished that they illumined the whole cavern; and one of them had arms that outshone the rest, and a crown of gold lay by his side. This was Arthur; and when the Welshman had taken as much as he could carry of the gold which lay in a heap amid the warriors, both men passed out; not, however, without the Welshman's accidentally touching the bell. It rang; but when the inquiry: "Is it day?" came from one of the warriors, he was prompt with the reply: "No; sleep thou on." The conjurer afterwards told him that the company he had seen lay asleep ready for the dawn of the day when the Black Eagle and the Golden Eagle should go to war, the clamour of which would make the earth tremble so much that the bell would ring loudly and the warriors would start up, seize their arms, and destroy the enemies of the Cymry, who should then repossess the island of Britain and be governed from Caerlleon with justice and peace so long as the world endured. When the Welshman's treasure was all spent he went back to the cavern and helped himself still more liberally than before. On his way out he touched the bell again: again it rang. But this time he was not so ready with his answer, and some of the warriors rose up, took the gold from him, beat him and cast him out of the cave. He never recovered the effects of that beating, but remained a cripple and a pauper to the end of his days; and he never could find the entrance to the cavern again. Merlin and the charm

"Of woven paces and of waving hands"

I need not do more than mention. A recess in the rock three miles eastward of Carmarthen, called Merlin's Cave, is generally accredited as the place where Vivien perpetrated her treachery. Merlin's county is possessed of another enchanted hero. On the northern side of Mynydd Mawr (the Great Mountain) near Llandilo, is a cave where Owen Lawgoch (Owen of the Red Hand), one of the last chieftains who fought against the English, lies with his men asleep. And there they will lie until awakened by the sound of a trumpet and the clang of arms on Rhywgoch, when they will arise and conquer their Saxon foes, driving them from the land. A more famous chieftain is the subject of a similar belief in the Vale of Gwent. Considerable obscurity overhangs the fate of Owen Glendower. What is certain about him is that he disappeared from history in the year 1415. What is believed in the Vale of Gwent is that he and his men still live and lie asleep on their arms in a cave there, called "Gogov y Ddinas," or Castle Cave, where they will continue until England become self-debased; but that then they will sally forth to reconquer their country, privileges, and crown for the Welsh, who shall be dispossessed of them no more until the Day of Judgment.[156]

In other Celtic lands the same superstition occurs. There is a hole called the Devil's Den at the foot of a mountain in the Isle of Man where it was believed in the last century that a great prince who never knew death had been bound by spells for six hundred years; but none had ever had courage enough to explore the hole. In Sutherlandshire it is said that a man once entered a cave and there found many huge men all asleep on the floor. They rested on their elbows. In the centre of the hall was a stone table, and on it lay a bugle. The man put the bugle to his lips and blew once. They all stirred. He blew a second blast, and one of the giants, rubbing his eyes, said: "Do not do that again, or you will wake us!" The intruder fled in terror, and never found the mouth of the cavern again. Earl Gerald of Mullaghmast sleeps with his warriors in a cavern under the castle, or Rath, of Mullaghmast. A long table runs down the middle of the cave. The Earl sits at the head, and his troopers in complete armour on either side, their heads resting on the table. Their horses, saddled and bridled, stand behind their masters in stalls on either side. The Earl was a leader of the Irish; he was very skilful at weapons, and deep in the black art. He could change himself into any shape he pleased. His lady was always begging him to let her see him in some strange shape; but he always put her off, for he told her that if during his transformation she showed the least fright he would not recover his natural form till many generations of men were under the mould. Nothing, however, would do for the lady but an exhibition of his powers; so one evening he changed himself into a goldfinch. While he was playing with her in this form a hawk caught sight of him and pursued him. The hawk dashed itself against a table and was killed; but the lady had given a loud scream at seeing her husband's danger, and neither goldfinch nor Earl did she behold again. Once in seven years the Earl rides round the Curragh of Kildare on a horse whose silver shoes were half an inch thick when he disappeared. When they are worn as thin as a cat's ear, a miller's son, who is to be born with six fingers on each hand, will blow his trumpet, the troopers will awake and mount their horses and with the Earl go forth to battle against the English; and he will reign King of Ireland for twoscore years. A horse-dealer once found the lighted cavern open on the night the Earl was riding round the Curragh and went in. In his astonishment at what he saw he dropped a bridle on the ground. The sound of its fall echoing in the recesses of the cave aroused one of the warriors nearest to him; and he lifted up his head and asked: "Is it time yet?" The man had the wit to say: "Not yet, but soon will;" and the heavy helmet sank down once more upon the table, while the man made the best of his way out. On Rathlin Island there is a ruin called Bruce's Castle. In a cave beneath lie Bruce and his chief warriors in an enchanted sleep; but some day they will arise and unite the island to Scotland. Only once in seven years the entrance to the cave is visible. A man discovered it on one of these occasions, and went in. He found himself in the presence of these men in armour. A sabre was half-sheathed in the earth at his feet. He tried to draw it, but every one of the sleepers lifted his head and put his hand on his sword. The intruder fled; but ere the gate of the cavern clanged behind him he heard voices calling fiercely after him: "Why could we not be left to sleep?"[157]

The population of the south and west of Yorkshire is largely Celtic. A tradition of Arthur seems to have been preserved among them to the effect that he and his knights sit spell-bound in the ruins of a castle, believed by the clergyman who communicated it to Mr. Alfred Nutt to be Richmond Castle. Wherever it was, a man named Potter Thompson penetrated by chance into the hall, and found them sitting around a table whereon lay a sword and a horn. The man did not venture, like the Sutherlandshire intruder, to blow the horn, but turned and fled at once. There, it seems, he made a mistake; for had he done so he would have released Arthur from the spell. And as he crossed the threshold again a voice sounded in his ears:—

"Potter Thompson, Potter Thompson, hadst thou blown the horn, Thou hadst been the greatest man that ever was born."

He had missed his chance, and could not return into the enchanted hall. By the twelfth century the legend of Arthur had reached Sicily, perhaps with the Normans. Gervase of Tilbury tells us that a boy was in charge of the Bishop of

Catania's palfrey, when it broke loose and ran away. He pursued it boldly into the dark recesses of Mount Etna, where, on a wide plain full of all delights, he found Arthur stretched on a royal couch in a palace built with wonderful skill. Having explained what brought him thither, the hero caused the horse to be given up to him, and added gifts which were afterwards beheld with astonishment by many. Arthur informed him, moreover, that he had been compelled to remain there on account of his wound, which broke out afresh every year.[158]

In Teutonic lands the legends of the sleeping host and the sleeping monarch are very numerous. Grimm in his Mythology has collected many of them. I select for mention a few only, adding one or two not included by him. Karl the Great lies in the Unterberg, near Salzburg, and also in the Odenberg, where Woden himself, according to other legends, is said to be. Siegfried, the hero of the Nibelungen Lied, dwells in the mountain fastness of Geroldseck. Diedrich rests in the mountains of Alsace, his hand upon his sword, waiting till the Turk shall water his horses on the banks of the Rhine. On the Grütli, where once they met to swear the oath which freed their country, lie the three founders of the Swiss Federation in a cleft of the rock. The Danes have appropriated Olger, who, Grimm says, really belongs to the Ardennes; and in a vaulted chamber under the castle of Kronburg he sits, with a number of warriors clad in mail, about a stone table, into which his beard has grown. A slave who was condemned to death received pardon and freedom on condition of descending to ascertain what was beneath the castle; for at that time no one knew, and no one could explain the clashing of armour sometimes heard below. He passed through an iron doorway and found himself in the presence of Olger and his men. Their heads rested on their arms, which were crossed upon the table. When Olger lifted up his head the table burst asunder. "Reach me thy hand," he said to the slave; but the latter, not venturing to give his hand, held out an iron bar instead, which Olger squeezed so that the marks remained visible. At length letting it go, he exclaimed: "It gladdens me that there are still men in Denmark!"[159]

But of all the great names appropriated by this myth, the one which has thus been made most famous is that of Frederick Barbarossa. When he was drowned in crossing the river Calycadmus in Asia Minor, the peasants of Germany refused to believe in his death, and constantly expected him to return. Poems which go back to the middle of the fourteenth century, or within a century and a half of Frederick's death, prove the existence of a tradition to this effect. More than this, they contain allusions to some of the details about to be mentioned, and foretell his recovery of the Holy Sepulchre. The Kyffhäuser in Thuringia is the mountain usually pointed out as his place of retreat, though other places also claim the honour. Within the cavern he sits at a stone table, and rests his head upon his hand. His beard grows round the table: twice already has it made the circuit; when it has grown round the third time the emperor will awake. He will then come forth, and will hang his shield on a withered tree which will break into leaf, and a better time will dawn. Gorgeous descriptions are given of the cavern. It is radiant with gold and jewels; and though it is a cavern deep in the earth, it shines within like the sunniest day. The most splendid trees and shrubs stand there, and through the midst of this Paradise flows a brook whose very mud is pure gold. Here the emperor's rest is not so profound as might have been expected. A strain of music easily seems to rouse him. A shepherd having once piped to him, Frederick asked: "Fly the ravens round the mountain still?" "Yes," replied the shepherd. "Then must I sleep another hundred years," murmured the emperor. The shepherd was taken into the armoury, and rewarded with the stand of a hand-basin, which turned out to be of pure gold. A party of musicians on their way home from a wedding passed that way, and played a tune "for the old Emperor Frederick." Thereupon a maiden stepped out, and brought them the emperor's thanks, presenting each of them with a horse's head by way of remembrance. All but one threw the gift away in contempt. One, however, kept his "to have a joke with his old woman," as he phrased it, and taking it home he put it under the pillow. In the morning, when his wife turned up the pillow to look at it, instead of a horse's head she brought forth a lump of gold. Other stories are told of persons who have penetrated into the emperor's presence and been enriched. A shepherd found the mountain open on St. John's Day, and entered. He was allowed to take some of the horse-meal, which when he reached home he found to be gold. Women have been given knots of flax, of the same metal. A swineherd, however, who went in, was less lucky. The emperor's lady-housekeeper made signs to him that he might take some of the treasure on the table before him; accordingly he stuffed his pockets full. As he turned to go out she called after him: "Forget not the best!" She meant a flower which lay on the table; but he heeded not, and the mountain, slamming behind him, cut off his heel, so that he died in great pain.[160]

Such are a few of the legends relating to the Kyffhäuser; but it should be observed that Frederick Barbarossa's is not the only name given to the slumbering hero. We have already seen in the last chapter that one tradition calls him the Marquis John. Another dubs him the Emperor Otto; and yet in another Dame Holle is identified with his housekeeper. Now this difference in the traditions about names, while they agree in the substance of the superstition, indicates that the substance is older and more important than the names, and that well-known names have become affixed to the traditions as they happened from time to time to strike the popular imagination. This is confirmed by the fact that in many places where similar traditions are located, no personal name at all is given to the hero. In the Guckenberg, near Fränkischgemünden, *an emperor* disappeared a long time ago with his army. A boy selling rolls once met an old man, to whom he complained of bad trade. The old man said he could show him a place where he could bring his rolls every day; but he must tell no one thereof. So saying, he led the boy into the mountain, where there were many people. The emperor himself sat at a table, round which his beard had grown twice: when it has grown round it once more he will come forth again with all his men. The boy's rolls were bought; and he daily repeated his visit. After a while, however, he could not pass the ancient coin wherein he was paid. The people in the village, grown suspicious, made him confess all; and he could never find his way to the mountain again. In the "Auersperg Chronicle," under the year 1223, it is recorded that from a certain mountain which Grimm identifies with the Donnersberg (Thor's mountain), near Worms, a multitude of armed horsemen used daily to issue, and thither daily to return. A man, who armed himself with the sign of the cross, and questioned one of the host in the name of Our Lord, was told by him: "We are not, as you think, phantoms, nor, as we seem, a band of soldiers, but the souls of slain soldiers. The arms and clothing, and horses, because they once were the instruments of sin, are now to us the materials of our punishment; for what you behold upon us is really on fire, although you cannot perceive it with your bodily eyes." We saw in an earlier chapter that a story influenced by the Welsh Methodist revival represented the midwife whose sight was cleared by fairy ointment as beholding herself surrounded by flames, and the fairies about her in the guise of devils. In the same way here the wonders recorded by a pious ecclesiastic have taken, though possibly not in the first instance from him, a strictly orthodox form, and one calculated to point a pulpit moral.[161]

Over against the last two legends we may place two from Upper Alsace. A body of the Emperor Karl the Great's warriors had become so puffed up by their successes that at last they pointed their guns and cannon against heaven itself. Scarcely had they discharged their pieces when the whole host sank into the earth. Every seventh year they may be seen by night on their horses, exercising. Concerning them it is said that a baker's daughter of Ruffach, in the Ochsenfeld valley, was carrying white bread to the next village, when she met a soldier on a white horse who offered to lead her to a place where she could sell the bread immediately for a good price. She accordingly followed him through a subterranean passage into a great camp quite full of long-bearded soldiers, who were all fast asleep. Here she sold all her bread, and was well paid; and for several years she continued daily to sell her bread there, so that her father became a rich man. One day she was ill and unable to go, whereupon she sent her brother, describing the place to him. He found it, but a door blocked up the passage, and he could not open it. The girl died soon after, and since then no one has entered the subterranean camp. From Bütow in Pomerania comes a saga similar to that of Olger at Kronburg. A mountain in the neighbourhood is held to be an enchanted castle, communicating by an underground passage with the castle of Bütow. A criminal was once offered his choice whether to die by the hangman, or to make his way by the passage in question to the enchanted castle, and bring back a written proof from the lord who sat enchanted within it. He succeeded in his mission; and the document he brought back is believed to be laid up among the archives of the town. According to another account a man once met two women who led him into the mountain, where he found a populous city. They brought him safely back after he had spent six hours within the mountain. A saga referred to by Grimm relates how a shepherd found in the cavern of the Willberg *a little man* sitting at a stone table through which his beard had grown; and in another three unnamed malefactors are spoken of. In Sweden there is a story that may remind us of the Sutherlandshire legend. In a large cleft of the mountain of

Billingen, in West Gothland, called the Giant's Path, it is said there was formerly a way leading far into the mountain, into which a peasant once penetrated, and found a man lying asleep on a large stone. No one knows how he came there; but every time the bell tolls for prayers in Yglunda church, he turns round and sighs. So he will continue until Doomsday.[162] In none of these stories is the hero identified with any known historical person.

Among the Slavonic peoples corresponding sagas are told. In Servia and Bulgaria King Marko is the enchanted hero. He is variously held to be in a palace on some mysterious island, or in a mountain not far from the Iron Gates. The traveller who crosses the mountain calls to him: "Marko, dost thou live?" and in the echo he believes that Marko gives him a reply. "Prince" Marko is also believed by the Serbs to be in the mountain Urvina with his horse Sharatz, asleep. His sword is rising slowly out of the mountain. When it is fully disclosed, Marko will awake and deliver his people. If other accounts may be trusted, however, he has retired to the Alps since the invention of gunpowder, and now lives as a hermit in a cave. So great pity was it

"This villainous saltpetre should be digg'd
Out of the bowels of the harmless earth."[163]

The Carpathian hero is Dobocz, the robber chief. He is bespelled by a jealous mistress in a cavern on the Czornahora, where he perpetually counts the gold he has hidden. On certain days of the year he comes out with his followers; and then he has often been seen by the mountaineers. Sometimes he visits his wife in her rock-dwelling by Polansko, where she too is enchanted; and on such occasions the nightly festivities may be seen and heard. Bold are they who endeavour to penetrate the depths of the mountain where Dobocz dwells. They never return, but are caught by the robber and added to his band. Strengthened with these reinforcements his companions will be with him when the charm shall one day be broken, and he will issue forth to take vengeance on the men who betrayed him. Some of the stories of Blanik Mountain, where Wenzel, the king of Bohemia, lies, have been set before the reader. The horses of himself and his followers stand ever ready saddled; and at midnight the mountain opens, and the king and his knights ride forth to exercise upon the plain. But other heroes than Wenzel dispute with him the honour of being the enchanted inhabitant of the Blanik. One clear moonlight night of spring the burgesses of Jung-Wositz were aroused from their slumbers by the beating of drums, and the clang of armour, and the trampling of horses. Terrified at such a rout, and not knowing what it might mean, they seized their weapons and stood on the defensive. Nor were they a little surprised to see on the open meadows a troop of horsemen engaged in knightly play. By and by, at the sound of the kettledrum, the troop formed into rank, and vanished into the mountain, which closed behind them with a crash. The burgesses offered a reward to whomsoever would explore the recesses of the mountain, and bring them sure tidings of the ghostly horsemen. Three years passed by ere the task was attempted. At last a clever man, Zdenko von Zasmuk, undertook the adventure. He was lucky enough to find the mountain open; and riding in, he came into a vast lighted hall where slept on stone benches the knights of the mountain, now changed into fine old men with long white beards. Their snow-white horses, ready saddled, stood fastened to the piers of the vault. Zdenko accidentally knocked down a spear; and the clangour, echoing round the hall, awakened the men. He explained to them why he had come, and politely offered, if they wished, to attempt their deliverance. Their leader informed him in reply that he was Ulrich von Rosenberg, that he with his companions had fallen gloriously against Chichka, in defence of the city of Litic, and that God, instead of admitting them into Paradise, had assigned them an abode in that place until Bohemia should be at its sorest need; then they would sally forth, and bring back peace and happiness to the land. And he enjoined Zdenko to make this known to the people. So saying, he sank again to sleep. It is said, moreover, that when the time of which Ulrich spoke shall come, a certain hazel-tree shall begin to blossom, though it will be winter. A quite different story alleges that it is the Knight Stoymir, who is under the spell at Blanik. His last struggle against the plundering hordes which overran the country took place there; and he with all his band perished. The next morning when the enemy had departed his friends searched the battlefield, but not a trace could be recovered of their bodies. It was first thought that the foes had carried them off to be ransomed. At night, however, the inhabitants of the neighbourhood were roused from slumber by the noise of a host; and they beheld the slain heroes exercising and afterwards watering their horses at the beck before they returned to the mountain. The herdsman who told the foregoing tale declared that he had been into the mountain, and had himself seen Stoymir and his companions in their sleep. There can be no doubt, therefore, of its truth.[164]

Legends of buried armies occur also at Trzebnica, in Silesia, where the Poles encountered the Turks, and at Matwa in the Prussian province of Posen. In the former a girl who is admitted into the cavern is warned against touching a bell that, as in the Welsh tale, hangs in the entrance. She cannot resist the temptation to transgress this command, and is ignominiously ejected. In the latter, an old man buys corn for the troops. Again, in the Carpathians, as in one of the sagas concerning the Blanik, a smith is summoned to shoe the steeds. The Rev. W. S. Lach-Szyrma, in addition to these stories, gave the Folklore Society some years ago, from a chap-book of Posen, the following abstract of a legend I have not met with elsewhere: "Once upon a time, in Mazowia, there were seven victorious leaders. After having won a hundred battles, finding their beards had grown white, they ordered their soldiers to build in their honour a very high tower. The soldiers built and built, but every day part of the tower tumbled down. This lasted a whole year. The leaders, after supper, assembled at the ruins of the tower. Here, at the sound of lutes and songs, immediately a tower grew up from the earth to heaven, and on its seven pinnacles shone the seven helmets of the seven leaders. Higher and higher they rose, but brighter and brighter they shone till they appeared as the seven stars in heaven. The soldiers sank down into graves which had been dug round the tower and fell asleep. The tower has melted out of view, but on fine nights we still see the seven helmets of the leaders, and the soldiers are sleeping till they are wanted."[165]

**FOOTNOTES:**

[148] "Choice Notes," p. 94.

[149] Curtin, p. 327. See also Kennedy, p. 240, and "F. L. Record," vol. ii. p. 15, where the late Mr. H. C. Coote quotes the "Transactions of the Ossianic Society."

[150] Comparetti, vol. i. p. 212. An English version is given by Mr. Coote, "F. L. Record," vol. ii. p. 12. Madame D'Aulnoy gives a similar story in her "Histoire d'Hypolite, Comte de Douglas," which seems to be the original of a tale in verse quoted by Mr. Baring-Gould from Dodsley's "Poetical Collection." See "F. L. Record," vol. ii. p. 8; Baring-Gould, p. 547.

[151] Des Michels, p. 38; Kreutzwald, p. 212. See also my article on "The Forbidden Chamber," "F. L. Journal," vol. iii. p. 193, where the relations of the Esthonian tale to the myth of the Forbidden Chamber are discussed.

[152] Dennys, p. 98, "Gent. Mag. Lib." (Eng. Trad. Lore), p. 22; "Revue des Trad. Pop." vol. iii. p. 566.

[153] "Thomas of Erceldoune," *passim*; Child, vol. i. p. 318; "Border Minstrelsy," vol. iii. p. 170.

[154] Malory, vol. iii. p. 339; Braga, vol. ii. p. 238; Liebrecht in a note to Gerv. Tilb., p. 95, quoting Aznar, "Expulsion de los Moriscos."

[155] "Athenæum," No. 2,400, 25 Oct. 1873, giving an account of Bishop Melchisedech's book, entitled "Lipovenismulu," on the creed and customs of the Raskolnics, or Russian schismatics.

[156] "Trans. Aberd. Eistedd.," p. 227, quoting Waring's "Recollections of Iolo Morganwg"; Black's "Picturesque Guide to Wales" (1872), p. 279; Howells, p. 104; "Iolo MSS." (Llandovery, 1848), pp. 68, 454, quoting from papers attributed to the Rev. Evan Evans, and said to be, when copied by Iolo Morganwg, in the possession of Paul Panton, Esq., of Anglesea.

[157] Waldron, p. 68; "F. L. Journal," vol. vi. p. 164; Kennedy, p. 172, Lady Wilde, vol. i. p. 161.

[158] "F. L. Journal," vol. i. p. 193; Gerv. Tilb., Dec. ii. c. 12. See Mr. Nutt's remarks on these in his admirable "Studies on the Legend of the Holy Grail" (London, 1888), pp. 123, 196.

[159] Grimm, "Teut. Myth." pp. 953, 955, 961; Thorpe, vol. ii. p. 222, translating Thiele; Certeux et Carnoy, vol. i. p. 65.

[160] Grimm, "Teut. Myth.," p. 955; Kuhn und Schwartz, p. 217. See also Thorpe, vol. iii. p. 101, translating Kuhn und Schwartz, and Grimm.

[161] Kuhn und Schwartz, pp. 220, 222; Grimm, "Teut. Myth." pp. 953, 954.

[162] Meier, pp. 122, 123; Jahn, p. 248; Grimm, "Teut. Myth." p. 961; Thorpe, vol. ii. p. 91, from Afzelius. In an Austrian *märchen* the Sleeping Host is a host of serpents. The king slept on a crystal table in the centre. During the winter serpents are believed to sleep. In the spring the oldest serpent awakes and wakens the others, crying: "It is time" (Vernaleken, p. 113).

[163] Grohmann, p. 10. Marko was a shepherd, who for a service rendered to a Vila was gifted by her with heroism, beauty, and other good fortune (Krauss, "Volksgl." p. 103).

[164] Grohmann, pp. 11, 13, 15.

[165] "F. L. Record," vol. iv. p. 67. Mr. Lach-Szyrma conjectures that the seven stars are the stars of *Ursa Major*.

# CHAPTER IX

# THE SUPERNATURAL LAPSE OF TIME IN FAIRYLAND

## (continued)

The story not an early one — Its weirdest developments European — Stories of short time appearing long — Mohammed's night-journey and its variants — The Sleeping Hero, a heathen god — The Wild Hunt — The Enchanted Princess, a heathen goddess.

The visits to Fairyland recorded in Chapter VII differ only in one respect from those mentioned in earlier chapters of this book. Like them, they are visits of business or of pleasure. Mortals are summoned to perform some service for the mysterious beings whose dwelling is beneath the earth, such as to stand sponsor to their children, or to shoe their horses; or they go to take a message from this world, or to bring a message back. Or else they are drawn into the regions over which the power of the supernatural extends, by curiosity, by the desire of pleasure, or else by the invitation, or unconsciously by the spell, of their superhuman inhabitants. The point at which the visits differ from those we have previously considered, and from a hundred others precisely parallel in all other respects, is in their length. To the entrammelled mortal the visit seems to last but a moment; for while under the fairy sway he is unconscious of the flight of time. In other stories deception is practised on the sight. The midwife, without the ointment, is deceived like Thor by Utgard-Loki: nothing is as it appears to her. Parents and husbands are deceived by changelings: they are made to believe that images of dead wood are living creatures, or human corpses. In these stories, on the other hand, the magic is directed against the sense of time. A subtler, a weirder, a more awful horror is thus added to the dread of communion with the supernatural.

This horror is one arising comparatively late in the history of culture. The idea of time must first grow up and be elaborated. Time is dependent on number. A savage who can barely count beyond five cannot know anything of stories which deal with the lapse of centuries. Even the vaguer, but shorter, period of a generation will be an idea he cannot grasp. We have therefore found no such tales in the lower savagery; and even among the Lapplanders and the Siberian tribes the stories we have been able to collect speak only of short periods, such as the transition from autumn to spring, where a man had slept through the winter, and the expansion of a day into a month, or a year. In these two cases not only the phases of the moon and the measurement of time by them, which must have been early in development, but also the cycle of the seasons had been observed. But the idea lying at the root of this group of tales is as yet only in germ. The full terror of the situation, as exhibited in the traditions of the more highly organized societies of Europe and of the extreme Orient, is unforeseen. For it is in proportion to the organization of society that such a catastrophe as the loss of years, and thereby of kindred and friends, becomes really dreadful. Indeed, it would seem to have been reserved for the European nations to put the final touches of gloom and horror upon the canvas. It may be sufficient to refer this to the more sombre imagination of Western peoples. But we ought not to overlook the influence of the Catholic Church in darkening the general tone of the imagination, and particularly the tone of the fairy sagas, by the absolute and unquestioned supremacy she demanded, and the frightful penalties, temporal and spiritual, she invoked upon those who dared to indulge in cults she was unable to incorporate. To men under such an influence, intercourse with fairies would be a thing unholy; and the greater the temptations to it, the severer, they would deem, should be the penalties. This is the frame of mind which would, if with shuddering, yet without a murmur, acquiesce in the justice of the doom suffered by Herla, to put an extreme case—a frame of mind undoubtedly countenanced by the equally uncompromising claims of various forms of Protestantism. But, while reprobating commerce with unhallowed spirits, intercourse with spirits sanctioned by the Church was believed to be almost equally possible, and was encouraged as much as the other was denounced. If such intercourse sometimes resulted in severance between the favoured mortal and his human friends, this was only an extension of the monastic idea; and, as in that case, the loss was held to be abundantly compensated by the favour of Heaven and the bliss received. At all events it is certain, from whatever cause, that the deepest depths and the loftiest heights of which this story-plot has been found capable, have been reached only under Christian influences. Pliny and Mohammed, the Taoist and the Shintoist, have recorded no tale that sways our emotions like those of Herla, the Aged Bride, and the Monk Felix.

But the magical power over time operates now and then in the contrary way, by making a short time appear long. A few examples may be interesting, though they will in no way affect the foregoing conclusions. In the tenth part of a night Mohammed, it will be remembered, was taken up to Paradise on the back of the beast Alborac, and passed through all the seven heavens into the presence of Allah himself, with whom he had a conversation, which could not have been a very short one, and was then brought back by the way he had gone. He remained long enough in each heaven to give a full, true and particular account of it and of its inhabitants, and performed various other feats during the journey. Nor will it be forgotten how one of the Sultans one day expressing doubts on the possibility of so much having happened to the Apostle in so short a time, a learned doctor of the Mohammedan law caused a basin of water to be brought and requested him to dip his head into it. When the Sultan dipped his head he found himself in a strange country, alone and friendless, on the seashore. He made his way to a neighbouring town, obtained employment, became rich, married, lived seven years with his wife, who afterwards, to his great grief, died, and then he lost all. One day he was wandering in despondency along the seashore, where he had first found himself; and in his despair he determined to cast himself into the sea. Scarcely had he done so when he beheld his courtiers standing around his throne: he was once more Sultan, and the basin of water into which he had dipped his head was before him. He began furiously to reproach the learned doctor for banishing him from his capital and sending him into the midst of vicissitudes and adventures for so many years. Nor was it without difficulty that he was brought to believe that he had only just dipped his head into the water and lifted it out again.

This type of story is less frequent than the other, but it is known in countries far apart. A stripling, in Pembrokeshire, joined a fairy dance, and found himself in a palace glittering with gold and pearls, where he remained in great enjoyment with the fairy folk for many years. One restriction was laid upon him: he was not to drink from a certain well in the midst of the palace gardens. But he could not forbear. In that well swam golden fishes and fishes of all colours. One day the youth, impelled by curiosity, plunged his hand into the water; but in a moment fishes and all disappeared, a shriek ran through the garden, and he found himself again on the hillside with his father's flocks around him. In fact, he had never left the sheep, and what seemed to him to be years had been only minutes, during which the fairy spell had been over him. In Count Lucanor, a Spanish work of the fourteenth century, is a story of a Dean of Santiago, who went to Don Illan, a magician of Toledo, to be instructed in necromancy. Don Illan made a difficulty, stating that the dean was a man of influence and consequently likely to attain a high position, and that men when they rise forget easily all past obligations, as well as the persons from whom they received them. The dean, however, protested that, no matter to what eminence he attained, he would never fail to remember and to help his former friends, and the magician in particular. This being the bargain, Don Illan led the dean into a remote apartment, first desiring his housekeeper to procure some partridges for supper, but not to cook them until she had his special commands. Scarcely had the dean and his friend reached the room when two messengers arrived from the dean's uncle, the archbishop, summoning him to his death-bed. Being unwilling, however, to forego the lessons he was about to receive, he contented himself with a respectful reply. Four days afterwards other messengers arrived with letters informing the dean of the archbishop's death, and again at the end of other seven or eight days he learned that he himself had been appointed archbishop in his uncle's place. Don Illan solicited the vacant deanery for his son; but the new archbishop preferred his own brother, inviting, however, Don Illan and his son to accompany him to his see. After awhile, the deanery was again vacant: and again the archbishop refused Don Illan's suit, in favour of one of his own uncles. Two years later, the archbishop was named cardinal and summoned to Rome, with liberty to name his successor in the see. Don Illan, pressing his suit more urgently, was again repulsed in favour of another uncle. At length the pope died, and the new cardinal was chosen pope. Don Illan, who had accompanied him to Rome, then reminded him that he had now no excuse for not fulfilling the promises he had so often repeated to him. The pope sought to put him off; but Don Illan complained in earnest of the many promises he had made, none of which had been kept, and declared that he had no longer any faith in his words. The pope, much angered, threatened to have Don Illan thrown into prison as a heretic and a sorcerer; for he knew that in Toledo he had no other means of support but by practising the art of necromancy. Don Illan, seeing how ill the pope had requited his services, prepared to depart; and the pope, as if he had not already shown sufficient ingratitude, refused even to grant him wherewith to support himself on the road. "Then," retorted Don Illan, "since I have nothing to eat, I must needs fall back on the partridges I ordered for to-night's supper." He then called out to his housekeeper and ordered her to cook the birds. No sooner had he thus spoken than the dean found himself again in Toledo, still dean of Santiago, as on his arrival, for, in fact, he had not stirred from the place. This was simply the way the magician had chosen to test his character, before committing himself to his hands; and the dean was so crestfallen he had nothing to reply to the reproaches wherewith Don Illan dismissed him without even a taste of the partridges.[166]

A modern folk-tale from Cashmere tells of a Brahmin who prayed to know something of the state of the departed. One morning, while bathing in the river, his spirit left him and entered the body of the infant child of a cobbler. The child grew up, learned his father's business, married, and had a large family, when suddenly he was made aware of his high caste, and, abandoning all, he went to another country. There the king had just died; and the stranger was chosen in his place, and put upon his throne. In the course of a few years his wife came to know where he was, and sought to join him. In this or some other way his people learned that he was a cobbler; and great consternation prevailed on account of his low caste. Some of his subjects fled; others performed great penances; and some indeed burnt themselves lest they should be excommunicated. When the king heard all this, he too burnt himself; and his spirit went and re-occupied the Brahmin's corpse, which still lay by the riverside. Thereupon the Brahmin got up and went home to his wife, who only said: "How quickly you have performed your ablutions this morning!" The Brahmin said not a word of his adventures, notwithstanding he was greatly astonished. To crown all, however, about a week afterwards a man came to him begging, and said he had eaten nothing for five days, during which he had been running away from his country because a cobbler had been made king. All the people, he said, were running away, or burning themselves, to escape the consequences of such an evil. The Brahmin, while he gave the man food, thought: "How can these things be? I have been a cobbler for several years; I have reigned as a king for several years;—and this man confirms the truth of my thoughts. Yet my wife declares I have not been absent from this house more than the usual time; and I believe her, for she does not look any older, neither is the place changed in any way." Thus were the gods teaching him that the soul passes through various stages of existence according to a man's thoughts, words, and acts, and in the great Hereafter a day is equal to a thousand years, and a thousand years are equal to a day.[167]

We may now turn to the types in which the spell is believed to be still powerful over heroes once mighty but now hidden within the hills, or in some far-off land, awaiting in magical sleep, or in more than human delight, the summons that shall bid them return to succour their distressed people in the hour of utmost need. As to the personality of these heroes there can be no doubt. Grimm long ago pointed out that the red-bearded king beneath the Kyffhäuser can be no other than Thor, the old Teutonic god of thunder, and that the long beard—sometimes described as white—attributed to other leaders was a token of Woden. The very name of Woden is preserved in the Odenberg, to which several of such legends attach; and the hidden king there is sometimes called Karl the Great, and sometimes Woden. In other countries Quetzalcoatl and Vishnu, we know, are gods of the native cults. Oisin, Merlin, and King Arthur all belong to the old Celtic Pantheon. And if some other sleeping or vanished heroes bear the names of personages who once had a real existence, they are but decked in borrowed plumes. In short, all these Hidden Heroes are gods of the earlier faiths, vanquished by Christianity but not destroyed.

If this be so, it may be inferred that these gods were at one time conceived as presently active, and that it is only since the introduction of the new faith that they have been thought to be retired beneath the overhanging hills or in the Islands of the Blest. But this was not so. In all regions the chief activity of the deities has always been placed in the past. Upon the stories told of the deeds of yesterday the belief of to-day is founded. Whether it be creation, or strife against evil spirits, or the punishment of men, or the invention of the civilizing arts, or the endless amours of too susceptible divinities, all is looked upon as past and done. The present is a state of rest, of suspension of labour, or at least of cessation of open and visible activity. These gods, like men, require an abode. In the later stages of culture this abode is a Paradise on some more or less imaginary mountain top, or effectually cut off from men by the magical tempests of the immeasurable main, or by the supreme and silent heights of heaven. But this exaltation of ideas took long to reach. At first a strange rock, a fountain, the recesses of a cavern, or the mysterious depths of the forest, enshrouded the divinity. In the earlier stages of savagery it would be almost truer to say that these *were* very often the divinity: at least they were often his outward and visible form. Mr. Im Thurn, who has had exceptional opportunities of observing the characteristics of the savage mind, and has made exceptionally good use of those opportunities, in describing the animism of the Indians of Guiana, says: "Every object in the whole world is a being consisting of body and spirit, and differs from every other object in no respect except that of bodily form, and in the greater or less degree of brute power and brute cunning consequent on the difference of bodily form and bodily habits." Then, after discussing the lower animals and plants as each possessed of body and soul, and particularizing several rocks which are supposed by the Indians to possess spirits like human beings, he goes on: "It is unnecessary to multiply instances, further than by saying that almost every rock seen for the first time, and any rock which is in any way abnormal whenever seen, is believed to consist of body and spirit. And not only many rocks, but also many waterfalls, streams, and indeed material bodies of every sort, are supposed to consist each of a body and a spirit as does man; and that not all inanimate objects have this dual nature avowedly attributed to them is probably only due to the chance that, while all such objects may at any time, in any of the ways above indicated, show signs of the presence of a spirit within them, this spirit has not yet been noticed in some cases."[168] From this belief to that in which the rocks and hills and other inanimate objects are looked upon as having the relation to spirits, not of body and soul, but of dwelling and dweller, is a step upward, and perhaps a long one. But it is a natural development, and one which would inevitably take place as the popular opinion of the power of certain spirits grew, and these spirits attracted to themselves superstitions and sagas current among the people whose civilization was by the same slow movement growing too.

The development spoken of would perhaps be assisted by the erection of monuments like piles of stones, or earthen barrows, over the dead. As formerly in their huts, so now in their graves, the dead would be regarded as the occupiers. Their spirits were still living, and would be seen from time to time haunting the spot. Food would be buried with them; and sacrifices at the moment of burial and on subsequent occasions would be offered to them. In process of time among illiterate races their identity would be forgotten, and then if the barrows were not large enough to attract attention the superstitions which had their seat there might cease. But if the barrows could not be overlooked, the spirits supposed to haunt them might merge into some other objects of reverence. In Denmark the barrows are invariably regarded as the haunt of fairies; and this is frequently the case in other countries.[169] When men once became habituated to think of a barrow as not the outward and visible form of some spirit, but simply its dwelling-place—still more, perhaps, if many interments took place within it, so that it became the dwelling-place of many spirits—they would be led by an easy transition to think of rocks, fountains, hills, and other natural objects in the same way. The spirits once supposed to be their inner identity would become perfectly separable in thought from them, because merely their tenants. Thus the gulf would be bridged between the savage philosophy of spirits described by Mr. Im Thurn, and the polytheism of the higher heathendom, represented by Mexico, Scandinavia, and Greece.

But whether they travelled by this, or any different road, certain it is that in the remoter times of the higher heathendom men had arrived no further than the belief that certain spots, and preferably certain striking objects, were the abodes of their gods. This was a doctrine developed directly from that which regarded the more remarkable objects of nature as the bodies of powerful spirits. Nor was it ever entirely abandoned; for even after the more advanced and thoughtful of the community had reached the idea of an Olympus, or an Asgard, far removed above the every-day earth of humanity, the gods still had their temples, and sacred legends still attached to places where events of the divine history had happened. Consequently some localities kept their reputation of sanctity. That they were really the abiding-places of the gods the common people would not cease to hold, whatever might be taught or held by those who had renounced that crudity. And, indeed, it may be doubted whether anybody ever renounced it altogether. Probably, at all events, most persons would see no difficulty in believing that the god dwelt on the sacred spot of earth and also at the same time in heaven. They would accept both traditions as equally true, without troubling themselves how to reconcile them.

But the gods did not always remain in their dwellings. The Wild Hunt, a tradition of a furious host riding abroad with a terrific noise of shouts and horns and the braying of hounds, common to Germany and England, has been identified beyond doubt by Grimm with Woden and his host. We cannot here discuss the subject except in its relations with the group of stories now under consideration. Woden, it will be borne in mind, is one of the figures of the old mythology merged in the Hidden Hero beneath the German hills. Now, nothing is more natural than that, when a company of warriors is conceived as lying ready for a summons, themselves all armed and their steeds standing harnessed at their sides, they should be thought now and then to sally forth. This was the sound which surprised the good burgesses of Jung-Wositz when Ulrich von Rosenberg and his train rode out by night upon the plain. In this way King Wenzel exercises his followers, and the unfortunate Stoymir vindicated his existence beneath the Blanik notwithstanding his death. In this way too, before a war, Diedrich is heard preparing for battle at one o'clock in the morning on the mountain of Ax. Once in seven years Earl Gerald rides round the Curragh of Kildare; and every seventh year the host at Ochsenfeld in Upper Alsace may be seen by night exercising on their horses. On certain days the Carpathian robber issues from his cavern in the Czornahora. Grimm mentions the story of a blacksmith who found a gap he had never noticed before in the face of a cliff on the Odenberg, and entering, stood in the presence of mighty men, playing there at bowls with balls of iron, as Rip van Winkle's friends were playing at ninepins. So a Wallachian saga connects the Wild Hunt with a mysterious forest castle built by the Knight Sigmirian, who was cursed with banishment for three hundred years from the society of men for refusing the daughter of the King of Stones. In the same category we must put the spectral host in the Donnersberg, and Herla's company, which haunted the Welsh marches, and is described by Walter Map as a great band of men and women on foot and in chariots, with pack-saddles and panniers, birds and dogs, advancing with trumpets and shouts, and all sorts of weapons ready for emergencies. Night was the usual time of Herla's wanderings, but the last time he and his train were seen was at noon. Those who then saw them, being unable to obtain an answer to their challenge by words, prepared to exact one by arms; but the moment they did so the troop rose into the air and disappeared, nor was it ever seen again.[170]

This is a different account of Herla from that previously quoted from an earlier part of Map's work; but perhaps, if it were worth while to spend the time, not altogether irreconcilable with it. The tradition, it should be observed, appears to have been an English, and not a Welsh, tradition, since the host received the English name of Herlething. Gervase of Tilbury, writing about the same time, reports that Arthur was said by the foresters, or woodwards, both in Britain and in Brittany, to be very often seen at midday, or in the evening moonlight at full of the moon, accompanied by a troop of soldiers, hunters, dogs, and the sound of horns. This is manifestly a Celtic tradition. But these occasions are not the last on which such appearances have been seen and heard in this country. If we may believe a tract published in 1643, spectral fights had taken place at Keniton, in Northamptonshire, during four successive Saturday and Sunday nights of the preceding Christmastide. By those who are reported to have witnessed the phenomenon—and among them were several gentlemen of credit mentioned by name as despatched by the king himself from Oxford—it was taken to be a ghostly repetition of the battle of Edgehill, which had been fought only two months before on the adjacent fields. The excitement of men's minds during periods of commotion has doubtless much to do with the currency of beliefs like this. Saint Augustine alludes to a story of a battle between evil spirits beheld upon a plain in Campania during the civil wars of Rome. As in the case of Edgehill, the vision was accompanied by all the noises of a conflict; and indeed the saint goes the length of declaring that after it was over the ground was covered with the footprints of men and horses. On the spot where this is said to have happened an actual battle took place not very long after.[171] These two instances are unconnected with the Sleeping Host; but many of the legends explicitly declare the exercises of the host when it emerges from its retirement to consist of a sham fight. Although the legends containing this account are not all found among Teutonic peoples, it cannot be deemed irrelevant to draw attention to the fact that similar fights are mentioned as the daily occupation of the heroes who attain to Valhalla, just as the nightly feasts of that roystering paradise correspond to the refreshments provided for the warriors around the tables of stone in their subterranean retreats. Whatever may have been the creed of other European races, it is hardly to be doubted that in these German superstitions we have an approach to the primitive belief, of which the Eddaic Valhalla was a late and idealized development.

But we may—nay, we must—go further. For in the history of traditional religions goddesses have been as popular as gods; and if we are right in seeing, with Grimm, the archaic gods in the Hidden Heroes, some where we must find their mates, the corresponding goddesses. We have already had glimpses of them in Morgan the Fay, in the Emperor Frederick's lady-housekeeper (*ausgeberin*) and in the maid who in another saga attended on his bidding. The lady-housekeeper is expressly called in one story Dame Holle. Now Dame Holle herself is the leader of a Furious Host, or Wild Hunt, and has been identified by Grimm beyond any doubt as a pagan goddess, like Berchta.

Let us take another story in which the female companion of the enchanted hero appears. Near the town of Garz, on the island of Rügen, lies a lake by which a castle formerly stood. It belonged to an old heathen king, whose avarice heaped up great store of gold and jewels in the vaults beneath. It was taken and destroyed by the Christians, and its owner was transformed into a great black dog ever watching his treasure. Sometimes he is still seen in human form with helm, or golden crown, and coat of mail, riding a grey horse over the city and the lake; sometimes he is met with by night in the forest, wearing a black fur cap and carrying a white staff. It is possible to disenchant him, but only if a pure virgin, on St. John's night between twelve and one o'clock, will venture, naked and alone, to climb the castle wall and wander backwards to and fro amid the ruins, until she light upon the spot where the stairway of the tower leads down into the treasure chamber. Slipping down, she will then be able to take as much gold and jewels as she can carry, and what she cannot herself carry the old king will bring after her, so that she will be rich for the rest of her life. But she must return by sunrise, and she must not once look behind her, nor speak a single word, else not only will she fail, but she will perish miserably. A princess who was accused of unchastity obtained her father's permission to try this adventure, in order to prove the falsehood of the charge against her. She safely gained the vault, which was illuminated with a thousand lights. The king, a little grey old man, bestowed the treasure upon her, and sent a number of servants laden with it to follow her. All would have gone well, but unhappily when she had climbed a few of the old steps she looked round to see if the servants were coming. At once the king changed into a great black dog, that sprang upon her with fiery throat and glowing eyes. She just had time to scream out when the door slammed to, the steps sank, and she fell back into the vault in darkness. She has sat there now for four hundred years, waiting until a pure youth shall find his way down in the same manner on St. John's night, shall bow to her thrice and silently kiss her. He may then take her hand and lead her forth to be his bride; and he will inherit such riches as a whole kingdom cannot buy.[172]

But goddesses do not always play so secondary a part. In a wood in Pomerania stands a round, flat hill called the Castle Hill, and at its foot lies a little lake known as the Hertha Lake. By its name it is thus directly connected with one of the old divinities, like that lake on the island of Rügen referred to in Chapter IV. And here, too, a mysterious lady has been seen to wash, a young and lovely maiden, clad in black—not in secret, as in the former instance, but openly, as if for the purpose of attracting attention from passers-by, and of being spoken to. At last a broad-shouldered workman, named Kramp, ventured to give the maiden "the time of day," and to get her into conversation. She told him she was a princess, who, with her castle, had been from time immemorial enchanted, and that she was still waiting for her deliverer. The mode of loosing the spell was by carrying her on his back in silence to the churchyard of Wusseken and there putting her down, being careful not to look round the while; for, happen what would, he could take no harm, even if it were threatened to tear his head off. He undertook the task, and had nearly accomplished it without troubling in the least about the troops of spirits which followed him, when suddenly, as he drew near the churchyard, a hurricane arose and took his cap off. Forgetful of his promise, he looked round; and the maiden rose into the air, weeping and crying out that she could never be delivered now. A story told in Mecklenburg is more picturesque. It concerns the daughter of a lake-king, who leagued himself with other knights against a robber, the owner of a castle called the Glamburg, which was a place of some strength, being entirely surrounded by the water of the Lake of Glam. The confederates were defeated; and nine large round barrows were raised the next day over the slain, among whom was the lake-king. His daughter wept upon her father's grave, and her tears, as they touched the earth, became lovely blue flowers. These flowers still grow upon the loftiest of the nine barrows, while the others are quite destitute of them. The princess threw herself that night—it was St. John's night—into the lake; and now every year on St. John's night, between twelve and one o'clock, a bridge of copper rises out of the lake, and the princess appears upon it, sighing for her deliverance.[173]

The typical form of the tale is as follows: In the Buchenberg by Doberan dwells an enchanted princess, who can only be released once in a hundred years, on St. John's Day between twelve and one. In the year 1818 a servant boy was watching sheep on the eastern side of the Buchenberg the day before St. John's day. About noon a white lady appeared to him and told him that he could deliver her, if he would, the next day at the same hour, kiss her. She would then come to him in the form of a toad with a red band round its neck. The shepherd promised; but the next day when he saw the toad he was so horrified that he ran away. A variant records the hour as between twelve and one at night, and the form of the lady as a snake which sought to twine round the shepherd's neck. A great treasure buried in the hill would have been his had he stood the proof; but now the lady will have to wait until a beech tree shall have grown up on the spot and been cut down, and of its timber a cradle made: the child that is rocked in that cradle will have power to save her. This is in effect the story told by Sir John Maundeville concerning the daughter of Hippocrates, the renowned physician, who was said to have been enchanted by Diana on the island of Cos, or (as he calls it) Lango, and given with so much of Mr. William Morris' power in "The Earthly Paradise."[174] "Then listen!" says the damsel in the ruined castle to the seaman whom she meets—

"Then listen! when this day is overpast,
A fearful monster I shall be again,
And thou may'st be my saviour at the last,
Unless, once more, thy words are nought and vain;
If thou of love and sovereignty art fain,
Come thou next morn, and when thou seest here
A hideous dragon, have thereof no fear,

"But take the loathsome head up in thine hands,
And kiss it, and be master presently
Of twice the wealth that is in all the lands,
From Cathay to the head of Italy;
And master also, if it pleaseth thee,
Of all thou praisest as so fresh and bright,
Of what thou callest crown of all delight.

"Ah, me! to hold my child upon my knees,
After the weeping of unkindly tears,
And all the wrongs of these four hundred years."

But the horrible apparition of the dragon was too much for the adventurer's courage:

"He cried out and wildly at her smote,
Shutting his eyes, and turned and from the place
Ran swiftly, with a white and ghastly face,"

to die within three days, a raving maniac. And

"Never any man again durst go
To seek her woman's form, and end her wo."

It would be too tedious to run through even a small proportion of the examples of this tale, almost innumerable in Germany alone. Fortunately, it will only be necessary to allude to a few of its chief features. When the enchanted princess assumes a monstrous form, the usual ordeal of the would-be deliverer is to kiss her. A toad or a snake is, perhaps, her favourite form; but occasionally she is half woman, half toad, or half woman, half snake. Further transformations now and then take place, as from a snake into a fiery dog, or from a bear into a lion, from a lion into a snake. Sometimes as a bear alone she threatens her deliverer. In a Carinthian saga he is to cut three birch rods at the full of the moon, and then wait at the appointed place. The damsel approaches in the guise of a snake, with a bunch of keys in her mouth, and menaces him, hissing and snorting fire. Unmoved by the creature's rage, he is to strike her thrice on the head with each rod and take the keys from her mouth. In the Duchy of Luxemburg the favourite form assumed by the princess is that of a fire-breathing snake, bearing in her mouth a bunch of keys, or a ring; and the deliverer's task then is to take the keys or ring away with his own mouth. It is believed that Melusina, whose story we shall deal with in the following chapters, is enchanted beneath the Bockfels, a rock near the town of Luxemburg. There she appears every seventh year in human form and puts one stitch in a smock. When she shall have finished sewing the smock she will be delivered; but woe then to the town! for its ruins will be her grave and monument. Men have often undertaken her earlier deliverance. This is to be effected at midnight, when she appears as a snake, by taking with the mouth a key from her mouth and flinging it into the Alzet. No one, however, has yet succeeded in doing this; and meantime when a calamity threatens the town, whose faithful guardian she is, she gives warning by gliding round the Bockfels uttering loud laments.[175]

But in many of the sagas the princess meets her hero in her own proper shape, and then the feat to be performed varies much more. In a Prussian tale she comes out of a deep lake, which occupies the site of a once-mighty castle, at sunset, clothed in black, and accompanied by a black dog. The castle belonged to the young lady's parents, who were wicked, though she herself was pious;

and it was destroyed on account of their evil doings. Since that time she has wandered around, seeking some bold and pious man who will follow her into the depths of the lake, and thus remove the curse. This would seem but another form of the tradition of the lake at the foot of the Herthaburg on the isle of Rügen. In another story the lady must be brought an unbaptized child to kiss. In yet another the deliverer is led down through a dark underground passage into a brilliantly lighted room, where sit three black men writing at a table, and is bidden to take one of two swords which lie on the table and strike off the enchanted lady's head. To cut off the head of a bewitched person is an effectual means of destroying the spell. So, in the Gaelic story of the Widow and her Daughters, the heroine decapitates the horse-ogre, who thereupon returns to his true form as a king's son, and marries her. A large number of parallel instances might easily be given; but they would lead us too far afield. The lady of the Princess Hill, near Warin, in Mecklenburg, has to be held fast from midnight until one o'clock in spite of all frightful apparitions of snakes, dragons, and toads which crowd around and threaten the adventurer. In the same way Peleus, desiring to secure Thetis, had to hold her fast through her various magical changes until she found resistance useless, and returned to her true form. In a modern Cretan tale the hero, by the advice of an old woman, seizes at night a Nereid by the hair and holds her until the cock crows, in spite of her changes successively into a dog, a snake, a camel, and fire. The process of disenchanting Tam Lin, in the ballad of that name, was for his lady-love to take him in her arms and hold him, notwithstanding his transformation into a snake, a bear, a lion, a red-hot iron, and lastly into a "burning gleed," when he was to be immediately flung into a well.[176]

We have already seen that the task is sometimes to carry the maiden to a churchyard. At the Castle Hill of Bütow she was to be carried to the Polish churchyard and there thrown to the ground with all the deliverer's might. A castle is said to have stood formerly on the site of Budow Mill in Eastern Pomerania. An enchanted princess now haunts the place. She is only to be freed by a bachelor who will carry her in silence, and without looking behind him, around the churchyard; but the spirits which hold her under their spell will seek in every way to hinder her deliverance. On the Müggelsberg is, or was (for it is said to be now destroyed), a large stone under which a treasure lies. It was called the Devil's Altar; and at night it often seemed, from the neighbouring village of Müggelsheim, to be in a blaze; but on drawing near the fire would vanish from sight. At Köpenick, another village not far off, it was called the Princesses' Stone, but the lake at the foot of the hill was called the Devil's Lake. The stone was said to occupy the site of a castle, now enchanted and swallowed up in the earth. Beneath it a hole ran deep into the mountain, out of which a princess was sometimes of an evening seen to come, with a casket of pure gold in her hand. He who would carry her thrice round the church of Köpenick without looking about him, would win the casket of gold and deliver her. The names of the stone and of the lake, as well as the attendant circumstances, are strong evidence in favour of the conclusion that we have in this superstition a relic of heathen times, and a record of some divinity believed to reside at that spot. A princess, clad in white and having a golden spinning-wheel in her hand, was believed to appear on the Castle Hill at Biesenthal, at midday. Once at midnight she appeared to a gardener who had often heard voices at night summoning him to the castle garden. At first he was frightened at the vision, but at length consented to carry her to the church, which stands near the hill. He took her on his back; but when he entered the churchyard gate he suddenly met a carriage drawn by coal-black horses, which vomited fire. So terrified was he that he shrieked aloud, whereupon the carriage vanished, and the princess flew away moaning: "For ever lost!" In a case where a prince had been enchanted, the feat was to wrestle with him three nights in succession.[177]

But it was not always that so hard a task was set before the deliverer. To our thinking, it says little for the German way of doing business that the difficulty in unspelling the castle near Lossin, and the maiden who dwelt therein, was to buy a pair of shoes without bargaining and cheapening their price, but to pay for them exactly the piece of money which the maiden handed to the youth who undertook the enterprise. In another case a maiden was seen to scour a kettle at a little lake. She was enchanted. The man who beheld her thought the kettle would prove useful at his approaching wedding, and borrowed it on the express condition of returning it at a fixed time. He failed to do so, and the Evil One came and fetched it; and the maiden had to wait longer for her deliverance. There are stories similar to this of fairies lending such articles on this condition. If the condition be not complied with, the fairies are never seen again. Aubrey relates that in the vestry of Frensham Church, in Surrey, is a great kettle, which was borrowed from the fairies who lived in the Borough Hill, about a mile away. It was not returned according to promise, and though afterwards taken back, it was not received, nor since that time had there been any borrowing there.[178]

A man who was in the habit of meeting in a certain wood an adder, which always sneezed thrice as he passed, consulted his parish priest on the subject. The priest advised him to say the next time, as he would to a human friend who sneezed: "God help thee!" The man did so, whereupon the adder shot forth before him with fiery body and terrible rattling, so startling him that he turned and fled. The snake hurried after him, crying out that it would not hurt him, but that if he would take (not, however, with naked hands) the bunch of keys that hung about its neck, it would then lead the way to a great treasure and make him happy. He turned a deaf ear to these entreaties; and as he ran away he heard the snake exclaim that now it must remain enchanted until yon little oak tree had grown great, and a cradle had been made out of the timber: the first child that lay in that cradle would be able to deliver it. The same incident reappears in another saga, in which some men passing through the forest hear a sneeze, and one of them says: "God help thee!" The sneeze and the blessing are repeated; but when the sneeze was heard a third time, the man exclaimed: "Oh, go to the devil!" "I believe somebody is making game of us," said another. But a mannikin stepped forward and said: "If you had said a third time 'God help thee!' I should have been saved. Now I must wait until an acorn falls from yonder tree and becomes an oak, and a cradle is made out of its timber. The child that comes to lie in that cradle will be able to deliver me." In this case all that was required was a thrice-repeated blessing. Another curious means of deliverance is found in a story from Old Strelitz. There an enchanted princess haunted a bridge a short distance from one of the gates of the town, on the road to Woldegk. Whoever in going over this bridge uttered a certain word, could unspell her if he would afterwards allow her to walk beside him the rest of the way over the bridge without speaking; but the difficulty was that nobody knew what the powerful word was.[179]

Two other legends may be noticed on the mode of undoing the spell. The White Lady who haunts the White Tower on the White Hill at Prague was married to a king. She betrayed him, and married his enemy, from whom she subsequently fled with an officer of his army. She was, however, caught, and walled up in the White Tower. From this she may be delivered if she can find any one who will allow her to give him three stabs in the breast with a bayonet without uttering a sound. Once she prevailed on a young recruit, who was placed as sentinel before the magazine of the castle, to stand the necessary trial; but on receiving the first blow he could not forbear crying aloud: "Jesus! Mary! thou hast given it me!" Another old castle in Bohemia has twelve ladies enchanted by day as fish in the fountain of the castle garden, and appearing only at night in their true shape. They can not be disenchanted unless by twelve men who will remain in the castle for twelve months without once going outside the walls.[180]

These bring us to a number of *märchen* in which the bespelled heroine is released by a youth who suffers torture on her account. The Transylvanian gipsies tell a tale of a very poor man who, instructed by a dream, climbed a certain mountain and found a beautiful maiden before a cavern, spinning her own golden hair. She had been sold by her heartless parents to an evil spirit, who compelled her to this labour; but she could be saved if she could find any one willing to undergo in silence, for her sake, an hour's torture from the evil spirit on three successive nights. The man expressed himself ready to make the attempt; he entered the cave, and at midnight a gigantic Prikulich, or evil spirit, appeared, and questioned him as to who he was and what he wanted there. Failing to get any reply, the Prikulich flung him to the ground and danced about madly on him. The man endured without a moan; and at one o'clock the Prikulich disappeared. The second night the man was beaten with a heavy hammer, and so tortured that the maiden had great difficulty in persuading him to stand the third proof. While she was praying him, however, to stay, the Prikulich appeared the third time, and beat him again with the hammer until he was half dead. Then the goblin made a fire and flung him into it. The poor fellow uttered not a single sound, in spite of all this torment; and the maiden was saved and wedded her deliverer. This is a tale by no means uncommon. Want of space forbids us to follow it in detail, but a few references in the note below will enable the reader to do so if he please. Meantime, I will only say that sometimes the princess who is thus to be rescued is enchanted in the form of a snake, sometimes of a she-goat, sometimes of a bird; and in one of the stories she herself, in the shape of a monster like a hedgehog, comes out of a coffin to tear the hero in pieces.[181] The group is allied, on the one hand, to that of Fearless Johnny who, passing the night in a haunted house, expelled the ghosts, or goblins, which had taken possession of it; on the other hand, to that of the Briar Rose, illustrated by Mr. Burne Jones' series of paintings.

The Briar Rose, or The Beauty of Sleeping Wood, as it comes to us from Perrault's hands, is the story of a maiden who was cursed by an offended fairy to pierce her hand with a spindle and to die of it—a curse afterwards mitigated into a sleep of a hundred years. Every effort was made by the king, her father, to avert the doom, but in vain; and for a whole century the princess and all her court remained in the castle in a magical sleep, while the castle itself and all within it were protected from intrusion by an equally magical growth of brambles and thorns, which not only prevented access, but entirely hid it from view. At length a king's son found his way in at the very moment the fated period came to an end; or, as we have it in other versions, he awakened the maiden with a kiss. In the old stories of the Niblungs and the Volsungs Odin has pricked the shield-maid Brynhild with a sleep-thorn, and thus condemned her to sleep within the shield-burg on Hindfell. Attracted by the appearance of fire, Sigurd comes to the shield-burg and, finding Brynhild, releases her from her slumber by ripping up her armour with his sword. This is chronologically the earliest form of the myth of the Enchanted Princess with which we are acquainted; and it is interwoven with the very fibres of the Teutonic mythology. It is no wonder, therefore, that the Germans have given it so prominent a place in their folklore. So far as now appears it is less conspicuous in the folklore of the other European races with the exception of the Slaves, and when it does show itself it shows itself chiefly as a *märchen*. But, although what we know of the folklore of the Teutonic and Slavonic races may suggest reasons for this, we must not forget how rarely we can dogmatize with safety on national characteristics. To this rule the folklore of a nation is no exception; nay, rather, the rule applies with a double emphasis to a subject the scientific investigation of which has so lately begun and has yet achieved so little.

Declining this speculation, therefore, we turn to a last point in the sagas before us, namely, the propitious time for the disenchantment. Different times of the year are spoken of for this purpose. In some stories it is Advent, or New Year's night, when the lady makes her appearance and may be delivered. In a Pomeranian saga, where a woman cursed her seven daughters and they became mice, a woman, who is of the same age as the mother when she uttered the curse, must come with seven sons of the same ages as the daughters were when they were cursed, on Good Friday at noon, to the thicket where the mice are, and put her sons on a certain round stone there. The seven mice will then return to human shape; and when the children are old enough they will marry, and become rich and happy for the rest of their lives. A Carinthian tale requires the deliverer to come the next full moon after "May-Sunday"; and May-night is the date fixed in another case. But the favourite time is St. John's Day, either at noon or midnight.[182] Some of these days are ecclesiastical festivals; but perhaps the only one which has not superseded an ancient heathen feast is Good Friday. The policy of the Church, in consecrating to Christian uses as many as possible of the seasons and customs she found already honoured among the peoples she had conquered, seized upon their holy days and made them her own. And if the science of Folklore has taught us anything, it is that the observances on these converted holy days external to the rites demanded by the Church are relics of the ceremonies performed in pagan days to pagan deities. In none of these instances has the proof been more conclusive than in that of St. John's, or Midsummer Day. Grimm, first, with abundant learning, and more recently Mr. Frazer, with a wealth of illustration surpassing that of Grimm himself, and indeed inaccessible in his day, have shown that the Midsummer festival was kept in honour of the sun; that it consisted of the ceremonial kindling of fire, the gathering and use of floral garlands, the offering of human and other sacrifices, and the performance of sacred dances; and that its object was to increase the power of the sun by magical sympathy, to obtain a good harvest and fruitfulness of all creatures, and to purge the sins of the people. It was, in fact, the chief ceremony of the year among the European races.

Prominent among the remnants of these ceremonies continued down to modern days are the Midsummer bonfires. These were lighted on the tops of mountains, hills, or even barrows. This situation may be thought to have symbolic reference to the solstice; but probably a still more powerful reason for it was the already sacred character of such places. But we need hardly consider whether the ceremonies of which the bonfires are the remnant, were observed on the hill-tops and other high places because the latter were already sacred, or, conversely, the hill tops and other high places were held sacred because of the ceremonies enacted there; for in either case the sanctity remains. Wells and pools, too, many of them still held sacred, were in various ways the objects of superstition at the Midsummer festival; for which the Church, when she chose to take the practices under her protection, had an ample excuse in St. John's mission to baptize.[183] Now, whatever spots were the haunt of pagan divinities, there it was doubtless that those divinities were expected to appear; and by the same reasoning they would be most likely to appear during the favoured hours of the holy days. This is exactly what we find to be the case with Enchanted Princesses, and, so far as the days are recorded, with Sleeping Heroes. The heroes lie within the hills, which in many legends are only open on certain days. The princesses appear upon the hills, or by the sides of pools, the sites, if we believe the legends, of ancient castles where they dwelt. Once in the year, or once in a cycle of years, on a certain day, usually Midsummer Day or Midsummer Eve, they come to wash, or to fetch water, in their own form, either compelled or permitted by the terms of the curse that has bound them; and then it is that mortals are admitted to an interview and may render them the service of disenchantment. The instances in which the days are specified are so frequent we may perhaps suspect that they were originally mentioned in all, but that time and other circumstances have caused them to be forgotten. However this may be, it is only reasonable to conclude that, in the number of instances remaining, we have a tradition of the honours long ago paid to these degraded divinities on the days appointed for their worship.

I may be going too far in suggesting that the feats to be performed afford some confirmation of this conclusion; yet it seems to me there is much to be said for such an opinion. The appearance of a god in animal form—even in a loathsome animal form—would not derogate from his essential godhead. Where in these stories the deliverer has to deal with an animal, a kiss is the usual task prescribed. Kissing is a very ancient and well-known act of worship, which survives among us in many a practice of the Roman Catholic Church, as well as in the form of oath taken daily in our law courts; and it may be that the more repulsive the object to be kissed, the greater the merit of kissing it. Again, the lady who required to be followed into the depths of a lake may be matched with the goddess Hertha, whose slaves were drowned in the self-same waters wherein they had washed her; nor does it seem more menial to carry a princess than to wash a goddess. The ceremony of carrying may indeed be the relic of a solemn procession, or of a sacred drama. The words of blessing following on a sneeze need no explanation; and the omission to return at the promised time a borrowed kettle would be more likely to provoke the anger of a god than to retard the deliverance of a mortal. This is implied by the statement that the devil fetched the kettle himself; and we need have little doubt that in an earlier form the story so described it. I am unable to explain the unknown word which would deliver the lady who haunted the bridge at Old Strelitz, unless it be a reminiscence of an incantation.

There remain the demand for an unbaptized child to kiss, the torture to which the heroes of the two Bohemian sagas submit, the requirement in the Pomeranian tale to place seven brothers on the stone haunted by the seven mice, and lastly the personal violence to the damsel involved in striking her with a birch-rod or a bunch of juniper and in beheadal. In all these we probably have traces of sacrifice. The offering of an innocent child is familiar, if not comprehensible, enough to any one who has the most superficial acquaintance with savage rites. We have already seen that an unbaptized child is regarded as a pagan, and is an object of desire on the part of supernatural beings. The same reasons which induce fairies to steal it would probably render it an acceptable offering to a pagan divinity. No words need be wasted on the torture, or the tale of the mice. But the personal violence, if indeed the remnant of a tradition of sacrifice, involves the slaughter of the divinity herself. This might be thought an insuperable objection; but it is not really so. For, however absurd it may seem to us, it is a very widespread custom to sacrifice to a divinity his living representative or incarnation, whether in animal or human form. It is believed in such cases that the victim's spirit, released by sacrifice, forthwith finds a home in another body. The subject is too vast and complex to be discussed here at length; the reader who desires to follow it out can do so in Mr. Frazer's profoundly interesting work on "The Golden Bough." Assuming, however, the custom and belief, as here stated, to be admitted, it will be seen that the underlying thought is precisely that which we want in order to explain this mode of disenchantment. For if, on the one hand, what looks like murder be enjoined in a number of stories for the purpose of disenchanting a bewitched person; and if, on the other hand, the result of solemnly slaughtering a victim be in fact held to be simply the release of the victim's spirit—nay, if it was the prescribed mode of releasing that spirit—to seek a new, sometimes a better, abode in a fresh body, we may surely be satisfied that both these have the same origin. We may then go further, and see in this unspelling incident, performed, as in the Enchanted Princess stories, in this way, at a haunted spot, frequently on a day of special sanctity, one more proof that the princess herself was in the earlier shape of the traditions no other than a goddess.

Finally: the myth of the Enchanted Princess has preserved in many of its variants a detail more archaic than any in that of the Sleeping Hero, and one which is decisive as to the lady's real status. If Frederick were to arise and come forth from his sleeping-place, the Kyffhäuser itself would remain. If Arthur were to awake and quit the Castle Rock, the rock itself wherein he lay would still be there. But the lake or mountain haunted by an enchanted maiden often owes its very existence, if not to her, at least to the spell which holds her enthralled. When she is delivered the place will be changed: the lake will give way to a palace; the earth will open and a buried castle will reascend to the surface; what is now nothing but an old grey boulder will forthwith return to its previous condition of an inhabited and stately building; or what is now a dwelling of men will become desolate. One of the best examples of this is the superstition I have already cited concerning Melusina. When she finishes her needlework she will be disenchanted, but only to die; and the ruins of the town of Luxemburg will be her grave and monument. In other words, the existence of the town is bound up with her enchantment,—that is to say, with her life. In the same way the bespelled damsel of the Urschelberg, near Pfullingen, in Swabia, is called by the very name of the mountain—the Old Urschel. This can only be the survival of a belief in the enchanted lady as the indwelling spirit, the soul, the real life of the spot she haunted: a belief which goes back to a deeper depth of savagery than one that regards her as a local goddess, and out of which the latter would be easily developed.[184]

These considerations by no means exhaust the case; but I have said enough in support of conclusions anticipated by Grimm's clear-sighted genius and confirmed by every fresh discovery. Let me, therefore, recapitulate the results of the investigations contained in this and the two preceding chapters. We have rapidly examined several types of fairy tales in which the hero, detained in Fairyland, is unconscious of the flight of time. These tales are characteristic of a high rather than a low stage of civilization. Connected with them we have found the story of King Arthur, the Sleeping Hero, "*rex quondam, rex que futurus,*" the expected deliverer, sometimes believed to be hidden beneath the hills, at other times in a far-off land, or from time to time traversing the world with his band of attendants as the Wild Hunt. This is a tradition of a heathen god put down by Christianity, but not destroyed in the hearts and memories of the people—a tradition independent of political influences, but to which oppression is apt to give special and enduring vitality. The corresponding tradition concerning a heathen goddess is discovered in the Enchanted Princess of a thousand sagas, whose peculiar home, if they have one, is in Teutonic and Slavonic countries.

**FOOTNOTES:**

[166] Howells, p. 120; "Count Lucanor," p. 77.

[167] Knowles, p. 17.

[168] Im Thurn, pp. 352, 354. *Cf.* Brett, p. 375. So Leland, p. 3: "The Indian *m'téoulin*, or magician, distinctly taught that every created thing, animate or inanimate, had its indwelling spirit. Whatever had an *idea* had a soul."

[169] *Cf.* Grimm, "Teut. Myth." p. 962, quoting Harry, "Nieders. Sagen"; Jahn, p. 228, quoting Temme. Many of the sanctuaries of the Celts were upon mounds, which were either barrows of the dead, or were expressly made for temples; and the god was called in Irish *Cenn Cruaich*, in Welsh *Penn Cruc* (now *Pen Crûg*), both meaning the Head or Chief of the Mound (Rhys, "Hibbert Lectures," p. 201). Many mounds in England, now crowned by churches, have been conjectured to be old Celtic temples. See an able paper by Mr. T. W. Shore on "Characteristic Survivals of the Celts in Hampshire," *Journ. Anthrop. Inst.*, vol. xx. p. 9. Mont St. Michel, near Carnac, in Brittany, is a chambered barrow surmounted by a little chapel. From the relics found in the tomb, as well as the size of the barrow itself, some person, or persons, of importance must have been buried there. The mound may well have been a haunted, a sacred spot ever since the ashes of the dead and their costly weapons and ornaments were committed to its keeping far back in the Neolithic age. Instances might easily be multiplied.

[170] Müller, p. 203; Map, Dist. iv. c. 13.

[171] Gerv. Tilb., Dec. ii. c. 12; "Book of Days," vol. i. p. 154; Augustine, "De Civ. Dei," l. ii. c. 25.

[172] Jahn, p. 182, quoting Arndt.

[173] Knoop, p. 10; Bartsch, vol. i. p. 273.

[174] Bartsch, vol. i. p. 271; "Early Trav.," p. 138.

[175] Bartsch, vol. i. pp. 269 (citing Niederhöffer, below), 271, 272, 273, 274, 318. In this last case it is a man who is to be saved by a kiss from a woman while he is in serpent form. Niederhöffer, vol. i. pp. 58, 168, vol. ii. p. 235; Meier, pp. 6, 31, 321; Kuhn und Schwartz, pp. 9, 201; Baring-Gould, p. 223, citing Kornemann, "Mons Veneris," and Prætorius, "Weltbeschreibung"; Jahn, p. 220; Rappold, p. 135. Gredt, pp. 8, 9, 215, 228, &c. In one of Meier's Swabian tales the princess appears as a snake and flings herself round the neck of her would-be deliverer—a woman—who is to strike her lightly with a

bunch of juniper: Meier, p. 27. In one of Kuhn und Schwartz' collection, where the princess becomes a toad, no ceremony is prescribed: Kuhn und Schwartz, p. 9.

[176] Von Tettau, p. 220; Kuhn, pp. 66, 99; Bartsch, vol. i. p. 272; Jahn, p. 249; Ovid, "Metam." l. xi. f. 5; Child, vol. i. pp. 336 (citing Schmidt, "Volkleben der Neugriechen," p. 115), 340.

[177] Knoop, pp. 6, 57; Kuhn, pp. 113, 172; Kuhn und Schwartz, p. 1. The prohibition to look back was imposed on Orpheus when he went to rescue Eurydice from Hades.

[178] Knoop, pp. 51, 59; Keightley, p. 295, quoting Aubrey's "Natural History of Surrey"; "Gent. Mag. Lib." (Pop. Supers.), p. 280.

[179] Meier, pp. 209, 87; Niederhöffer, vol. iii. p. 251.

[180] Grohmann, pp. 56, 50.

[181] Von Wlislocki, p. 76; Campbell, vol. ii. p. 293; Luzel, "Contes," vol. i. pp. 198, 217; "Annuaire des Trad. Pop." 1887, p. 53; Pitré, vol. v. pp. 238, 248; Grundtvig, vol. i. p. 148; Schneller, pp. 103, 109.

[182] Meier, p. 26; Bartsch, vol. i. pp. 271, 272, 274; Jahn, p. 185; Rappold, p. 135; Bartsch, vol. i. pp. 269, 270, 271, 272, 273, 283, 308, 318; Niederhöffer, vol. i. p. 168, vol. ii. p. 235, vol. iii. p. 171; Knoop, p. 10; Jahn, pp. 182, 185, 206, 207, 217, 220, 221; and many others.

[183] "Gent. Mag. Lib." (Pop. Superst.) p. 51; Brand, vol. i. p. 250, note; Pitré, vol. xii. pp. 304, 307; Bartsch, vol. ii. p. 288; "Antiquary," vol. xxi. p. 195, vol. xxii. p. 67. *Cf.* a legend in which the scene haunted by the enchanted lady is a Johannisberg on the top of which is a chapel dedicated to St. John the Baptist, to which pilgrimages were made and the lady appeared on Midsummer Day (Gredt, pp. 215, 219, 225, 579).

[184] Von Tettau, p. 220; Kuhn und Schwartz, pp. 9, 200; Meier, pp. 6, 8; Gredt, pp. 7, 228, 281. In another story, quoted by Meier (p. 34), from Crusius' "Schwäb. Chron.", the enchanted maiden is called "a heathen's daughter"—pointing directly to pagan origin.

# CHAPTER X

# SWAN-MAIDENS

The *märchen* of Hasan of Bassorah — The Marquis of the Sun — The feather robe and other disguises — The taboo — The Star's Daughter — Melusina — The Lady of the Van Pool and other variants — The Nightmare.

The narratives with which we have hitherto been occupied belong to the class called Sagas. But our discussions of them have led us once and again to refer to the other class mentioned in the second Chapter—that of Nursery Tales or *Märchen*. For, as I have already pointed out, there is no bridgeless gulf between them. We have seen the very same incidents narrated in Wales or in Germany with breathless awe as a veritable occurrence which in India, or among the Arabs, are a mere play of fancy. Equally well the case may be reversed, and what is gravely told at the antipodes as a series of events in the life of a Maori ancestor, may be reported in France or England as a nursery tale. Nay, we need not go out of Europe itself to find the same plot serving for a saga in one land and a *märchen*, detached from all circumstances of time and place, in another.

An excellent example of this is furnished by the myth of the Swan-maiden, one of the most widely distributed, and at the same time one of the most beautiful, stories ever evolved from the mind of man. As its first type I shall take the tale of Hasan of Bassorah, where it has been treated with an epic grandeur hardly surpassed by any of its companions in the famous "Nights," and perhaps only by one of the less famous but equally splendid Mabinogion of old Wales.

Hasan is a worthless boy who falls under the influence of a Magian, who professes to be an alchemist, and who at length kidnaps him. Having used him with great cruelty the Magian takes him fifteen days' journey on dromedaries into the desert to a high mountain, at the foot whereof the old rascal sews him up in a skin, together with a knife and a small provision of three cakes and a leathern bottle of water, afterwards retiring to a distance. One of the vultures which infest the mountain then pounces on Hasan and carries him to the top. In accordance with the Magian's instructions, the hero, on arriving there, slits the skin, and jumping out, to the bird's affright, picks up and casts down to the Magian bundles of the wood which he finds around him. This wood is the means by which the alchemy is performed; and having gathered up the bundles the Magian leaves Hasan to his fate. The youth, after despairing of life, finds his way to a palace where dwell seven maidens, with whom he remains for awhile in Platonic friendship. When they are summoned away by their father for a two months' absence, they leave him their keys, straitly charging him not to open a certain door. He disregards their wishes, and finds within a magnificent pavilion enclosing a basin brimful of water, at which ten birds come to bathe and play. The birds for this purpose cast their feathers; and Hasan is favoured with the sight of "ten virgins, maids whose beauty shamed the brilliancy of the moon." He fell madly in love with the chief damsel, who turns out to be a daughter of a King of the Jann. On the return of the maidens of the palace he is advised by them to watch the next time the birds come, and to take possession of the feather-suit belonging to the damsel of his choice, for without this she cannot return home with her attendants. He succeeds in doing so, and thus compels her to remain with him and become his wife. With her he departs to his own country and settles in Bagdad, where his wife bears him two sons. During his temporary absence, however, she persuades her mother-in-law—who, unfortunately for the happiness of the household, lives with the young couple—to let her have the feather-suit which her husband has left under her charge. Clad with this she takes her two boys in her arms and sails away through the air to the islands of Wák, leaving a message for the hapless Hasan that if he loves her he may come and seek her there. Now the islands of Wák were seven islands, wherein was a mighty host, all virgin girls, and the inner isles were peopled by satans and marids and warlocks and various tribesmen of the Jinn, and whoso entered their land never returned thence; and Hasan's wife was one of the king's daughters. To reach her he would have to cross seven wadys and seven seas and seven mighty mountains. Undaunted, however, by the difficulties wherewith he is threatened, he determines to find her, swearing by Allah never to turn back till he regain his beloved, or till death overtake him. By the help of sundry potentates of more or less forbidding aspect and supernatural power, to whom he gets letters of introduction, and who live in gorgeous palaces amid deserts, and are served by demons only uglier and less mighty than themselves, he succeeds in traversing the Land of Birds, the Land of Wild Beasts, the country of the Warlocks and the Enchanters, and the Land of the Jinn, and enters the islands of Wák—there to fall into the hands of that masterful virago, his wife's eldest sister. After a preliminary outburst against Hasan, this amiable creature pours, as is the wont of women, the full torrent of her wrath against her erring sister. From the tortures she inflicts, Hasan at length rescues his wife, with their two sons, by means of a cap of invisibility and a rod conferring authority over seven tribes of the Jinn, which he has stolen from two boys who are quarrelling over them. When his sister-in-law with an army of Jinn pursues the fugitives, the subjects of the rod overcome her. His wife begs for her sister's life and reconciles her husband to her, and then returns with her husband to his home in Bagdad, to quit him no more.[185]

Such in meagre outline is this wonderful story. Its variants are legion, and I can only refer to a few of them which are of special interest. In dealing with these I shall confine my attention to the essential points of the plot, touching only such details as are germane to the questions thus evoked. We shall accordingly pass in review the maiden's disguise and capture, her flight and her recapture; and afterwards turning to other types of the tale, we shall look at the corresponding incidents to be met with therein, reserving for another chapter the consideration of the meaning of the myth, so far as it can be traced.

The bird whose shape is assumed by the Jinn in the foregoing tale is not specified; but in Europe, where beauty and grace and purity find so apt an emblem in the swan, several of the most important variants have naturally appropriated that majestic form to the heroine, and have thus given a name to the whole group of stories. In Sweden, for example, we are told of a young hunter who beheld three swans descend on the seashore and lay their plumage aside before they plunged into the water. When he looked at the robes so laid aside they appeared like linen, and the forms that were swimming in the waves were damsels of dazzling whiteness. Advised by his foster-mother, he secures the linen of the youngest and fairest. She, therefore, could not follow her companions when they drew on their plumage and flew away; and being thus in the hunter's power, she became his wife. The hero of a story current among the Germans of Transylvania opens, like Hasan, a forbidden door, and finds three swan-maids bathing in a blue pool. Their clothes are contained in satchels on its margin, and when he has taken the satchel of the youngest he must not look behind until he has reached home. This done, he finds the maiden there and persuades her to marry him. Mikáilo Ivanovitch, the hero of a popular Russian ballad, wanders by the sea, and, gazing out upon a quiet bay, beholds a white swan floating there. He draws his bow to shoot her, but she prays him to desist; and rising over the blue sea upon her white wings, she turns into a beautiful maiden. Surprised with love, he offers to kiss her; but she reveals herself as a heathen princess and demands first to be baptized, and then she will wed him. In a Hessian story a forester sees a fair swan floating on a lonely lake. He is about to shoot it when it warns him to desist, or it will cost him his life. Immediately the swan was transformed into a maiden, who told him she was bewitched, but could be freed if he would say a Paternoster for her every Sunday for a twelvemonth, and meantime keep silence concerning his adventure. The test proved too hard, and he lost her.[186]

The swan, however, by no means monopolizes the honour of concealing the heroine's form. In a Finnish tale from Œsterbotten, a dead father appears in dreams to his three sons, commanding them to watch singly by night the geese on the sea-strand. The two elder are so frightened by the darkness that they scamper home. But the youngest, despised and dirty, watches boldly, till at the first flush of dawn three geese fly thither, strip off their feathers, and plunge, as lovely maidens, into the water to bathe. Then the youth chooses the most beautiful of the three pairs of wings he finds on the shore, hides them, and awaits events; nor does he give them up again to the owner until she has betrothed herself to him. Elsewhere the damsels are described as ducks; but a more common shape is that of doves. A story is current in Bohemia of a boy whom a witch leads to a spring. Over the spring stands an old elm-tree haunted by three white doves, who are enchanted princesses. Catching one and plucking out her wings, he restores her to her natural condition; and she brings him to his parents, whom he had lost in the sack of the city where they dwelt. The Magyars speak of three pigeons coming every noontide to a great white lake, where they turn somersaults and are transformed into girls. They are really fairy-maidens; and a boy who can steal the dress of one of them and run away with it, resisting the temptation to look back when she calls in caressing tones, succeeds in winning her. In the "Bahar Danush" a merchant's son perceives four doves alight at sunset by a piece of water, and, resuming their natural form (for they are Peries), forthwith undress and plunge into the water. He steals their clothes, and thus compels the one whom he chooses to accept him as her husband. The extravagance characteristic of the "Arabian Nights," when, in the story of Janshah, it represents the ladies as doves, expands their figures to the size of eagles, with far less effect, however, than where they retain more moderate dimensions. No better illustration of this can be given than the story from South Smaland of the fair Castle east of the Sun and north of the Earth, versified so exquisitely in "The Earthly Paradise." There a peasant, finding that the fine grass of a meadow belonging to him was constantly trodden down during the summer nights, set his three sons, one after another, to watch for the trespassers. The two elder, as usual in these tales, are unsuccessful, but the youngest keeps wide awake until the sun is about to rise. A rustling in the air, as of birds, then heralds the flight of three doves, who cast their feathers and become fair maidens. These maidens begin to dance on the green grass, and so featly do they step that they scarce seem to touch the ground. To the watching youth, one among them looked more beautiful than all other women; and he pictured to himself the possession of her as more to be longed for than that of every other in the world. So he rose and stole their plumage, nor did he restore it until the king's daughter, the fairest of them all, had plighted her troth to him.[187]

The story is by no means confined to Europe and Asia. The Arawàks, one of the aboriginal tribes of Guiana, relate that a beautiful royal vulture was once captured by a hunter. She was the daughter of Anuanima, sovereign of a race whose country is above the sky, and who lay aside there the appearance of birds for that of humanity. Smitten with love for the hunter, the captive divested herself of her feathers and exhibited her true form—that of a beautiful girl. "She becomes his wife, bears him above the clouds, and, after much trouble, persuades her father and family to receive him. All then goes well, until he expresses a wish to visit his aged mother, when they discard him, and set him on the top of a very high tree, the trunk of which is covered with formidable prickles. He appeals pathetically to all the living creatures around. Then spiders spin cords to help him, and fluttering birds ease his descent, so that at last he reaches the ground in safety. Then follow his efforts, extending over several years, to regain his wife, whom he tenderly loves. Her family seek to destroy him; but by his strength and sagacity he is victorious in every encounter. The birds at length espouse his cause, assemble their forces, and bear him as their commander above the sky. He is at last slain by a valiant young warrior, resembling himself in person and features. It is his own son, born after his expulsion from the upper regions, and brought up there in ignorance of his own father. The legend ends with the conflagration of the house of the royal vultures, who, hemmed in by crowds of hostile birds, are unable to use their wings, and forced to fight and die in their human forms."[188] This tale, so primitive in form, can hardly have travelled round half the globe to the remote American Indians among whom it was discovered. And yet in many of its features it presents the most striking likeness to several of the versions current in the Old World.

Sometimes, however, as in the tale of Hasan, the species is left undescribed. Among the Eskimo the heroine is vaguely referred to as a sea-fowl. The Kurds have a strange tale of a bird they call the Bird Simer. His daughter has been ensnared by a giant when she and three other birds were out flying; but she is at length rescued by two heroes, one of whom she weds. When she becomes homesick she puts on her feather-dress and flies away.[189]

A Pomeranian saga forms an interesting link between the Swan-maiden group and the legends of Enchanted Princesses discussed in the last chapter. A huntsman, going his rounds in the forest, drew near a pool which lies at the foot of the Hühnerberg. There he saw a girl bathing; and thinking that she was from the neighbouring village, he picked up her clothes, with the intention of playing her a trick. When she saw what he had done, she left the water and hastened after him, begging him to give back her clothes—or at any rate her shift. He, however, was not to be moved; and she then told him she was an enchanted princess, and without her shift she could not return. Now he was fully determined not to give up the precious article of apparel. She was, therefore, compelled to follow him to his hut, where his mother kept house for him. The huntsman there put the shift into a chest, of which he took the key, so that the maiden could not escape; and after some time she accepted the position, and agreed to become his wife. Years passed by, and several children had been born, when one day he went out, leaving the key of the chest behind. When the heroine saw this she begged her mother-in-law to open the chest and show her the shift; for, we are told, the enchanted princess could not herself open the trunk. She begged so hard that her mother-in-law at last complied; and no sooner had she got the shift into her hands than she vanished out of sight. When the husband returned and heard what had happened, he made up his mind to seek her. So he climbed the Hühnerberg and let himself down the opening he found there. He soon arrived at the underground castle. Before its closed gate lay a great black dog, around whose neck a paper hung which conveniently contained directions how to penetrate into the castle. Following these, he presently found himself in the presence of the princess, his wife, who was right glad to see him, and gave him a glass of wine to strengthen him for the task before him; for at midnight the Evil One would come to drive him out of the castle and prevent the lady's deliverance. At this point, unfortunately, the reciter's memory failed: hence we do not know the details of the rescue. But we may conjecture, from the precedents, that the huntsman had to endure torture. The issue was that he was successful, the castle ascended out of the earth, and husband and wife were reunited.[190]

This story differs in many important respects from the type; and it contains the incident, very rare in a modern European saga belonging to this group, of the recovery of the bride. I shall have occasion to revert to the curious inability of the enchanted princess to open the chest containing the wonderful shift. Meanwhile, let me observe that in most of the tales the feather-dress, or talisman, by which the bride may escape, is committed to the care of a third person—usually a kinswoman of the husband, and in many cases his mother; and that the wife as a rule only recovers it when it is given to her, or at least when that which contains it has been opened by another: she seems incapable of finding it herself.

There is another type of the Swan-maiden myth, which appears to be the favourite of the Latin nations, though it is also to be met with among other peoples. Its outline may, perhaps, best be given from the nursery tale of the Marquis of the Sun, as told at Seville. The Marquis of the Sun was a great gamester. A man played with him and lost all he had, and then staked his soul—and lost it. The Marquis instructed him, if he desired to recover it, to come to him when he had worn out a pair of iron shoes. In the course of his wanderings he finds a struggle going on over a dead man, whose creditors would not allow him to be buried until his debts had been paid. Iron Shoes pays them, and one shoe goes to pieces. He afterwards meets a cavalier, who reveals himself as the dead man whose debts had been paid, and who is desirous of requiting that favour. He therefore directs Iron Shoes to the banks of a river where three white doves come, change into princesses, and bathe. Iron Shoes is to take the dress of the smallest, and thus get her to tell him whither he has to go. Obeying this direction, he learns from the princess that the Marquis is her father; and she shows him the way to his castle. Arrived there, he demands his soul. Before conceding it the Marquis sets him tasks: to level an inconvenient mountain, so that the sun may shine on the castle; to sow the site of the mountain with fruit trees, and gather the fruit of them in one day for dinner; to find a piece of plate which the Marquis's great-grandfather had dropped into the river; to catch and mount a horse which is no other than the Marquis himself; and to choose a bride from among the princesses, his daughters. The damsel who had shown Iron Shoes the way to the palace performs the first two of these tasks: and she teaches him how to perform the others. For the third, he has to cut her up and cast her into the river, whence she immediately rises whole again, triumphantly bringing the lost piece of plate. In butchering her he has, however, clumsily dropped a piece of her little finger on the ground. It is accordingly wanting when she rises from the river; and this is the token by which Iron Shoes recognizes her when he has to choose a bride; for, in choosing, he is only allowed to see the little fingers of these candidates for matrimony. He and his bride afterwards flee from the castle; but we need not follow their adventures now.[191]

In stories of this type doves are the shape usually assumed by the heroine and her comrades; but swans and geese are often found, and in a Russian tale we are even introduced to spoonbills. Nor do the birds I have mentioned by any means exhaust the disguises of these supernatural ladies. The stories comprised under this and the foregoing type are nearly all *märchen*; but when we come to other types where sagas become more numerous, we find other animals favoured, well-nigh to the exclusion of birds. In the latter types there is no recovery of the wife when she has once abandoned her husband. An inhabitant of Unst, one of the Shetland Islands, beholds a number of the seafolk dancing by moonlight on the shore of a small bay. Near them lie several sealskins. He snatches up one, the property, as it turns out, of a fair maiden, who thereupon becomes his wife. Years after, one of their children finds her sealskin, and runs to display it to his mother, not knowing it was hers. She puts it on, becomes a seal, and plunges into the waters. In Croatia it is said that a soldier once, watching in a haunted mill, saw a she-wolf enter, divest herself of her skin, and come out of it a damsel. She hangs the skin on a peg and goes to sleep before the fire. While she sleeps the soldier takes the skin and nails it fast to the mill-wheel, so that she cannot recover it. He marries her, and she bears him two sons. The elder of these children hears that his mother is a wolf. He becomes inquisitive, and his father at length tells him where the skin is. When he tells his mother, she goes away and is heard of no more. A Sutherlandshire story speaks of a mermaid who fell in love with a fisherman. As he did not want to be carried away into the sea he, by fair means or foul, succeeded in getting hold of her pouch and belt, on which her power of swimming depended, and so retained her on land; and she became his bride. But we are not surprised to hear that her tail was always in the way: her silky hair grew tangled too, for her comb and glass were in the pouch; the dogs teased her, and rude people mocked her. Thus her life was made wretched. But one day in her husband's absence the labourers were pulling down a stack of corn. As she watched them, weeping for her lost freedom, she espied her precious pouch and belt, which had been built in and buried among the sheaves. She caught it and leaped into the sea.[192]

In the last tale there is no change of form: the hero simply possesses himself of something without which the supernatural maiden has no power to leave him. Even in the true Hasan of Bassorah type, the magical change does not always occur. A variant translated by Jonathan Scott from a Syrian manuscript merely enwraps the descending damsels in robes of light green silk. When her robe is taken the chosen beauty is kept from following her companions in their return flight. Similar to this is the Pomeranian saga already cited. In the New Hebrides there is a legend of seven winged women whose home was in heaven, and who came down to earth to bathe. Before bathing, they put off their wings. According to the version told in Aurora island, Qatu one day, seeing them thus bathing, took the wings of one and buried them at the foot of the main post of his house. In this way he won their owner as his wife; and she so remained until she found her wings again. In modern Greece it is believed that Nereids can be caught by seizing their wings, their clothes, or even their handkerchiefs. The Bulgarians, who have similar tales, call the supernatural ladies Samodivas; and they are captured by means of their raiment. A number of parallels have been cited from various sources by M. Cosquin, a few of which may be mentioned. A Burmese drama, for instance, sets before us nine princesses of the city of the Silver Mountain, who wear enchanted girdles that enable them to fly as swiftly as a bird. The youngest of these princesses is caught while bathing, by means of a magical slip-knot. A divine ancestress of the Bantiks, a tribe inhabiting the Celebes Islands, came down from the sky with seven companions to bathe. A man who saw them took them for doves, but was surprised to find that they were women. He possessed himself of the clothes of one of them, and thus obliged her to marry him. In a story told by the Santals of India, the daughters of the sun make use of a spider's thread to reach the earth. A shepherd, whom they unblushingly invite to bathe with them, persuades them to try which of them all can remain longest under water; and while they are in the river he scrambles out, and, taking the upper garment of the one whom he loves, flees with it to his home. In another Indian tale, five apsaras, or celestial dancers, are conveyed in an enchanted car to a pool in the forest. Seven supernatural maidens, in a Samoyede *märchen*, are brought in their reindeer chariot to a lake, where the hero possesses himself of the best suit of garments he finds on the shore. The owner prays him to give them up; but he refuses, until he obtains a definite pledge of marriage, saying: "If I give thee the garments thou wilt fare up again to heaven."[193]

In none of these stories (and they are but samples of many) does the feather dress occur; yet it has left reminiscences which are unmistakable. The variants hitherto cited have all betrayed these reminiscences as articles of clothing, or conveyance, or in the pardonable mistake of the Bantik forefather at the time of capture. I shall refer presently to cases whence the plumage has faded entirely out of the story—and that in spite of its picturesqueness—without leaving a trace. But let me first call attention to the fact that, even where it is preserved, we often do not find it exactly how and where we should have expected it. Witness the curious Algonkin tale of "How one of the Partridge's wives became a Sheldrake Duck." A hunter, we are told, returning home in his canoe, saw a beautiful girl sitting on a rock by the river, making a moccasin. He paddled up softly to capture her; but she jumped into the water and disappeared. Her mother, however, who lived at the bottom, compelled her to return to the hunter and be his wife. The legend then takes a turn in the direction of the Bluebeard myth; for the woman yields to curiosity, and thus deprives her husband of his luck. When he finds this out he seizes his bow to beat her. "When she saw him seize his bow to beat her she ran down to the river, and jumped in to escape death at his hands, though it should be by drowning. But as she fell into the water she became a sheldrake duck." The Passamaquoddies, who relate this story, have hardly yet passed out of the stage of thought in which no steadfast boundary is set between men and the lower animals. The amphibious maiden, who dwelt in the bottom of the river, could not be drowned by jumping into the stream; and it is evident that she only resumes her true aquatic form in escaping from her husband, who, it should be added, is himself called Partridge and seems to be regarded as, in fact, a fowl of that species. A still more remarkable instance is to be found among the Welsh of Carnarvonshire, who, it need hardly be said, are now on a very different level of civilization from that of the Passamaquoddies. They tell us that when the fairy bride of Corwrion quitted her unlucky husband, she at once flew through the air and plunged into the lake; and one account significantly describes her as flying away *like a wood-hen*. Can it have been many generations since she was spoken of as actually changing into a bird?[194]

We may now pass to wholly different types of the tradition. In all the stories where the magical dress appears, whether as a feather-skin, the hide of a quadruped, or in the modified form of wings, a robe, an apron, a veil or other symbol, the catastrophe is brought about by the wife's recovery, usually more or less accidental, of the article in question. But it is obvious that where the incident of the dress is wanting, the loss of the supernatural bride must be brought about by other means. In some traditions, the woman's caprice, or the fulfilment of her fate, is deemed enough for this purpose; but in the most developed stories it is caused by the breach of a *taboo*. *Taboo* is a word adopted from the Polynesian languages, signifying, first, something set apart, thence holy and inviolable, and lastly something simply forbidden. It is generally used in English as a verb of which the nearest equivalent is another curious verb—to boycott. A person or thing *tabooed* is one avoided by express or tacit agreement on the part of any class or number of persons; and *to taboo* is to avoid in pursuance of such an agreement. In Folklore, however, the word is used in a different and wider sense. It includes every sort of prohibition, from the social or religious boycott (if I may use the word), to which it would be more properly applied, down to any injunction addressed by a supernatural being to the hero or heroine of a tale. Folklore students of the anthropological school are so apt to refer these last prohibitions for their origin to the more general prohibitions of the former kind, that perhaps this indiscriminate use of the word may be held to beg some of the questions at issue. It is certain, however, that the scholars who originally applied it to what I may call private prohibitions, had no such thought in their minds. They found it a convenient term, applicable by no great stretch of its ordinary meaning, and they appropriated it to the purposes of science. I shall therefore use it without scruple as a well recognized word, and without any question-begging intent.

Having premised so much, I will proceed to set forth shortly the balder type of the story, where there is no taboo, then the fuller type. Their relations to one another will be dealt with in the next chapter.

An Algonkin legend relates that a hunter beheld a basket descend from heaven, containing twelve young maidens of ravishing beauty. He attempted to approach, but on perceiving him they quickly re-entered the basket and were drawn up again out of his sight. Another day, however, he succeeded, by disguising himself as a mouse, in capturing the youngest of the damsels, whom he married and by whom he had a son. But nothing could console his wife for the society of her sisters, which she had lost. So one day she made a small basket; and having entered it with her child she sang the charm she and her sisters had formerly used, and ascended once more to the star from whence she had come. It is added that when two years had elapsed the star said to his daughter: "Thy son wants to see his father; go down, therefore, to the earth and fetch thy husband, and tell him to bring us specimens of all the animals he kills." This was done. The hunter ascended with his wife to the sky; and there a great feast was given, in which the animals he brought were served up. Those of the guests who took the paws or the tails were transformed into animals. The hunter himself took a white feather, and with his wife and child was metamorphosed into a falcon.[195] I will only now remark on the latter part of the tale that it is told by the same race as the Sheldrake Duck's adventures; and if we deem it probable that the heroine of that narrative simply resumed her pristine form in becoming a duck, the same reasoning will hold good as to the falcons here. This type of the myth we may call the "Star's Daughter type."

The other type may be named after Melusina, the famous Countess of Lusignan. The earliest writer to mention the legend which afterwards became identified with her name, was Gervase of Tilbury, who relates that Raymond, the lord of a certain castle a few miles from Aix in Provence, riding alone on the banks of the river, unexpectedly met an unknown lady of rare beauty, also alone, riding on a splendidly caparisoned palfrey. On his saluting her she replied, addressing him by name. Astonished at this, but encouraged, he made improper overtures to her; to which she declined to assent, intimating, however, in the most unabashed way, that she would marry him if he liked. He agreed to this; but the lady imposed a further condition, namely, that he should never see her naked; for if once he did so, all the prosperity and all the happiness with which he was about to be blessed would depart, and he would be left to drag out the rest of his life in wretchedness. On these terms they were married; and every earthly felicity followed,—wealth, renown, bodily strength, the love of his fellow-men, and children—boys and girls—of the greatest beauty. But one day his lady was bathing in the bedroom, when he came in from hunting and fowling, laden with partridges and other game. While food was being prepared the thought struck him that he would go and see her in her bath. So many years had he enjoyed unalloyed prosperity that, if there ever were any force in her threat, he deemed it had long since passed away. Deaf to his wife's pleadings, he tore away the curtain from the bath and beheld her naked; but only for an instant, for she was forthwith changed into a serpent, and, putting her head under the water, she disappeared. Nor ever was she seen again; but sometimes in the darkness of night the nurses would hear her busy with a mother's care for her little children. Gervase adds that one of her daughters was married to a relative of his own belonging to a noble family of Provence, and her descendants were living at the time he wrote.[196]

The story, as told of Melusina, was amplified, but in its substance differed little from the foregoing. Melusina does not forbid her husband to see her naked, but bargains for absolute privacy on Saturdays. When Raymond violates this covenant he finds her in her bath with her lower extremities changed into a serpent's tail. The lady appears to be unconscious of her husband's discovery; and nothing happens until, in a paroxysm of anger and grief, arising from the murder of one of his children by another, he cries out upon her as an odious serpent, the contaminator of his race. It will be remembered that in the Esthonian tale cited in Chapter VIII the youth is forbidden to call his mistress mermaid; and all goes well until he peeps into the locked chamber, where she passes her Thursdays, and finds her in mermaid form. Far away in Japan we learn that the hero Hohodemi wedded Toyotamahime, a daughter of the Sea-god, and built a house for her on the strand where she might give birth to her child. She strictly forbade him to come near until the happy event was over: he was to remain in his own dwelling, and on no account to attempt to see her until she sent for him. His curiosity, however, was too much for his happiness. He peeped, and saw his wife writhing to and fro on the floor in the shape of a dragon. He started back, shocked; and when, later on, Toyotamahime called him to her, she saw by his countenance that he had discovered the secret she had thought to hide from all mankind. In spite of his entreaties she plunged into the sea, never more to see her lord. Her boy, notwithstanding, was still the object of her care. She sent her sister to watch over him, and he grew up to become the father of the first Emperor of Japan. In a Maori tale the hero loses his wife through prematurely tearing down a screen he had erected for her convenience on a similar occasion. A Moravian tale speaks of a bride who shuts herself up every eighth day, and when her husband looks through the keyhole, he beholds her thighs clad with hair and her feet those of goats. This is a *märchen*; and in the end, having paid the penalty of his rashness by undergoing adventures like those of Hasan, the hero regains his love. A Tirolese *märchen* tells us of a witch who, in the shape of a beautiful girl, took service with a rich man and made a conquest of his son. She wedded him on condition that he would never look upon her by candlelight. The youth, like a masculine Psyche, breaks the taboo; and a drop of the wax, falling on her cheek, awakens her. It was in vain that he blew out the taper and lay down. When he awoke in the morning she was gone; but a pair of shoes with iron soles stood by the bed, with a paper directing him to seek her till the soles were worn out, and then he should find her again. By the aid of a mantle of invisibility, and a chair which bore him where he wished, he arrived in the nick of time to prevent her marriage with another bridegroom. The proper reconciliation follows, and her true husband bears her home in triumph. Not so happy was the hero of a Corsican saga, who insisted on seeing his wife's naked shoulder and found it nothing but bones—the skeleton of their love which he had thus murdered.[197]

At the foot of the steep grassy cliffs of the Van Mountains in Carmarthenshire lies a lonely pool, called Llyn y Fan Fach, which is the scene of a variant of Melusina, less celebrated, indeed, but equally romantic and far more beautiful. The legend may still be heard on the lips of the peasantry; and more than one version has found its way into print. The most complete was written down by Mr. William Rees, of Tonn (a well-known Welsh antiquary and publisher), from the oral recitation of two old men and a woman, natives of Myddfai, where the hero of the story is said to have dwelt. Stated shortly, the legend is to the following effect: The son of a widow who lived at Blaensawdde, a little village about three-quarters of a mile from the pool, was one day tending his mother's cattle upon its shore when, to his astonishment, he beheld the Lady of the Lake sitting upon its unruffled surface, which she used as a mirror while she combed out her graceful ringlets. She imperceptibly glided nearer to him, but eluded his grasp and refused the bait of barley bread and cheese that he held out to her, saying as she dived and disappeared:

"Cras dy fara;
Nid hawdd fy nala!"
("Hard-baked is thy bread;
It is not easy to catch me!")

An offer of unbaked dough, or *toes*, the next day was equally unsuccessful. She exclaimed:

"Llaith dy fara!
Ti ni fynna'."
("Unbaked is thy bread!
I will not have thee.")

But the slightly baked bread, which the youth subsequently took, by his mother's advice, was accepted: he seized the lady's hand and persuaded her to become his bride. Diving into the lake she then fetched her father—"a hoary-headed man of noble mien and extraordinary stature, but having otherwise all the force and strength of youth"—who rose from the depths with *two* ladies and was ready to consent to the match, provided the young man could distinguish which of the two ladies before him was the object of his affections. This was no small test of love, inasmuch as the maidens were exactly alike in form and features. One of them, however, thrust her foot a little forward; and the hero recognized a peculiarity of her shoe-tie, which he had somehow had leisure to notice at his previous interviews. The father admits the correctness of his choice, and bestows a dowry of sheep, cattle, goats, and horses, but stipulates in the most business-like way that these animals shall return with the bride, if at any time her husband prove unkind and strike her thrice without a cause.

So far Mr. Rees' version. A version published in the "Cambro-Briton" is somewhat different. Three beautiful damsels appear from the pool, and are repeatedly pursued by the young farmer, but in vain. They always reached the water before him and taunted him with the couplet:

"Cras dy fara,
Anhawdd ein dala!"

One day some moist bread from the lake came floating ashore. The youth seized and devoured it; and the following day he was successful in catching the ladies. The one to whom he offers marriage consents on the understanding that he will recognize her the next day from among the three sisters. He does so by the strapping of her sandal; and she is accompanied to her new home by seven cows, two oxen, and a bull from the lake. A third version presents the maiden as rowing on New Year's Eve up and down the lake in a golden boat with a golden oar. She disappears from the hero's gaze, without replying to his adjurations. Counselled by a soothsayer, who dwells on the mountain, he casts loaves and cheese night after night from Midsummer Eve to New Year's Eve into the water, until at length the magic skiff again appears, and the fairy, stepping ashore, weds her persistent wooer.

In all three versions the bridegroom is forbidden to strike "three causeless blows." Of course he disobeys. According to the "Cambro-Briton" version it happened that one day, preparing for a fair, he desired his wife to go to the field for his horse. Finding her dilatory in doing so, he tapped her arm thrice with his glove, saying, half in jest: "Go, go, go!" The blows were slight, but they were blows; and, the terms of the marriage contract being broken, the dame departed—she and her cattle with her—back into the lake. The other two accounts agree in spreading the blows over a much greater length of time. Mr. Rees' version relates that once the husband and wife were invited to a christening in the neighbourhood. The lady, however, seemed reluctant to go, making the feminine excuse that the distance was too far to walk. Her husband told her to fetch one of the horses from the field. "I will," said she, "if you will bring me my gloves, which I left in the house." He went, and, returning with the gloves, found that she had not gone for the horse, so he jocularly slapped her shoulder with one of the gloves, saying: "Go, go!" Whereupon she reminded him of the condition that he was not to strike her without a cause, and warned him to be more careful in future. Another time, when they were together at a wedding, she burst out sobbing amid the joy and mirth of all around her. Her husband touched her on the shoulder and inquired the cause of her weeping. She replied: "Now people are entering into trouble; and your troubles are likely to commence, as you have the second time stricken me without a cause." Finding how very wide an interpretation she put upon the "causeless blows," the unfortunate husband did his best to avoid anything which could give occasion for the third and last blow. But one day they were together at a funeral, where, in the midst of the grief, she appeared in the highest spirits and indulged in immoderate fits of laughter. Her husband was so shocked that he touched her, saying: "Hush, hush! don't laugh!" She retorted that she laughed "because people, when they die, go out of trouble"; and, rising up, she left the house, exclaiming: "The last blow has been struck; our marriage contract is broken, and at an end! Farewell!" Hurrying home, she called together all her fairy cattle, walked off with them to the lake, and vanished in its waters. Even a little black calf, slaughtered and suspended on the hook, descended alive and well again to obey his mistress' summons; and four grey oxen, which were ploughing, dragged the plough behind them as they went, leaving a well-marked furrow, that remains to this day "to witness if I lie." The remaining version, with some differences of detail, represents the same eccentric pessimism on the lady's part (presumably attributable to the greater spiritual insight of her supernatural character), as the cause of the husband's not unwarranted annoyance and of his breach of the agreement. She had borne him three fair sons; and although she had quitted her husband for ever, she continued to manifest herself occasionally to them, and gave them instruction in herbs and medicine, predicting that they and their issue would become during many generations the most renowned physicians in the country.[198]

Such is the legend of the Van Pool. It has a number of variants, both in Wales and elsewhere, the examination of which I postpone for the present. Hitherto I have been guided in the mention of variants of this myth chiefly by the desire of showing how one type insensibly merges into another. The only type I have now left for examination may be called the "Nightmare type." It is allied not so much to the stories of Melusina and the Lady of the Van Pool as to stories like that of the Croatian wolf-maiden. According to German and Slavonic belief the nightmare is a human being—frequently one whose love has been slighted, and who in this shape is enabled to approach the beloved object. It slips through the keyhole, or any other hole in a building, and presses its victim sometimes to death. But it can be caught by quickly stopping the hole through which it has entered. A certain man did so one night; and in the morning he found a young and lovely maiden in the room. On asking her whence she came, she told him from Engelland (angel-land, England). He hid her clothes, married her, and had by her three children. The only thing peculiar about her was that she used constantly to sing while spinning:

"Now calls my mother (*or*, blows my father) in Engelland,
Mary Catharine,
Drive out thy swine."

One day her husband came home and found that his wife had been telling the children that she had come as a nightmare from Engelland. When he reproached her for it, she went to the cupboard where her clothes were hidden, threw them over herself, and vanished. Yet she could not quite forsake her husband and little ones. On Saturdays she came unseen and laid out their clean clothes; and every night she appeared while others slept, and taking the baby out of the cradle quieted it at her breast. The allusion to the nightmare's clothes is uncommon; but it is an unmistakable link with the types we have been considering. In other tales she is caught in the shape of a straw; and she is generally released by taking the stopper out of the hole whereby she entered. The account she gives of herself is that she has come out of England, that the pastor had been guilty of some omission in the service when she was baptized, and hence she became a nightmare, but to be re-christened would cure her. She often hears her mother call her. In one story she vanished on being reproached with her origin, and in another on being asked how she became a nightmare.[199]

An Esthonian tale speaks of a father who found his little boy one night in an unquiet slumber. He noticed over the bed a hole in the wall through which the wind was whistling, and thought it was this which was disturbing him. Wherefore he stopped it up; and no sooner had he done so than he saw on the bed by the boy's side a pretty little girl, who teased and played with him so that he could not sleep in peace. The child was thus forced to stay in the house. She grew up with the other children, and being quick and industrious was beloved by all. Specially was she dear to the boy in whose bed she was found; and when he grew up he married her. One Sunday in church she burst out laughing during the sermon. After the service was over the husband inquired what she was laughing at. She refused to tell him, save on condition of his telling her in return how she came into his father's house. When she had extracted this promise from him, she told him she saw stretched on the wall of the church a great horse-skin, on which the Evil One was writing the names of all those who slept or chattered in church, and paid no heed to God's word. The skin was at last full of names; and in order to find room for more the Devil had to pull it with his teeth, so as to stretch it further. In so doing he bumped his head against the wall, and made a wry face: whereat she, who saw it, laughed. When they got home her husband pulled out the piece of wood which his father had put into the hole; and the same instant his wife was gone. The husband was disconsolate, but he saw her no more. It was said, however, that she often appeared to his two children in secret, and brought them precious gifts. In Smaland a parallel legend is current, according to which the ancestress of a certain family was an elf-maid who came into the house with the sunbeams through a knot-hole in the wall, and, after being married to the son and bearing him four children, vanished the same way as she had come. In North Germany it is believed that when seven boys, or seven girls, are born in succession, one among them is a nightmare. A man who had unknowingly wedded such a nightmare found that she disappeared from his bed at nights; and on watching her he discovered that she slipped through the hole for the strap by which the latch was lifted, returning the same way. So he stopped up the opening, and thus always retained her. After a considerable time he wanted to use the latch, and thinking she had forgotten her bad habit and he might safely take the peg out, he did so; but the next night she was missing, and never came back, though every Sunday morning the man found clean linen laid out for him as usual.[200]

A Pomeranian tradition relates the adventure of an officer who was much troubled by the nightmare. He caught her in the usual manner and wedded her, although he could not persuade her to say whence she came. After some years she induced her husband to open the holes he had stopped up; and the next morning she had disappeared. But he found written in chalk on the table the words: "If thou wilt seek me, the Commander of London is my father." He sought her in London and found her; and having taken the precaution to rechristen her he lived happily with her ever after.[201] This is the only instance I have met with where the nightmare-wife is recovered. It would be interesting to know why England is assigned as the home of these perturbed spirits.

**FOOTNOTES:**

[185] Burton, "Nights," vol. viii. p. 7.

[186] Thorpe, vol. ii. p. 69, quoting Afzelius; Haltrich, p. 15; Hapgood, p. 214; Meier, "Volksmärchen," p. 39; Baring-Gould, p. 575. No authority is given by Mr. Baring-Gould, and I have been unable to trace the Hessian tale; but I rely on his correctness. He also cites an incoherent Swan-maiden tale from Castrén, of which he manages to make more sense than I can (Castrén, "Altaischen Völker," p. 172). In an Irish tale Oengus, the son of the Dagda,

falls in love, through a dream, with Caer ib Ormaith, who is one year in the form of a swan and the next in human shape. After union with her he seems to have undergone the same alternation of form (*Revue Celtique*, vol. iii. p. 342, from a MS. in the British Museum).

[187] Schreck, p. 35; Vernaleken, pp. 274, 287; Jones and Kropf, p. 95; "Bahar-Danush," vol. ii. p. 213 (an abstract of this story will be found in Keightley, p. 20); Burton, "Nights," vol. v. p. 344; Steere, p. 349; Cavallius, p. 175, freely translated by Thorpe, "Yule-Tide Stories," p. 158. Mr. Morris turns the doves into swans. *Cf.* a South-Slavonic tale from Varazdina, Krauss, vol. i. p. 409.

[188] Brett, "Legends and Myths," p. 29. This legend is told with further details by Im Thurn, p. 381.

[189] Rink, p. 145; Prym und Socin, p. 51.

[190] Knoop, p. 104.

[191] "F. L. Españ." vol. i. p. 187.

[192] Keightley, p. 169, from Hibbert, "Description of the Shetland Islands"; Wratislaw, p. 290; "F. L. Journal," vol. vi. p. 165. As a point of resemblance with the Lady of the Van Pool, quoted further on, it may be noted that these seal-women (the legend of their capture is a common one in the Shetland Islands) had the power to conjure up from the deep a superior breed of horned cattle, many of whose offspring are still to be seen (Dr. Karl Blind in "Contemp. Rev." 1881, quoted by Mac Ritchie, p. 4).

[193] Kirby, p. 319; "Arch. Rev." vol. ii. p. 90; Schmidt, p. 133; Bent, p. 13; Von Hahn, vol. i. p. 295 (*cf.* vol. ii. p. 82); Garnett, p. 352, translating Dozon's "Chansons Populaires Bulgares"; Cosquin, vol. ii. p. 18. *Cf.* Ralston, "Tibetan Tales," p. 53; Landes, p. 123; Comparetti, vol. i. p. 212, translated "F. L. Record," vol. ii. p. 12; Grimm, "Tales," vol. ii. p. 331; Poestion, p. 55; Vernaleken, p. 274; Pitré, vol. iv. p. 140; Sastri, p. 80.

[194] Leland, p. 300. *Cf.* ibid. p. 140, where the maidens are called weasels, and ultimately marry stars. "Y Cymmrodor," vol. iv. p. 201. In a tale rendered from the modern Greek by Von Hahn the name Swan-maiden is preserved in the title, though the plumage has disappeared from the text. Stress can hardly be laid upon this, as the title is no part of the tale. Von Hahn, vol. i. p. 131.

[195] "La Tradition," March 1889, p. 78, quoting the Abbé Domenech, "Voyage pittoresque dans les déserts du Nouveau Monde," p. 214. Mr. Farrer gives the same story from "Algic Researches" (Farrer, "Primitive Manners," p. 256).

[196] Gerv. Tilb. Dec. i. c. 15.

[197] Brauns, p. 138; White, vol. ii. p. 141; Vernaleken, p. 294; Schneller, p. 23; Ortoli, p. 284.

[198] "The Physicians of Myddfai—Meddygon Myddfai," translated by John

Pughe, Esq., F.R.C.S., and edited by Rev. John Williams ab Ithel, M.A. (1861), p. xxi. "Cambro-Briton," vol. ii. p. 315; Sikes, p. 40. Mr. Sikes gives no authority for the third version. I have assumed its genuineness, though I confess Mr. Sikes' methods are not such as to inspire confidence.

[199] Jahn, p. 364, *et seqq.*; Knoop, pp. 26, 83, 103; Kuhn, pp. 47, 197, 374; Kuhn und Schwartz, pp. 14, 91, 298; Schleicher, p. 93; Thorpe, vol. ii. p. 169, quoting Thiele. Note the suggestion of Pope Gregory's pun in the name of the native land of the nightmare. Elsewhere a child becomes a nightmare who is born on a Sunday and baptized on a Sunday at the same hour, or one at whose baptism some wicked person has secretly muttered in response to one of the priest's questions some wrong words, or "It shall become a nightmare" (Lemke, p. 42). Similar superstitions attached to somnabulism; see Lecky, "History of Rationalism," vol. i. p. 81, note 2.

[200] Jannsen, vol. i. p. 53; Thorpe, vol. iii. p. 70, quoting Afzelius, vol. ii. p. 29, quoting Müllenhoff. It is a common Teutonic belief that knot-holes are attributable to elves (Grimm, "Teut. Myth." p. 461).

[201] "Am Urds-Brunnen," vol. vi. p. 58.

# CHAPTER XI
# SWAN-MAIDENS (*continued*)

The incident of the recovery of the bride not found in all the stories — New Zealand sagas — Andrianòro — Mother-right — The father represented under a forbidding aspect — Tasks imposed on the hero — The Buddhist theory of the Grateful Animals — The feather-robe a symbol of bride's superhuman character — Mode of capture — The Taboo — Dislike of fairies for iron— Utterance of name forbidden — Other prohibitions — Fulfilment of fate — The taboo a mark of progress in civilization — The divine ancestress — Totems and Banshees — Re-appearance of mother to her children — The lady of the Van Pool an archaic deity.

I hope I have made clear in the last chapter the connection between the various types of the Swan-maiden group of folk-tales. The one idea running through them all is that of a man wedding a supernatural maiden and unable to retain her. She must return to her own country and her own kin; and if he desire to recover her he must pursue her thither and conquer his right to her by undergoing superhuman penance or performing superhuman tasks,— neither of which it is given to ordinary men to do. It follows that only when the story is told of men who can be conceived as released from the limitations we have been gradually learning during the progress of civilization to regard as essential to humanity—only when the reins are laid upon the neck of invention,—is it possible to relate the narrative of the recovery of the bride. These conditions are twice fulfilled in the history of a folk-tale. They are fulfilled, first, when men are in that early stage of thought in which the limitations of man's nature are unknown, when speculations of the kind touched upon in our second chapter, and illustrated repeatedly in the course of this work, are received as undisputed opinions. They are fulfilled again when the relics of these opinions, and the memories of the mythical events believed in accordance with such opinions, are still operative in the mind, though no longer with the vividness of primitive times; when some of them still hold together, but for the most part they are decaying and falling to pieces, and are only like the faded rags of a once splendid robe which a child may gather round its puny form and make believe for the moment that it is a king. To the genuine credulity of the South-Sea Islander, and to the conscious make-believe of the Arab story-teller and the peasant who repeats the modern *märchen*, all things are possible. But to the same peasant when relating the traditional histories of his neighbours, and to the grave mediæval chronicler, only some things are possible, though many more things than are possible to us. The slow and partial advance of knowledge destroys some superstitions sooner, others later. Some branches of the tree of marvel flourish with apparently unimpaired life long after others have withered, and others again have only begun to fade. Hence, where the adventures of Tawhaki, the mythical New Zealander, are incredible, the legend of the origin of the Physicians of Myddfai from the Lady of the Lake may still be gravely accepted. Gervase of Tilbury would probably have treated the wild story of Hasan's adventures in the islands of Wák as what it is; but he tells us he has seen and conversed with women who had been captives to the Dracs beneath the waters of the Rhone, while a relative of his own had married a genuine descendant of the serpent-lady of that castle in the valley of Trets.

Accordingly, the episode of the recovery of the bride is scarcely ever found in the sagas of modern Europe, or indeed of any nation that has progressed beyond a certain mark in civilization. But it is common in their *märchen*, as well as in the sagas of more backward nations. In the sagas of the advanced races, with rare exceptions, the most we get is what looks like a reminiscence of the episode in the occasional reappearance of the supernatural wife to her children, or as a Banshee. Putting this reminiscence, if it be one, aside for the present, we will first discuss some aspects of the bride's recovery. In doing so, though the natural order may seem to be inverted, we shall in effect clear the ground for the proper understanding of the main features of the myth.

Many variants of the legend of Tawhaki are current among the Maories. According to that adopted by Sir George Grey, he was a hero renowned for his courage, whose fame had reached to heaven. There Tango-tango, a maiden of heavenly race, fell in love with him from report; and one night she descended to the earth and lay down by his side. She continued to do this nightly, stealing away again before dawn to her home. But when she found herself likely to become a mother she remained with him openly; and when her daughter was born she gave her to her husband to wash. Evidently he did not like the work, for while carrying out his wife's instructions, Tawhaki made a very rude remark about the child. Hearing this, Tango-tango began to sob bitterly, and at last rose up from her place with the child and took flight to the sky. Her husband determined to seek her. He found his way to the place where a creeper hung down from heaven and struck its roots into the earth. It was guarded there by a blind old ancestress of his, whom he restored to sight, and from whom he obtained directions how to climb the plant. Arrived in heaven, he disguised himself and had to undergo the indignity—he, a mighty chieftain—of being enslaved by his wife's relatives, for whom he was compelled to perform menial work. At length, however, he manifested himself to his wife and was reconciled to her. He is still in heaven, and is worshipped as a god. Another version represents a cloud swooping upon the wife and taking her away. Tawhaki endeavoured in vain to follow her by mounting on a kite. A third version simply relates that the lady returned to her friends. Her husband, on arriving at the *pa*, or settlement, where she dwelt, found among the children his own son, by whom he sent his wife a love-token she had formerly given him. This led to recognition, and she eventually returned with him to his home. A more interesting variant tells us that the fame of the nobleness of Tini-rau was heard by Hine-te-iwaiwa, who determined to set her cap (or whatever might be its equivalent in her scanty costume) at him. She obtained an interview with him, by a device recalling the conduct of the ladies in The Land East of the Sun, for she broke and destroyed some bathing-pools belonging to the hero. A quest of the intruder naturally followed, with the result that Tini-rau took her to live with him. She made short work of her rivals, his elder wives; and all went smoothly until Hine, one unlucky day, asked her husband to perform an operation upon her head as necessary as familiar in some strata of civilization. In doing this he made disrespectful observations about her, when lo! a mist settled down upon them, from the midst of which her elder brother came and took his sister away. Tini-rau, unable to endure her absence, determined to go after his wife, accompanied by a flight of birds, by whose cries he was informed, as he passed one settlement after another, whether or not his wife was there. At length he discovered her whereabouts, and made himself known to her sister by a token which Hine understood. Then he came to her, and she announced his arrival to all the people, who assembled and welcomed him. He abode there; and when his wife's relatives complained that he did not go and get food, he obtained it in abundance by the exercise of magical powers; and so they lived happy ever after.[202]

Now let us turn to the Malagasy tale of the way in which Andrianòro obtained a wife from heaven. There three sisters, whose dwelling-place is in heaven, frequent a lake in the crystal waters whereof they swim, taking flight at once on the approach of any human being. By a diviner's advice the hero changes into three lemons, which the youngest sister desires to take; but the others, fearing a snare, persuade her to fly away with them. Foiled thus, the hero changes into bluish water in the midst of the lake, then into the seed of a vegetable growing by the waterside, and ultimately into an ant. He is at length successful in seizing the youngest maiden, who consents to be his wife in spite of the difference of race; for, while her captor is a man living on the earth, her father dwells in heaven, whence the thunderbolt darts forth if he speak, and she herself drinks no spirits, "for if spirits even touch my mouth I die." After some time, during his absence, his father and mother force *tòaka*, or rum, into the lady's mouth, and she dies; but on his return he insists on opening her grave, and, to his joy, finds her alive again. But she will not now stay on earth: she must return to her father and mother in the sky. They are grieving for her, and the thunder is a sign of their grief. Finding himself unable to prevail upon her to stay, he obtains permission to accompany her. She warns him, however, of the dangers he will have to encounter,—the thunderbolt when her father speaks, and the tasks her father will lay upon him. Before he goes he accordingly calls the beasts and the birds together; he slays oxen to feed them; he tells them the tests he is about to undergo, and takes promises from them to accomplish the things that trouble him. Obedient to his wife, he displays great humility to his father-in-law; and by the aid of the lower animals he comes triumphant out of every trial. The beasts with their tusks plough up the spacious fields of heaven; the beasts and birds uproot the giant trees; from the Crocodile Lake the crocodiles themselves bring the thousand spades; between cattle which are exactly alike the cattle-fly distinguishes the cows from the calves; and the little fly, settling on the nose of the heroine's mother, enables the hero to point her out among her daughters. The wife's father is astonished, and gives his daughter anew to the hero to be his wife, dismissing them with a dower of oxen, slaves and money.[203]

It will be observed that the adventures undergone by Andrianòro in heaven are very different from those of the Maori heroes. Tawhaki and Tini-rau have certainly to submit to hardships and indignities before they can be reunited to their wives; and they perform actions of superhuman power. But these actions are not performed as the condition of reunion; nor are the tasks and the indignities laid upon them by any parental ogre. In fact the parental ogre is as conspicuous by his absence from the New Zealand stories as he is by his presence in those of Andrianòro and the Marquis of the Sun. How is this to be explained? The reason seems to lie in the different organization of society under which the tale attained its present form in either case. At an early period of civilization, kinship is reckoned exclusively through the mother: even the father is in no way related to his children. This is a stage hardly ever found complete in all its consequences, but of which the traces remain in the customs and in the lore of many nations who have long since passed from it, becoming, as we might expect, fainter and fewer as it recedes into the distance. Such traces are abundant in Maori tradition; and they point to a comparatively recent emergence from female kinship. Among these traces is the omission of the heavy father from the stories before us. Tango-tango and Hine-te-iwaiwa were both maidens of more than mortal race; and presumably their parents would be conceived of as still alive. But they are not so much as alluded to—a sure sign that there was no paternal authority to which these ladies would be accountable. Indeed, if accountable at all, they are so to the whole circle of their relatives, or to their tribe in general. It is their brothers who assist them in time of need. Tawhaki becomes the slave of his brothers-in-law. To her "people" Hine announces her husband's arrival: she simply announces it; nor does it appear that any consent on their part is required. Tini-rau takes his place at once as a tribesman, and is expected to contribute by his labour and skill to the sustenance of the whole brotherhood.

One of the consequences of reckoning descent only through females, which may be noticed here, is that the children belong to the mother and the mother's family. A trace of this lingers about the story of Tawhaki in the affront to Tango-tango caused by her husband's offensive remark upon their little one. In a society where the offspring are the father's, or even where, as in modern civilized life, they are treated as belonging to both parents and partaking of the nature of both, no such offence could be taken. Another consequence is that in the organization of society the wife still continues after marriage to reside with, and to be part of, the community to which she belongs by birth. The man leaves his father and his mother and cleaves to his wife. Hence it would be natural for her to return home to her own kindred, and for him to seek her and dwell with her there. This is illustrated not only in the Maori legends just cited, but also in the Arawàk story given in the last chapter, where the husband is received into the vulture race until he desires to visit his mother. He is then discarded as if he had committed some unpardonable breach of custom; and he cannot be restored to his former privileges. Although the Greeks had before the dawn of history ceased to practise mother-right, a trace of it lingers in a modern folk-tale from Epirus. There a man had by the ordinary device obtained an elf as a wife; and she bore him a child. After this her own kinsmen came and begged her to return to them; but she refused on the ground that she had a husband and child. "Then bring them with you," they replied. Accordingly, she took her husband and child, and went back with them to dwell among the elves. It seems, however, to be felt that this was an unusual proceeding; otherwise it would have been needless to plead with the lady to return, and to extend a special invitation to those whom she would not abandon: an indication, this, that the story has been adapted to a higher plane of civilization, in which it was no longer the custom for the husband to go and dwell among his wife's people.[204]

On the other hand, Andrianòro's wife lives under patriarchal government. The Malagasy have advanced further on the path of civilization than the Maories; and at the stage of progress they have reached, the father is much more like an absolute monarch. In the story referred to, the lady had married without her father's consent. Accordingly her marriage is ignored, and her lover has to perform a number of services for his father-in-law, and so purchase formal consent to their union. Nor will it escape the reader that when the wielder of the thunderbolt at last gives his daughter to her husband, he dismisses them back to the home of the latter. Hasan, too, it will be remembered, returns to Bagdad with his wife and children, though we probably have a survival of an older form of the story in his relations with her redoubtable sister. This lady holds a position impossible in an Arab kingdom. Her father is a mere shadow, hardly mentioned but to save appearances; so much more substantial is her power and her opposition to the match. The variants of the Marquis of the Sun are found chiefly among European nations,[205] whose history, institutions, and habits of thought lead them to attach great value to paternal authority. In the tasks performed in *märchen* of this type, and the precipitate flight which usually takes place on the wedding night from the ogre's secret wrath, it would seem that we have a reminiscence of the archaic institutions of marriage by purchase and marriage by capture,—both alike incidents of the period when mother-right (as the reckoning of descent solely through females is called) has ceased to exist in a pure form, and society has passed, or is passing, into the patriarchal stage. The Marquis of the Sun type is, therefore, more recent than the other types of the Swan-maiden tradition, none of which so uniformly in all their variants recognize the father's supreme position.[206]

If the tasks and the flight be a reminiscence of purchase and capture, we may find in that reminiscence a reason why nearly all the stories concur in representing the father under a forbidding aspect. As his daughter's vendor,— her unwilling vendor,—as her guardian from capture, he would be the natural foe of her lover. He is not always so ready as the Bird Simer to give up to another his rights over her; but perhaps the Bird Simer's readiness may be partly explained by the husband's having already performed the feat of rescuing the maiden from a giant, beside slaying his own brother for her sake. Usually the father is a frightful ogre or giant; not infrequently he is no less a personage than the Devil himself. And the contrast between him and his lovely daughter would be more and more strongly felt as purchase and capture ceased to be serious methods of bride-winning. Hence, probably, the thought of real relationship would be abandoned, and the maiden would often be conceived of as enchanted and captive in the hands of a malevolent being.

We will not now stop to discuss the tasks in detail: we can only afford time to glance at one of them, namely, that of distinguishing the maid from her sisters. There are three chief means by which the lover or husband is enabled to identify the object of his devotion. Two of these depend upon the lady herself: in the one she slily helps her lover; in the other he recognizes an insignificant peculiarity of her person or attire. The third means is an indication given by one of the lower animals, which has better means of knowledge than the suitor, due probably to its greater cleverness—a quality, as I have already pointed out in Chapter II., universally credited in a certain stage of culture to these creatures. We will deal first with the second means.

The most usual personal idiosyncrasy of the damsel is the want of a finger, or some deformity in it, the result of her previous efforts to aid the hero. Thus, in a Basque tale the lad is set to find a ring lost by the ogre in a river. This is accomplished by cutting up the maiden and throwing the pieces into the stream; but a part of the little finger sticks in his shoe. When he afterwards has to choose between the ogre's daughters with his eyes shut, he recognizes his love by the loss of her little finger. The giant's daughter, in a West Highland tale, makes a ladder with her fingers for her lover to climb a tree to fetch a magpie's eggs; and, in the hurry, she leaves her little finger at the top. This accident arises sometimes, as in the Marquis of the Sun, from the dropping of a piece of flesh on the ground when the hero cuts up his beloved; or, according to a story of the Italian Tirol, from spilling some of her blood. In the latter case, three drops of blood fall into the lake, instead of the bucket prepared to receive them, and thereby almost cause the failure of his task. When the magician afterwards leads the youth to his daughters and bids him choose, he takes the youngest by the hand, and says: "I choose this one." We are not told that there was any difference in the maidens' hands, but this is surely to be inferred. In the Milanese story of the King of the Sun the hero also chooses his wife blindfold from the king's three daughters by touching their hands; and here, too, we must suppose previous help or concert, though it has disappeared from the text. In a story from Lorraine, John has to take the devil's daughter, Greenfeather, to pieces to find a spire for the top of a castle that he is compelled to build; and in putting her together again he sets one of her little fingers clumsily. With bandaged eyes he has to find the lady who has assisted him; and he succeeds by putting his hand on hers. The lad who falls into the strange gentleman's hands in a Breton tale, forgets to put the little toe of the girl's left foot into the caldron; and when she and her two sisters are led before him veiled and clad in other than their ordinary garb, he knows her at once by the loss of her toe. As it is told in Denmark the enchanted princess agrees with the king's son to wind a red silken thread around her little finger; and by this means he identifies her, though in the form of a little grey-haired, long-eared she-ass, and again of a wrinkled, toothless, palsied old woman, into which the sorceress, whose captive she is, changes her. In a Swedish story the damsel informs her lover that when the mermaid's daughters appear in various repulsive forms she will be changed into a little cat with her side burnt and one ear snipped. The Catalonian *märchen* of Joanescas represents the heroine as wanting a joint of her finger, from her lover having torn off some of her feathers by accident when he stole her robe. "Monk" Lewis in his "Journal of a West India Proprietor" gives an Ananci tale in which the heroine and her two sisters are changed into black cats: the two latter bore scarlet threads round their necks, the former a blue thread.[207] According to the Carmarthenshire saga, the lady is recognized by the strapping of her sandal.

In several of the stories just cited, and many of their congeners, the maiden forewarns her suitor how she will be disguised, or by what marks she will be known. Sometimes, however, she makes a sign to him on the spot. The Lady of the Van Pool only thrusts her foot forward that he may notice her shoe-tie; but Cekanka in a Bohemian tale is bold enough to wink at him. In a Russian variant of the Marquis of the Sun, to which I have already referred, the hero is in the power of the Water King. On his way to that potentate's palace he had, by the advice of the Baba Yaga, gone to the seashore and watched until twelve spoonbills alighted, and, turning into maidens, had unrobed for the purpose of bathing. Then he had stolen the eldest maiden's shift, to restore it only on her promise to aid him against her father, the Water King. She redeems the pledge by performing for him the usual tasks, the last of which is to choose the same bride thrice among the king's twelve daughters. The first time she secretly agrees with him that she will wave her handkerchief; the second time she is to be arranging her dress; and the third time he will see a fly above her head.[208]

Here we are led to the third means of recognition. The incident of help rendered by one or more of the lower animals to man is a favourite one in folk-tales; and it has furnished a large portion of the argumentative stock-in-trade of those scholars who contend for their Indian origin. We are assured that every tale which contains this incident must be referred to a Buddhist source, or at least has been subjected to Buddhist influence. This theory is supported by reference to the doctrine of love for all living creatures which Buddha is said to have promulgated. The command to overcome hatred by love, the precepts of self-sacrifice and devotion to others' good were not limited in the Buddha's discourses, if those discourses be correctly reported, to our conduct towards our fellow-men: they included all creation. And they were enforced by parables which represented good as done in turn to men by all sorts of creatures, even the wildest and the most savage. Stories of grateful beasts, of the type familiar to us in Androcles and the Lion, became favourites among the disciples of the Light of Asia. Scholars, therefore, have told us that wherever a grateful beast thrusts his muzzle into the story, that story must have come from India, and must have come since the rise of Buddhism. Nay, they go further. In every instance where a beast appears as helping the hero, we are taught to presume that the hero has first helped the beast, even though no trace of such an incident be actually found. It must have been so, otherwise the beast would have had no motive for helping the hero,—and, it may be added, the theorist would have had no ground for claiming the story as proceeding from a Buddhist source.

Now all this would have been seen at once to be very poor reasoning, but for one fact. A number, sufficient to be called large, of parables, have actually made their way from India to Europe in historic times, and since the age of Gautama. The literary history of these parables can be traced; and it must be acknowledged that, whatever their origin, they have been adopted into Buddhist works and adapted to Buddhist doctrine. Further, it seems demonstrated that some of them have descended into the oral tradition of various nations in Europe, Asia, and even Africa. But when so much as this is conceded, it still fails to account for the spread of the story of the Grateful Beasts and, even more signally, for the incident of the Beast-helpers where there is no gratitude in the case. A very slight examination of the incident as it appears in the group of legends now before us will convince us of this.

First of all, let it be admitted that in several of these tales the service rendered by the brute is in requital for a good turn on the part of the hero. Andrianòro, as we have seen, begins by making friends with various animals by means of the mammon of unrighteousness in the shape of a feast. Jagatalapratâpa, in the narrative already cited from the Tamil book translated into English under the title of "The Dravidian Nights Entertainments," pursuing one of Indra's four daughters, is compelled by her father, after three other trials, to choose her out from her sisters, who are all converted into one shape. He prays assistance from a kind of grasshopper; and the little creature, in return for a previous benefit, hops upon her foot. But it is somewhat curious, if the theory be true, that even in stories told among peoples distinctly under Buddhist influence the gratitude is by no means an invariable point. Thus the princess in the Burmese drama is betrayed by "the king of flies" to her husband, though the abstract we have of the play gives us no hint of any previous transaction between the puny monarch and the hero; and it is worthy of note that the Tibetan version of the same plot given by Mr. Ralston from the Kah-Gyur knows nothing of this entomological agency. There the hero is a Bodisat, who, if he does not recognize his beloved among the thousand companions who surround her, at least has a spell the utterance of which compels her to step out from among them. It does not appear that Kasimbaha, the Bantik patriarch, is required to undergo this particular test. But he is indebted to a bird for indicating the lady's residence; a glow-worm places itself at her chamber door; and a fly shows him which of a number of dishes set before him he must not uncover. M. Cosquin, who is an adherent of the Buddhist hypothesis, in relating this instance, is compelled expressly to say that "one does not see why" these animals should render such services. Neither, on M. Cosquin's principle, can one see why, in the Arawàk story, the spiders should spin cords to help the outcast husband down from heaven, or the birds take his part against the vulture-folk to enable him to recover his wife.[209] The proof of Buddhist influence must rest heavily on its advocates here, both on account of the absence of motive for gratitude, and of the distance of the Arawàk people from India and the utter disparity of civilizations.

The agency of recognition, when attributed to one of the lower animals, is ordinarily an insect; but the reason is, as often as not, a prior arrangement with the lady, as in the Russian story of the Water King. The Polish *märchen* of Prince Unexpected follows this line. In it, the princess warns her lover that she will have a ladybird over her right eye. When a thousand maidens all alike are produced to poor Hans in a Bohemian tale, he has no difficulty in selecting the right one; for a witch has bidden him "choose her on whom, from the roof of the chamber, a spider descends."[210]

These considerations are sufficient to prove that the incident of the Helpful Beasts, as found in the Swan-maiden group of stories, cannot be attributed to a Buddhist origin.

We have now dealt with an episode of the mythical narrative, necessary, indeed, to its completion, but found only under certain conditions which I have pointed out. We have seen this episode in two distinct forms whose respective sources we have assigned to two distinct stages of culture. The form characteristic of the European *märchen* is apparently more barbarous in several respects than that yielded by the islanders of the Southern Ocean; but the latter bears testimony to a state of society more archaic than the other. Presumably, therefore, it represents more nearly the primitive form of the story.

We turn next to the central incidents. In the previous chapter I have taken pains to show the unmistakable relation between the different types of the myth, in spite of the omission of the feather-robe, or indeed of any substitute for it. The truth is that the feather-robe is no more than a symbol of the wife's superhuman nature. From the more archaic variants it is absent; but frequently the true form of the lady is held to be that of a member of what we contemptuously call "the brute creation." Men in savagery, as we have already seen, have quite different feelings from those of contempt for brutes. On the contrary, they entertain the highest respect and even awe for them. They trace their descent from some of them; and a change of form from beast to man, or from man to beast, while still preserving individual identity, would not seem at all incredible, or even odd, to them. By and by, however, the number of creatures having these astonishing powers would decrease, as the circle of experience widened. But there would linger a belief in remarkable instances, as at Shan-si, in China, where it is believed that there is still a bird which can divest itself of its feathers and become a woman. Not every swan would then be deemed capable of turning when it pleased into a fair maiden; and when this change happened, it would be attributed to enchantment, which had caused the maiden merely to assume the appearance of a swan for a time and for a special purpose. This often occurs, as we have seen, in *märchen*, where the contrast between the heroine and her father, or, as it is then often put, her master, is very strong. It occurs, too, in tales belonging to other types. A *märchen* told by Dr. Pitré relates that a man had a pet magpie, which by enchantment had the power of casting its wings and becoming a woman. She always practised this power in his absence; but he came home one day and found her wings on the chair. He burnt them, and she remained permanently a woman and married him. In a saga from Guiana a warlock's daughter persuades her father to transform her into a dog that she may venture near a hunter whom she loves. He accordingly gives her a skin, which she draws over her shoulders, and thus becomes a hound. When the hunter finds her in his hut as a maiden, the charmed skin hanging up and revealing her secret, he flings the skin into the fire and weds her.[211]

But enchantment is not the only explanation. The lady may, like Hasan's bride, be held to belong to a superior race to men, though properly in human form. In either case the peltry would be a mere veil hiding the true individuality for a while. It would thus acquire a distinct magical efficacy; so that when deprived of it, the maiden would be unable to effect the change. A remarkable instance of this occurs in an Arab saga. There a man, at Algiers, puts to death his three daughters, who afterwards appear to a guitar-player and dance to his playing. As they dance they throw him the rind of the oranges they hold in their hands; and this rind is found the next day changed into gold pieces and into jewels. The following year the maidens appear again to the guitar-player. He manages to get hold of their shrouds, which he burns. They thereupon come back to life, and he weds the youngest of them. This is said to have happened no longer ago than sixty years before the French conquest of Algiers.[212]

Nothing of the sort is found in the Maori tales. To the natives of New Zealand no change seemed needful: the lady was of supernatural birth and could fly as she pleased. The same may be said of Andrianòro's wife, notwithstanding that the Malagasy variant, as a whole, bespeaks a higher level of culture than the adventures of Tawhaki and Tini-rau. As little do we find the magical robe in the Passamaquoddy story of the Partridge and the Sheldrake Duck. The Dyaks of Borneo are unconscious of the need of it in the saga of their ancestral fish, the *puttin*, which was caught by a man, and when laid in his boat turned into a girl, whom he gave to his son for a bride. The Chinese have endless tales about foxes which assume human form; but the fox's skin plays no part in them. And in a Japanese tale belonging to the group under consideration, the lady changes into a fox and back again into a lady without any apparatus of peltry.[213]

Again, in the nursery tales of the higher races, the dress when cast seems simply an article of human clothing, often nothing but a girdle, veil, or apron; and it is only when donned by the enchanted lady, or elf, that it is found to be neither more nor less than a complete plumage. Thence it easily passes into a mere instrument of power, like the mermaid's belt and pouch in the Scottish story, or the book of command in the *märchen* of the Island of Happiness, and is on its way to final disappearance.

The maiden's capture is effected in those types of the tale where the enchanted garment is worn, by the theft of the garment. These cases will not detain our attention: we will pass at once to the discussion of those where there is no transformation to be effected or dreaded. Perhaps the most interesting of all are the Welsh sagas; and of these not the least remarkable is the suit by offerings of food. Andrianòro tried this device in the Malagasy story; but it was unsuccessful. In a Carnarvonshire analogue from Llanberis, the youth entices his beloved into his grasp by means of an apple:[214] in the Van Pool variants the offering assumes almost a sacramental character. Until the fairy maiden has tasted earthly bread, or until her suitor has eaten of the food which sustains her, he cannot be united to her. Here we are reminded on the one hand of the elfin food considered in a former chapter, to partake of which sealed the adventurer's fate and prevented him for ever from returning to his human home; and on the other hand of the ceremony of eating together which among so many nations has been part of the marriage rites.

Walter Map relates a curious story of Llangorse Lake having affinities for the Land East of the Sun, and still more with one of the Maori sagas. Wastin of Wastiniog watched, the writer tells us, three clear moonlit nights and saw bands of women in his oat-fields, and followed them until they plunged into the pool, where he overheard them conversing, and saying to one another: "If he did so and so, he would catch one of us." Thus instructed, he of course succeeded in capturing one. Here, as in many of the stories, the lady has obviously designs upon the mortal of opposite sex, and deliberately throws herself in his way. But she lays a taboo upon him, promising to serve him willingly and with all obedient devotion, until that day he should strike her in anger with his bridle. After the birth of several children he was unfortunate enough on some occasion, the details of which Walter Map has forgotten, to break the condition; whereupon she fled with all her offspring, of whom her husband was barely able to save one before she plunged with the rest into the lake. This one, whom he called Triunnis Nagelwch, grew up, and entered the service of the King of North Wales. At his royal master's command, Triunnis once led a marauding expedition into the territory of the King of Brecknock. A battle ensued, when he was defeated and his band cut to pieces. It is said that Triunnis himself was saved by his mother, and thenceforth dwelt with her in the lake. "But, indeed," adds the truth-loving Walter, "I think it is a lie, because a delusion of this kind is so likely to account for his body not having been found."[215]

In spite, however, of such unwonted incredulity, Map, having once begun by telling this story, proceeds to tell another like it, which he seems to have no difficulty in believing. The second tale concerns a hero of the Welsh border, Wild Edric, of whose historic reality as one of the English rebels against William the Conqueror there is ample proof. It appears that Edric, returning from hunting, lost his way in the Forest of Dean, and accompanied only by one boy, reached about midnight a large house which turned out to be a drinking-shop, such as the English, Map says, call a *guildhouse*. On approaching it he saw a light, and looking in, he beheld a number of women dancing. They were beautiful in countenance, bigger and taller than ordinary women. He noticed one among them fairer than the rest, and (Walter, perhaps, had Fair Rosamund in his mind when he says) more to be desired than all the darlings of kings. Edric rushed round the house and, finding an entrance, dashed in and with the help of his boy dragged her out, despite a furious resistance in which the nails and teeth of her companions made themselves felt. She brooded in sullen silence for three whole days; but on the fourth day she exclaimed to her new master: "Bless you, my dearest, and you will be blessed too, and enjoy health and prosperity until you reproach me on account of my sisters, or the place, or the grove whence you have snatched me away, or anything connected with it. For the very day you do so your happiness will forsake you. I shall be taken away; and you will suffer repeated misfortune, and long for your own death." He pledged himself to fidelity; and to their splendid nuptials nobles came from far and near. King William heard of the wonder, and bade the newly wedded pair to London, where he was then holding his court, that he might test the truth of the tale. They proved it to him by many witnesses from their own country; but the chief testimony was that of the lady's superhuman beauty; and he dismissed them in admiration to their home. After many years of happiness Edric returned one evening late from hunting, and could not find his wife. He spent some time in vainly calling for her before she came. "Of course," he began, angrily, "you have not been detained so long by your sisters, have you?" The rest of his wrath fell upon the empty air; for at the mention of her sisters she vanished. And neither her husband's self-reproaches, nor his tears, nor any search could ever find her again.[216]

A point far more interesting than the actual mode of capture is the taboo. The condition on which the heroine remains with her captor-spouse is, in stories of the Hasan of Bassorah type, his preservation of the feather-garb; in those of the Melusina type (with which we are now dealing), his observance of the taboo. In the tales just cited from Walter Map we have two important forms of the taboo, and in the legend of Melusina herself we have a third. The latter is an example of the ordinary objection on the part of supernatural beings to be seen otherwise than just how and when they please, which we have dealt with in a previous chapter; and little need be added to what I have already said on the subject. The other two are, however, worth some consideration.

In the account of Wastin of Wastiniog we are told that he was forbidden to strike his wife with the bridle. Let us compare this prohibition with that of the fairy of "the bottomless pool of Corwrion," in Upper Arllechwedd, Carnarvonshire, who wedded the heir of the owner of Corwrion. The marriage took place on two conditions—first, that the husband was not to know his wife's name, though he might give her any name he chose; and, second, that if she misbehaved towards him, he might now and then beat her with a rod, but that he should not strike her with iron, on pain of her leaving him at once. "This covenant," says Professor Rhys in repeating the tale, "was kept for some years, so that they lived happily together, and had four children, of whom the two youngest were a boy and a girl. But one day, as they went to one of the fields of Bryn Twrw, in the direction of Penardd Gron, to catch a pony, the fairy wife, being so much nimbler than her husband, ran before him and had her hand in the pony's mane in no time. She called out to her husband to throw her a halter; but instead of that he threw towards her a bridle with an iron bit, which, as bad luck would have it, struck her. The wife at once flew through the air, and plunged headlong into Corwrion Lake. The husband returned sighing and weeping towards Bryn Twrw (Noise Hill), and when he reached it, the *twrw* (noise) there was greater than had ever been heard before, namely, that of weeping after 'Belene'; and it was then, after he had struck her with iron, that he first learnt what his wife's name was."[217]

The perusal of this saga will raise a suspicion that the original form of the taboo in Wastin's case was a prohibition against striking with iron, and that the prohibition was eventually infringed by means of a bridle. Whether the alteration was due to a blunder on Map's part in relating the story is of no importance; but the suspicion will be raised to a certainty by turning to some other sagas in Professor Rhys' admirable collection. It is related at Waenfawr, near Carnarvon, that a youth broke, like Wild Edric, into a dance of the fairies on the banks of the Gwyrfai, near Cwellyn Lake, one moonlit night, and carried off a maiden. She at first refused to wed him, but consented to remain his servant. One evening, however, he overheard two of her kindred speaking of her, and caught her name—Penelope. When she found that he had learnt her name she gave way to grief: evidently she now knew that her fate was sealed. On his importunity being renewed, she at length consented to marry him, but on the condition that he should not strike her with iron. Here again the taboo was broken by the flinging of a bridle while chasing a horse. A similar tale was related in the vale of Beddgelert, wherein the stolen lady would only consent to be the servant of her ravisher if he could find out her name. When he had discovered it, she asked in astonishment; "O mortal, who has betrayed my name to thee?" Then, lifting up her tiny folded hands, she exclaimed: "Alas! my fate, my fate!" Even then she would only marry him on condition that if ever he should touch her with iron she would be free to leave him and return to her family. Catastrophe, as before. In a variant the maiden, pressed by her human lover, promises to marry, provided he can find out her name. When he succeeds in doing this she faints away, but has to submit to her doom. In doing so, she imposes one more proviso: he is not to touch her with iron, nor is there to be a bolt of iron, or a lock, on their door. The servant-girl, in another story cited in Chapter VII., who was rescued from Fairyland, could only stay, it will be remembered, in her master's service so long afterward, as he forebore to strike her with iron; and the fatal blow was struck accidentally with a bit.[218]

Mr. Andrew Lang has remarked, following Dr. Tylor, that in this taboo the fairy mistress is "the representative of the stone age." This is so; and the reason is, because she belongs to the realm of the supernatural. When the use of metals was discovered, stone implements were discarded in ordinary life; but for ages afterwards knives of stone were used for religious purposes. There is evidence, for instance, that the Hebrews, to seek no further, employed them in some of their sacred rites; an altar of stone was forbidden to be hewn; and when King Solomon built the temple, "there was neither hammer, nor axe, nor any tool of iron heard in the house while it was in building." Although there may be no direct evidence of such a practice among the Cymric Britons, they were probably no exception to the rule, which seems to have been general throughout the world; and the Druids' custom of cutting the mistletoe with a golden, not with an iron, sickle, points in this direction. The retention of stone instruments in religious worship was doubtless due to the intense conservatism of religious feeling. The gods, having been served with stone for so long, would be conceived of as naturally objecting to change; and the implements whose use had continued through so many revolutions in ordinary human utensils, would thereby have acquired a divine character. Changes of religion, however, brought in time changes even in these usages. Christianity was bound to no special reverence for knives and arrowheads of flint; but they seem to have been still vaguely associated with the discarded deities, or their allies, the Nymphs and Oreads and Fairies of stream or wood or dell, and with the supernatural generally. A familiar example of this is the name of Elfbolts given by the country people in this and other lands to these old-world objects, whenever turned up by the harrow or the spade. Now the traditional preference on the part of supernatural beings for stone instruments is only one side of the thought which would, as its reverse side, show a distinct abhorrence by the same mythical personages for metals, and chiefly (since we have long passed out of the bronze age) for iron. Not only do witches and spirits object to the horseshoe; axes and iron wedges are equally distasteful to them—at all events in Denmark. So in Brittany, when men go to gather the *herbe d'or*, a medicinal plant of extraordinary virtue, they go barefooted, in a white robe and fasting, and no iron may be employed; and though all the necessary ceremonies be performed, only holy men will be able to find it. The magical properties of this plant, as well as the rites requisite to obtain it, disclose its sacredness to the old divinities. It shines at a distance like gold, and if one tread on it he will fall asleep, and will come to understand the languages of birds, dogs, and wolves.[219]

In previous chapters we have already had occasion to note this dislike for iron and steel. Hence the placing of scissors and fire-steel in an unchristened babe's cradle. Hence the reason for the midwife's casting a knife behind her when she left the troll's dwelling laden with his gifts; and for the Islay father's taking the precaution of striking his dirk into the threshold when he sought his son in the fairy hill. So, too, in Sweden people who bathed in the sea were gravely advised to cast into it close to them a fire-steel, a knife, or the like, to prevent any monster from hurting them. The bolts and locks to which the fairy of Beddgelert objected would have prevented her free passage into and out of the house.

In the Pomeranian saga quoted in the last chapter, the enchanted princess is unable to open the trunk which contains her magical shift: she must wait for another to open it and give her the garment. In the same way Hasan's bride could not herself go to the chest and get her feather-dress. The key was committed to her mother-in-law's care, and was forced from the old woman by Zubaydah, the Caliph's wife; nor did it ever come into the fairy's hands, for her dress was fetched for her by Masrur at Zubaydah's bidding. It is not unlikely that the reason for the supernatural wife's difficulty in these and analogous cases is the metal lock and key. But we must not forget that the robe is not always locked up in a chest. Sometimes it is hidden in a hole in the wall, sometimes in a stack of corn, sometimes beneath the main-post of the wooden hut in which the wedded pair are dwelling. Moreover, we must not leave out of account that in the Nightmare type the wife cannot herself take the wooden stopper out of the hole through which she entered; but directly it is removed by another she vanishes. These things go to show that such supernatural beings cannot themselves undo charms expressly performed against them. So evil spirits cannot penetrate a circle drawn around him by one who invokes them. So, too, the sign of the cross is an efficient protection against them; and it is therefore made upon churches and altars at the time of consecration.

But the stipulation made by the lady of Corwrion was twofold. Not only was her bridegroom to forbear striking her with iron, but he was not even to know her name. It is so difficult for us to put ourselves into the mental attitude of savages, that we do not understand the objection they almost all entertain to the mention of their names. The objection itself is, however, well known and widely spread; but it is not always manifested in exactly the same form. In some cases a man only refuses to utter his own name, while he will utter another's name readily enough. Sometimes it is deemed an unpardonable thing to call another by name; he must be addressed, or spoken of by an epithet. And frequently a man's real name is a profound secret, known only to himself, all others knowing him only by some epithet or title. Sometimes it is only forbidden to relatives by marriage to speak one another's names. Thus in various ways etiquette has prescribed a number of customs limiting the utterance of names among savage and barbarous peoples all the world over. The origin of these rules and customs seems to have been the dread of sorcery. A personal name was held to be a part of its owner; and, just as the possession of a lock of another's hair, or even a paring of his nail, was believed to confer power over him, so was the knowledge of his name. Similarly men in the lower culture have a great fear of having their likenesses taken; and everybody is familiar with the belief that a witch, who has made a waxen image and given it the name of any one whom she wants to injure, can, by sticking pins in it, or melting it in a flame, inflict pain, and even death, upon the person whom the doll represents.[220]

Illustrations of this superstition might easily be multiplied from every nation under heaven. But we need not go so far afield; for if we compare the taboo in the story of Corwrion with the other stories I have cited from the same county, we shall have no difficulty in satisfying ourselves as to its meaning. It can only belong to the stage of thought which looks with dread on the use that may be made of one's name by an enemy,—a stage of thought in which the fairy might naturally fear for a man of another race, albeit her husband, to become possessed of her real name. What else can we infer from the evident terror and grief with which the captive ladies hear their names from their suitors' lips? It is clear that the knowledge of the fairy's name conferred power over her which she was unable to resist. This is surely the interpretation also of the Danish tale of a man from whom a Hill-troll had stolen no fewer than three wives. Riding home late one night afterwards, he saw a great crowd of Hill-folk dancing and making merry; and among them he recognized his three wives. One of these was Kirsten, his best beloved, and he called out to her and named her name. The troll, whose name was Skynd, or Hurry, came up to him and asked him why he presumed to call Kirsten. The man explained that she had been his favourite wife, and begged him with tears to give her back to him. The troll at last consented, but with the proviso that he should never hurry (*skynde*) her. For a long time the condition was observed; but one day, as she was delayed in fetching something for her husband from the loft, he cried out to her: "Make haste (*skynde dig*), Kirsten!" And he had hardly spoken the words when the woman was gone, compelled to return to the troll's abode. Here we have the phenomenon in a double form; for not only does the husband regain his wife from the troll by pronouncing her name, but he loses her once more by inadvertently summoning her captor. It is a German superstition that a mara, or nightmare, can be effectually exorcised if the sufferer surmises who it is, and instantly addresses it by name.[221] We can now understand how, in the Carmarthenshire story mentioned in Chapter VII., the farmer was rescued from the fairies under whose spell he had been for twelve months. A man caught sight of him dancing on the mountain and broke the spell by speaking to him. It must have been the utterance of his name that drew him out of the enchanted circle.

Returning, however, to the legend of Wastin, we may observe how much narrower and less likely to be infringed is the taboo imposed on him than that imposed on the youth of Blaensawdde. Yet the lady of the Van Pool, whatever her practice, had in theory some relics of old-fashioned wifely duty. She did not object to the chastisement which the laws of Wales allowed a husband to bestow. A husband was permitted to beat his wife for three causes; and if on any other occasion he raised his hand against her, she had her remedy in the shape of a *sarâd*, or fine, to be paid to her for the disgrace. But a *sarâd* would not satisfy this proud lady; nothing less than a divorce would meet the case. The Partridge's wife, as we have seen, was still more exacting: she declined to be struck at all. In the same way the fish who had become a girl, in the Dyak story, cautioned her husband to use her well; and when he struck her she rushed back screaming into the water. In another Bornoese tradition, which is quoted by Mr. Farrer, the heroine is taken up to the sky because her husband had struck her, there having been no previous prohibition.[222] A different sort of personal violence is resented in the Bantik legend cited above. There the husband is forbidden to tear out one white hair which adorns Outahagi, his wife's head. He disobeys after she has given birth to a son; and she vanishes in a tempest and returns to the sky, where her husband is forced to seek her again.

The stipulation made by Wild Edric's bride is still more arbitrary, according to our notions, than these. Her husband was forbidden to reproach her on account of her sisters, or the place from which he snatched her away. In other words, he was forbidden to charge her with her supernatural character. When Diarmaid, the daughter of King Underwaves, comes in the form of a beggar to Fionn and insists on sharing his couch, she becomes a beautiful girl, and consents to marry him on condition that he does not say to her thrice how he found her. In a variant, the hero, going out shooting, meets with a hare, which, when hard pressed by the dogs, turns into a woman. She promises to wed him on his entering into three vows, namely, not to ask his king to a feast without first letting her know (a most housewifely proviso), not to cast up to her in any company that he found her in the form of a hare, and not to leave her in the company of only one man. Both these are West Highland tales; and in the manner of the taboo they closely resemble that given by Map. In an Illyrian story, a Vila is by a youth found one morning sleeping in the grass. He is astonished at her beauty, and plants a shade for her. When she wakes she is pleased, and asks what he wants for such kindness. He asks nothing less than to take her to wife; and she is content, but, avowing herself a Vila, forbids him to utter that name, for if he should do so she must quit him at once. Keats has glorified one of these stories by his touch; and it was a true instinct that guided him to make Lamia's disappearance follow, not on Apollonius' denunciation of her real character, but on the echo of the words "A serpent!" by her astounded husband, Lycius. What matter that the philosopher should make a charge against her? It was only when her lover repeated the foul word that she forsook him. The nightmare-wife in one of the stories mentioned in the last chapter vanishes, it will be remembered, on being reproached with her origin, and in another on being asked how she became a nightmare; and the lady in the Esthonian tale warns her husband against calling her Mermaid. In this connection it is obvious to refer to the euphemistic title Eumenides, bestowed by the Greeks on the Furies, and to the parallel names, Good People and Fair Family, for fays in this country. In all these cases the thought is distinguishable from that of the Carnarvonshire sagas; for the offence is not given by the utterance of a personal name, but by incautious use of a generic appellation which conveys reproach, if not scorn.[223]

The heroine of a saga of the Gold Coast was really a fish, but was in the form of a woman. Her husband had sworn to her that he would not allude in any way to her home or her relatives; and, relying on this promise, his wife had disclosed her true nature to him and taken him down to her home. He was kindly received there, but was speared by some fishermen, and only with difficulty rescued by his new relatives, who enjoined him when he returned to earth with his wife to keep the spearhead carefully concealed. It was, however, found and claimed by its owner; and to escape the charge of theft the husband reluctantly narrated the whole adventure. No evil consequences immediately ensued from this breach of his vow. But he had lately taken a second wife; and she one day quarrelled with the first wife and taunted her with being a fish. Upbraiding her husband for having revealed the secret, the latter plunged into the sea and resumed her former shape. So in the Pawnee story of The Ghost

Wife, a wife who had died is persuaded by her husband to come back from the Spirit Land to dwell again with himself and her child. All goes well until he takes a second wife, who turns out ill-tempered and jealous of the first wife. Quarrelling with her one day, she reproaches the latter with being nothing but a ghost. The next morning when the husband awoke, his first wife was no longer by his side. She had returned to the Spirit Land; and the following night both he and the child died in their sleep—called by the first wife to herself.[224] These sagas bring us back to that of Melusina, who disappears, it will be recollected, not when the count, her husband, breaks the taboo, but when, by calling her a serpent, he betrays his guilty knowledge.

A name, indeed, is the cause of offence and disappearance in many other of these stories. The chieftain of the Quins, who owned the Castle of Inchiquin on the lake of that name, near the town of Ennis in Ireland, found in one of the many caves of the neighbourhood a lady who consented to become his bride, only stipulating that no one bearing the name of O'Brien should be allowed to enter the castle gate. When this prohibition was infringed she sprang through a window with her child into the lake. The property has long since passed into the hands of the O'Briens; and amid the ruins of the castle the fatal window is still shown nearly as perfect as when the supernatural lady leaped through it into the waters. It may be safely said that the primitive form of the taboo has not come down to us in this tale, and that it owes its present form to the fact that the O'Briens have acquired the estates once owned by the Quins. Probably the utterance of some hateful name was forbidden. But whatever name may have been able to disturb the equanimity of the Lady of Inchiquin, we are now familiar enough with these superstitions to understand why a holy name should be tabooed by the goat-footed fairy wife of Don Diego Lopez in the Spanish tale narrated by Sir Francis Palgrave. "Holy Mary!" exclaimed the Don, as he witnessed an unexpected quarrel among his dogs, "who ever saw the like?" His wife, without more ado, seized her daughter and glided through the air to her native mountains. Nor did she ever return, though she afterwards, at her son's request, supplied an enchanted horse to release her husband when in captivity to the Moors. In two Norman variants the lady forbids the utterance in her presence of the name of Death.[225]

These high-born heroines had, forsooth, highly developed sensibilities. The wife of a Teton (the Tetons are a tribe of American natives) deserted him, abandoned her infant to her younger brother's care, and plunged into a stream, where she became what we call a mermaid,—and all because her husband had scolded her. In another American tale, where the wife was a snake, she deserted him from jealousy. A Tirolese saga speaks of a man who had a wife of unknown extraction. She had bidden him, whenever she baked bread, to pour water for her with his right hand. He poured it once with the left, to see what would happen. He soon saw, to his cost; for she flew out of the house. The Queen of Sheba, according to a celebrated Arab writer, was the daughter of the King of China and a Peri. Her birth came about on this wise. Her father, hunting, met two snakes, a black one and a white, struggling together in deadly combat. He killed the black one, and caused the white one to be carefully carried to his palace and into his private apartment. On entering the room the next day, he was surprised to find a lovely lady, who announced herself as a Peri, and thanked him for delivering her the day before from her enemy, the black snake. As a proof of her gratitude she offered him her sister in marriage, subject, however, to the proviso that he should never question her why she did this or that, else she would vanish, never to be seen again. The king agreed, and had every reason to be pleased with his beautiful bride. A son was born to them; but the lady put it in the fire. The king wept and tore his beard, but said nothing. Then a daughter of singular loveliness—afterwards Balkis, Queen of Sheba—was born: a she-bear appeared at the door, and the mother flung her babe into its jaws. The king tore out not only his beard, but the hair of his head, in silence. A climax, however, came when, in the course of a war, he and his army had to effect a seven days' march across a certain desert. On the fifth day came the queen, a large knife in her hand, and, slitting the provision-bags and the waterskins, strewed the whole of the food upon the ground, and brought the king and his army face to face with death. Her husband could no longer restrain himself from questioning her. Then she told him that his vizier, bribed by the enemy, had poisoned the food and water in order to destroy him and his army, and that his son had a constitutional defect which would have prevented him from living three days if she had not put him in the fire. The she-bear, who was no other than a trusty old nurse, brought back his daughter at her call; but the queen herself disappeared, and he saw her no more. The Nereid in the Cretan tale referred to in Chapter IX obstinately refused to speak, although her lover had fairly conquered her. But after she bore him a son, the old woman of whom he had previously taken counsel advised him to heat the oven and threaten his mistress that if she would not speak he would throw the boy into it. The Nereid seized the babe, and, crying out: "Let go my child, dog!" tore it from his arms and vanished. It is related by Apollodorus that Thetis, who was also a Nereid, wished to make her son immortal. To this end she buried him in fire by night to burn out his human elements, and anointed him with ambrosia by day. Peleus, her husband, was not informed of the reason for this lively proceeding; and, seeing his child in the fire, he called out. Thetis, thus thwarted, abandoned both husband and child in disgust, and went back to her native element. In the great Sanskrit epic of the Mahábhárata we are told that King Sántanu, walking by a riverside one day, met and fell in love with a beautiful girl, who told him that she was the river Ganges, and could only marry him on condition that he never questioned her conduct. To this he, with a truly royal gallantry, agreed; and she bore him several children, all of whom she threw into the river as soon as they were born. At last she bore him a boy, Bhíshma; and her husband begged her to spare his life, whereupon she instantly changed into the river Ganges and flowed away. Incompatibility of temper, as evidenced by three simple disagreements, was a sufficient ground of divorce for the fairy of Llyn Nelferch, in the parish of Ystradyfodwg, in Glamorganshire, from her human husband. In a variant of the Maori sagas, to which I have more than once referred, the lady quits her spouse in disgust because he turns out *not* to be a cannibal, as she had hoped from his truculent name, Kai-tangata, or man-eater. Truly a heartrending instance of misplaced confidence![226]

Many of these stories belong to the Star's Daughter type,—that is to say, are wanting in the taboo. But in every variant of the Swan-maiden group, to whatsoever type it may belong, the catastrophe is inevitable from the beginning. Whether or not it depends on the breach of an explicit taboo, it is equally the work of doom. A legend of the Loo-Choo Islands expresses this feeling in its baldest form. A farmer sees a bright light in his well, and, on drawing near, beholds a woman diving and washing in the water. Her clothes, strange in shape and of a ruddy sunset colour, are hanging on a pine-tree near at hand. He takes them, and thus compels her to marry him. She lives with him for ten years, bearing him a son and a daughter. At the end of that time her fate is fulfilled; she ascends a tree during her husband's absence, and, having bidden her children farewell, glides off on a cloud and disappears. Both in its approximation to the Hasan of Bassorah type and in its attributing the separation of husband and wife to fate, this tale agrees remarkably with the Lay of Weyland Smith, where we are told: "From the south through Mirkwood, to fulfil their fates, the young fairy maidens flew. The southern ladies alighted to rest on the sea-strand, and fell to spinning their goodly linen. First Allrune, Cear's fair daughter, took Egil to her bright bosom. The second, Swanwhite, took Slagfin. But Lathgund, her sister, clasped the white neck of Weyland. Seven winters they stayed there in peace, but the eighth they began to pine, the ninth they must needs part. The young fairy maidens hastened to Mirkwood to fulfil their fates." A Vidyádhari, too, who, in the Kathá-sarit-ságara, is caught in the orthodox manner, dwells with a certain ascetic until she brings forth a child. She then calmly remarks to her holy paramour: "My curse has been brought to an end by living with you. If you desire to see any more of me, cook this child of mine with rice and eat it; you will then be reunited to me!" Having said this, she vanished. The ascetic followed her directions, and was thus enabled to fly after her. In one of the New Zealand variants we are told that the time came for Whai-tiri to return to her home. The same thing is indicated to the wife in a Tirolese tale by means of a voice, which her husband hears as he passes through the forest. The voice cried: "Tell Mao that Mamao is dead." When he repeated this to his wife she disappeared; and he never saw or heard of her after. In view of these narratives there can be little doubt as to the meaning of the Arab tradition of the she-demon, from whom one of the clans was descended. Her union with their human father came suddenly to an end when she beheld a flash of lightning.[227]

The Star's Daughter, however, returned to the sky because she was homesick. Nor is she the only heroine of these tales who did so; but homesick heroines are not very interesting, and I pass to one who had a nobler reason for quitting her love. The saga is told at Rarotonga of a girl of dazzling white complexion who came up out of a fountain and was caught. She became the wife of a chief. It was the custom of the inhabitants of the world from which she came to perform the Cæsarean operation on females who were ready to give birth; so that the birth of a child involved the mother's death. When she found on the earth, to her surprise, that by allowing nature to take its course the mother as well as the child was saved, she persuaded her husband to go with her to the lower world to endeavour to put a stop to the cruel custom. He was ready to accompany her; but after five several efforts to dive with her through the fountain to the regions below he was obliged to abandon the attempt. Sorrowfully embracing each other, the "peerless one" said: "I alone will go to the spirit-world to teach what I have learnt from you." At this she again dived down into the clear waters, and was never more seen on earth.[228]

It will not have escaped the reader's attention, that among the more backward races the taboo appears generally simpler in form, or is absent altogether. Among most, if not all, of the peoples who tell stories wherein this is the case, the marriage bonds are of the loosest description; and there is, therefore, nothing very remarkable in the supernatural bride's conduct. We might expect to find that as advances are made in civilization, and marriage becomes more regarded, the reason for separation would become more and more complex and cogent. Am I going too far in suggesting that the resumption by the bride of her bird or beast shape marks a stage in the development of the myth beyond the Star's Daughter type; and the formal taboo, where the human figure is not abandoned, a stage later still? In our view, indeed, the taboo is not less irrational, as a means of putting an end to the marriage, than the retrieved robe or skin. But we forget how recent in civilization is the sanctity of the marriage-tie. Even among Christian nations divorce was practised during the Middle Ages for very slight reasons, despite the authority of popes and priests. In Eastern countries the husband has always had little check on his liberty of putting away a wife for any cause, or no cause at all; and, though unrecognized by the religious books, which have enforced the husband's rights with so stern a sanction, this liberty on his part may have been counterbalanced, oftener than we think, by corresponding liberty on the wife's part. Beyond doubt this has been so in India, where it is effected by means of marriage settlements. In Bengal, for instance, a bridegroom is sometimes compelled to execute a deed in which he stipulates never to scold his wife, the penalty being a divorce; and deeds are not unknown empowering the wife to get a divorce if her husband ever so much as disagree with her.[229] This is incompatibility of temper with a vengeance! Even the fairy of Llyn Nelferch was willing to put up with two disagreements; and no taboo in story has gone, or could go, further.

Moreover, some of the taboos are such as the etiquette of various peoples would entirely approve, though breaches of them might not be visited so severely as in the tales. I have already pointed out that the Lady of the Van Pool would have had a legal remedy for blows without cause. The romance lies in the wide interpretation she gave to the blows, and their disproportionate punishment. These transfer the hearer's sympathies from the wife to the husband. Precisely parallel seems to be the injunction laid upon Hohodemi, by Toyotamahime, daughter of the Sea-god. I know not what may be the rule in Japan; but it is probably not different from that which obtains in China.

There, as we learn from the Li Kì, one of the Confucian classics, a wife in Toyotamahime's condition would, even among the poor, be placed in a separate apartment; and her husband, though it would be his duty to send twice a day to ask after her, would not see her, nor apparently enter her room until the child was presented to him to be named. Curiously enough the prohibition in the Japanese tale is identical with that imposed by Pressina, herself a water-fay, the mother of Melusina, according to the romance of Jean d'Arras written at the end of the fourteenth century. Melusina and the Esthonian mermaid laid down another rule: they demanded a recurring period during which they would be free from marital intrusion. India is not Europe; but it cannot be thought quite irrelevant to observe that much more than this is commonly secured to a bride in many parts of India. For by the marriage settlement it is expressly agreed that she is to go to her father's house as often as she likes; and if her husband object, she is empowered in the deed to bring an action against him for false imprisonment.[230]

Here we may leave the subject of the taboo. Something, however, must be said on the Swan-maiden as divine ancestress. But first of all, let me advert to one or two cases where divinity is ascribed without progenitorship. The Maori heroine and her husband are worshipped. They do not appear to be considered actual parents of any New Zealand clan; but the husband at all events would be deemed one of the same blood. Passing over to New Guinea, we find a remarkable saga concerning the moon. The moon is a daughter of the earth, born by the assistance of a native of the village of Keile, about twenty miles to the eastward of Port Moresby. A long while ago, digging deeper than usual, he came upon a round, smooth, silvery, shining object, which, after he had got it out and lifted it up, grew rapidly larger and larger until it floated away. He set out to search for it; nor did he desist until one day he came upon a large pool in the river and found a beautiful woman bathing. On the bank lay her grass petticoat where she had cast it off. He sat down upon it; and when her attention was attracted to him by his dogs, they recognized one another. She was the moon, and he was the man who had dug her up out of the earth; and he claimed her as his wife. "If I marry you," she replied, "you must die; but as you have touched my clothes you must die in any case, and so for one day I will marry you, and then you must go home to your village and prepare for death." Accordingly they were married for one day; and the man then went home, made his funeral feast and died. The moon in due course married the sun, as it was her doom to do; but his intolerable jealousies rendered their union so wretched that they at last agreed to see as little of one another as possible. This accounts for their conduct ever since. An Annamite legend relates that a woodcutter found some fairies bathing at a lovely fountain. He took possession of the raiment of one, and hid it at the bottom of his rice-barn. In this way he compelled its owner to become his wife; and they lived together happily for some years. Their son was three years old when, in her husband's absence, she sold their stock of rice. On clearing out the barn her clothes were found. She bade farewell to the child, left her comb stuck in his collar, donned her clothes and flew away. When her husband returned and learned how matters stood, he took his son and repaired to the fountain, where happily they fell in with some of his wife's servants who were sent thither to draw water. Engaging them in conversation, he caused his son to drop the comb into one of the water-jars. By this means his wife recognized them, and sent an enchanted handkerchief which enabled him to fly and follow her servants to her home. After awhile she sent him and her son back to the earth, promising to get permission in a short time to return and live with them. By the carelessness of one of her servants, however, both father and son were dropped into the sea and drowned. Apprised of the catastrophe by ravens, the fairy transformed her servant, by way of punishment, into—or according to a variant, became herself—the morning star, while father and son became the evening star. And now the morning star and the evening star perpetually seek one another, but never again can they meet.[231]

Turning to the instances where ancestry is claimed, we find that the chiefs of the Ati clan are descended from "the peerless one" of Rarotonga. The Arawàk Indians of Guiana reckon descent in the female line. One of their families takes its name from its foremother, the warlock's daughter who was provided with the dogskin mentioned on a previous page. Another family deduces its name and pedigree from an earth-spirit married to one of its ancestors; but it does not appear whether any Swan-maiden myth attaches to her. The fish *puttin* is sacred among the Dyaks. On no account will they eat it, because they would be eating their relations, for they are descended from the lady whose first and last form was a *puttin*. In other words, the *puttin* is their totem. A family of the town of Chama on the Gold Coast claims in like manner to be descended from the fish-woman of whose story I have given an outline; and a legend to the same effect is current at the neighbouring town of Appam; nor in either instance do the members of the family dare to eat of the fish of the kind to which they believe their ancestress belonged. The totem superstition is manifest in the case of the Phœnician, or Babylonian, goddess Derceto, who was represented as woman to the waist and thence downward fish. She was believed to have been a woman, the mother of Semiramis, and to have thrown herself in despair into a lake. Her worshippers abstained from eating fish; though fish were offered to her in sacrifice, and golden fish suspended in her temple. Melusina was the mother of the family of Lusignan. She used to appear and shriek on one of the castle towers as often as the head of the family, or a King of France, was to die, or when any disaster was about to happen to the realm, or to the town of Luxemburg. She was also the author of certain presages of plenty or famine. Similar legends are told of the castles of Argouges and Rânes in Normandy. If the Irish Banshee tales could be minutely examined, it is probable that they would resolve themselves into stories of supernatural ancestresses. To the Vila of the Illyrian story, and the fairy of Sir Francis Palgrave's Spanish story, noble families attribute their origin. A family in the Tirol is descended from the lady who insisted on her husband's pouring water with his right hand; and the members of a noble Greek family have the blood of a Nereid in their veins.[232]

Though the heroine of the Van Pool might never return to her husband, she was drawn back to earth by the care of her three sons, who, by means of her instructions, became celebrated physicians. On one occasion she accompanied them to a place still called Pant-y-Meddygon (the hollow, or dingle, of the physicians), and there pointed out to them the various herbs which grew around, and revealed their medicinal virtues. It is added that, in order that their knowledge should not be lost, the physicians wisely committed the same to writing for the benefit of mankind throughout all ages. A collection of medical recipes purporting to be this very work still exists in a manuscript preserved at Jesus College, Oxford, which is now in course of publication by Professor Rhys and Mr. J. Gwenogvryn Evans, and is known as the Red Book of Hergest. An edition of the "Meddygon Myddfai," as this collection is called, was published by the Welsh MSS. Society thirty years ago, with an English translation. It professes to have been written under the direction of Rhiwallon the Physician and his sons Kadwgan, Gruffydd, and Einion; and they are called "the ablest and most eminent of the physicians of their time and of the time of Rhys Gryg, their lord, and the lord of Dinevor, the nobleman who kept their rights and privileges whole unto them, as was meet." This nobleman was Prince of South Wales in the early part of the thirteenth century; and his monumental effigy is in the cathedral of St. David's. Mr. Gwenogvryn Evans, than whom there is no higher authority, is of opinion that the manuscript was written at the end of the fourteenth century—that is to say, about two hundred years after the date at which the marriage between the youth of Blaensawdde and his fairy love is alleged to have taken place; and it is believed by the editor of the published volume to be a copy of a still more ancient manuscript now in the British Museum. Yet it contains no reference to the legend of the Van Pool. The volume in question includes a transcript of another manuscript of the work, which is ascribed in the colophon to Howel the Physician, who, writing in the first person, claims to be "regularly descended in the male line from the said Einion, the son of Rhiwallon, the physician of Myddfai, being resident in Cilgwryd, in Gower." This recension of the work is much later in date than the former. A portion of it cannot be older than the end of the fifteenth century; and the manuscript from which it was printed was probably the result of accretions extending over a long period of time, down to the year 1743, when it was copied "from the book of John Jones, Physician of Myddfai, the last lineal descendant of the family." The remedies it contains, though many of them are antique enough, and superstitious enough, are of various dates and sources; and, so far from being attributed to a supernatural origin, they are distinctly said to "have been proved to be the best and most suitable for the human body through the research and diligent study of Rhiwallon" and his three sons. The negative evidence of the "Meddygon Myddfai," therefore, tends to show that the connection of the Van Pool story with the Physicians is of comparatively recent date.[233]

And yet it is but natural (if we may use such an expression) that a mythical creature like the Lady of the Lake should be the progenitor of an extraordinary offspring. Elsewhere we have seen her sisters the totems of clans, the goddesses of nations, the parents of great families and renowned personages. Melusina gave birth to monsters of ugliness and evil,[234] and through them to a long line of nobles. So the heroine of the Llanberis legend had two sons and two daughters, all of whom were remarkable. The elder son became a great physician, and all his descendants were celebrated for their proficiency in medicine. The second son was a Welsh Tubal-cain. One of the daughters invented the small ten-stringed harp, and the other the spinning wheel. "Thus," we are told, "were introduced the arts of medicine, manufactures, music, and woollen work!" If, then, there were a family at Myddfai celebrated for their leechcraft, and possessed of lands and influence, as we know was the fact, their hereditary skill would seem to an ignorant peasantry to demand a supernatural origin; and their wealth and material power would not refuse the additional consideration which a connection with the legend of the neighbouring pool would bring them.

But for all that the incident of the reappearance by the mother to her children may have been part of the original story. The Carnarvonshire fairies of various tales analogous to that of the Van Pool are recalled by maternal love to the scenes of their wedded life; and the hapless father hears his wife's voice outside the window chanting pathetically:

"If my son should feel it cold,
Let him wear his father's coat;
If the fair one feel the cold,
Let her wear my petticoat!"

Whatever he may have thought of these valuable directions, they hardly seem to us sufficient to have brought the lady up from "the bottomless pool of Corwrion" to utter. There is more sense in the mother's song in a Kaffir tale. This woman was not of purely supernatural origin. She was born in consequence of her (human) mother's eating pellets given her by a bird. Married to a chief by whom she was greatly beloved, it was noticed that she never went out of doors by day. In her husband's absence her father-in-law forced her to go and fetch water from the river for him in the daytime. Like the woman by the waters of the Rhone, she was drawn down into the river. That evening her child cried piteously; and the nurse took it to the stream in the middle of the night, singing:

"It is crying, it is crying,
The child of Sihamba Ngenyanga;
It is crying, it will not be pacified."

The mother thereupon came out of the water, and wailed this song as she put the child to her breast:

"It is crying, it is crying,
The child of the walker by moonlight.
It was done intentionally by people whose names are unmentionable.[235]
They sent her for water during the day.
She tried to dip with the milk-basket, and then it sank.

Tried to dip with the ladle, and then it sank.
Tried to dip with the mantle, and then it sank."

The result of the information conveyed in these words was her ultimate recovery by her husband with the assistance of her mother, who was a skilful sorceress.[236]

A Finnish tale belonging to the Cinderella group represents the heroine as changed into a reindeer-cow by an ogress who takes her place as wife and mother. But her babe will not be comforted; so a woman, to whose care he is committed, carries him into the forest, and sings the following incantation:

"Little blue eyes, little red-fell,
Come thou thine own son to suckle,
Feed whom thou hast given birth to!
Of that cannibal nought will he,
Never drinks from that bloodsucker;
For her breasts to him are loathsome,
Nor can hunger drive him to them."

The reindeer cannot withstand this appeal. She casts her skin, and comes in human form to suckle her child. This results, after two repetitions in the husband's burning the reindeer hide and clasping her in his arms. But, like Peleus, he has to hold her fast in spite of various transformations, until he has overcome the charm and has her once more in her pristine shape![237]

It was not strength so much as boldness and tenacity that conquered here. In the Kaffir story the husband's first attempt to pull his wife out of the water by sheer force failed. Thus, too, in one of the Tirolese stories already mentioned the husband lies in wait for his wife when she returns, as usual, to comb her little girl's hair on a Saturday. He catches her by the arm as she enters; and she tells him that if he can hold her for a little while she must stay: otherwise she will never come again. All his strength is, however, too little to struggle successfully with her. The mother's visits to her children are, indeed, a frequent sequel to the story; and occasionally the tie which compels her to return is taken advantage of by the forsaken husband to obtain possession of her again. But fraud, not force, is the means employed, as in the Lapp story of the Maiden out of the Sea, where the mermaid's clothes are once more confiscated. In a legend of Llyn y Dywarchen (the Lake of the Sod), not very far from Beddgelert, the water-nymph subsequently appears to her husband, conversing with him from a floating turf while he stands on the shore. Here the motive of the reappearance is the unusual one of conjugal, rather than parental, affection.[238]

I must not omit to add that the first Sunday in August is kept in the neighbourhood of the Van Pool as the anniversary of the fairy's return to the lake. It is believed that annually on that day a commotion takes place in the lake; its waters boil to herald the approach of the lady with her oxen. It was, and still is (though in decreasing force), the custom for large numbers of people to make a pilgrimage to witness the phenomenon; and it is said that the lady herself appears in mermaid form upon the surface, and combs her tresses. I have little doubt that in this superstition we have the relic of a religious festival in honour of an archaic divinity whose abode was in the lake. She has, perhaps, only escaped being an enchanted princess by being a Welsh rather than a German goddess. If the mermaid form be of genuine antiquity,—about which I confess to a lurking suspicion,—it is another bond with the Scottish stories, with Melusina and with Derceto.[239]

We have now considered the principal points of the myth. The feather-robe, or skin, we found absent from all its more archaic examples. There, no change of form occurs, or when it does occur it is accomplished by simple transformation. When present, the robe is a mere symbol of the lady's superhuman nature, or else the result of enchantment. These are more recent types, and are all, or nearly all, *märchen*. In the later sagas, such as those of Melusina and the Lady of the Van Pool, it is again absent; though relics of the change of form frequently remain.

Capture of the Swan-maiden proper is effected by theft of her robe: in other types either by main force, or more frequently with her consent, more or less willingly given, or by her own initiative.

We then passed to the more important subject of the taboo. The taboo, strictly speaking, only appears where the peltry is absent. Several of its forms correspond with rules of antique etiquette. Others recall special points connected with savage life, such as the dislike of iron and steel, and the prejudice against the mention of a personal name. Other prohibitions are against reproaching the wife with her origin, against reminding her of her former condition, or against questioning her conduct or crossing her will. But whether the taboo be present or absent, the loss of the wife is equally inevitable, equally foreseen from the beginning. It is the doom of the connection between a simple man and a superhuman female. Even where the feather-robe is absent the taboo is not always found. Among savages the marriage-bond is often very loose: notably in the more backward races. And among these the superhuman wife's excuse for flight is simpler; and sometimes it is only an arbitrary exercise of will. The taboo grows up with the advance in civilization.

Lastly, we considered the Swan-maiden as divine ancestress. We found her resident in heaven, we found her worshipped, we found her as the totem of a clan. The totemistic stories are widely spread,—so widely, indeed, as to afford a presumption that we have in them a clue to the whole meaning of the myth. For not only have we the complete totemistic form, as among the Dyaks and the tribes of the Gold Coast; but we find the superstition fading through the goddess Derceto into modern sagas of the supernatural mother of a family, who to her sometimes owe extraordinary powers, and over whose fate she continually watches.

Here, then, our study of this beautiful myth must close. I am far from suggesting that the subject is exhausted. On the contrary, it is so large and so complex that I have rigidly abstained from anything more than a very imperfect examination of its principal features. On some of the points here partially discussed I shall have something more to add in our final chapter, when discussing certain theories on the fairy beliefs.

**FOOTNOTES:**

[202] Grey, p. 66; Taylor, p. 138; White, vol. i. pp. 95, 115, *et seqq.*, vol. ii. p. 127, *et seqq.*

[203] "F. L. Journal," vol. i. p. 202; "Revue des Trad. Pop." vol. iv. p. 305.

[204] Von Hahn, vol. ii. p. 78. In illustration of these remarks on marital relations in a society where female kinship only is recognized, let me quote the following paragraph concerning Maori customs. The Maories, it must be borne in mind, have only recently emerged from this stage; and many relics of it remain.

"Sometimes the father simply told his intended son-in-law he might come and live with his daughter; she was thenceforth considered his wife, he lived with his father-in-law, and became one of the tribe, or *hapu*, to which his wife belonged, and in case of war, was often obliged to fight against his own relatives. So common is the custom of the bridegroom going to live with his wife's family, that it frequently occurs, when he refuses to do so, she will leave him, and go back to her relatives; several instances came under my notice where young men have tried to break through this custom, and have so lost their wives" (Taylor, p. 337).

[205] Not entirely: see Burton, "Suppl. Nights," vol. vi. p. 363; "F. L. Journal," vol. i. p. 284; Sastri, p. 148.

[206] In speaking of a type as more or less recent than another, it must be recollected that I am not speaking of chronological order, but of the order of development. For aught we know, the story of the Marquis of the Sun may as a matter of date be actually older, could we trace it, than the far more archaic story of Tawhaki. But the society in which it took shape was more advanced than that disclosed in the Maori legend.

[207] Webster, p. 120; Campbell, vol. i. p. 25; "Mélusine," vol. i. p. 446; "F. L. Españ." vol. i. p. 187; Schneller, p. 71; Imbriani, p. 411; Cosquin, vol. i. pp. 9, 25; Sébillot, "Contes," vol. i. p. 197; Grundtvig, vol. i. p. 46; Cavallius, p. 255; Maspons y Labros, p. 102; "F. L. Journal," vol. i. p. 284, quoting Lewis.

[208] Waldau, p. 248; Ralston, "R. F. Tales," p. 120, from Afanasief.

[209] Compare the assistance rendered by the birds to Tini-rau, *suprà*, p. 286. The Eskimo hero is conveyed to his wife on a salmon's tail (Rink, p. 145). Where is the Buddhist pedigree of this incident, or the evidence of Buddhist influence which produced it?

[210] Sastri, p. 80; Cosquin, vol. ii. pp. 19, 18; Ralston, "Tibetan Tales," p. 72; "F. L. Journal," vol. ii. p. 9; Vernaleken, p. 280.

[211] "F. L. Journal," vol. vii. p. 318; Pitré, vol. iv. pp. 391, 410. A variant given by Prof. De Gubernatis is nearly allied to the Cinderella group ("Novelline," p. 29); Brett, p. 176.

[212] Basset, p. 161, quoting Bresnier, "Cours de langue Arabe." In a Maya story given by Dr. Brinton, the husband prevents his wife's transformation in a different way—namely, by throwing salt ("F. L. Journal," vol. i. p. 251).

[213] "Journ. Ethnol. Soc." N. S., vol. ii. p. 26; Giles, *passim*; Brauns, p. 388.

[214] "Y Cymmrodor," vol. v. p. 94.

[215] Map, Dist. ii. c. 11.

[216] Map, Dist. ii. c. 12.

[217] "Y Cymmrodor," vol. iv. p. 201. Nothing turns on the actual names in these stories; they have been evidently much corrupted,—probably past all recognition.

[218] Ibid. p. 189; vol. v. pp. 59, 66; vol. vi. p. 196.

[219] Pliny l. xvi. c. 95; Thorpe, vol. ii. pp. 275, 277; Stephens, p. 248, citing the "Barzas Breiz."

[220] The above paragraphs had scarcely been written when the London papers (June 1890) reprinted extracts from a letter in the *Vossische Zeitung* relating the adventures of Dr. Bayol, the Governor of Kotenon, who was recently imprisoned by the bloodthirsty King of Dahomey. The king was too suspicious to sign the letter written in his name to the President of the French Republic. In all probability he was unwilling to let the President have his sign manual, for of course M. Carnot would have no hesitation in bewitching him by its means.

[221] Keightley, p. 121, quoting from Thiele; Thorpe, vol. iii. p. 155.

[222] Ancient Laws and Institutes of Wales (Public Record Comm., 1841) pp. 44, 252. (The Dimetian code was the one in force at Myddfai; but that of Gwynedd was similar in this respect.) Farrer, p. 256.

[223] Campbell, vol. iii. p. 403; Mac Innes, p. 211; Wratislaw, p. 314. *Cf.* a similar story told by a peasant to Dr. Krauss' mother no longer ago than 1888, as having recently happened at Mrkopolje: he "knew the parties!" (Krauss, "Volksgl." p. 107).

[224] Ellis, p. 208; Grinnell, p. 129.

[225] "Choice Notes," p. 96; *cf.* Jahn, p. 364, cited above, p. 279. (Kennedy relates the story of the Lady of Inchiquin differently. According to him the husband was never to invite company to the castle. This is probably more modern than the other version. Kennedy, p. 282.) Keightley, p. 458, quoting

the *Quarterly Review*, vol. xxii. Sir Francis Palgrave, though an accurate writer, was guilty of the unpardonable sin of invariably neglecting to give his authorities. Ibid. p. 485, quoting Mdlle. Bosquet, "La Normandie Romanesque."

[226] "Journal Amer. F. L." vol ii. p. 137; vol. i. p. 76; Schneller, p. 210; "Rosenöl," vol. i. p. 162; Child, vol. i. p. 337, quoting Schmidt and Apollodorus; "Panjab N. & Q.," vol. ii. p. 207. (In this form the story is found as a tradition, probably derived from the Mahábhárata.) "Trans. Aberd. Eistedd." p. 225; White, vol. i. p. 126.

[227] Dennys, p. 140; "Corpus Poet. Bor." vol. i. p. 168; "Kathá-sarit-ságara," vol. ii. p. 453, *cf.* p. 577; White, vol. i. p. 88; Schneller, p. 210; Robertson Smith, p. 50.

[228] Gill, p. 265.

[229] "Indian N. & Q." vol. iv. p. 147.

[230] "Sacred Books of the East," vol. xxvii. pp. 471, 475, 476; "Indian N. & Q." vol. iv. p. 147.

[231] Romilly, p. 134; Landes, p. 123.

[232] Bent, p. 13. The Nereids in modern Greek folklore are conceived in all points as Swan-maidens. They fly through the air by means of magical raiment (Schmidt, p. 133).

[233] See my article on the "Meddygon Myddfai," entitled "Old Welsh Folk Medicine," "Y Cymmrodor," vol. ix. p. 227.

[234] A certain German family used to excuse its faults by attributing them to a sea-fay who was reckoned among its ancestors; Birlinger, "Aus Schwaben," vol. i. p. 7, quoting the "Zimmerische Chronik."

[235] Namely, her husband's father, whose name she was not permitted by etiquette to utter. See above, p. 309.

[236] Theal, p. 54. The Teton lady who became a mermaid was summoned, by singing an incantation, to suckle her child; "Journal Amer. F. L." vol. ii. p. 137.

[237] Schreck, p. 71.

[238] Poestion, p. 55; "Cymru Fu," p. 474.

[239] "Y Cymmrodor," vol. iv. p. 177, vol. vi. p. 203. I have also made inquiries at Ystradgynlais, in the neighbourhood of the lake, the results of which confirm the statements of Professor Rhys' correspondents; but I have failed to elicit any further information.

# CHAPTER XII

# CONCLUSION

Retrospect — The fairies of Celtic and Teutonic races of the same nature as the supernatural beings celebrated in the traditions of other nations — All superstitions of supernatural beings explicable by reference to the conceptions of savages — Liebrecht's Ghost Theory of some Swan-maiden myths — MacRitchie's Finn Theory — The amount of truth in them — Both founded on too narrow an induction — Conclusion.

We have in the preceding pages examined some of the principal groups of tales and superstitions relating to Fairies proper,—that is to say, the Elves and Fays of Celtic and Teutonic tradition.

Dealing in the first instance with the sagas found in this country, or in Germany, our investigations have by no means ended there; for in order to understand these sagas, we have found occasion to refer again and again to the *märchen*, as well as the sagas, of other European nations,—nay, to the traditions of races as wide apart from our own in geographical position and culture, as the South Sea Islanders, the Ainos, and the Aborigines of America. And we have found among peoples in the most distant parts of the globe similar stories and superstitions. Incidentally, too, we have learned something of the details of archaic practices, and have found the two great divisions of Tradition,—belief and practice,—inseparably interwoven.

I do not pretend to have touched upon all the myths referring to Fairies, as thus strictly defined; and the Kobolds and Puck, the Household Spirits and Mischievous Demons, have scarcely been so much as mentioned. Want of space forbids our going further. It is hoped, however, that enough has been said, not merely to give the readers an idea of the Fairy Mythology correct as far as it goes, but, beyond that, to vindicate the method pursued in the investigation, as laid down in our second chapter, by demonstrating the essential identity of human imagination all over the world, and by tracing the stories with which we have been dealing to a more barbarous state of society and a more archaic plane of thought. It now remains, therefore, to recall what we have ascertained concerning the nature and origin of the Fairies, and briefly to consider two rival theories.

We started from some of the ascertained facts of savage thought and savage life. The doctrine of Spirits formed our first proposition. This we defined to be the belief held by savages that man consists of body and spirit; that it is possible for the spirit to quit the body and roam at will in different shapes about the world, returning to the body as to its natural home; that in the spirit's absence the body sleeps, and that it dies if the spirit return not; further, that the universe swarms with spirits embodied and disembodied, because everything in the world has a spirit, and all these spirits are analogues of the human spirit, having the same will and acting from the same motives; and that if by chance any of these spirits be ejected from its body, it may continue to exist without a body, or it may find and enter a new body, not necessarily such an one as it occupied before, but one quite different. The doctrine of Transformation was another of our premises: that is to say, the belief held by savages in the possibility of a change of form while preserving the same identity. A third premise was the belief in Witchcraft, or the power of certain persons to cause the transformations just mentioned, and to perform by means of spells, or symbolic actions and mystical words, various other feats beyond ordinary human power. And there were others to which I need not now refer, all of which were assumed to be expressed in the tales and songs, and in the social and political institutions, of savages. Along with these, we assumed the hypothesis of the evolution of civilization from savagery. By this I mean that just as the higher orders of animal and vegetable life have been developed from germs which appeared on this planet incalculable ages ago; so during a past of unknown length the civilization of the highest races of men has been gradually evolving through the various stages of savagery and barbarism up to what we know it to-day; and so every nation, no matter how barbarous, has arisen from a lower stage than that in which it is found, and is on its way, if left to its natural processes, to something higher and better. This is an hypothesis which does not, of course, exclude the possibility of temporary and partial relapses, such as we know have taken place in the history of every civilized country, any more than it excludes the possibility of the decay and death of empires; but upon the whole it claims that progress and not retrogression is the law of human society. The different stages of this progress have everywhere left their mark on the tales and songs, the sayings and superstitions, the social, religious and political institutions—in other words, on the belief and practice—of mankind.

Starting from these premises, we have examined five groups, or cycles, of tales concerning the Fairy Mythology. We have found Fairyland very human in its organization. Its inhabitants marry, sometimes among themselves, sometimes into mankind. They have children born to them; and they require at such times female assistance. They steal children from men, and leave their own miserable brats in exchange; they steal women, and sometimes leave in their stead blocks of wood, animated by magical art, or sometimes one of themselves. In the former case the animation does not usually last very long, and the women is then supposed to die. Their females sometimes in turn become captive to men. Unions thus formed are, however, not lasting, until the husband has followed the wife to her own home, and conquered his right to her afresh by some great adventure. This is not always in the story: presumably, therefore, not always possible. On the other hand, he who enters Fairyland and partakes of fairy food is spell-bound: he cannot return—at least for many years, perhaps for ever—to the land of men. Fairies are grateful to men for benefits conferred, and resentful for injuries. They never fail to reward those who do them a kindness; but their gifts usually have conditions attached, which detract from their value and sometimes become a source of loss and misery. Nor do they forget to revenge themselves on those who offend them; and to watch them, when they do not desire to be manifested, is a mortal offence. Their chief distinction from men is in their unbounded magical powers, whereof we have had several illustrations. They make things seem other than they are; they appear and disappear at will; they make long time seem short, or short time long; they change their own forms; they cast spells over mortals, and keep them spell-bound for ages.

All these customs and all these powers are asserted of the Fairies properly so called. And when we look at the superstitions of other races than the Celts and Teutons, to which our inquiries have been primarily directed, we find the same things asserted of all sorts of creatures. Deities, ancestors, witches, ghosts, as well as animals of every kind, are endowed by the belief of nations all over the world with powers precisely similar to those of the Fairies, and with natures and social organizations corresponding with those of men. These beliefs can only be referred to the same origin as the fairy superstitions; and all arise out of the doctrine of spirits, the doctrine of transformations, and the belief in witchcraft, held by savage tribes.

But here I must, at the risk of some few repetitions, notice a theory on the subject of the Swan-maiden myth enunciated by Liebrecht. That distinguished writer, in his book on Folklore, devotes a section to the consideration of the group which has occupied us in the last two chapters, and maintains, with his accustomed wealth of allusion and his accustomed ingenuity, that some at least of the Swan-maidens are nothing more nor less than ghosts of the departed, rescued from the kingdom of darkness for a while, but bound to return thither after a short respite here with those whom they love. Now it is clear that if Swan-maiden tales are to be resolved into ghost stories, all other supernatural beings, gods and devils as well as fairies and ghosts, will turn out to be nothing but spectres of the dead. A summary of his argument, and of the reasons for rejecting it, will, therefore, not only fill up any serious gaps in our discussion of the main incidents of the myth in question; but it will take a wider sweep, and include the whole subject of the present volume.

His argument, as I understand it, is based, first, on the terms of the taboo. The object of the taboo, he thinks, is to avoid any remark being made, any question being asked, any object being presented, which would remind these spirits of their proper home, and awaken a longing they cannot withstand to return. There is an old Teutonic legend of a knight who came in a little boat drawn by a swan to succour and wed a distressed lady, on whom he laid a charge never to ask whence he came, or in what country he was born. When she breaks this commandment the swan reappears and fetches him away. So the nightmare-wife, as we have seen, in one of the tales vanishes on being asked how she became a nightmare. Again, the fay of Argouges disappears on the name of Death being mentioned in her presence. A fair maiden in an Indian tale, who is found by the hero in the neighbourhood of a fountain, and bears the name of Bheki (Frog), forbids her husband ever to let her see water.

When she is thirsty and begs him for water, the doom is fulfilled on his bringing it to her. A similar tale may be added from Ireland, though Liebrecht does not mention it. A man who lived near Lough Sheelin, in County Meath, was annoyed by having his corn eaten night after night. So he sat up to watch; and to his astonishment a number of horses came up out of the lake driven by a most beautiful woman, whom he seized and induced to marry him. She made the stipulation that she was never to be allowed to see the lake again; and for over twenty years she lived happily with him, till one day she strolled out to look at the haymakers, and caught sight of the distant water. With a loud cry she flew straight to it, and vanished beneath the surface.[240]

Liebrecht's next reason is based upon the place where the maiden is found,—a forest, or a house in the forest. In this connection he refers to the tavern, or drinking-shop, on the borders of the forest, where Wild Edric found his bride, and points to a variant of the story, also given by Walter Map, in which she is said, in so many words, to have been snatched *from the dead*.[241] The forest, he fancies, is the place of the dead, the underworld. Lastly, he gives numerous legends of the Middle Ages,—some of which found their way into the "Decameron," that great storehouse of floating tales, and other literary works of imagination, as well as into chronicles,—and instances from more modern folklore, wherein a mistress or wife dies, or seems to die, and is buried, yet is afterwards recovered from the tomb, and lives to wed, if a maiden, and to bear children. He supports these by references to the vampire superstitions, and to the case of Osiris, who returned after death to Isis and became the father of Horus. And, following Uhland, he compares the sleep-thorn, with which Odin pricked the Valkyrie, Brynhild, and so put her into a magic slumber, to the stake which was driven into the corpse suspected of being a vampire, to prevent its rising any more from the grave and troubling the living.

Now it may be admitted that there is much that is plausible, much even that is true, in this theory. It might be urged in its behalf that (as we have had more than one occasion in the course of this work to know) Fairyland is frequently not to be distinguished from the world of the dead. Time is not known there; and the same consequences of permanent abode follow upon eating the food of the dead and the food of the fairies. Further, when living persons are stolen by fairies, mere dead images are sometimes left in their place. These arguments, and such as these, might well be added to Liebrecht's; and it would be hard to say that a formidable case was not made out. And yet the theory fails to take account of some rather important considerations. Perhaps the strongest point made—a point insisted on with great power—is that of the taboo. The case of the lady of Argouges is certainly very striking, though, taken by itself, it is far from conclusive. It might very well be that a supernatural being, in remaining here, would be obliged to submit to mortality, contrary perhaps to its nature; and to remind it of this might fill it with an irresistible impulse to fly from so horrible a fate. I do not say this is the explanation, but it is as feasible as the other. In the Spanish story it was not the utterance of the name of Death, but of a holy name—the name of Mary—which compelled the wife to leave her husband. Here she was unquestionably regarded by Spanish orthodoxy, not as a spirit of the dead, but as a foul fiend, able to assume what bodily form it would, but bound to none. The prohibition of inquiry as to the bride's former home may arise not so much from a desire to avoid the recollection, as from the resentment of impertinent curiosity, which we have seen arouses excessive annoyance in supernatural bosoms. The resentment of equally impertinent reproaches, or a reminiscence of savage etiquette that avoids the direct name, may account at least as well for other forms of the taboo. Liebrecht suggests most ingeniously that assault and battery must strike the unhappy elf still more strongly than reproaches, as a difference between her present and former condition, and remind her still more importunately of her earlier home, and that this explains the prohibition of the "three causeless blows." It may be so, though there is no hint of this in the stories; and yet her former condition need not have been that of a ghost of the dead, nor her earlier home the tomb. By far the greater number of these stories represent the maiden as a water-nymph; but it is the depths of the earth rather than the water which are commonly regarded as the dwelling-place of the departed. Moreover, the correspondence I have tried to point out between the etiquette of various peoples and the taboo,—such, for instance, as the ban upon a husband's breaking into his wife's seclusion at a delicate moment in his family history,—would remain, on Liebrecht's theory, purely accidental. Nor would the theory account for the absence of a taboo in the lower savagery, nor for the totemistic character of the lady, nor, least of all, for the peltry which is the most picturesque, if not the most important, incident in this group of tales.

In fact, the only direct evidence for Liebrecht's contention is the variant of Wild Edric's legend alluded to by Map. His words are, speaking of Alnoth, Edric's son, a great benefactor of the see of Hereford: "The man whose mother vanished into air openly in the sight of many persons, being indignant at her husband's reproaching her that he had carried her off by force from among the dead (*quod cam a mortuis rapuisset*)." Upon this it is to be observed that the expression here made use of cannot be regarded as one which had accidentally dropped out of the narrative previously given; but it is an allusion to an independent and inconsistent version, given in forgetfulness that the writer had already in another part of his work related the story at large and with comments. There he had explicitly called Alnoth—the heir and offspring of a devil (*dæmon*), and had expressed his wonder that such a person should have given up his whole inheritance (namely, the manor of Ledbury North, which he made over to the see of Hereford in gratitude for the miraculous cure of his palsy) to Christ in return for his restored health, and spent the rest of his life as a pilgrim. Mediæval writers (especially ecclesiastics) were in a difficulty in describing fairies. They looked upon them as having an objective existence; and yet they knew not how to classify them. Fairies were certainly neither departed saints nor holy angels. Beside these two kinds of spirits, the only choice left was between devils and ghosts of the wicked dead, or, at most, of the dead who had no claims to extraordinary goodness. They did not believe in any other creatures which could be identified with these mysterious elves. It is no wonder, therefore, if they were occasionally perplexed, occasionally inconsistent, sometimes denouncing them as devils, at other times dismissing them as ghosts.[242]

This is what seems to have happened to Map. In the two chapters immediately preceding, he has given two legends illustrating each horn of the dilemma. One of these relates the marriage of Henno With-the-Teeth, who found a lovely maiden in a grove on the coast of Normandy. She was sitting alone, apparelled in royal silk, and weeping. Her beauty and her tears attracted the gallant knight, to whom, in response to his questions, she told a cock-and-bull story about her father having brought her, all unwilling as she was, by sea to be married to the King of France; but having been driven by a storm on the shore, she said she had landed, and then her father had taken advantage of a sudden change of wind to sail away, leaving her to her fate. Henno was an easy conquest: he took her home and married her. Unluckily, however, he had a mother who had her suspicions. She noticed that her fair daughter-in-law, though she went often to church, always upon some trumpery excuse came late, so as to avoid being sprinkled with holy water, and as regularly left before the consecration of the elements. So this virtuous old vixen determined to watch one Sunday morning; and she discovered that after Henno had gone to church, his wife, transformed into a serpent, entered a bath, and in a little while, issuing upon a cloth which her maid had spread out for her, she tore it into pieces with her teeth before resuming human form. The maid afterwards went through the like performance, her mistress waiting upon her. All this was in due course confided to Henno, who, in company with a priest, unexpectedly burst in the next time upon his wife and her servant, and sprinkled them with holy water. Mistress and maid thereupon with a great yell bounded out through the roof and disappeared.

Clearly these ladies were devils: no other creatures with self-respect would be guilty of such transformations and such constant disregard of the proprieties at church. Ghosts get their turn in Map's other narrative. It concerns a man whose wife had died. After sorrowing long for her death, he found her one night in a deep and solitary dale amid a number of women. With great joy he seized her, and, carrying her off, lived with her again for many years and had a numerous progeny. Not a few of her descendants were living when Map wrote, and were known as *the children of the dead woman*. This, of course, is not a Swan-maiden story at all. At the end of Chapter V. I have referred to some similar tales; and what we learned during our discussion of the subject of Changelings may lead us to suspect that we have here in an imperfect form a story of the exchange of an adult woman for a lifeless image, and her recovery from the hands of her ravishers. This is by no means the same plot as that of the stories recounted by Liebrecht in which the wife or the betrothed is rescued from the grave. Those stories, at least in warm climates where burials are hurried, and in rude ages when medical skill is comparatively undeveloped, are all within the bounds of possibility. There does not appear in them any trace of mythology,—hardly even of the supernatural; and he would be a bold man who would deny that a substratum of fact may not underlie some of them. To establish their relationship with the group we are now considering, links of a much more evident character are wanting. The fact that they are traditional is not of itself sufficient. The fairy of the Forest of Dean had not revived after death, or supposed death; nor had she been recovered from supernatural beings who had stolen her away. Map's account, to whatever his expression *from the dead* may point, is inconsistent with either the one or the other. Rather she was stolen from her own kindred, to become the wife of him who had won her by his own right arm.

But a single instance, and that instance either inconsistent with the analogous traditions, or unable to supply a cogent or consistent explanation of them, is not a very safe basis for a theory. What is it worth when it is inconsistent even with the theory itself? Indeed, if it were consistent with the theory, we might match it with another instance wholly irreconcilable. Mikáilo Ivanovitch in the Russian ballad marries a Swan-maiden, who, unlike some of the ladies just mentioned, insists upon being first baptized into the Christian faith. She makes the stipulation that when the one of them dies the other shall go living into the grave with the dead, and there abide for three months. She herself dies. Mikáilo enters the grave with her, and there conquers a dragon which comes to feast on the dead bodies. The dragon is compelled to fetch the waters of life and death, by means of which the hero brings his dead love back to life. Marya, the White Swan, however, proved herself so ungrateful that after awhile she took another husband, and twice she acted the part of Delilah to Mikáilo. The third time she tried it he was compelled in self-defence to put an end to her wiles by cutting off her head. This is honest, downright death. There is no mistaking it. But then it is impossible that Marya, the White Swan, was a mere ghost filched from the dead and eager to return. Yet the story of Marya is equally a Swan-maiden story, and is just as good to build a theory on as Map's variant of Wild Edric.[243]

In replying, however, to the arguments of so learned and acute a writer as Liebrecht, it is not enough to point out these distinctions and inconsistencies: it is not enough to show that the terms of the taboo do not warrant the construction he has put upon them, nor that he has failed to account for very significant incidents. If he has mistaken the meaning of the legends, we should be able to make clear the source of his error. It arises, I hold, from an imperfect apprehension of the archaic philosophy underlying the narratives. Liebrecht's comparisons are, with one exception, limited to European variants. His premises were thus too narrow to admit of his making valid deductions. Perhaps even yet we are hardly in a position to do this; but at all events the sources of possible error are diminished by the wider area we are able to survey, and from the evidence of which we reason. We have compared the stories, both mediæval and modern, mentioned by Liebrecht, with *märchen* and sagas told among nations outside European influence in various degrees of civilization, down to the savagery of Kaffirs and Dyaks. We have succeeded in classifying their differences, and in spite of them we have found all the tales in substantial agreement. They are all built on the same general plan; the same backbone of thought runs through them; and between them all there is no greater divergence than that which in the physical realm separates mammal from bird, or bird from reptile. It is inevitable to conclude that even the most recently discovered folk-tale of them has come to us from a distant period when our forefathers were in the same rude state as Dyaks and South Sea Islanders. No actual adventure of Wild Edric or Raymond of Lusignan gave rise to these stories. English patriot and Burgundian Count were only the names whereon they fastened,—the mountains which towered above the plain and gathered about their heads the vapours already floating in the atmosphere. We must therefore go back far beyond the Middle Ages to learn in what manner we are to understand these stories,—back to the state of savagery whence the inhabitants of Europe had long emerged when Map and Gervase wrote, but of which the relics linger among us even yet.

The necessarily meagre exposition of some of the most salient characteristics of savage thought with which we started has been illustrated and its outlines filled in to some extent in the course of the subsequent discussions. I need not, therefore, do more than draw attention as briefly as possible to those characteristics that are relevant here. First and foremost, we have found some of the Swan-maiden tales boldly professing to account for the worship of totems; and so thoroughly does totemism appear to be ingrained in the myth that there is some reason for thinking that here we have a clue to the myth's origin and meaning. But the intellect to which totemism is a credible theory draws no line of demarcation between humanity and the life and consciousness it recognizes in the whole encircling universe. To it, accordingly, a story of union between a man and a fish, a swan or a serpent, involves no difficulty. When advancing knowledge, and with knowledge repulsion from such a story, begins to threaten it, another belief advances to its defence. For nothing is easier to creatures as clever as the lower animals than a change of form. They can, whenever they please, assume the appearance of man or woman: it is as natural to them as the shape under which they are usually seen. Again, the life that swarms about the savage philosopher does not always manifest itself visibly. It is often unseen. The world is filled with spirits, of whom some have inhabited human bodies, others have not. To the savage they are all alike; for those who have not hitherto inhabited human bodies may do so at will, or may inhabit other bodies, either animal or vegetable, and those who have once done so may do so again.

All these—Totemism, the equality and essential identity of nature between man and all other objects in the universe, the doctrine of Transformation, the doctrine of Spirits—are phases of savage thought, every one of which has been incorporated in the myth of the Swan-maidens, and every one of which, except one special and very limited development of the doctrine of Spirits, is ignored in Liebrecht's theory. The theory is, indeed, an admirable illustration of the danger of reasoning without a sufficiently wide area of induction. Liebrecht's mistake on the present occasion was twofold: he only dealt with one or, at most, two types of the myth; and he ignored the savage variants. Had he taken into consideration other types—such as Hasan, the Marquis of the Sun, the Star's Daughter;—had he been aware of the savage variants all over the world, he would not have formed a theory so inconsistent with the facts, and so little fitted to solve the problems propounded, not merely by the phenomena of the Swan-maiden group, but by those of other tales in which supernatural beings intervene.

In reasoning by induction, the greater the number of facts taken into account, the greater the probability of sound reasoning; and therefore the greater the number of facts a theory will explain, the more likely it is to be true. Had Liebrecht's theory touched only the Swan-maiden group, it would have been more convenient to discuss it in the last chapter. But inasmuch as its truth would involve much wider issues, it seemed better to reserve it to be dealt with here. For if the theory be valid for Melusina, the Lady of the Van Pool, and other water-nymphs, it is valid also for the "water-woman" who, in a Transylvanian story, dwelt in a lake in the forest between Mehburg and Reps. She had two sons, whose father was a man, and the younger of whom became king of that land. But when the Saxon immigration took place the incomers cut down the wood; the lake dried up, and as it dried up, the lives of the water-spirit and her son gradually sank lower and lower, and at last were extinguished with the extinction of the lake.[244] Now I will venture to say that this story is to be explained satisfactorily on no theory yet broached, unless it be the theory that we have in it a survival of the savage doctrine of Spirits. Least of all it is to be explained by any adaptation of what I may call the Ghost theory,—namely, that the water-spirit and her son were already the spirits of dead human beings.

Leaving this one example of the value of Liebrecht's theory, as applied to water-spirits, to stand for all, I turn to another order of beings with supernatural powers referred to several times in the foregoing pages: I mean Witches. I adduced in Chapter X. a Tirolese tale, a variant of the Melusina type, wherein the wife was a witch. It will have been obvious to every reader that the tale is simply that of Cupid and Psyche with the parts reversed; and I might urge that Cupid and the witch were beings of precisely the same nature. Waiving this for the moment, however, no one will deny that the witch takes the place of the Swan-maiden, or fairy, in other stories of the group. But perhaps it may be suggested that the name *witch* (*Angana, Hexe*) has got into the story by accident; and that not a witch in our sense of the word, but a ghost from the dead, is really meant. There might be something to be said for this if there were any substantial distinction to be made between ghosts and witches and fairies. In the tales and superstitions discussed in the present volume we have found no distinction. Whether it be child-stealing, transformation, midnight meetings, possession and gift of enchanted objects, spell-binding, or whatever function, or habit, or power be predicted of one, it will be found to be common to the three. I conclude, therefore, that they are all three of the same nature. This is what a consideration of the superstitions of savages would lead me to expect. The belief in fairies, ghosts, and witches is a survival of those superstitions. It is, of course, not found in equal coherence, equal strength of all its parts, equal logic (if I may so express it) everywhere. We must not be surprised if, as it is gradually penetrated by the growing forces of civilization, it becomes fragmentary, and the attributes of these various orders of supernatural beings begin to be differentiated. They are never completely so; and the proof of this is that what is at one place, at one time, or by one people, ascribed to one order, is at another place, at another time, or by another people, ascribed to another order. The nature of the classical deities was identical too; and hence Cupid and the witch of the Tirolese tale are the masculine and feminine counterparts of the same conception.

Lastly, a few words must be expended on a totally different theory lately put forward by Mr. MacRitchie. This theory is not altogether a new one; it has been before the world for many years. But Mr. MacRitchie has, first in "The Archæological Review," and since then more elaborately in a separate book, entitled "The Testimony of Tradition," worked it out and fortified it with an array of arguments philological, historical, topographical, and traditional. He claims to have established that the fairies of the Celtic and Teutonic races are neither more nor less than the prehistoric tribes whom they conquered and drove back, and whose lands they now possess. He identifies these mysterious beings with the Picts of Scotland, the Feinne of the Scottish Highlands and of Ireland, and the Finns and Lapps of Scandinavia. And he suggests that the Eskimo, the Ainos, and I know not what other dwarfish races, are relics of the same people; while Santa Klaus, the patron saint of children, is only a tradition of the wealthy and beneficent character borne by this ill-used folk. Primarily his arguments are concerned with Scotland and Ireland. He builds much on the howes or barrows, called in Scotland Picts' houses, which in both countries bear the reputation of being the haunt of fairies or dwarfs, and some of which seem to have been in fact dwelling-places. He quotes Dr. Karl Blind to show that Finns intermarried with the Shetlanders, and that they were believed to come over in the form of seals, casting aside their sealskins when they landed. In this connection he relates how the Finn women were captured by taking possession of their sealskins, without which they could not get away from their captors. He also shows that illimitable riches and magical powers were ascribed to the Picts and to the Finns, and that the Lapps were pre-eminent in witchcraft.

I shall leave it to Celtic scholars to deal with Mr. MacRitchie's remarkable etymologies and with his historical arguments, confining myself to one or two observations on the traditional aspect of the theory. Now I should be the last to undervalue any traces of history to be found in tradition. I have elsewhere drawn attention to the importance of the study of this element in folk-tales;[245] and I am quite ready to admit that nothing is more likely than the transfer to the mythical beings of Celtic superstition of some features derived from alien races. Savages and barbarians are in the habit of imputing to strangers and foes in greatly extended measure the might of witchcraft they claim for themselves. And the wider the differences between themselves and the foreigners, the more mysterious to them are the habits and appearance of the latter, and the more powerful do they believe them. All this might account for many details that we are told concerning the dwarfs, the Picts, the Finns, or by whatever other names the elvish race may have been known to Scots and Irishmen. But further than this I cannot go with Mr. MacRitchie. I hold his error, like that of Liebrecht already discussed, to be founded on too narrow an induction. This volume will have been written in vain, as it appears that for Mr. MacRitchie the vastly more important works of Dr. Tylor and Mr. Andrew Lang have been written in vain, unless I have made it clear that the myths of nations all over the world follow one general law and display common characteristics. I am not astonished to find the Shetland tale of marriage with a seal-woman reproduced on the Gold Coast and among the Dyaks of Borneo. But Mr. MacRitchie ought to be very much astonished; for he can hardly show that the historical Finns were known in these out-of-the-way places. It seems to me natural to find that in Scotland and Ireland fairies dwelt in barrows, and in Annam and Arabia in hills and rocks; and that both in this country and in the far East they inveigled unhappy mortals into their dwellings and kept them for generations—nay, for centuries. That the Shoshone of California should dread their infants being changed by the Ninumbees, or dwarfs, in the same way as the Celts of the British Islands, and the Teutons too, dreaded their infants being changed, does not seem at all incredible to me. That to eat the food of the dead in New Zealand prevents a living man from returning to the land of the living, just as Persephone was retained in Hades by partaking of the pomegranate, and just as to eat the food of fairies hinders the Manx or the Hebrew adventurer from rejoining his friends on the surface of the earth, is in no way perplexing to me. But all these things, and they might be multiplied indefinitely, must be very perplexing to Mr. MacRitchie, if he be not prepared to prove that Annamites and Arabs, Hebrews and Shoshone, New Zealanders and classical Greeks alike, were acquainted with the Picts and the Finns, and alike celebrated them in their traditions.

The truth Mr. MacRitchie does not reckon with is, that no theory will explain the nature and origin of the fairy superstitions which does not also explain the nature and origin of every other supernatural being worshipped or dreaded by uncivilized mankind throughout the world. And until he shall address himself to this task, however ingenious his guesses, however amusing his philology, however delightfully wild his literary and historical arguments, he will not succeed in convincing any serious student.

Here then we must pause. Obvious are the differences between the nations of mankind: differences of physical conformation,—that is to say, of race; divergences of mental and moral development,—that is to say, of civilization. Hitherto the task attempted by folklore has been to show that underlying all these differences there is a broad foundation of common agreement; that distinctions of race do not extend to mental and moral constitution; that the highest nation on the ladder of culture has climbed from the same rung on which the lowest are yet standing; and that the absurd and incongruous customs and institutions and the equally absurd and impossible stories and beliefs found imbedded in the civilization of the more advanced nations are explicable, and explicable only, as relics of the phases wherethrough those nations have passed from the depths of savagery.

If it be admitted in general terms that the evidence collected and marshalled up to the present time has established among sure scientific facts so much of the past of humanity, this achievement is but the beginning of toil. A wide field has been opened to the student for the collection and arrangement of details, before the true meaning of many a strange custom and stranger tale will be thoroughly understood. I have tried to do something of the kind in the foregoing pages. But beyond this there is the more delicate investigation of the ethnic element in folklore. Can we assign to the various races their special shares in the development of a common tradition? Can we show what direction each race took, and how and why it modified the general inheritance?

On the other hand, it is not asserted that the status of savagery was the primitive condition of men. Of course it may have been. But if not, there is work to be done in endeavouring to ascertain what lies behind it. The questions started from this point wander across the border of folklore into pure psychology; but it is a psychology based not upon introspection and analysis of the mind of the civilized man, developed under the complex influences that have been acting and reacting during untold years of upward struggling, always arduous and often cruel, but a psychology which must be painfully reconstructed from the simplest and most archaic phenomena disclosed by anthropological research. Who can say what light may not thus be thrown as well on the destiny as on the origin of mankind?

**FOOTNOTES:**

[240] Liebrecht, p. 54; "F. L. Journal," vol. vii. p. 312.

[241] Map, Dist. iv. c. 10.

[242] The sect of the Cabalists, indeed, believed in the existence of spirits of nature, embodiments or representatives of the four elements, which they called respectively gnomes, sylphs, salamanders, and ondines. To this strange sect some of the savage opinions on the subject of spirits seem to have been transmitted in a philosophical form from classical antiquity. They taught that it was possible for the philosopher by austerity and study to rise to intercourse with these elemental spirits, and even to obtain them in marriage. But the orthodox regarded the Cabalists as magicians and their spirits as foul incubi. See Lecky, "History of Rationalism," vol. i. p. 46.

[243] Hapgood, p. 214.

[244] Müller, p. 33.

[245] "Folklore," vol. i. pp. 113, 116.

# BIBLIOGRAPHY

*Aberd. Eistedd.* See *Trans. Aberd. Eistedd.*

Alpenburg. See Von Alpenburg.

Amélineau. Contes et Romans del' Égypte Chrétienne par E. Amélineau. 2 vols. Paris, 1888.

*Amer. F. L.* See *Journal Amer. F. L.*

*Am Urds-Brunnen.* Am Urds-Brunnen. Mittheilungen für Freunde volksthümlich-wissenschaftlicher Kunde. 6 vols. [The first two volumes entitled *Am Urds-Brunnen, Organ des Vereins für Verbreitung volksthümlich-wissenschaftlicher Kunde.*] Rendsburg, 1881-89.

*Antiquary.* The Antiquary, a Magazine devoted to the study of the Past. 22 vols. London, 1880-90, still proceeding.

*Archivio.* Archivio per lo studio delle Tradizioni Popolari Rivista Trimestrale diretta da G. Pitré e S. Salomone-Marino. 9 vols. Palermo, 1882-90, still proceeding.

*Arch. Rev.* The Archæological Review. 4 vols. London, 1888-90.

Arnaudin. Contes Populaires recueillis dans la Grande Lande le Born les Petites Landes et le Marensin par Félix Arnaudin. Paris, 1887.

Aubrey, *Miscellanies.* Miscellanies upon various subjects. By John Aubrey, F.R.S. 4th edition. London, 1857.

—— *Remaines.* Remaines of Gentilisme and Judaisme. By John Aubrey, R.S.S. 1686-87. Edited and annotated by James Britten, F.L.S. London, 1881. (Folk-Lore Society.)

*Bahar-Danush.* Bahar-Danush; or Garden of Knowledge. An Oriental Romance. Translated from the Persic of Einaiut Oollah. By Jonathan Scott. 3 vols. Shrewsbury, 1799.

Baring-Gould. Curious Myths of the Middle Ages. By S. Baring-Gould, M.A. New edition. London, 1869.

Bartsch. Sagen, Märchen und Gebräuche aus Mecklenburg. Gesammelt und herausgegeben von Karl Bartsch. 2 vols. Wien, 1879-80.

Basset. Contes Populaires Berbères recueillis, traduits et annotés par René Basset. Paris, 1887.

Bent. The Cyclades, or Life among the Insular Greeks. By J. Theodore Bent, B.A. London, 1885.

Birlinger, *Aus Schwaben*. Aus Schwaben Sagen, Legenden, Aberglauben, Sitten, Rechtsbräuche, Ortsneckereien, Lieder, Kinderreime Neue Sammlung von Anton Birlinger. 2 vols. Wiesbaden, 1874.

—— *Volksthümliches*. Volksthümliches aus Schwaben. Herausgegeben von Dr. Anton Birlinger. 2 vols. and Wörterbüchlein. Freiburg im Breisgau, 1861-62.

Bladé. Contes Populaires de la Gascogne par M. Jean-François Bladé. 3 vols. Paris, 1886.

*Border Minstrelsy*. Minstrelsy of the Scottish Border: consisting of Historical and Romantic Ballads, collected in the Southern Counties of Scotland. 3rd edition. 3 vols. Edinburgh, 1806.

Bowker. Goblin Tales of Lancashire. By James Bowker, F.R.G.S.I. London, N.D.

Braga. Ethnographia Portugueza. O Povo Portuguez nos seus Costumes, Crenças e Tradições por Theophilo Braga. 2 vols. Lisboa, 1886.

Brand. Observations on Popular Antiquities: chiefly illustrating the origin of our vulgar Customs, Ceremonies, and Superstitions. By John Brand, M.A., F. and Sec. S.A. Arranged and revised, with additions by Henry Ellis, F.R.S., Sec. S.A. 2 vols. London, 1813.

Brauns. Japanische Märchen und Sagen gesammelt und herausgegeben von David Brauns. Leipzig, 1885

Bray. See Mrs. Bray.

Brett. The Indian Tribes of Guiana: their condition and habits. By the Rev. W. H. Brett. London, 1868.

—— *Legends and Myths*. Legends and Myths of the Aboriginal Indians of British Guiana. Collected and edited by the Rev. William Henry Brett, B. D. London, N.D.

*Brython*. See *Y Brython*.

Burton, *Nights*. A plain and literal translation of the Arabian Nights' Entertainments, now entitled The Book of the Thousand Nights and a Night, with introduction, explanatory notes, &c. by Richard F. Burton. 10 vols. Privately printed. 1885.

—— *Suppl. Nights*. Supplemental Nights to The Book of the Thousand Nights and a Night with notes anthropological and explanatory by Richard F. Burton. 6 vols. Privately printed. 1886-88.

Busk, *Sagas*. Sagas from the Far East; or Kalmouk and Mongolian Traditionary Tales. With historical preface and explanatory notes by the author of Patrañas, &c. [Miss R. H. Busk]. London, 1873.

Campbell. Popular Tales of the West Highlands orally collected with a translation by J. F. Campbell. 4 vols. Edinburgh, 1860-62.

Campbell, Lord A. See Lord A. Campbell.

Carnoy. Littérature Orale de la Picardie par E. Henry Carnoy. Paris, 1883.

Castrén, *Altaischen Völker*. M. Alexander Castrén's Ethnologische Vorlesungen über die Altaischen Völker nebst Samojedischen Märchen und Tartarischen Heldensagen. Herausgegeben von Anton Schiefner. St. Petersburg, 1857.

Cavallius. Schwedische Volkssagen und Märchen. Nach mündlicher Ueberlieferung gesammelt und herausgegeben von Gunnar Olof Hyltén Cavallius und George Stephens. Mit Varianten und kritischen Anmerkungen. Deutsch von Carl Oberleitner. Wien, 1848.

Certeux et Carnoy. Contributions au Folk-Lore des Arabes. L'Algérie Traditionnelle Légendes, Contes, &c., par A. Certeux et E. Henry Carnoy. First vol. only published. Paris, 1884.

Chambers. Popular Rhymes of Scotland. Robert Chambers. London, 1870.

Child. The English and Scottish Popular Ballads edited by Francis James Child. Boston, U.S.A. Privately printed. [The prospectus is dated 1882. It announced "about 8 parts": only six of these (making three volumes) have been issued to date.]

*Choice Notes*. Choice Notes from "Notes and Queries." Folk Lore. London, 1859.

Comparetti. Novelline Popolari Italiane pubblicate ed illustrate da Domenico Comparetti. First vol. only published. Roma, 1875.

*Corpus Poet. Bor.* Corpus Poeticum Boreale. The Poetry of the Old Northern Tongue from the earliest times to the thirteenth century. Edited by Gudbrand Vigfusson, M.A., and F. York Powell, M.A. 2 vols. Oxford, 1883.

Cosquin. Emmanuel Cosquin. Contes Populaires de Lorraine comparés avec les Contes des autres Provinces de France et des Pays Étrangers. 2 vols. Paris, N.D.

*Count Lucanor*. Count Lucanor; or The Fifty Pleasant Stories of Patronio. Written by the Prince Don Juan Manuel and first done into English by James York, M.D., 1868. London, 1888.

Cromek. Remains of Nithsdale and Galloway Song with Historical and Traditional Notices relative to the Manners and Customs of the Peasantry, now first published by R. H. Cromek, F.A.S. Ed. London, 1810. Reprint: Paisley, 1880.

Curtin. Myths and Folk-Lore of Ireland by Jeremiah Curtin. London, 1890.

*Cymmrodor.* See *Y Cymmrodor.*

*Cymru Fu.* "Cymru Fu"; yn cynwys Hanesion, Traddodiadau, yn nghyda Chwedlau a Dammegion Cymreig (oddiar lafar gwlad a gweithiau y prif awduron). Wrexham, N.D. [Preface dated October 1862.]

*Cymru Fu N. and Q.* Cymru Fu: Notes and Queries relating to the past History of Wales and the Border Countries. 2 vols. Cardiff, 1887-90, still proceeding.

Davies, *Mythology.* The Mythology and Rites of the British Druids by Edward Davies, author of Celtic Researches. London, 1809.

Day. Folk-Tales of Bengal by the Rev. Lal Behari Day. London, 1883.

De Gubernatis, *Novelline.* Le Novelline di Santo Stefano raccolte da Angelo De Gubernatis. Torino, 1869.

—— *Usi Natal.* A. De Gubernatis. Storia comparata degli Usi Natalizi in Italia e presso gli altri-popoli Indo-Europei. Milano, 1878.

—— *Zool. Myth.* Zoological Mythology or The Legends of Animals by Angelo De Gubernatis. 2 vols. London, 1872.

Dennys. The Folk-Lore of China, and its affinities with that of the Aryan and Semitic Races. By N. B. Dennys, Ph.D., F.R.G.S. London, 1876.

Des Michels. Contes Plaisants Annamites traduits en Français pour la première fois par Abel Des Michels. Paris, 1888.

Dorman. The Origin of Primitive Superstitions and their Development, &c., among the Aborigines of America. By Rushton M. Dorman. Philadelphia, 1881.

Dorsa. La Tradizione Greco-Latina negli usi e nelle credenze popolari della Calabria citeriore per Vincenzo Dorsa. 2a edizione. Cozenza, 1884.

*Early Trav.* Early Travels in Palestine, edited by Thomas Wright Esq., M.A., F.S.A., &c. London, 1848.

Ellis. The Tshi-speaking Peoples of the Gold Coast of West Africa. Their religion, manners, customs, laws, language, &c. By A. B. Ellis. London, 1887.

Farrer. Primitive Manners and Customs. By James A. Farrer. London, 1879.

*F. L. Españ.* Folk-Lore Español. Biblioteca de las Tradiciones Populares Españolas. 11 vols. Sevilla, 1883-90, still proceeding.

*Folk-Lore.* Folk-Lore, a quarterly Review of Myth, Tradition, Institution, and Custom. London, 1890, still proceeding. [Organ of the Folk-Lore Society.]

*F. L. Journal.* The Folk-Lore Journal. 7 vols. London, 1883-89. [Organ of the Folk-Lore Society.]

*F. L. Record.* The Folk-Lore Record. 5 vols. N.D. [1878-82. Organ of the Folk-Lore Society.]

Fleury. Littérature Orale de la Basse-Normandie (Hague et Val-de-Saire) par Jean Fleury. Paris, 1883.

Garnett. The Women of Turkey and their Folklore by Lucy M. J. Garnett. The Christian Women. London, 1890.

*Gent. Mag. Lib.* The Gentleman's Magazine Library: being a classified collection of the chief contents of the Gentleman's Magazine from 1731 to 1868. Edited by George Lawrence Gomme, F.S.A. 11 vols. London, 1883-90, still proceeding. [Vols. not numbered, but distinguished by the title of their contents.]

Gerv. Tilb. Des Gervasius von Tilbury Otia Imperialia. In einer Auswahl neu herausgegeben und mit Anmerkungen begleitet von Felix Liebrecht. Hannover, 1856.

*Gesta Romanorum.* Gesta Romanorum translated from the Latin by the Rev. Charles Swan, revised and corrected by Wynnard Hooper, B.A. London, 1877.

Giles. Strange Stories from a Chinese Studio. Translated and annotated by Herbert A. Giles. 2 vols. London, 1880.

Gill. Myths and Songs from the South Pacific. By the Rev. William Wyatt Gill, B.A. London, 1876.

Girald. Cambr. The Itinerary of Archbishop Baldwin through Wales, translated by Sir Richard Colt Hoare, Bart., in The Historical Works of Giraldus Cambrensis, edited by Thomas Wright Esq., M.A., F.S.A. London, 1887.

Gonzenbach. Sicilianische Märchen. Aus dem Volksmund gesammelt von Laura Gonzenbach. 2 vols. Leipzig, 1870.

Gredt. Sagenschatz des Luxemburger Landes. Gesammelt von Dr. N. Gredt. Luxemburg, 1885.

Gregor. Notes on the Folk-Lore of the North-East of Scotland. By the Reverend Walter Gregor, M.A. London, 1881. (Folk-Lore Society.)

Grey. See Sir G. Grey.

Grimm, *Märchen.* Kinder- und Haus-Märchen gesammelt durch die Brüder Grimm. 17te Auflage. Berlin, 1880.

—— *Tales.* Grimm's Household Tales. With the author's notes translated from the German and edited by Margaret Hunt. 2 vols. London, 1884.

—— *Teut. Myth.* Teutonic Mythology by Jacob Grimm translated from the fourth edition with notes and appendix by James Steven Stallybrass. 4 vols. with continuous pagination. London, 1880-88.

Grinnell. Pawnee Hero Stories and Folk Tales with notes on the Origin, Customs, and Character of the Pawnee People by George Bird Grinnell. New York, 1889.

Grohmann. Sagen aus Böhmen gesammelt und herausgegeben von Dr. Josef Virgil Grohmann. Prag, 1883.

Grundtvig. Dänische Volksmärchen von Svend Grundtvig. Übersetzt von Willibald Leo. Neue Ausgabe. 2 vols. Leipzig, 1885.

Gubernatis. See De Gubernatis.


Hahn. See Von Hahn.

Haltrich. Deutsche Volksmärchen aus dem Sachsenlande in Siebenbürgen. Gesammelt von Josef Haltrich. 4te Auflage. Wien, 1885.

Hapgood. The Epic Songs of Russia by Isabel Florence Hapgood. New York, N.D. [Preface dated August 1885.]

Harland and Wilkinson. Lancashire Legends, Traditions, Pageants, Sports, &c. By John Harland, F.S.A., and T. T. Wilkinson, F.R.A.S. London, 1873.

Hazlitt, *Fairy Tales.* Fairy Tales, Legends and Romances illustrating Shakespeare and other Early English writers to which are prefixed two preliminary dissertations by Joseph Ritson. [Edited by W. C. Hazlitt.] London, 1875.

Henderson. Notes on the Folk-Lore of the Northern Counties of England and the Borders. New Edition. By William Henderson. London, 1879. (Folk-Lore Society.)

Howells. Cambrian Superstitions, comprising Ghosts, Omens, Witchcraft, Traditions, &c. By W. Howells. Tipton, 1831.

Hunt. Popular Romances of the West of England or the Drolls, Traditions and Superstitions of Old Cornwall collected and edited by Robert Hunt, F.R.S. 3rd edition, revised and enlarged. London, 1881.


Imbriani. La Novellaja Fiorentina fiabe e novelline stenografate in Firenze dal dettato popolare da Vittorio Imbriani. Ristampa accresciute di molte novelle inedite, &c., nelle quali è accolta La Novellaja Milanese dello stesso raccoglitore. Livorno, 1877.

Im Thurn. Among the Indians of Guiana being sketches chiefly anthropologic from the interior of British Guiana. By Everard F. im Thurn, M.A. London, 1883.

*Indian N. and Q.* Indian Notes and Queries (late "Panjab Notes and Queries"), a Monthly Periodical conducted by Captain R. C. Temple and others. 7 vols. Allahabad, 1883-90, still proceeding.

*Irish Folk Lore*, or *Irish F. L.* Irish Folk Lore: Traditions and Superstitions of the Country; with humorous tales. By "Lageniensis." Glasgow, N.D. [Preface dated April 1870.]

Jahn. Volkssagen aus Pommern und Rügen. Gesammelt und herausgegeben von Dr. Ulrich Jahn. Stettin, 1886.

Jannsen. Märchen und Sagen des estnischen Volkes gesammelt und übersetzt von Harry Jannsen. Two series. 1st ser. Dorpat, 1881: 2nd ser. Riga, 1888.

Jones and Kropf. The Folk-Tales of the Magyars. Collected by Kriza, Erdélyi, Pap and others. Translated and edited by the Rev. W. Henry Jones and Lewis L. Kropf. London, 1889. (Folk-Lore Society.)

*Journal. Amer. F. L.* The Journal of American Folk-Lore. 3 vols. Boston, 1888-90, still proceeding. [Organ of the American Folk-Lore Society.]

*Kalewala.* Kalewala, des National-Epos der Finnen, nach der zweiten Ausgabe ins Deutsche übertragen von Anton Schiefner. Helsingfors, 1852.

*Kathá Sarit Ságara.* The Kathá Sarit Ságara, or Ocean of the Streams of Story translated from the original Sanskrit by C. H. Tawney, M.A. 2 vols. Calcutta, 1880-84.

Keightley. The Fairy Mythology, illustrative of the Romance and Superstition of various Countries by Thomas Keightley. New Edition, revised and greatly enlarged. London, 1882.

Kennedy. Legendary Fictions of the Irish Celts. Collected and narrated by Patrick Kennedy. London, 1866.

Kirby. The New Arabian Nights. Select Tales, not included by Galland or Lane. Translated and edited by W. F. Kirby. London, N.D.

Knoop. Volkssagen, Erzählungen, Aberglauben, Gebräuche und Märchen aus dem östlichen Hinterpommern. Gesammelt von Otto Knoop. Posen, 1885.

Knowles. Folk-Tales of Kashmir. By the Rev. J. Hinton Knowles. London, 1888.

Krauss. Sagen und Märchen der Südslaven. Zum grossen Teil aus ungedruckten Quellen von Dr. Friedrich S. Krauss. 2 vols. Leipzig, 1883-84.

—— *Volksgl.* Volksglaube und religiöser Brauch der Südslaven. Vorwiegend nach eigenen Ermittlungen von Dr. Friedrich S. Krauss. Münster i W. 1890.

Kreutzwald. Ehstnische Märchen. Aufgezeichnet von Friedrich Kreutzwald. Aus dem Ehstnischen übersetzt von F. Löwe. Halle, 1869.

Kuhn. Märkische Sagen und Märchen nebst einem Anhange von Gebräuchen und Aberglauben gesammelt und herausgegeben von Adalbert Kuhn. Berlin, 1843.

Kuhn und Schwartz. Norddeutsche Sagen, Märchen und Gebräuche aus Mecklenburg, &c. Aus dem munde des Volkes gesammelt und herausgegeben von A. Kuhn und W. Schwartz. Leipzig, 1848.

Lady Wilde. Ancient Legends, Mystic Charms and Superstitions of Ireland. By Lady Wilde. 2 vols. London, 1887.

La Croix. Manners Customs and Dress during the Middle Ages and during the Renaissance Period by Paul La Croix (Bibliophile Jacob). 4th thousand. London, 1876.

Landes. Contes et Légendes Annamites par A. Landes. Saigon, 1886.

*La Tradition.* La Tradition Revue Générale des Contes, Légendes, Chants, Usages, Traditions et Arts populaires. 4 vols. Paris, 1887-90, still proceeding. [Organ of the Société des Traditionnistes.]

Leland. The Algonquin Legends of New England, or Myths and Folk-Lore of the Micmac, Passamaquoddy, and Penobscot Tribes by Charles G. Leland. London, 1884.

Lemke. Volksthümliches in Ostpreussen von E. Lemke. 2 vols. Mohrungen, 1884-87.

Liebrecht. Zur Volkskunde. Alte und neue Aufsätze von Felix Liebrecht. Heilbronn, 1879.

*Llyvyr Coch.* See *Y Llyvyr Coch.*

Lord A. Campbell, *Waifs and Strays.* Waifs and Strays of Celtic Tradition. I. Argyllshire Series. Edited by Lord Archibald Campbell. London, 1879.

Luzel, *Contes.* Contes Populaires de Basse-Bretagne par F. M. Luzel. 3 vols. Paris, 1887.

—— *Légendes Chrét.* Légendes Chrétiennes de la Basse-Bretagne par F. M. Luzel. 2 vols. Paris, 1881.

—— *Veillées.* Veillées Bretonnes par F. M. Luzel. Morlaix, 1879.

MacInnes. Waifs and Strays of Celtic Tradition. Folk and Hero Tales. Collected, Edited and Translated by the Rev. D. Mac Innes. With Notes by the Editor and Alfred Nutt. London, 1890.

MacRitchie. The Testimony of Tradition by David MacRitchie. London, 1890.

Malory. La Mort d' Arthure. The History of King Arthur and of the Knights of the Round Table. Compiled by Sir Thomas Malory, Knt. Edited from the text of the edition of 1634 by Thomas Wright Esq., M.A., F.S.A. 2nd edition. 3 vols. London, 1866.

Map. Gualteri Mapes De Nugis Curialium Distinctiones Quinque. Edited from the unique manuscript in the Bodleian Library at Oxford by Thomas Wright Esq., M.A., F.S.A., &c. London, 1850.

*Masnavi i Ma'navi.* Masnavi i Ma'navi. The Spiritual Couplets of Maulána Jalálu-'d-Dín Muhammad i Rúmí. Translated and abridged by E. H. Whinfield, M.A. London, 1887.

Maspons y Labros. Folk-Lore Catalá. Cuentos Populars Catalans per lo Dr. Francisco de S. Maspons y Labros. Barcelona, 1885.

Meier. Deutsche Sagen, Sitten und Gebräuche aus Schwaben, gesammelt von Ernst Meier. Stuttgart, 1852.

—— *Märchen.* Deutsche Volksmärchen aus Schwaben. Aus dem Munde des Volks gesammelt und herausgegeben von Dr. Ernst Meier. 3te Auflage. Stuttgart, N.D.

*Mélusine.* Mélusine Recueil de Mythologie, Littérature Populaire, Traditions et Usages publié par H. Gaidoz et E. Rolland. [Since vol. iii. by H. Gaidoz alone.] 5 vols. Paris, 1878-90, still proceeding.

Michels. See Des Michels.

Mrs. Bray. The Borders of the Tamar and the Tavy; their Natural History, &c., by Mrs. Bray. New Edition. 2 vols. London, 1879.

Müller. Siebenbürgische Sagen gesammelt und herausgegeben von Dr. Friedrich Müller. Zweite veränderte Auflage. Wien, 1885.

Napier. Folk Lore: or Superstitious Beliefs in the West of Scotland within this Century. By James Napier, F.R.S.E., F.C.S., &c. Paisley; 1879.

Nicholson. Folk Lore of East Yorkshire. By John Nicholson. London, 1890.

Niederhöffer. Mecklenburg's Volkssagen. Gesammelt und herausgegeben von M. Dr. A. Niederhöffer. 4 vols. Leipzig, N.D. [Vorwort dated Februar 1857.]

Ortoli. Les Contes Populaires del' Ile de Corse par J. B. Frédéric Ortoli. Paris, 1883.

*Panjab N. and Q.* See *Indian N. and Q.*

Pitré. Biblioteca delle Tradizioni Popolari Siciliane per cura di Giuseppe Pitré. 18 vols. Palermo, 1871-88.

Poestion. Lappländische Märchen, Volkssagen, Rätsel und Sprichwörter. Nach lappländischen, norwegischen und schwedischen Quellen von J. C. Poestion. Wien, 1886.

Powell and Magnusson. Icelandic Legends (collected by Jón Arnason) Translated by George E. J. Powell and Eiríkr Magnusson. 2nd series. London, 1866.

Preller, *Röm. Myth.* Römische Mythologie von L. Preller. 3te Auflage. 2 vols. Berlin, 1881-83.

Prym und Socin. Kurdische Sammlungen. Erzählungen und Lieder im dialekte des Tûr 'Abdîn. Gesammelt, herausgegeben und übersetzt von Eugen Prym und Albert Socin. St. Petersburg, 1887. [A second part, by Socin only, consisting of tales and songs in the dialect of Bohtan, has since been published, 1890.]


Radloff. Proben der Volkslitteratur der Türkischen Stämme Süd-Sibiriens, gesammelt und übersetzt von Dr. W. Radloff. 6 vols. [the last two entitled P. der V. der Nördlichen Türkischen Stämme.] St. Petersburg, 1866-86.

Ralston, *R. F. Tales.* Russian Folk-Tales by W. R. S. Ralston, M.A. London, 1873.

—— *Tibetan Tales.* Tibetan Tales derived from Indian Sources. Translated from the Tibetan of the Kah-Gyur by F. Anton von Schiefner. Done into English from the German by W. R. S. Ralston, M.A. London, 1882.

Rappold. Sagen aus Kärnten. Zusammengestellt und theilweise neu erzählt von Professor J. Rappold. Augsburg, 1887.

*Revue des Trad. Pop.* Revue des Traditions Populaires. 5 vols. Paris, 1886-90, still proceeding. [Organ of the Société des Traditions Populaires.]

Rhys, *Hibbert Lectures.* The Hibbert Lectures, 1886. Lectures on the Origin and Growth of Religion as illustrated by Celtic Heathendom. By John Rhys. London, 1888.

Rink. Tales and Traditions of the Eskimo by Dr. Henry Rink. Translated from the Danish by the author. Edited by Dr. Robert Brown. Edinburgh, 1875.

Robertson Smith. Lectures on the Religion of the Semites. First Series. The Fundamental Institutions. By W. Robertson Smith, M.A., LL.D. Edinburgh, 1889.

Romero. Contos Populares do Brazil collegidos pelo Dr. Sylvio Romero. Lisboa, 1885.

Romilly. From my Verandah in New Guinea Sketches and Traditions by Hugh Hastings Romilly, C.M.G. London, 1889.

*Rosenöl.* Rosenöl oder Sagen und Kunden des Morgenländes aus arabischen, persischen und türkischen Quellen gesammelt. 2 vols. Stuttgart, 1813.

Rudder. A New History of Gloucestershire. Cirencester, Samuel Rudder, 1779.


Sastri. The Dravidian Nights Entertainments: being a translation of Madanakamarajankadai. By Pandit S. M. Natesa Sastri. Madras, 1886.

Saxo, *Gesta Dan.* Saxonis Grammatici Gesta Danorum, herausgegeben von Alfred Holder. Strassberg, 1886.

Schleicher. Litaüische Märchen, Sprichwörter, Rätsel und Lieder. Gesammelt und übersetzt von August Schleicher. Weimar, 1857.

Schmidt. Griechische Märchen, Sagen und Volkslieder gesammelt, übersetzt und erläutert von Bernhardt Schmidt. Leipzig, 1877.

Schneller. Märchen und Sagen aus Wälschtirol. Gesammelt von Christian Schneller. Innsbruck, 1867.

Schreck. Finnische Märchen übersetzt von Emmy Schreck. Weimar, 1887.

Sébillot, *Contes.* Paul Sébillot. Contes Populaires de la Haute Bretagne. Paris, 1880. Do. 2me série. Contes des Paysans et des Pécheurs. Paris, 1881. Do. 3me série. Contes des Marins. Paris, 1882.

—— *Litt. Orale.* Littérature Orale de la Haute Bretagne par Paul Sébillot. Paris, 1881.

—— *Trad. et Super.* Traditions et Superstitions de la Haute Bretagne par Paul Sébillot. 2 vols. Paris, 1882.

Shortland. Traditions and Superstitions of the New Zealanders: with illustrations of their manners and customs. By Edward Shortland, M.A. 2nd edition. London, 1856.

Sikes. British Goblins: Welsh Folk-Lore, Fairy Mythology, Legends and Traditions. By Wirt Sikes. London, 1880.

Simrock. Handbuch der Deutschen Mythologie mit Einschluss der nordischen. Von Karl Simrock. 3te Auflage. Bonn, 1869.

Sir G. Grey. Polynesian Mythology, and Ancient Traditional History of the New Zealand Race, as furnished by their Priests and Chiefs. By Sir George Grey. London, 1855.

Spitta Bey. Contes Arabes Modernes recueillis et traduits par Guillaume Spitta-Bey. Leide, 1883.

Steere. Swahili Tales, as told by natives of Zanzibar. With an English translation. By Edward Steere, LL.D. London, 1870.

Stephens. The Literature of the Kymry: being a critical essay on the history of the Language and Literature of Wales during the twelfth and two succeeding centuries. By Thomas Stephens. 2nd edition. London, 1876.

Sternberg. The Dialect and Folk-Lore of Northamptonshire. By Thomas Sternberg. London, 1851.

Taylor. Te Ika a Maui; or New Zealand and its Inhabitants. By the Rev. Richard Taylor, M.A., F.G.S. 2nd edition. London, 1870.

Temple, *Legends of the Panjab*. The Legends of the Panjab. By Captain R. C. Temple. 2 vols. Bombay, N.D. [Preface to vol. i. dated May 1884.] Still proceeding.

Tettau. See Von Tettau.

Theal. Kaffir Folk-Lore; a Selection from the Traditional Tales current amongst the people living on the eastern border of the Cape Colony. By George M'Call Theal. London, N.D. [Preface dated Jan. 1882.]

Thomas of Erceldoune. The Romance and Prophecies of Thomas of Erceldoune, printed from five manuscripts. Edited, with introduction and notes, by James A. H. Murray, LL.D. London 1875 (Early Eng. Text Soc.).

Thorburn. Bannú; or, Our Afghan Frontier. By S. S. Thorburn. London, 1876.

Thorpe. Northern Mythology, comprising the principal popular traditions and superstitions of Scandinavia, North Germany, and the Netherlands. Compiled by Benjamin Thorpe. 3 vols. London, 1851-52.

—— *Yule-Tide Stories*. Yule-Tide Stories. A collection of Scandinavian and North German Popular Tales and Traditions. Edited by Benjamin Thorpe. London, 1853.

*Tradition.* See *La Tradition.*

*Trad. Pop. Revue des.* See *Revue des Trad. Pop.*

Train. An Historical and Statistical Account of the Isle of Man, from the earliest times to the present date. By Joseph Train, F.S.A. Scot. 2 vols. Douglas, 1845.

*Trans. Aberd. Eistedd.* Eisteddfod Genedlaethol y Cymry. Cofnodion a Chyfansoddiadau Buddugol Eisteddfod Aberdar, 1885. Transactions of the National Eisteddfod of Wales, Aberdare, 1885. Caerdydd, 1887.

Tylor. Primitive Culture: Researches into the development of Mythology, Philosophy, Religion, Art, and Custom. By Edward B. Tylor. 2 vols. London, 1871.

Vernaleken. In the Land of Marvels. Folk-Tales from Austria and Bohemia by Theodor Vernaleken. London, 1889.

*Volkskunde.* See *Zeits. f. Volkskunde.*

Von Alpenburg. Mythen und Sagen Tirols. Gesammelt und herausgegeben von Johann Nepomuk Ritter von Alpenburg. Zürich, 1857.

Von Hahn. Griechische und albanesiche Märchen. Gesammelt übersetzt und erläutert von J. G. von Hahn. 2 vols. Leipzig, 1864.

Von Tettau. Die Volkssagen Ostpreussens, Litthauens und Westpreussens. Gesammelt von W. J. A. von Tettau und J. D. H. Temme. Berlin, 1837.

Von Wlislocki. Märchen und Sagen der Transsilvanischen Zigeuner Gesammelt und übersetzt von Dr. Heinrich von Wlislocki. Berlin, 1886.

Waldau. Böhmisches Märchenbuch. Deutsch von Alfred Waldau. Prag, 1860.

Waldron. A Description of the Isle of Man by George Waldron, Gent. Edited by William Harrison, Esq. Douglas, 1865.

Webster. Basque Legends: collected chiefly in the Labourd by Rev. Wentworth Webster, M.A. 2nd edition. London, 1879.

Wenzig. Westslawischer Märchenschatz. Deutsch bearbeitet von Joseph Wenzig. Neue Ausgabe. Leipzig, 1886.

White. The Ancient History of the Maori, his Mythology and Traditions by John White. 4 vols. Wellington, 1887-89, still proceeding.

*Wide Awake Stories.* Wide Awake Stories. A collection of tales told by little children, between sunset and sunrise, in the Panjab and Kashmir. By F. A. Steel and R. C. Temple. Bombay, 1884.

Wilde. See Lady Wilde.

Wirt Sikes. See Sikes.

Wlislocki. See Von Wlislocki.

Wratislaw. Sixty Folk-Tales from exclusively Slavonic sources. Translated, with brief introductions and notes, by A. H. Wratislaw, M.A. London, 1889.

Wright, *Middle Ages.* Essays on subjects connected with the Literature, Popular Superstitions and History of England in the Middle Ages. By Thomas Wright, M.A., F.S.A. 2 vols. London, 1846.

*Y Brython.* Y Brython: Cylchgrawn Llenyddol Cymru; dan olygiad y Parch. D. Silvan Evans. 5 vols. Tremadog, 1858-63.

*Y Cymmrodor.* Y Cymmrodor, embodying the Transactions of the Cymmrodorion Society of London. 10 vols. London, 1877-90, still proceeding.

*Y Llyvyr Coch.* Y Llyvyr Coch o Hergest. Y gyvrol I. The Text of the Mabinogion and other Welsh Tales from the Red Book of Hergest edited by John Rhys, M.A. and J. Gwenogvryn Evans. Oxford, 1887.

The Mabinogion, from the Welsh of the Llyfr Coch o Hergest (The Red Book of Hergest) in the Library of Jesus College, Oxford. Translated, with notes, by Lady Charlotte Guest. London, 1877.

*Zeits. f. Volksk.* Zeitschrift für Volkskunde in Sage und Mär, Schwank und Streich, Lied, Rätsel und Sprichwörter, Sitte und Brauch herausgegeben von Dr. Edmund Veckenstedt. 2 vols. Leipzig, 1889-90, still proceeding.

www.ingramcontent.com/pod-product-compliance
Lightning Source LLC
Chambersburg PA
CBHW022356040426
42450CB00005B/201